FASCINATING FACTS FROM YOUR FAVORITE FILMS!

- Columbia Pictures bought the original C. S. Forester novel *The African Queen,* intending to cast Charles Laughton and Elsa Lanchester in the starring roles.
- For the finale of *The Birds,* Alfred Hitchcock placed Tippi Hedren in a cagelike room representing an attic and then had crew members throw hundreds of live seagulls at her.
- Burt Lancaster loudly proclaimed *Airport* "a piece of junk," but the film proved his most financially rewarding role ever.
- Director Miloš Forman chose his native Prague to film *Amadeus* because it remained the only large baroque city in Europe untouched by the bombings of World War II.

FOR A BOOK THAT IRISES IN, SPREADS WIDE ANGLE, GETS CLOSEUP, AND GOES DEEP FOCUS...REACH FOR *RETAKES*.

Also by John Eastman:

WHO LIVED WHERE

WHO LIVED WHERE IN EUROPE

RETAKES:

Behind the Scenes of 500 Classic Movies

John Eastman

BALLANTINE BOOKS • NEW YORK

 Published in the United States of America by Ballantine Books, a division of Random House, Inc., New York, and simultaneously in Canada by Random House of Canada Limited, Toronto.

Library of Congress Catalog Card Number: 89-90699

ISBN 0-345-35399-4

Manufactured in the United States of America

First Edition: July 1989

To four movie lovers, stars in their own right—
Cal Everly, Jackie Ladwein, John Murphy, Bob O'Daniel

It did not seem possible that the hunger of people for a story could be strong enough to call into being an entire industry, strong enough to make millionaires, to transform private persons into public stars, to impose ways of dress and thought upon us all.

Jessamyn West

There is nothing that says more about its creator than the work itself.

Akira Kurosawa

Preface

Behind the scenes of many favorite movies lies a rich lore that adds intriguing dimensions to what we see on the screen. This is a book that rummages some of that lore. Call it a video home companion.

But this is also a subversive book about crafted illusions. The light-and-shadow product designed, created, and sold by the movie industry not only decorates our lives but feeds us in some essential way. Though the technical means of providing these illusions cannot be fully understood without a knowledge of modern electronics, our hunger for them is as ancient as our cave ancestors. The figures they saw dancing in the flames of a campfire, while shaman or ceremony fulfilled a community need by telling a story, became refined and confined—even as the fire itself became a domesticated servant, sparks channeled through wires, tubes, transistors. A good story remains, among other things, an answer to a question we were just about to ask. Today the VCR is our cave campfire.

But there is also a frame that surrounds, exists outside the movie frame. This larger context consists of an unscripted historical moment, unseen events of real life that enclose and refocus the shadows intended for us to see. To move outside the screen boundary to the drama occurring beyond that edge is the purpose of this book.

Why? Why tamper with illusions that have been so artfully and expensively framed in precise dimensional ratios to satisfy our needs for them? Why must we search for hidden wires, clay feet, optical tricks in order to know something that may destroy believability or the suspension of disbelief, the very goal of it all? Isn't it enough to be ingeniously fooled by the best that cinema art and industry can provide? Isn't that what we pay for and obviously want?

Well, yes and no. For some of us, the package just isn't enough, no matter how well wrapped and framed. The reason why is as simple and complicated as human curiosity. As for destroying illusions, we will never be crucially desperate for another good campfire story. We seem to know how to preserve the illusions that matter to us.

Thus we can still suspend disbelief while knowing that many a combat soldier experienced more real battlefield action in five minutes than screen hero John Wayne saw throughout his entire superpatriotic career; that the cosmic artistry of clowns like Buster Keaton and Charles Chaplin burned through to the screen despite their desperate and unfunny private lives: that such masters of film drama as Spencer Tracy, Alfred Hitchcock, and Chaplin himself remained, behind all the marvelous scenes, deeply troubled men of uncertain aim; that the physical grace of an Errol Flynn, an Alan Ladd, masked staggering physical/emotional weaknesses: that drugs or alcohol ruled the off-screen lives of many legendary performers; but also that the private lives of numerous screen idols were marked by nothing if not a deep commitment to conventionality. Still, these mortals convince us otherwise when we see them move, immortal as gods and goddesses, on the screen—and some part of us preserves them, despite our best knowing, as indeed larger than life.

Repeatedly, as I researched behind such masks of movie bravado as Humphrey Bogart, Jean Harlow, Richard Burton, I was struck with the heartrending pathos of the Movie Star existence. So common to that existence was the child at bored wit's end, the lack of pointed endeavor while awaiting the next script, the next spouse, the next picture in which to play adult. So many of them apparently defined their lives in terms not of individuality but of image. Rarer than invitations to Pickfair seemed a true case of self-awareness in all of Hollywood. The unsentimental fact was that many if not most performers during Hollywood's golden age saw themselves almost entirely through the eyes of their studio employers—i.e., mainly as commodities, ultimately replaceable parts of the factory product. And never for an instant out of their minds was the consciousness of the fickle movie audience. *We* set the cues, called the tune. And, eager to idolize, to exude worship upon projected ideals of ourselves, we still do.

For those viewers who want nothing more from the movies than the packaged, calculated images that corporate wisdom provides, this, frankly, may not be the book. But unwritten in any script—beyond the frame measured for us to see—there's something else happening; and that drama, for many of us, adds much to the pleasure of watching a movie.

While film has, in the past few decades, become the rightful subject for a whole new realm of studies in the humanities, my own qualifications for writing this book amount to little except personal interest, curiosity, and a love of research on the topic. I am not a film scholar, and my appreciation for the types of analysis that film scholars value is minimal and uncultivated. Thus any expertise I may claim in the subject is quite limited to its historical aspects. My sources included numerous film biographies, memoirs, and journalistic and film trade accounts. While most of the information has thus been previously published in some form, the advantages of bringing it together and making it conveniently accessible to the video viewer are obvious. I avoided all studio publicity and fan-magazine-type material, since it was (and is) notoriously inaccurate and unreliable. While I have tried to render faithfully the information from sources I believe to be trustworthy, the ultimate "truth" of an account must, of course, rely upon the integrity, both personal and corporate, of those sources. If there seemed doubts on this matter, the questionable material got filed in the well-known appropriate place.

I based my choice of films on four main criteria: (1) films available on videocassette to date; (2) of videos available, the ones ranked as best by critical, popular, and movie industry standards from 1930, when sound in films was young, up through 1988; (3) of *those* videos, the ones that offered most in the way of behind-the-scenes information; and (4) of the latter list, after consultation with persons whose opinions I respect, the videos I arbitrarily selected for inclusion. If your favorite doesn't appear here, lay the reason to one of the four "filters" mentioned. While a different list of 500 films could as easily have been chosen, I think this selection includes *most* of the available classics as well as many of the most successful efforts of the past five decades. The emphasis here is on American productions, but a large sampling of foreign works, especially British, is also included. Also, I haven't been nearly so interested in the nuts-and-bolts technology of special effects or "how was that done?" types of information—many excellent books have covered these topics—as in the people and events of a given film context. Numerous books about the making of certain well-known movies also exist; within the appropriate entries, I've named these, for the possible interest of diehard devotees.

In the film headings, note that studio designations do not *necessarily* refer to the studio that financed the production but to the studio premises where actual filming occurred. Most often the two were the same—but not invariably. In some cases, there is no studio mentioned at all because most or all of the filming occurred on nonstudio locations. Also, some studios shifted their own premises in California during their history, which accounts for the occasional variation in studio city locales.

My foremost appreciation and gratitude goes to my dear companion, Susan Woolley Stoddard, not only for her countless hours at the word processor but for loving support in every way. This book wouldn't exist without her. I also owe much to Professor John M. Murphy, film scholar and old friend, for valuable preliminary suggestions, advice, and resources. Others whose vital interest and generous aid made this book possible include senior editor Joe Blades of Ballantine Books, himself a notable film scholar; Peter L. Ginsberg of Curtis Brown Associates, Ltd.; and Chris Thommen and her interlibrary loan staff at the Portage Public Library, Portage, Michigan. For finding and loaning materials, I especially thank Richard A. Johnson, Jacqueline Ladwein, Sandra O'Daniel, and Susan Park-Mason. Far from least goes my eternal gratitude to William J. Mills for providing Mills Manor, a solitary cabin in the Michigan north woods where priorities balance, words join, and things are all right.

RETAKES:

Behind the Scenes of 500 Classic Movies

A

A NOUS LA LIBERTÉ. 1931. Filmed autumn 1931; Studio Tobis, Epinay-sur-Seine, France.
Cast: Raymond Cordy, Henri Marchand, Rolla France, Paul Olivier.
Director: René Clair.

While viewing a scene of wildflowers growing against factory chimneys, René Clair was inspired to write and direct this classic satire on the work ethic. The opening sequence was said to have influenced Charles Chaplin in making *Modern Times*; conversely, the dreamer Emile, played by Henri Marchand, was based on Chaplin's little tramp. The career of French producer-industrialist Charles Pathé inspired the character of Louis, played by Raymond Cordy. German-owned Studio Tobis at first opposed Clair's plans for the film, labeling its theme communistic; but when Clair's *Le Million* proved so popular, the studio let him go ahead. Ironically, *A Nous la Liberté* drew the wrath of French Communists for its "anarchistic tendencies," and Hungary banned it as "dangerous propaganda." Clair, in short, couldn't please anybody. In 1971, though, he professed himself delighted to have made a "hippie" movie forty years before.

ADAM'S RIB. 1949. Filmed May–June 1949; New York City. MGM Studios, Culver City.
Cast: Spencer Tracy, Katharine Hepburn, David Wayne, Tom Ewell, Judy Holliday, Jean Hagen.
Director: George Cukor.

During filming, Katharine Hepburn gave much moral support to Judy Holliday, who literally trembled at performing with high-powered stars Tracy and Hepburn. Holliday's insecurity worked to her advantage in her early monologue scene with Hepburn, since her role required her to show nervousness and fear, and the first and only take of that scene is what you see. Holliday was at this time performing nights on stage in *Born Yesterday*, a role she was later chosen to recreate (thanks to the enthusiastic plugging of Tracy and Hepburn) in the film of that title. Screenwriters Garson Kanin and Ruth Gordon hatched the idea for this film from circumstances surrounding the divorce of actor Raymond Massey and his wife. The name of the character played by Hepburn was changed, at her request, to accommodate the song "Farewell, Amanda," composed by Cole Porter. Tracy insisted on top billing, as usual. When asked if he'd ever heard of "ladies first," he replied, "This is a movie, not a lifeboat."

THE ADVENTURES OF ROBIN HOOD. 1938. Filmed September 1937–January 1938; California: Bidwell Park, Chico; Busch Gardens, Pasadena; Lake Sherwood, Thousand Oaks; Corrigan Ranch, Simi Valley; Warner Bros. Studio Ranch, Calabasas; Warner Bros. Studios, Burbank.

Cast: Errol Flynn, Olivia de Havilland, Basil Rathbone, Claude Rains, Patric Knowles, Alan Hale.

Directors: William Keighley, Michael Curtiz.

To most film buffs, Errol Flynn will always be *the* Robin Hood. Yet he professed himself bored with the role, insisting that the part "sends me off to sleep." His frequent tardiness on the set annoyed cast and crew, and most of his speaking scenes had to be reshot several times because of his bad memory for dialogue. With costar Olivia de Havilland, who had carried an unrequited torch for him for three years, he teased and bantered, kissing her far more ardently than the censors would pass, thus requiring more retakes. Flynn's habits provoked constant arguments between himself, director Michael Curtiz, and studio chief Jack Warner, who wanted to fire him but was tied by contract—fortunately, for the film became a minor classic. Alan Hale, a Flynn drinking buddy, had originated his Little John role in the 1922 silent *Robin Hood* starring Douglas Fairbanks, and he played it again in the 1950 *Rogues of Sherwood Forest*. Basil Rathbone, cast as the villainous Sir Guy of Gisbourne, handled a sword far better than Flynn but was injured during the filming of Robin's escape from the castle; knocked down and trampled by extras, he suffered a spear wound in his right foot that required eight stitches to close. Sweltering weather and studio dissatisfaction with director William Keighley, who was fired and replaced by Curtiz, also plagued the production. Watch for the horse ridden by de Havilland; it's none other than the palomino that, a short time later, became Roy Rogers's Trigger.

THE ADVENTURES OF SHERLOCK HOLMES. 1939. Filmed spring 1939; 20th Century-Fox Studios, Los Angeles.
Cast: Basil Rathbone, Nigel Bruce, Ida Lupino, George Zucco, E. E. Clive.
Director: Alfred Werker.

English actors Basil Rathbone and Nigel Bruce not only played their Holmes-Watson roles in a total of fourteen films and numerous radio shows over a period of seven years, but also created the prototypes against which all subsequent performers of these roles were (and are) measured. Being Holmes was ultimately not kind to Rathbone's career, for this versatile actor soon found himself rigidly typecast as the sleuth. Becoming bored and frustrated with the increasingly inferior scripts, he grew to deplore Holmes's egotism and his cruel put-downs of Watson. Bruce, on the other hand, never lost his own enthusiasm for playing Watson; for him, the role was bread and butter, and toward the end of the series, the two actors (who were close friends off-camera) approached their roles with far different attitudes. But this second film of the series, loosely based on William Gillette's play *Sherlock Holmes*, saw both actors still fresh and eager, and the script, costumes, and settings were authentic to Victorian London. Zucco, a fine character actor who played Moriarty in the film, went insane and died in 1960.

AN AFFAIR TO REMEMBER. 1957. Filmed February–April 1957; 20th Century-Fox Studios, Los Angeles.
Cast: Cary Grant, Deborah Kerr, Cathleen Nesbitt, Richard Denning.
Director: Leo McCarey.

This remake of *Love Affair* (1939), which had also been directed by Leo McCarey, cast Cary Grant and Deborah Kerr together for the second time. (They first teamed in *Dream Wife*, released in 1953.) Initially reluctant to follow Charles Boyer in his role, Grant agreed when he found out who his director and costar would be. At home during this period, Grant and his wife, Betsy Drake, were experimenting with hypnotism. Munching health foods, he would arrive on the set complaining that hypnosis had killed his taste for cigarettes. A benign but enlarging lump on Grant's forehead, vestige of a childhood injury, caused lighting problems in his close-ups, so he had it surgically removed while McCarey shot around him for a few days. Kerr's only genuine vocalizing in the film is the song "The Tiny Scout"; for all the other songs, she lip-synched to Marni Nixon, whose dubbed voice made songbirds of many an unmelodic actress through the years.

THE AFRICAN QUEEN. 1951. Filmed May–August 1951; Ruiki River and Butiaba, Belgian Congo (now Zaire). Murchison (Kabalega) Falls and Lake Albert, Uganda. England: Islesworth Studios, London; Shepperton Studios, Shepperton.

Cast: Humphrey Bogart, Katharine Hepburn, Robert Morley, Peter Bull.

Director: John Huston.

Columbia Studios bought the original C. S. Forester novel for Charles Laughton and Elsa Lanchester, then, in 1939, sold it to Warner Bros. for Bette Davis and David Niven. When Davis fell out with the producer, 20th Century-Fox bought the property, and John Huston unearthed it there twelve years later. Plagued by army ants, black wasps, dysentery, and steaming jungle heat, cast and crew suffered miserably in the African location scenes. Only Huston and Bogart escaped sickness (owing, they maintained, to their daily Scotch intake). The actual *African Queen*, a retired riverboat, towed four rafts down the Ruiki. On one, a mock-up replica of the boat provided a stage set, while others held equipment and private quarters for Hepburn. Bogart, at first lukewarm about his role and hating any sort of location work, gradually absorbed himself in the character of Charlie Allnutt (thereby winning his only Academy Award), but he never ceased complaining about the jungle discomforts and Hepburn's incessant, bewildering cheerfulness. Though severely ill with dysentery much of the time, Hepburn remained fascinated with every aspect of the African locations, even (decades later) writing a book about the filming (*The Making of The African Queen*, 1987). For her role as the spinster missionary, she was encouraged by Huston to emulate Eleanor Roosevelt, which she found a splendid bit of direction. The entire production, virtually wiped out by illness, transferred to London, where the early scenes with Robert Morley and late ones with Peter Bull were shot. Also recreated in London studios were all sequences in which Bogart or Hepburn were actually in the water, the torrential rainfall scenes, and back-projected views of the boat riding the rapids. Screenwriter James Agee, whose disabling heart attack put an end to his work on the script, intended the river journey to symbolize the act of love, and he strongly criticized the upbeat finale concocted by Huston and writer Peter Viertel.

AGUIRRE, THE WRATH OF GOD (AGUIRRE, DER ZORN GOTTES). 1972. Filmed January–February 1972; Peru: Urubama River Valley; Huallaga and Nanay Rivers.

Cast: Klaus Kinski. Ruy Guerra, Helena Rojo, Cecilia Rivera, Peter Berling, Del Negro.

Director: Werner Herzog.

Incessant rainfall, financial difficulties, and primitive hardships plagued the filming of this harsh, beautiful picture, paralleling the actual disastrous expedition led in 1561 by the mutinous conquistador Lope de Aguirre (played by Klaus Kinski). Dysentery, the lack of civilized comforts, and eroding tempers threatened to wipe out the production. Tales of Werner Herzog's slavedriving techniques and erratic behavior toward his crew and actors during the making of this film became legend. At one strained point, he and Kinski apparently threatened to kill each other with pistols. Even though the two didn't subsequently speak to each other for four years, both men teamed again in several films after *Aguirre* that brought them international reputations. Herzog "borrowed" the troupe of monkeys for the film's final sequence from an airport baggage room at Iquitos, claiming he was an animal health inspector.

AIRPORT. 1970. Filmed February–March 1969; Minneapolis-St. Paul International Airport, Minneapolis. Universal Studios, Universal City.

Cast: Burt Lancaster, Dean Martin, Jean Seberg, Helen Hayes, Van Heflin, Jacqueline Bisset, George Kennedy, Dana Wynter.

Director: George Seaton.

For Burt Lancaster, who loudly proclaimed this film "a piece of junk," *Airport* was a godsend; it not only restored his flagging box-office fortunes, but proved his most financially rewarding role. This was Jean Seberg's last American film; she, too, thought her role as an airline public relations flack insipid, and she detested the gray uniform she had to wear. Dean Martin initially turned down his part as not fitting his laid-back persona. Almost the only performer who didn't consider the film beneath contempt was veteran Helen Hayes, who launched into her role with typical enthusiasm. To the alarm of cast and crew, she insisted on doing her wrestling scene with Van Heflin herself rather than using a stand-in. (For her performance the Academy voted her the best supporting actress of 1970.) Exterior scenes of the snowbound plane used an actual 707 in a real snowstorm, but cockpit and cabin sequences were filmed in a studio mock-up.

THE ALAMO. 1960. Filmed September–December 1959; Brackettville, Texas. Los Angeles.
Cast: John Wayne, Richard Widmark, Laurence Harvey, Richard Boone, Frankie Avalon, Linda Cristal, Chill Wills.
Director: John Wayne.

John Wayne had planned to make this film, a reasonable if hardly precise facsimile of the 1836 Battle of the Alamo, for at least fourteen years before he was finally able to do so. He mortgaged all he owned and invested over $1 million (possibly accounting for his bothersome ulcer during filming), which he didn't recoup until years later when he sold his interest in the film. He intended *The Alamo* as a statement of his own patriotic principles, tying its publicity into the 1960 Kennedy-Nixon presidential campaign through a piece he wrote for *Life*. Two of his children played minor roles: Patrick as Captain Bonham, and four-year-old Aissa as the daughter of Captain Dickinson (played by *Gunsmoke*'s Festus, Ken Curtis). The Alamo building and the frontier town of San Antonio were reconstructed to scale on a 22,000-acre ranch near Brackettville, where all exterior scenes were filmed. Wayne combed seven states to obtain 1,500 horses and a herd of rare Texas longhorn cattle. A retired Marine sergeant drilled Santa Anna's "army" (actually 4,000 extras recruited from southwest Texas towns) in how to charge, using real bayonets on actual flintlock rifles; each full volley that was fired cost

$1,500. Laurence Harvey, superbly masking his British accent, suffered an injury when a cannon wheel rolled over his foot; refusing to be hospitalized, he successfully treated himself with hot and cold foot baths.

ALFIE. 1966. Filmed winter–spring 1966; London.
Cast: Michael Caine, Vivien Merchant, Shirley Anne Field, Julia Foster, Millicent Martin, Shelley Winters, Denholm Elliott.
Director: Lewis Gilbert.

The abortion procurement scene scared off three actors to whom Michael Caine's title role was first offered: Terence Stamp, Anthony Newley, and Laurence Harvey. Caine was hungrier at the time, however, and the film's frankness and box-office success, as well as his stunning performance, made him a major star. Filmed for only $350,000 (normally the sort of money spent on executives' cigar bills, said director Lewis Gilbert), *Alfie* brought Caine mixed blessings; so convincing was his performance that people often identified him with the role in real life. If that were true, he said, "I couldn't have made him such a bastard" on the screen. In one scene, where Caine had to roll off a sofa on top of the redoubtable Shelley Winters, a whalebone from her corset dislodged and "stabbed me half to death." Speaking directly to the camera, as portions of his role required, was difficult for Caine. He finally hit on the solution of placing a warm body whom he could address just out of camera range. Because of the low budget, Gilbert filmed most scenes in only one take.

ALGIERS. 1938. Filmed winter–spring 1938; Walter Wanger Studio, Los Angeles.
Cast: Charles Boyer, Hedy Lamarr, Sigrid Gurie, Gene Lockhart, Joseph Calleia, Alan Hale.
Director: John Cromwell.

Charles Boyer, a thorough professional, balked at making this film, only acceding as a favor to producer Walter Wanger. Boyer's chief concern was the script, a virtual scene-by-scene remake of the compelling French film *Pépé le Moko* (1936). That picture had starred Jean Gabin, whom Boyer admired and had no desire to emulate or reinterpret in *Algiers*. Also, the weak acting of newcomer Hedy Lamarr, a beautiful Austrian actress making her American debut, embarrassed and frustrated him—though he did his best to coach her in their scenes together. (Wanger had wanted Dolores del Rio or Sylvia Sidney for the female lead.) For Lamarr, despite being clearly out of her league, the film meant international stardom. Her white turban headgear, which she personally created, became briefly stylish in the fashion world. Cameraman James Wong Howe's overhead lights created a vibrant sunlight effect, and he burned resin on the studio floor to cause a dry, atmospheric haze. His intricately lighted close-ups of Lamarr in her love scene with Boyer, requiring three days to film, remain classics of portrait photography. The Casbah set, a long, narrow, three-level maze of cobblestone streets and passages, was reconstructed from photos of the actual area in Algiers. Boyer spent the rest of his life affably denying the famous line "Come wiz me to ze Casbah" attributed to him—but never actually spoken—in the film.

ALICE DOESN'T LIVE HERE ANYMORE. 1975. Filmed 1974; Tucson, Arizona. Columbia Studios, Burbank.
Cast: Ellen Burstyn, Kris Kristofferson, Diane Ladd, Jodie Foster, Alfred Lutter, Vic Tayback, Harvey Keitel.
Director: Martin Scorsese.

Using the leverage of her star performance in *The Exorcist*, Ellen Burstyn became the impelling force behind this film, collaborating on both scripting and casting and choosing Martin Scorsese as director. Rejecting the all's-well ending of Robert Getchell's original screenplay, she worked with Kris Kristofferson on the set to achieve, if not the ringing feminist statement she wanted, at least a psychologically real fade-out she could live with. Her son, Jefferson Burstyn, played a bit part as next-door neighbor kid, Harold. For Scorsese, one challenge lay in working with young Alfred Lutter, who had never acted before. Scorsese filmed many interior scenes with a hand-held camera because of space limitations and his wish to create a degree of subconscious tension in the viewer. The beginning dream vignette was the last scene ever filmed in the old Columbia Studios (used by Warner Bros. for this film) and included a dresser used on a set of *Citizen Kane*. Burstyn won an Academy Award as best actress, and the movie inspired the TV sitcom *Alice*, in which only Vic Tayback remained from the original cast.

ALICE'S RESTAURANT. 1969. Filmed winter–spring 1969; Massachusetts: Trinity Church, Stockbridge; Stockbridge, Pittsfield, and Great Barrington areas. New York: Millerton Scrambling Track, Millerton; New York City.
Cast: Arlo Guthrie, Pat Quinn, James Broderick, Michael McClanathan, Geoff Outlaw.
Director: Arthur Penn.

This paean to the flower-child culture of the 1960s combined nonactors with professionals in a story that required every ounce of Arthur Penn's directorial skills. Almost all the participants either played themselves or actual living persons. Half the story derived from folksinger Arlo Guthrie's autobiographical title song; the part where he is arrested for dumping trash illegally had actually happened to him five years earlier. One scene required many retakes to get the stolid, androgynous Guthrie to show a modicum of anger. The Alice of the title, played by Pat Quinn, was in real life Alice Brock who, with her husband Ray (played by James Broderick), watched filming from the sidelines; despite the film's depiction of their generally rosy marriage, they were divorcing at the time. Brock, bearing a striking resemblance to Quinn, played a bit part. The mixture of persons and impersonations on the set led to some strange confusions of identity, in which the real Alice and Ray reacted spontaneously to their opposite-sex acting counterparts. Brock said she didn't want to play Alice herself because she "had already done it." William Obanhein, the Stockbridge cop who played himself, became known on the set as "One-Shot Obie" because "somehow I got what Mr. Penn wanted right off." Broderick confessed that he loved his young hippie costars but felt depressed about them in what he called a "very sad movie."

ALIEN. 1979. Filmed summer–autumn 1978; Shepperton Studios, Shepperton, England.
Cast: Tom Skerritt, Sigourney Weaver, Veronica Cartwright, Harry Dean Stanton, John Hurt, Yaphet Kotto, Ian Holm.
Director: Ridley Scott.

This outer-space chiller owed its intense realism and terror to superb sets and special effects. The adult alien monster (called Big Chap on the set) was actually seven-foot-two Bolaji Badejo, an African Masai tribesman dressed in a rubber suit (he was a student in England at the time). Technicians built three space monster heads for long, medium, and close-up shots; the fully mechanized "near head" had multiple moving parts remotely controlled by a 45-foot cable. That's K-Y Jelly coating its drooling chops, and shredded condoms simulated its ghastly jaw tendons. Real blood and entrails, shipped from a London slaughterhouse, spurted plentifully on the sets, sometimes inspiring genuine sickness and distress. The baby monster (actually a puppet) that suddenly burst from John Hurt's false chest (another intricate construction that lined up his torso with a cutaway table) shocked the other players who had been kept off the set while Hurt was being prepared. Their horrified reactions were not faked. Veronica Cartwright was especially shaken; and cameraman Derek Vanlint, who filmed the scene, almost passed out when he saw rushes of it later. Produced entirely in a studio interior, the filming combined enormous constructions with duplicate miniatures. Intricate spacecraft interiors used tons of jet engine scrap, but the main exterior model of the spacecraft measured only eight feet. The huge alien planet landscape, bathed in incense smoke to heighten the other worldly aura, was further enlarged by matte paintings. An Academy Award went to the visual effects team. Sigourney Weaver, who remembered the film as a "nightmare" and felt at the time that she never wanted to make another, reprised her role in the 1986 sequel, *Aliens*.

ALL ABOUT EVE. 1950. Filmed April–June 1950; New York City. New Haven, Connecticut. California: Curran Theatre, San Francisco; 20th Century-Fox Studios, Los Angeles.

Cast: Bette Davis, Anne Baxter, George Sanders, Celeste Holm, Gary Merrill, Gregory Ratoff, Marilyn Monroe, Thelma Ritter.

Director: Joseph L. Mankiewicz.

Claudette Colbert, scheduled for the Bette Davis role, canceled out because of a back injury, a circumstance she never ceased to regret. For Davis, this film represented a professional comeback after her career had nose-dived. Her role of Margo Channing, possibly her best ever, was inspired by English stage actress Peg Woffington. Davis and Gary Merrill began an off-camera romance that culminated in their marriage. Tallulah Bankhead accused Davis of imitating her husky voice for the role, but Davis swore it was unintentional; the emotional stress of her recent divorce from William Grant Sherry, she said, had caused her hoarseness. She received voice treatments throughout most of the filming and rerecorded her early dialogue for the soundtrack. Anne Baxter found the reticent George Sanders (who won an Academy Award as best supporting actor) difficult to "key up" for their scenes together—he slept in his dressing room betweentimes, and Baxter said that filming a scene with him usually required seven takes before he was fully awake. The shorter of the two scenes between Sanders and Marilyn Monroe, who was then a virtual unknown, required twenty-five takes to get right. Offscreen, Sanders's wife, Zsa Zsa Gabor, took an instant dislike to Monroe, causing Sanders to plead with Marilyn to greet him on the set only "from afar." Davis, never easy to please, confessed herself delighted with the film, calling it "a charmed production from the word go." The Broadway musical *Applause* was based on this film.

ALL QUIET ON THE WESTERN FRONT. 1930. Filmed 1930. California: Balboa; Irvine Ranch, Irvine; Sherwood Forest and Malibu Lakes, San Fernando Valley; Universal City; RKO-Pathé Studios, Culver City.

Cast: Lew Ayres, Louis Wolheim, Slim Summerville, John Wray, Russell Gleason, Beryl Mercer, Ben Alexander.

Director: Lewis Milestone.

Filmed mainly in the same sequence in which it appears on screen, this classic antiwar film won two Academy Awards—for best picture and for director Lewis Milestone, who strived for precise authenticity, importing tons of World War I German and French army equipment and building a training camp from actual German blueprints. More than 2,000 extras, mostly war veterans, played in the camp and battle scenes; the battles were photographed without sound (added later) on the twenty-acre Irvine Ranch. ZaSu Pitts originally played hero Lew Ayres's mother, but her renown as a comic performer signaled preview audiences to laugh; so her scenes were reshot with Beryl Mercer. Silent film comedian Raymond Griffith begged for and got the brief role of the dying French soldier. Cameraman Karl Freund suggested the brilliant concluding butterfly sequence, and the "dead" hand we see supporting the butterfly is Milestone's. The young Ben Alexander (playing Franz Kemmerich) was the same actor who, years later, became Jack Webb's sidekick in TV's *Dragnet*. As for Ayres, his genuine pacifism all but shattered his career a decade later, though he valiantly served in dangerous noncombat positions during World War II. Overseas, as Europe prepared for another war, the film's humanist message aroused huge controversy. Poland banned *All Quiet on the Western Front* as being pro-German, as did France (until 1962); and the rising Nazi Party in Germany reacted furiously, instigating riots at German cinemas that dared show it.

ALL THAT JAZZ. 1979. Filmed 1979; Astoria Studios, Queens, New York.
Cast: Roy Scheider, Jessica Lange, Ann Reinking, Leland Palmer, Ben Vereen, Cliff Gorman, Erzsebet Foldi, John Lithgow.
Director: Bob Fosse.

A man bent on self-destruction (played by Roy Scheider) is how Bob Fosse viewed himself in this semiautobiographical portrait, probably the most unusual musical ever filmed. Fosse worked with two of his former lovers in this film. He and Ann Reinking, who played Scheider's girlfriend, had ended a six-year relationship; and his subsequent brief affair with Jessica Lange, playing the white-gauzed angel of death, was also finished. Of all the females on the set, he most enjoyed thirteen-year-old Erzsebet Foldi and her endless stream of bad jokes. A ballet student, Foldi had been one of thirty girls to audition for the part of Scheider's daughter. Many scenes, including the open-heart surgery sequence, reflected episodes from the director's own frenetic life. Fosse said he found inspiration for many of the dance sequences in John Huston's *Moulin Rouge* (1952).

ALL THE KING'S MEN. 1949. Filmed summer 1949; California: Stockton; Columbia Studios, Burbank.
Cast: Broderick Crawford, John Ireland, Mercedes McCambridge, Joanne Dru, John Derek.
Director: Robert Rossen.

Broderick Crawford, whose Academy Award for best actor hardly helped his later career, broke out of B films in his role of demagogue politician Willie Stark, a character based on the late Louisiana senator Huey Long. John Wayne had angrily turned down the role, saying that Robert Penn Warren's original novel (as well as the screenplay) disgusted him. Stockton residents, who figured prominently as extras in the film, got caught up in the drama as the domineering Stark became a well-publicized presence in the civic life of the town. Director Robert Rossen gave speaking lines to scores of citizens who had never acted before. To capture spontaneity, he sometimes filmed crowd scenes when the participants thought he was just rehearsing a shot. This was Mercedes McCambridge's first movie appearance, and she won a supporting-actress Oscar for it.

ALL THE PRESIDENT'S MEN. 1976. Filmed June–November 1975; Washington, D.C. Warner Bros. Studios, Burbank.

Cast: Robert Redford, Dustin Hoffman, Jason Robards, Jr., Martin Balsam, Hal Holbrook, Jack Warden, Jane Alexander, Stephen Collins.

Director: Alan J. Pakula.

As coproducer, Robert Redford not only bought film rights to the yet-unwritten book about President Nixon's downfall by *Washington Post* reporters Carl Bernstein and Bob Woodward; he had also encouraged the team to write the book in the first place. Redford then offered Dustin Hoffman the role of Bernstein. A meticulous researcher of his roles, Hoffman spent weeks with Bernstein, absorbing atmosphere at the *Post*, before ever seeing a script. Screenwriter William Goldman, who penned countless revisions, encountered plenty of opposition: from director Alan Pakula, who had his own concept; from Redford, who demanded (but ultimately relinquished) a love interest; and from a competing script that Bernstein and his wife, Nora Ephron, suddenly launched into the fray. (Woodward apologized for his partner to the incensed Goldman, and the new script was never used.) Authenticity of newsroom scenes, along with carefully noted bantering of the editorial staff, was of prime concern to the filmmakers. A 33,000-square-foot replica of the *Post* newsroom arose in the Burbank studio; several tons of paper trash, even, were trucked from the *Post* to recreate the office litter. Look for Watergate security guard Frank Wills, playing himself, in the actual corridors where he noticed the break-in and set in motion the events that brought down a president. Writer Goldman and Robards (as best supporting actor) won Academy Awards. Jack Hirshberg's book, *A Portrait of All the President's Men* (1976), details each aspect of the production.

AMADEUS. 1984. Filmed spring 1984; Prague, Czechoslovakia: Grypek Palace; Kromerz Palace; Tyl Theatre; Barrandov Studio.

Cast: F. Murray Abraham, Tom Hulce, Elizabeth Berridge, Jeffrey Jones, Simon Callow.

Director: Miloš Forman.

Miloš Forman chose his native Prague in which to make this film because it remained the only large baroque city in Europe untouched by World War II bombing. Officials at first declined to permit use of the wooden Tyl Theatre, where Mozart himself had conducted *Don Giovanni* in 1787, because of the fire hazard involved in lighting the auditorium with eleven chandeliers, each with forty to sixty candles. After long negotiations, scaffolding was erected to support the 700-pound chandeliers, and firemen stood guard while opening-night opera sequences were filmed. Tom Hulce described the experience of playing the role of Mozart in this theatre as "eerie and awe inspiring." Rivalry similar to that between Mozart and Salieri (played by F. Murray Abraham) operated on the sets as the two actors increasingly identified with their roles. Hulce found himself growing unaccountably "suspicious" of Abraham, and the latter resented being "pushed out" of the private jokes shared between Hulce and Meg Tilly, the actress first cast in the role of Constanze Mozart. (Tilly broke her ankle playing soccer, and Elizabeth Berridge came in as a last-minute replacement.) Abraham, however, believed that such tensions ultimately helped their performances. The film reaped eight Academy Awards, including honors for best film, for Forman as director, and for Abraham as leading actor.

AMERICAN GRAFFITI. 1973. Filmed June–August 1972; California: Petaluma; San Rafael.

Cast: Richard Dreyfuss, Ronny Howard, Paul Le Mat, Charlie Martin Smith, Cindy Williams, Candy Clark, Mackenzie Phillips, Harrison Ford.

Director: George Lucas.

Scripted by George Lucas as a fond memorial to his own

adolescence in Modesto, California, *American Graffiti* didn't inspire anybody's confidence at the outset or during production. Even Lucas himself was not optimistic. On a shoestring budget, he recruited dozens of 1950s-vintage automobiles from all over northern California for the many cruising scenes, an assemblage that attracted hordes of car freaks and would-be greasers to location sites in Petaluma. Private jokes abound in the film: the license plate of Paul Le Mat's 1932 deuce coupe, THX-1138 was the title of Lucas's first film (1970); *Dementia 13*, displayed on the marquee of the local movie house, was coproducer Francis Ford Coppola's first mainstream directorial effort (1963). A near-tragedy occurred during the climactic car crash: a cameraman filming from ground level was almost run over. The teen angel character was Suzanne Somers's first professional acting job, and twelve-year-old Mackenzie Phillips also made her screen debut here. Johnny Weissmuller, Jr., son of the movies' best-known Tarzan, played a bit part as Badass I. Lucas was later criticized—rightfully, he agreed—for failing to include the fate of the female characters in the epilogue. The film grossed more than $55 million, not only making Lucas respectably bankable again, but also financing his 1977 *Star Wars* epic and inspiring the popular TV series *Happy Days*.

AN AMERICAN IN PARIS. 1951. Filmed August–October 1950; MGM Studios, Culver City.
Cast: Gene Kelly, Leslie Caron, Oscar Levant, Nina Foch, Georges Guetary.
Director: Vincente Minnelli.

Only the opening panoramic views of Paris were actually filmed there—all the rest was studio creation, though Vincente Minnelli insisted on meticulous authenticity of details. This was nineteen-year-old French ballet dancer Leslie Caron's screen debut. Discovered by Gene Kelly in 1948, she became his protégée for this film (which he also choreographed). But Caron's memories were mostly unpleasant. She spoke little English, found Hollywood mores mystifying and her dance routines tedious when not exhausting, and also suffered from a chronic case of anemia throughout the filming. Her charming but offbeat facial features nettled the Hollywood ideal of glamour, provoking hostility toward her—but also created a significant breakthrough in the casting of women. Georges Guetary, unknown to American audiences, was chosen for his role after Maurice Chevalier refused it and the studio had turned down Yves Montand for his supposed "Communist tendencies." Oscar Levant enjoyed making the film as a tribute to his old friend George Gershwin. He created the idea for his own musical "ego fantasy," in which he plays all the instruments and conducts the orchestra as well—this entire trick-photo sequence was filmed in one day. Levant was noted for his many and varied neuroses. During the prerecording session, which produced the actual soundtrack music, he said he found himself abysmally distracted at the keyboard by a candy wrapper staring at him from the floor; *Butterfinger*, it ominously declared. The film made a popular hit of "Our Love is Here to Stay," the last song Gershwin composed. Kelly's tap-dancing on screen is not the tap-dancing you hear; each routine had to be sound-synchronized in a post-recording session. The climactic, seventeen-minute ballet sequence had not been formulated by the time production wrapped on the rest of the film. Nina Foch's three-week absence because of chicken pox proved fortuitous to Kelly and Minnelli, giving them time to create the spectacular ballet, which they rehearsed for about eight weeks. The cement staircase they used in the ballet came from the retrieved 1944 set of *Kismet*; and the Paris street set rested on a hill created of dumped debris from *The Wizard of Oz*. Kelly's movable bed in his starving-artist garret cost $10,000 by the time all the rigging was installed to make it rise correctly. The black-and-white ball sequence came out overlong and disorganized; this passage was later entirely recreated in the editing room. For real devotees of *An American in Paris*, Donald Knox's book *The Magic Factory* (1973) provides design details of various sequences and of the intricate sets built to resemble Raoul Dufy paintings.

ANATOMY OF A MURDER. 1959. Filmed March–May 1959; Michigan: Marquette; Ishpeming.

Cast: James Stewart, Lee Remick, Ben Gazzara, Eve Arden, Arthur O'Connell, George C. Scott, Kathryn Grant, Orson Bean, Brooks West, Joseph N. Welch.

Director: Otto Preminger.

The set for James Stewart's law office occupied the Ishpeming house where Robert Traver, author of the original novel, was born and had practiced law; and trial scenes were filmed in the Marquette County Courthouse, where Traver had served fourteen years as a prosecutor. Because of winter weather, Otto Preminger filmed the trial scenes first, leaving exterior scenes until later. Both Spencer Tracy and Burl Ives had rejected the role of the trial judge, and Preminger's last-minute casting of Boston attorney Joseph Welch, famed for his surgical destruction of Senator Joseph R. McCarthy in 1954, was inspired. Welch enjoyed his brief foray into show business. (His new wife played a jury member. And there was another real-life married couple in the cast: Brooks West and Eve Arden.) Explaining how he instructed a nonactor for the part, Preminger said he was careful not to require Welch to move and talk at the same time. The film made a major star of Lee Remick, a new mother just five weeks before shooting began; Preminger had wanted Lana Turner, who declined because he wouldn't allow her a glamorous wardrobe. This was also George C. Scott's first notable screen role. The courtroom audience consisted of three hundred local townspeople, most of them unemployed in Michigan's chronically depressed Upper Peninsula. Along with all the California celebrities who descended on the suddenly bedazzled North Woods came Duke Ellington, who scored the film and briefly appeared in it. *Anatomy* evoked much controversy for its frank treatment (for 1959) of rape, and Preminger fought off several legal challenges to its exhibition. Among louder critics was Stewart's aged father, who publicly scolded his son for making a "dirty picture" and placed an ad in his hometown newspaper advising people not to see it. Richard Griffith's book, *Anatomy of a Motion Picture* (1959), gives many behind-the-scenes details of production.

ANGELS WITH DIRTY FACES. 1938. Filmed July–August 1938; Warner Bros. Studios, Burbank.

Cast: James Cagney, Pat O'Brien, Humphrey Bogart, Ann Sheridan, Leo Gorcey, the Dead End Kids.

Director: Michael Curtiz.

Imported to Hollywood from Brooklyn, the Dead End Kids (later called the Bowery Boys) were a tough, unruly bunch of adolescent stage actors who liked to raise much more hell than their scripts called for. James Cagney, no cream puff himself, had an early run-in with Leo Gorcey. Tiring of the latter's smart remarks and impulsive ad libs on the set, Cagney grabbed him by the shirt and told him in no uncertain terms to behave. Recognizing a genuine street kid when they saw one, the Kids thereafter shaped up. Cagney, who played hoodlum Rocky Sullivan, modeled his body language and speech on a street-corner pimp he had once known in Manhattan. The early scene in which the two boys playing Cagney and Pat O'Brien as youngsters run across the railroad tracks in front of an oncoming train terrified the boys and angered the locomotive engineer, who hadn't been properly briefed. Realism extended to the live machine-gun bullets you see popping around Cagney as police fire at him through a building window; studios in the 1930s used real ammunition, not blanks, for gunfire scenes. Though long-accustomed to such dangers as part of the job, Cagney this time stubbornly refused to stand in the window as bullets tore into the sash. Sure enough, one of the bullets passed exactly where his head would have been. Ironically, there were protests complaining of not enough realism in Cagney's performance—he stood off the entire New York police force, it seems, without once reloading his gun. In his next film, *The Oklahoma Kid*, he took pains to fire not more than six shots per scene.

ANIMAL CRACKERS. 1930. Filmed spring 1930; Paramount Studios, Astoria, Queens, New York.
Cast: Groucho, Chico, Harpo, and Zeppo Marx, Margaret Dumont, Lillian Roth.
Director: Victor Heerman.

Director Victor Heerman couldn't get all four Marx brothers to show up at the same time for rehearsals, so in desperation he had four small jail cells moved to the sound stage from another set for the wandering brothers to "rest in" when they weren't on camera. The Marxes essentially repeated onscreen their hugely popular stage show of the same title that had toured the country. Heerman held them to the script about as well as anyone could. The budget soared, however, because of all the Marxian horseplay—described by Lillian Roth as "one step removed from a circus"—that occurred *between* takes. For the female lead, the acting assignment was intended as severe penance by studio executives unhappy with Roth's erratic behavior as a Paramount contract player. (Alcoholism later forced her retirement, and in 1955 Susan Hayward played Roth in *I'll Cry Tomorrow.*) One of Roth's dialogues with Groucho in the fake painting scene had to be reshot at least ten times because she kept bursting into giggles. Tripping to the camera to deliver himself of mock-profound observations, Groucho parodied the mannered asides in *Strange Interlude*, the solemn Eugene O'Neill play that was popular at the time. And "Hooray for Captain Spaulding," first sung in this film, became Groucho's theme song for his later radio and TV shows.

ANNA CHRISTIE. 1930. Filmed winter 1930; MGM Studios, Culver City.
Cast: Greta Garbo, Charles Bickford, Marie Dressler.
Director: Clarence Brown.

Widely billed as Greta Garbo's first sound film, this adaptation of Eugene O'Neill's play brought the Swedish star a role she had long yearned to play. Her English was so good, however, that some scenes had to be refilmed with more accented speech to jibe with the part. In the end, she didn't revere her own performance, but she thought Marie Dressler was superb. For Dressler, whom the studio cast only reluctantly because "her day is past," the part heralded a career comeback. Charles Bickford, no Garbo fan and a thorny, difficult man to direct, accepted his role only after Garbo and producer Irving Thalberg charmed him into it. Though harmony reigned on the set, Bickford finally opined that the film was badly acted by the entire cast, "not excepting myself." O'Neill (deliberately) never saw this version of his play.

ANNA KARENINA. 1935. Filmed spring 1935; MGM Studios, Culver City.
Cast: Greta Garbo, Fredric March, Basil Rathbone, Freddie Bartholomew, Maureen O'Sullivan, Constance Collier.
Director: Clarence Brown.

Fredric March at 37 was tired of acting in costume epics and did this one only by studio order when producer David O. Selznick couldn't get Clark Gable for the male lead. Garbo, ever aloof from her public and her fellow cast members (except for Constance Collier, who became her confidante), insisted on closed sets for her scenes, and retakes were seldom necessary. Basil Rathbone believed he gave one of his best performances, attributing his inspiration to Garbo, whom he greatly admired. From her performance, he maintained that he learned the secret of good screen acting: using "mental projection" combined with "the least possible physical movement." Yet the enigmatic Garbo ignored even this cultured gentleman's attempts to be friendly, and Rathbone never quite forgave the personal slight. The production code office saw to it that many important scenes of Tolstoy's novel were precensored before scripting.

ANNIE. 1982. Filmed April–September 1981; New Jersey: Monmouth College, West Long Branch; Passaic River, East Newark. Radio City Music Hall, New York City. Burbank Studios, Burbank.
Cast: Albert Finney, Carol Burnett, Aileen Quinn, Bernadette Peters, Ann Reinking, Tim Curry, Edward Herrmann.
Director: John Huston.

Based on Harold Gray's vintage comic strip "Little Orphan Annie," the screenplay for this musical was, by critical consensus, much better than the script for the 1977 Broadway show. Neither John Huston nor most of the cast had ever made a musical before. Some 8,000 moppets were auditioned for the title role. Ten-year-old Aileen Quinn, an understudy in the Broadway *Annie* and a veteran of several TV commercials, won the highly publicized contest reminiscent of the 1938 search for an actress to play Scarlett O'Hara. Her brown hair was dyed red, and her exuberant fitness for the part led Huston to call her "a prodigy." Annie's famous dog Sandy, actually an otter hound named Bingo, had three stand-ins. The large mansion of Shadow Lawn (Woodrow Wilson Hall) on the Monmouth College campus became the Daddy Warbucks manor—and the college library, formerly the Murry Guggenheim mansion, served as the White House lawn set, where 6,000 rosebuds were hand-wired to the bushes in order to display a rose garden. Huston scrapped much of the Radio City Music Hall song footage—"Let's Go to the Movies"—in favor of incorporating scenes of Greta Garbo in *Camille*. Rotting crossties and an 85-degree incline made the railroad drawbridge scenes near the Passaic River hazardous, though the top thirty feet, where most of the action occurred, was a studio creation. Four-foot-nine stunt man Bobby Porter, dressed as Annie, performed in these scenes. The film created a merchandising bonanza when prearranged licensing and franchise deals spawned *Annie* toys, clothing, and other products.

ANNIE HALL. 1977. Filmed May–summer 1976; New York: Long Island; New York City. Los Angeles.
Cast: Woody Allen, Diane Keaton, Tony Roberts, Carol Kane, Paul Simon, Shelley Duvall.
Director: Woody Allen.

Anhedonia, defined as the chronic inability to experience pleasure, was Woody Allen's working title, changed only three weeks before the premiere. (*Hall* is Diane Keaton's real surname.) The retitling reflected a shift in Allen's whole concept of the film, from a comedic survey of almost every issue that plagued his own life to the exploration of a love affair—and it happened, he said, only during the final editing process. More or less autobiographical, *Annie Hall* explored fragments of Allen and Keaton's real-life relationship (amiably platonic by the time the film was made). Allen derived the scene in which he visits his childhood self from *Wild Strawberries* (1957), the masterpiece by Allen's favorite director, Ingmar Bergman. The scene where he sneezes into the cocaine powder was pure improvisation. Look for Sigourney Weaver in her screen debut as Allen's date outside the movie theatre. *Annie Hall* won four Oscars: for best picture, Keaton as best actress, Allen as director, and Allen and Marshall Brickman for best screenplay. Yet Allen was characteristically disappointed in the result, feeling that he hadn't achieved the balance of comedy and drama he intended. At the box office, he noted, the film made less money than had any previous Academy Award-winner.

THE APARTMENT. 1960. Filmed November 1959–February 1960; New York City. Samuel Goldwyn Studios, Los Angeles.
Cast: Jack Lemmon, Shirley MacLaine, Fred MacMurray, Ray Walston, Edie Adams, Jack Kruschen.
Director: Billy Wilder.

The oversize stage converted into the insurance company office set had previously housed Catfish Row in the film version of *Porgy and Bess*; here Billy Wilder shot the office party scene in one take on December 23, 1959. Jack Lemmon described his sequence with a comatose Shirley MacLaine in the apartment set as one of the most demanding he ever played. Note the painting over her bed: Rousseau's *Sleeping Gypsy*, the composition of which Wilder tried to emulate in the scene. Lemmon's improvised business with his character's ubiquitous nose spray (actually milk to make the spray visible) enlivened his dialogue with a genuinely startled Fred MacMurray. (Paul Douglas, originally cast for the MacMurray role, died two weeks before filming began.) The public response to his heel role stunned MacMurray, who quickly resumed playing only nice guys. Famously tight with a buck, MacMurray revised one slight bit for his character by tipping his shoe shiner only a dime instead of the fifty cents specified in the script—Wilder, who always insisted on absolute fidelity to the screenplay, merely shook his head and allowed it. He belatedly added the gin-playing scene between Lemmon and MacLaine because the latter was always playing gin off-camera. *The Apartment* won Academy Awards for best picture and for Wilder as director and (with I. A. L. Diamond) best writer.

APOCALYPSE NOW. 1979. Filmed March 1976–June 1977; Philippines: Baler; Pagsanjan River; Luzon.
Cast: Marlon Brando, Robert Duvall, Martin Sheen, Frederic Forrest, Dennis Hopper, Harrison Ford.
Director: Francis Ford Coppola.

Inspired by Joseph Conrad's *Heart of Darkness*, this film became a seemingly endless nightmare for everyone involved. A typhoon, an earthquake, equatorial weather, jungle fevers, personality clashes, a constantly changing script, a money sinkhole, and director Francis Coppola's one-shot-a-day perfectionism abruptly halted production at several points. Martin Sheen, whose role had been turned down by Steve McQueen, Harvey Keitel, and Jack Nicholson, suffered a nervous breakdown and a heart attack, requiring a further delay to await his recovery. For the hotel room scene early in the film, Sheen stayed drunk for two days while listening to Coppola's diatribes on the evils of mankind, finally hitting the mirror and cutting his hand in the unscripted sequence shown. Marlon Brando's character, Colonel Kurtz, was based on a real person, Green Beret Colonel Robert B. Rheault. Embarrassed by his 285-pound girth, Brando insisted on using a body double for long shots, and he originated much of his own dialogue. Dennis Hopper reportedly wore the same clothes for two months; crew members finally refused to ride in the same bus with him. For Coppola, who briefly appeared in one scene as director of a camera crew, making the film became an agonizing, apocalyptic metaphor, inspiring and symbolizing emotional crises of his own. He also mortgaged his entire financial capital. The film's logistics were awesome. Set designers built an entire fishing village of tile and bamboo plus replicas of the jungle Buddhist temple and the infamous Saigon street of Tu-Do. Pilots of the Philippine Air Force flew the fifty helicopters used. Language problems arising from the use of numerous South Vietnamese extras and the Italian camera crew caused formidable communications problems for Coppola in directing both ground action and aircraft. Mountain tribesmen, the Ifugaos, were also used as extras on the Kurtz compound set; for the camera they reenacted their actual ceremony of slaying a water buffalo. Coppola never denied that some of his bloated, $30-million budget went to grease the hands of General Ferdinand Marcos's Filipino officials. The U.S. Defense Department, leery of all screen attempts to show the Vietnam War as it was, refused all cooperation. Finally, however, the film more than paid its way and also won two Academy Awards—for sound and cinematography.

AROUND THE WORLD IN 80 DAYS. 1956. Filmed summer 1955–spring 1956; Chinchón, Spain. Elstree Studios, Borehamwood, England. Paris. Hong Kong. Tokyo. U.S.: Durango, Colorado; and six Hollywood studios, Los Angeles.

Cast: David Niven, Cantinflas, Robert Newton, Shirley MacLaine, plus forty-four guest stars.

Director: Michael Anderson.

This multimillion-dollar extravaganza, based on Jules Verne's classic novel and produced by flamboyant showman Mike Todd, originated the term *cameo role*, meaning a brief appearance of a familiar performer—and this film was full of them. According to one cameo star, Sir Cedric Hardwicke, Todd only succeeded in hiring his major bit players because he began doing it in England, "where an actor loses no prestige by taking a small part"—then the American actors he approached readily joined in. Ronald Colman received a new yellow Cadillac for his half-day stint before the camera. Sir Noel Coward wrote his own dialogue after being bullied into playing the role, he said, "over an inferior lunch." Todd replaced Gregory Peck as leader of a cavalry charge with old-time cowboy star Tim McCoy because he thought Peck didn't take the role seriously enough. As for the film's featured stars, David Niven had been suggested to the unsuspecting Todd by Todd's then-current housemate Evelyn Keyes (who also played a cameo role), a former flame of Niven's. Surrounded by some of England's finest actors in his initial London club scene, Niven fluffed his lines in take after take, but eventually gained confidence. He also feared heights but finally accomplished the balloon-ascent scene over "the Alps" (by means of a crane 180 feet above a Universal Studios back lot) with the help of champagne that Todd had imported to fortify him. The film proved the biggest money-maker of Niven's long career. Mexican comedian Cantinflas (i.e., Mario Moreno), though immensely popular in South America, was almost unknown elsewhere until his performance as Niven's sidekick. This was Robert Newton's last movie; beset for years by alcoholism, he remained on the wagon for the duration of filming but died soon after. Shirley MacLaine, another virtual unknown at the time, later deplored her own performance, feeling she had been dismally miscast. Filmed in 140 location setups throughout the world, the production underwent several sudden halts while Todd went scrounging for completion money. The enterprise was mainly financed by Todd's old friend Lorraine Manville, heiress of the Johns-Manville fortune. Academy Awards for best picture, writing, photography, and music followed; and, along with wealth and respectability for Todd, a new wife: Elizabeth Taylor.

ARSENIC AND OLD LACE. 1944. Filmed November–December 1941; Warner Bros. Studios, Burbank.
Cast: Cary Grant, Josephine Hull, Jean Adair, Raymond Massey, Peter Lorre, Priscilla Lane.
Director: Frank Capra.

Made as the Japanese bombed Pearl Harbor, this comedy first appeared in movie houses three years later because contract agreements prevented its release until the long-running

Broadway play of the same title closed. (Ironically, director-producer Capra had chosen the property because he wanted some quick financial security for his family.) Bob Hope turned down the male lead, which at Cary Grant's insistence was then considerably enlarged. Boris Karloff was unavailable for the part that went to Raymond Massey. The film used only two studio-bound sets, one interior and one exterior. Jean Adair had helped nurse a very ill vaudeville performer called Archibald Leach (who later changed his name to Cary Grant) some twenty years before, so the two were old friends. In memory of that occasion, Grant had one of the tombstones in the cemetery set inscribed with his former name. *Arsenic*, however, was his least favorite performance. He thought that James Stewart would have been a better choice for the role. The film's mockery of death was innovative, and Capra's lightning dialogue whizzed by the bluenoses. Only Grant's final line—"I'm a bastard!"—didn't make it past the censors; "bastard" became "son of a sea cook."

THE ASPHALT JUNGLE. 1950. Filmed autumn–December 1949; Lexington, Kentucky. MGM Studios, Culver City.
Cast: Sterling Hayden, Sam Jaffe, Louis Calhern, Jean Hagen, Marilyn Monroe, James Whitmore.
Director: John Huston.

The Asphalt Jungle spawned a cinema genre—the caper or big heist film—endlessly imitated but rarely equaled. A nervous Sterling Hayden, fighting severe alcohol and psychiatric problems, landed his first major starring role over the opposition of skeptical studio chief Dore Schary, and his performance restored his Hollywood status. The film also gave Marilyn Monroe her breakthrough part; John Huston had originally sought Lola Albright—and though the original screen credits didn't even list Monroe, she judged her small climactic scene with Calhern as one of her best performances. The last scene was filmed first—in Lexington. Three remakes: *The Badlanders* (1958), *Cairo* (1963), and *Cool Breeze* (1972).

THE AWFUL TRUTH. 1937. Filmed June–July 1937; Columbia Studios, Los Angeles.
Cast: Irene Dunne, Cary Grant, Ralph Bellamy.
Director: Leo McCarey.

One of the first sound films in which divorce was considered an apt subject for comedy, this was a reworking of a 1922 stage hit and two previous silent movies. Leo McCarey was a director who brought new lines of dialogue, scrawled on scraps of paper, to the set each morning, also instructing his cast to improvise lines liberally. This procedure irked an already nervous and insecure Cary Grant, still festering from his own 1935 divorce from actress Virginia Cherrill. At first, Grant sought to exchange roles with Ralph Bellamy—then he offered studio chief Harry Cohn $5,000 to release him entirely from the project. That action thoroughly disgusted McCarey, who offered to chip in another $10,000. Cohn finally interceded, but years later McCarey still shook his head over Grant's behavior on the set. Ironically, *The Awful Truth* proved one of the actor's biggest successes. He made one more film (two decades later) for McCarey and teamed twice more with Irene Dunne. Stealing many scenes was the wirehaired terrier called Mr. Smith in this film but known as Asta in *The Thin Man* (1934). McCarey won an Academy Award as best director. *Let's Do It Again* was a 1953 musical remake.

B

BABES IN ARMS. 1939. Filmed May–June 1939; MGM Studios. Culver City.

Cast: Judy Garland, Mickey Rooney, Charles Winninger, Douglas MacPhail, Betty Jaynes, Margaret Hamilton.

Director: Busby Berkeley.

This was the first movie matchup of Garland and Rooney, who subsequently made nine more films together. Never romantically teamed in real life, they both adored each other in a brother-sister sort of way that lasted until Garland's death. Behind the music and high spirits of this movie lurked pain and ultimate tragedy. Both stars trembled on the edge of physical collapse, having just completed an exhausting nationwide tour of personal appearances. Garland turned seventeen during the production (her first screen appearance after making *The Wizard of Oz*), and director Berkeley pushed her hard to match Rooney's determined vigor. Garland was already a pill addict, consuming uppers to hold down her weight and key up her energy level. Douglas MacPhail and Betty Jaynes married during the making of the film; following their divorce in 1944, MacPhail killed himself. The happy endings of *Babes in Arms* were all, unfortunately, in the script.

BABY DOLL. 1956. Filmed November 1955–February 1956; Benoit, Mississippi. Warner Bros. Vitagraph Studios, Brooklyn, New York.
Cast: Karl Malden, Carroll Baker, Eli Wallach, Mildred Dunnock, Rip Torn.
Director: Elia Kazan.

Condemned by the Catholic Legion of Decency for its "carnal suggestiveness" (the first major-studio film to receive such valuable publicity), *Baby Doll* looks innocuous by today's standards. But things got plenty steamy in Benoit, many of whose 444 townsfolk played bit parts. Carroll Baker, a Method actress in a part that Marilyn Monroe had wanted and Diane Cilento had refused, said she reflected the demands of her role in her attitude of unreasonable antagonism toward Karl Malden and her turned-on feelings toward Eli Wallach (in his screen debut). She confessed that she habitually worked herself into a lathering "state of desire" before cameras rolled. (An amused Wallach repeated for years afterward his account of the house hallway scene, in which Baker kept on kissing him long after the camera had moved away.) She claimed to have modeled her speech and mannerisms on Ellie May, a genteel, eighty-year-old Mississippi belle she met on location. The house in which most of the filming occurred was the "Old Burras Place," which had been vacant for twenty-five years. The entire company took pains to make friends and enlist cooperation in Benoit; Mildred Dunnock, Elia Kazan joked, could have been elected mayor by the time they left. Kazan never rigidly plotted his scenes, preferring his cast to remain unaware of the camera; instead, he ordered his camera crew merely to follow the actors. He said he preferred this film to his much more acclaimed *A Streetcar Named Desire*.

THE BAD AND THE BEAUTIFUL. 1952. Filmed spring 1952; MGM Studios, Culver City.
Cast: Lana Turner, Kirk Douglas, Walter Pidgeon, Dick Powell, Barry Sullivan, Gloria Grahame, Gilbert Roland, Leo G. Carroll, Elaine Stewart.

Director: Vincente Minnelli.

Hollywood's favorite topic—itself—provided the backdrop for this drama, in which writer Charles Schnee patterned the major roles on several Tinseltown figures of the time. Gossip had it that Kirk Douglas's character was based on the producer Val Lewton (but it was David O. Selznick who considered suing MGM). Lana Turner's role was identified with Diana Barrymore, and Dick Powell's with F. Scott Fitzgerald. Leo G. Carroll and Ivan Trisseult reputedly caricatured Alfred Hitchcock and Fritz Lang, respectively. Vincente Minnelli and producer John Houseman were reluctant to cast Turner, questioning her ability to sustain such a demanding role. Minnelli guided her closely, obtaining needed retakes by faking mistakes in lighting and sound setups so as not to make the actress more nervous and insecure than she already was. In the end, he was pleased with her performance. Turner's most difficult moment, her mounting hysteria in a brakeless car, was also the final scene shot, some eleven weeks after everybody else had gone home. Seated in a car chassis mounted on a turntable and springs atop planks, she endured take after take from different camera angles as crew members swayed the chassis and sprayed "rain" at her; by the end of the day, she was close to genuine hysteria. Miscellanea: Louis Calhern, unbilled, recited Shakespeare as the voice of Turner's actor father on the phonograph; Douglas's studio wardrobe numbered seventy-three items of clothing, all of which he kept; and Ned Glass, who played the wardrobe manager, was barely allowed to finish his scene after giving "unsatisfactory" answers to the infamous House Un-American Activities Committee—he was thereafter blacklisted for several years. Academy Award winners: Gloria Grahame for supporting actress and Robert Surtees for cinematography.

THE BAND WAGON. 1953. Filmed September 1952–January 1953; MGM Studios, Culver City.
Cast: Fred Astaire, Cyd Charisse, Oscar Levant, Nanette Fabray, Jack Buchanan.
Director: Vincente Minnelli.

Betty Comden and Adolph Green wrote this musical as a satire of themselves (as played by Nanette Fabray and Oscar Levant) and of Fred Astaire (as played at age fifty-four by himself). The fan club scene at the train station was a real episode from Comden and Green's own hungry days as struggling composers. In setting up the small hotel room set, Vincente Minnelli constantly changed lines and positions, causing Astaire to suffer a brief mental lapse in the confusion—he uncharacteristically stormed off the set in frustration. Levant, felled by a heart attack only six weeks before filming, had been ordered by his doctor not to stride down the long ramp used in filming the song "That's Entertainment"—but when Astaire disgustedly offered to carry him, Levant did the walk. Minnelli conceived the Mickey Spillane "Girl Hunt" ballet and filmed it in seven days. (Spillane was, at the time, at the peak of his popularity for his ultrahardboiled detective novels.) English music hall star Jack Buchanan was a second choice for his role after Clifton Webb turned it down, Buchanan performing despite severe pain from dental surgery. Cyd Charisse, slightly taller than Astaire, often played her scenes with him on bent legs. Fabray's memories were mostly unpleasant; she cut her leg on a barrel edge during one routine, and she recalled the set as a cold, unfriendly place—"nobody talked to anybody." The genuine dancing bootblack from downtown Los Angeles, named LeRoy Daniels, had inspired the 1950 song "Chattanooga Shoe Shine Boy." "That's Entertainment," written for this film, became the title for a 1974 compilation movie, part of which Astaire narrated on the same train station set used in *The Band Wagon*.

THE BANK DICK. 1940. Filmed September–October 1940; Universal Studios, Universal City.
Cast: W. C. Fields, Franklin Pangborn, Shemp Howard, Jack Norton, Grady Sutton, Cora Witherspoon.
Director: Eddie Cline.

The script for *The Bank Dick*, authored by Mahatma Kane Jeeves (one of W. C. Field's many noms de plume), was savaged by studio heads before filming began. Fields conducted a long, hilarious correspondence with his censors, finally preserving most of his ideas intact. He often changed dialogue during production, however (directors on his films were usually positions of mere formality), and he postdubbed some of his best lines with no attempt to lip-synch them. Fields had wanted Gloria Jean, Ann Sothern, and Mickey Rooney for this film but couldn't get them. Repulsive Rogan was played by a reputed mobster, Al Hill, supposedly planted on the set to launder money. Fields took a shine to him, and Hill liked acting so much he stayed in Hollywood. The name of the Black Pussy saloon, bartended by Shemp Howard (one of the Three Stooges), evoked executive gasps until Fields pointed out that a café of that name, operated by comedian Leon Errol, actually existed on Santa Monica Boulevard. Citizens of Lompoc, California, weren't so easily mollified, however, by Fields's constant mispronunciation of the town's name and depiction of the place as dull and backward. At age sixty and rapidly declining in health, Fields suffered from a painful kidney ailment during production. Observers noted that his malicious versions of housewives, American home life, banks, salesmen, and doctors seemed to square many old personal accounts.

BAREFOOT IN THE PARK. 1967. Filmed November 1966–January 1967; New York City. Paramount Studios, Los Angeles.
Cast: Robert Redford, Jane Fonda, Mildred Natwick, Charles Boyer, Herb Edelman.
Director: Gene Saks.

This first screen collaboration of Neil Simon and director Gene Saks top-billed Redford for the first time. He hadn't expected to be offered the film role. As it turned out, he enjoyed working with Jane Fonda, his costar in *The Chase* (1966), but hated the preppy costuming; off-camera, he lounged in cowboy boots and hat. Fonda nosed out Elizabeth Ashley for the female lead, and the film proved her biggest box-office success up to that time. Based on Simon's long-running Broadway success, which also starred Redford, Mildred Natwick, and Herb Edelman.

BARRY LYNDON. 1975. Filmed December 1973–July 1974; England: Corsham Court, Corsham; Wilton House, Wilton; Petworth House, Petworth; Longleat House, Warminster; Castle Howard, Malton. Ireland: Powerscourt House, Ennis Kerry. West Germany.
Cast: Ryan O'Neal, Marisa Berenson, Patrick Magee, Hardy Kruger, Michael Hordern.
Director: Stanley Kubrick.

Stanley Kubrick intended each frame of this film as a master composition. Pressing the pause button on your VCR at almost any point gives you a replica of an 18th-century canvas. Note Kubrick's juxtapositions of sunlight and candlelight—using, for the latter, newly developed lenses. Clothing designs were all copies from drawings and paintings of the period, and Kubrick used no constructed sets. Several English mansions and country houses provided both exterior and interior scenes, which he integrated to represent one manor. He filmed battle scenes at Powerscourt in Ireland, where he had originally intended to make the entire movie. (Anonymous threats to his family caused him to remove the production to England.) Working with both novice and professional actors, Kubrick shot numerous retakes, but he pushed only the pros for perfection. Ryan O'Neal, who had never faced such a demanding role, at first disparaged his costar, international fashion model Marisa Berenson, as "lazy"; he changed his mind, however, as filming proceeded and Kubrick coaxed the best from both of them. The movie took four Academy Awards, though none for acting. (Based on a novel by William Makepeace Thackeray.)

BEAT THE DEVIL. 1954. Filmed autumn 1953; Ravello, Italy. Shepperton Studios, Shepperton, England.
Cast: Humphrey Bogart, Gina Lollobrigida, Jennifer Jones, Edward Underdown, Peter Lorre, Robert Morley, Ivor Barnard.
Director: John Huston.

The script was a piecemeal job by Truman Capote, who worked about one day ahead of actual filming—his dialogue was always "mint fresh," said a bemused Robert Morley. Capote shifted the original screenplay from heavy drama to comedy played straight. Elements of parody from previous Bogart-Huston films, including *The Maltese Falcon*, *The Treasure of the Sierra Madre*, and *Key Largo*, crept into the screenplay. (*Beat the Devil* was their last collaboration.) Bogart, as coproducer, had bought the property for Huston, but the production turned into a series of elaborate in-jokes, with finally no very clear idea of what the entire film was supposed to be *about*. Most of the Italians in the supporting cast knew no English and spoke their lines phonetically. A bewildered Gina Lollobrigida (whom Bogart nicknamed Frigidaire on the set because he couldn't pronounce her name) earned his high respect for her dogged professionalism—he had at first considered her just another sexy starlet. An efficient Italian Communist crew worked on the actual filming, while Huston kept another, inept Italian crew and an English crew out of his hair by assigning them to the construction of unnecessary towers and scaffolds. In an offscreen car accident, Bogart split his tongue so badly that production halted for several days while he recovered from stitches and awaited the arrival of new dentures from Hollywood. In the film, the car that goes over the cliff was supposed to stop, while the camera halted, letting Bogart climb out before it was pushed over. But the Italian technician engaged to hide below the front seat to operate the brakes had disappeared, and Bogart bailed out only seconds before the car sailed into space. Part of the Ravello monastery had to be decloistered to allow location filming and the entry of women; it was later reconsecrated. The villa where many scenes were filmed had been the romantic hideaway of conductor Leopold Stokowski and actress Greta Garbo in 1937. Despite being a textbook example on how not to make a movie, *Beat the Devil* proved enjoyable, if baffling.

BEAUTY AND THE BEAST (LA BELLE ET LA BÊTE). 1947. Filmed August 1945–January 1946; France: Rochecorbon; Château de Raray, Raray; Saint-Maurice Studios, Joinville.

Cast: Jean Marais, Josette Day, Michel Auclair, Marcel André, Mila Parély.

Director: Jean Cocteau.

Hardships plagued Jean Cocteau's production of this surreal fantasy based on the 18th-century fairy tale and begun just months after World War II hostilities had ended in Europe. The director encountered constant obstacles that at times became overwhelming. Supplies were short or altogether unavailable; camera and lighting equipment were antique and unreliable; the film stock proved inferior; and the electric power periodically failed. In addition, Jean Marais and Mila Parély became virtual invalids—Marais from painful boils on his thigh and head, and Parély from injuries received offscreen when the spirited circus horse Aramis (called Magnifique in the film) rolled over on her. Cocteau himself endured eruptions of facial eczema that almost drove him wild. Despite these problems, he somehow managed to complete the film, shooting on location at the villages of Rochecorbon (Beauty's house) and Raray (Beast's castle). Designer Christian Bérard created sets combining the styles of Jan Vermeer and Gustave Doré. Marais, who played three roles, required five hours to apply his intricate Beast makeup; the fragile mask, devised in three separate facial parts, consisted of gum and hair on a webbing base, with fangs attached to his teeth. Between takes, he hardly dared open his mouth lest his fearful face would come unglued. Local children watching the location shooting ran off terrified when he emerged from the bushes. Marais also subjected himself to extreme hazard in the scene where he is shot by Diana's arrow; despite his padding of mail and cork, the angle of safety was marginal and the offscreen archer nervous. Cocteau detailed the making of this movie in his book *Diary of a Film* (1950).

BECKET. 1964. Filmed May–September 1963; England: Newcastle; Shepperton Studios, Shepperton.
Cast: Richard Burton, Peter O'Toole, Donald Wolfit, John Gielgud, Martita Hunt, Pamela Brown, Sian Phillips.
Director: Peter Glenville.

Richard Burton, given the choice of playing either Becket or Henry II, inclined to the latter role—but on the advice of Elizabeth Taylor, with whom he had just finished making *Cleopatra*, he selected the title character, thus varying his frequent casting as a king. He and Peter O'Toole, both earnest drinkers, agreed to stay on the wagon until after they had mastered their roles, which didn't take long. The two enjoyed a friendly rivalry on the set and much active roistering off-camera. Though both often showed up tipsy, they invariably recovered instantly for their takes. O'Toole was quite far gone in the scene where he slips a ring on Burton's finger, but he managed nicely. Likewise, when repeating the famous line "Will no one rid me of this meddlesome priest?" O'Toole thought best to be actually drunk, as Henry II was on that occasion. Despite their boozy frolics, however, both actors took their characters and performances seriously. O'Toole read deeply on Henry II, studying Paul Robeson recordings for the voice he sought and lowering his normal pitch. Sian Phillips, O'Toole's wife, disliked acting with her husband, but was enlisted for her role because she could read music and sing Welsh songs. Burton had suggested John Gielgud, whose future career looked bleak at the time, for the role of Louis VII, a job he badly needed. The Canterbury Cathedral set, a plaster replica, approximated the cathedral's 12th-century appearance. It took seventeen weeks to build on Stage H at Shepperton, the largest sound stage in Europe. Ten days of filming on this set resulted in only eight minutes of release-print footage. Scriptwriter Edward Anhalt won an Academy Award for his adaptation of Jean Anouilh's original play. Five years later, O'Toole played Henry II again in *The Lion in Winter*.

BEING THERE. 1979. Filmed January–April 1979; Washington, D.C. Biltmore Estate, Asheville, North Carolina. California: Craven Estate, Pasadena; MGM/United Artists Studios, Culver City.

Cast: Peter Sellers, Shirley MacLaine, Jack Warden, Melvyn Douglas, Richard Basehart.

Director: Hal Ashby.

Jerzy Kosinski, who adapted his novel into the screenplay of *Being There*, originally wanted to play the role of Chance the gardener himself, as well as direct the film; but he professed himself pleased at the final casting. Peter Sellers, considering Chance the role of a lifetime, had lobbied with Kosinski for the part since 1972. He tried out numerous walks and accents, settling on a voice resembling that of film comic Stan Laurel. Characteristically, he didn't abandon the role when he went home at night; his wife, Lynne Frederick, said he seemed to become an old man for the duration. Apprehensive about his health, Sellers recalled to Shirley MacLaine that it was on the same stage in 1964, during the making of *Kiss Me Stupid*, that he had felt the first symptoms of his heart disease; he had to resign from the production. Sellers had acted once before with MacLaine (in *Woman Times Seven*, 1967) and apparently believed, falsely, that they had had a brief affair at that time. MacLaine found him "a dream" to work with despite his sudden moods of abstraction. She fretted long about the prospect of her bedroom masturbation scene. Director Hal Ashby delayed it as long as possible, but the scene required seventeen takes. Because of this sequence in the script, Sir Laurence Olivier had turned down the role that went to Melvyn Douglas, saying MacLaine's scene was "immoral."

BEN-HUR. 1959. Filmed May 1958–January 1959; Rome: Castle Antonio; Cinecittà Studios.
Cast: Charlton Heston, Haya Harareet, Jack Hawkins, Stephen Boyd, Hugh Griffith.
Director: William Wyler.

It was the most expensive production ($15 million) in movie history up to that time. During location shooting, the eighteen-acre main set attracted thousands of visitors from all over the world. William Wyler decided that all Romans in the film would be portrayed by British actors, and all Hebrews by Americans (except for Israeli actress Haya Harareet). Roman summer heat made filming an endurance contest. Charlton Heston trained for weeks under the direction of veteran stunt man Yakima Canutt to learn how to drive the chariot for the climactic race. Canutt fought lengthy, frustrating battles with studio chiefs over the proper kind of pavement to lay for horses and chariots. His son, doubling for Heston, performed in the scene where the chariot crashes against a wall and the rider is thrown. The scene was shot only once; the younger Canutt, using improper hand-holds in the chariot, narrowly escaped serious injury. Another dangerous scene, in which the rival chariot wheels interlock, was filmed by chaining the camera car to the chariots as they careened. The single most honored film in history, *Ben-Hur* won eleven Academy Awards, including Oscars for best picture, and for Wyler, Heston, and supporting actor Hugh Griffith.

THE BEST YEARS OF OUR LIVES. 1946. Filmed April–August 1946; California: Ontario Army Air Field, Chino; Los Angeles Airport and Samuel Goldwyn Studios, Los Angeles.
Cast: Myrna Loy, Fredric March, Teresa Wright, Dana Andrews, Hoagy Carmichael, Harold Russell, Virginia Mayo.
Director: William Wyler.

Nonactor Harold Russell, discovered by William Wyler in an army Signal Corps film about disabled veterans, had lost both hands in an explosion accident at a Georgia training camp. (His only other feature film appearance came in 1980 in *Inside Moves*.) Despite much drilling, Russell remained unable to modify his Boston accent. Wyler insisted that he *not* take acting lessons. In order to get Russell properly enraged in his fight scene with actor Ray Teal, Wyler told him that Teal was secretly a Fascist. Teresa Wright, playing Myrna Loy's daughter, was only twelve years younger than Loy. And Hoagy Carmichael worried that his saloon-keeper role wasn't dignified enough. The entire cast dressed in their own clothes and performed, at Wyler's insistence, with little or no makeup. Both Loy and Fredric March were initially reluctant to join the cast. March signed on only because he was at loose ends after William Powell landed the lead role in *Life With Father*, that March had sought, Samuel Goldwyn himself persuaded Loy, and both she and March finally judged this their best film. The subject of returning war veterans and their personal problems was a controversial topic at the time, and Wyler was apprehensive about making the film—which ultimately collected seven Oscars: best picture, best actor (March) and supporting actor (Russell), director, screenplay (Robert E. Sherwood), editing (Daniel Mandell), and musical score (Hugo Friedhofer).

THE BICYCLE THIEF (LADRI DI BICICLETTE). 1948.
Filmed 1945; Rome.

Cast: Lamberto Maggiorani, Enzo Staiola, Lianella Carell.
Director: Vittorio De Sica.

Filmed just after the end of World War II, using no constructed sets and no experienced actors, *The Bicycle Thief* catapulted both Vittorio De Sica and Italian neorealism to international attention. An American company had offered to bankroll De Sica if he would hire Cary Grant for the starring role, an offer promptly refused. After a Milanese banker rescued the project, De Sica sought his cast in the streets of Rome. He hired Lamberto Maggiorani, an unemployed steelworker, and radio interviewer Lianella Carell for the adult parts, and he discovered seven-year-old street waif Enzo Staiola in a gang of noisy children. His extras, recruited off the streets, included a group of thieves and ex-convicts, whose experience of prison discipline made them ideal subjects for the carefully planned crowd scenes. While the director took pains to allow the personal qualities of his actors to shape scenes, this was not an improvised film—its script plotted each shot to the last detail. *The Bicycle Thief* earned many international awards as well as special Oscars for best foreign film and for writer Cesare Zavattini.

THE BIG SLEEP. 1946. Filmed October 1944–January 1945; Warner Bros. Studios, Burbank.
Cast: Humphrey Bogart, Lauren Bacall, Martha Vickers, Dorothy Malone, Regis Toomey, Elisha Cook, Jr.
Director: Howard Hawks.

Raymond Chandler, author of the original detective novel, refused to cooperate after other writers, including William Faulkner, were assigned to adapt *The Big Sleep*. (Howard Hawks ended up rewriting much of the material as shooting progressed but confessed that he could never figure the story out; even Chandler couldn't positively state "who done it.") But fast action and fine performances made the film one of Hawks's best. Bogart's third marriage, to actress Mayo Methot, had reached its final violent stages, and Hawks considered Bogart's ongoing love affair with Lauren Bacall a disruptive influence on the set. Believing that Bacall was hurting her mint-fresh career by continuing the affair, he lectured them both sternly but to no avail; they married before the film was released. In January 1946, a year after production had wrapped up, studio chiefs decided to reinforce the sultry screen persona Bacall had developed in her previous film with Bogey (*To Have and Have Not*) and called the couple back to shoot two additional sequences.

THE BIRDS. 1963. Filmed March–July 1962; California: Bodega Bay; Revue Studios and Universal Studios, Universal City.
Cast: Rod Taylor, Tippi Hedren, Jessica Tandy, Suzanne Pleshette, Ethel Griffies, Veronica Cartwright.
Director: Alfred Hitchcock.

Birds in sinister or symbolic guises appeared in several Hitchcock thrillers, but never with such overt hostility as in this shocker. Hitchcock spent $200,000 trying to develop menacing mechanical birds but, except for a few fakes used in certain attack scenes, ended up using real birds, mostly gulls that expert Ray Berwick trained to swoop, dive, mass, and nip at clothing and arms. In some scenes, notably of the fleeing schoolchildren, the attacking birds were later added by optical processing, though a few mechanical stuffed ravens were also tied to the kids. The film, a mosaic of trick photography, achieved some 370 different optical effects by superimposed images and creative snipping. The final scene combined thirty-two separate pieces of film. Tippi Hedren, whom Hitchcock had discovered in a Sego TV commercial and envisioned as another Grace Kelly, got the worst of it in this, her first film. For one notable sequence, sadistic even for Hitchcock, he placed his star in a cagelike room representing an attic, then had crew members throw hundreds of living gulls at her; other gulls were tied by nylon threads to her arms and legs. Filming of this scene, which occupied only one minute of screen time, went on for a week until a gull pecked at Hedren's eye. She fled hysterically from the set and filming was suspended for a few days. Normally Hitchcock never improvised or changed scenes on the set, but in *The Birds* he found many weaknesses in the script and revised as filming progressed, making the viewpoint far more subjective than originally planned. Look for the director's brief cameo appearance walking his own two pet Sealyham terriers.

THE BLACKBOARD JUNGLE. 1955. Filmed autumn 1954; MGM Studios, Culver City.
Cast: Glenn Ford, Anne Francis, Louis Calhern, Richard Kiley, Sidney Poitier, Vic Morrow.
Director: Richard Brooks.

Richard Brooks swapped assignments with William Wyler to make this film, a far less ambitious project than Wyler's *Ben-Hur*. But Brooks probably took the greater risk. Not only banned in Memphis and Georgia for depicting a racially integrated classroom, this film was also barred from the prestigious Venice Film Festival by Ambassador Clare Boothe Luce. Its enduring significance, however, lies in its fame as the first film to use a rock 'n' roll theme: "Rock Around the Clock," performed by Bill Haley and the Comets. Sidney Poitier, a main source of the bigoted reactions to this film, went through a degree of private harassment before production began. A little-known actor at the time (though this was his fifth film), he was asked to sign a loyalty oath by MGM's legal department, apparently because of his associations with actors Paul Robeson and Canada Lee. Poitier refused to sign, Brooks backed him, and the matter was quietly dropped. On the set, Glenn Ford had problems addressing Poitier in a conflict scene as "You black . . ." Poitier pulled him aside and persuaded him to speak the line as written. After filming was completed, Poitier went back to work at his family's restaurant in Harlem, finally achieving major stardom in *The Defiant Ones* (1958). In 1967, he played a harassed teacher himself in *To Sir, with Love*.

BLOW-UP. 1966. Filmed May–August 1966; England: London; Elstree Studios, Borehamwood.
Cast: David Hemmings, Sarah Miles, Vanessa Redgrave.
Director: Michelangelo Antonioni.

Michelangelo Antonioni's first English-language film, as many viewers have discovered, is not solely the suspense thriller that it first appears. His primary aim, the auteur said, was to question "the nature of reality." Despite the fact that the London photographer's studio rented for the main set had no soundproofing, all sound recording was done synchronously, with no postdubbing of voices (contrary to usual studio practice since the mid-1930s). Vanessa Redgrave, starring in a stage play at night and putting in sixteen-hour days during filming, wanted so much to work with Antonioni that she accepted the part before reading the script. *Blow-Up* won the Cannes Film Festival best picture award.

THE BLUE ANGEL (DER BLAUE ENGEL). 1930. Filmed November 1929–January 1930; UFA Studios, Berlin.
Cast: Emil Jannings, Marlene Dietrich, Kurt Gerron, Hans Albers.
Director: Josef von Sternberg.

Marlene Dietrich only reluctantly agreed to be cast. She hated playing a whore but also considered screen acting an inferior chore, and she continued to perform nights in a Berlin stage play even as filming proceeded. Josef von Sternberg originally wanted Brigitte Helm for the role but later insisted on Dietrich over the objections of almost everybody else. Emil Jannings, a difficult man of protean ego, declared the director would "rue the day" he chose Dietrich over Lucie Mannheim for the role. Von Sternberg, no modest man himself, fell in love with his new star, rigorously coached her off-camera as well as on. He dyed her hair a brassy blonde and drew a silver line down the middle of her nose to "straighten" it for the camera; the nose line became her stage trademark for years after. A jealous Jannings, who considered the film *his* vehicle, grew increasingly perturbed as filming progressed (von Sternberg insisted on shooting sequentially, making German and English versions on alternate days). So enraged became Jannings that, in the scene where he attacks Dietrich, he was actually strangling her, and her terror was genuine; Hans Albers had to strike Jannings to make him stop, and Dietrich carried painful bruises on her neck for several days. Two of the actors—Kurt Gerron, playing Kiepert, a magician, and Karl Huszar-Puffy, in the role of a publican—later died in Nazi concentration camps while Jannings was making propaganda films for Joseph Goebbels. (Jannings died disgraced in 1950.) Frederick Hollander said he wrote most of the songs while seated on the toilet, his most creative place. In Dietrich's English version of her song "Falling in Love Again," the word *moths* always came out as *moss* in her Teutonic accent; von Sternberg reshot it 235 times over two days to no avail, finally upping the crowd noises to drown out the word. He added fifteen meters of black film after Dietrich's number "I Am Switched On to Love" to cue audience applause, an action that caused a fearful row between Jannings and musical arranger Peter Kreuder. Filming was done on a cold set, since heat-radiator noises would have interfered with the sound (this was the first talkie made in Germany); and all the performers, especially thin-clad Dietrich, shivered throughout. The picture inspired countless Blue Angel nightclubs in Paris and Berlin —but during production, unemployment riots ominously raged just outside the studio.

THE BLUES BROTHERS. 1980. Filmed July 1979–January 1980; Chicago. Universal Studios, Universal City.
Cast: John Belushi, Dan Aykroyd, Cab Calloway, John Candy, James Brown.
Director: John Landis.

The many cameo roles in *The Blues Brothers* were mostly performed in the studio, but director John Landis shot the exteriors including chase and car-crash sequences right on Chicago streets, not without some close calls. In the chase down Lake Street, one police car went out of control, rolled over, collided with a cameraman's parked station wagon from which he was filming, and knocked it a hundred feet down the street. John Belushi by this time was heavily addicted to the drugs that would finally kill him in 1982. Just getting him to the set was often a major task for Landis, who at one point slugged his uncooperative star when he couldn't stir him from his more-or-less constant, offscreen torpor.

BODY AND SOUL. 1947. Filmed spring 1947; Enterprise Studios, Los Angeles.
Cast: John Garfield, Lilli Palmer, Hazel Brooks, Anne Revere, William Conrad, Joseph Pevney, Canada Lee, Lloyd Gough.
Director: Robert Rossen.

Just before major studio blacklisting began, John Garfield personally financed this classic prizefight picture and hired many of his so-called left-wing friends, including Anne Revere, Joseph Pevney, Canada Lee, and Lloyd Gough for supporting roles. Some of his intimates saw the film as an allegorical commentary on his own rise from street kid to major Hollywood star. Certainly he threw himself into his own role body and soul: he suffered a mild heart attack (his second) after strenuous rope skipping in a scene with Hazel Brooks; and, in a scene with former welterweight pro Art Darrell, he knocked himself cold against a camera boom, requiring six stitches to close a scalp wound. Cameraman James Wong Howe captured many of the fight sequences by roller-skating around the ring with a hand-held camera. A 1981 remake had little to do with the original.

THE BODY SNATCHER. 1945. Filmed October–November 1944; California: RKO Ranch, Encino; RKO Studios, Culver City.
Cast: Boris Karloff, Henry Daniell, Bela Lugosi, Edith Atwater.
Director: Robert Wise.

Producer Val Lewton cowrote the screenplay under the name Carlos Keith. This grim classic was the final teaming of horror masters Karloff and Lugosi. Lugosi's role, though minimal, was almost his last decent one—Hollywood wasted him thereafter in a roster of increasingly bad films that marked the long decline of his career. Between scenes in this picture, Karloff took time out to make another Lewton classic, *Isle of the Dead*. Exterior scenes, reproducing the Edinburgh of 1831, were filmed on old sets of *The Hunchback of Notre Dame* (1939) at Encino. So precise was Lewton's attention to historical authenticity that this film has been screened in medical colleges for its value in showing details of 19th-century anatomy instruction. Subsequent versions included *The Flesh and the Fiends* (1959) and *The Doctor and the Devils* (1985).

BONNIE AND CLYDE. 1967. Filmed 1966; Texas: Dallas; various small towns near Dallas. Warner Bros. Studios, Burbank.
Cast: Warren Beatty, Faye Dunaway, Gene Hackman, Estelle Parsons, Michael J. Pollard, Gene Wilder.
Director: Arthur Penn.

Though its details were largely fictional (also incorporating the lore of another outlaw, John Dillinger), this influential comedy-drama showed much of the authentic Clyde Barrow country ranged by the outlaw and his gang during the early 1930s, including three of the actual banks he robbed (closed since the Depression but reopened especially for the filming). Warren Beatty, whose lover at the time, French actress Leslie Caron, said she encouraged him to buy the script, also produced the film. He approached two famed French directors—François Truffaut and Jean-Luc Godard, both of whom were interested but declined—before lining up Arthur Penn. Caron desperately wanted to play Bonnie Parker, but Beatty turned her down and sought Sue Lyon for the role; Jane Fonda and Tuesday Weld also refused it along the line. Beatty didn't like Faye Dunaway in the part at first but later realized the wisdom of his final choice, and the role brought her stardom. In preparation, she shed twenty pounds by hauling sandbags, which also helped her achieve a tense, strained look. Penn required three days to film the Dexter, Iowa, shoot-out scene (actually filmed at Lemmon Lake near Dallas), consuming some 3,000 blank bullets. Another three-day job, using four cameras set at varying speeds, was the famous ambush choreography, in which Bonnie and Clyde are killed in slow motion. Dunaway's right leg was tied to the gear shift so she wouldn't fall from the car. (There is also a one-second shot that most viewers don't catch, that of bullets tearing off a portion of Clyde's skull—Penn said he wanted it to be subliminal.) While many critics greeted *Bonnie and Clyde* harshly, it ushered in a new cinematic style of violent realism. Bonnie Parker's relatives sued Warner Bros., as did lawman Frank Hamer's widow and son for Denver Pyle's "wholly fictitious and unwarranted" portrayal of Hamer. Look for a brief excerpt from Busby Berkeley's *Gold Diggers of 1933*. Academy Awards: Estelle Parsons (in her film debut) for best supporting actress; Burnett Guffey for cinematography.

BORN YESTERDAY. 1950. Filmed summer 1950; Washington, D.C. Columbia Studios, Los Angeles.
Cast: Judy Holliday, Broderick Crawford, William Holden, Howard St. John.
Director: George Cukor.

Studio executive Harry Cohn wanted Rita Hayworth for the lead role of Billie Dawn. The plum assignment went, of course, to Judy Holliday, who had played Billie Dawn in Garson Kanin's Broadway play for two years; but getting her to Hollywood over Cohn's fierce oppostion was a major project involving a conspiracy between Spencer Tracy and Katharine Hepburn. In order to showcase her talents for Cohn, they cast her in *Adam's Rib*. The scheme worked, Holliday shed fifteen pounds for the role, and *Born Yesterday* made her a major star, winning her an Academy Award for best actress. Kanin had named the male lead character Harry Brock after Cohn himself and gave him many of Cohn's personality traits. The part went to Broderick Crawford after Broadway lead Paul Douglas turned it down. Most extras in the film were unemployed Washingtonians.

THE BOUNTY. 1984. Filmed 1983; London. Matavai Bay, Tahiti. New Zealand.
Cast: Mel Gibson, Anthony Hopkins, Laurence Olivier, Edward Fox.
Director: Roger Donaldson.

Historical accuracy was the strong suit of this third remake of the famed mutiny story (see *Mutiny on the Bounty*). A steel-hulled boat cost $4 million to convert into an exact replica of the ninety-foot HMS *Bounty*. Among thousands of Tahitian extras employed, many of the otherwise beautiful women had bad teeth or none, so new dentures numbered among the many location expenses; after a day's work, the teeth were collected to insure the women's return the next day (they finally got to keep them). For the Dutch colony of Timor, where Capt. Bligh (played by Anthony Hopkins) and his castaways finally land, an entire native village, authentically copying the colony's rustic architecture, arose—for only one day of filming—on the island of Mooréa twelve miles off Tahiti. Both Hopkins and Mel Gibson (playing Fletcher Christian) scrupulously researched their roles. Famed director David Lean originated this production, a project he had anticipated for years, but he was replaced by New Zealander Roger Donaldson.

BREAKING AWAY. 1979. Filmed August–September 1978; Bloomington, Indiana: Indiana University campus; Woolery Stone Mill.
Cast: Dennis Christopher, Dennis Quaid, Daniel Stern, Jackie Earle Haley, Paul Dooley, Barbara Barrie.
Director: Peter Yates.

Hundreds of Bloomington citizens participated as extras, and the performers' wardrobe came from local department stores and their own closets. Screenwriter Steve Tesich, who had once attended Indiana University, based Dennis Christopher's role (Dave Stohler) on one of his student friends there. English producer-director Peter Yates insisted on using new faces rather than established stars. One unfortunate local result of the film (which the crew nicknamed *Bambino*) stemmed from its use of the word *cutter* as a disparaging term for the town residents—as contrasted with the student population; before the release of *Breaking Away*, few locals had been aware of the label. Steve Tesich won an Academy Award for his screenplay, and the film hugely benefited the university in fund-raising campaigns.

BREATHLESS (À BOUT DE SOUFFLE). 1959. Filmed August–September 1959; France: Marseille; Paris.
Cast: Jean-Paul Belmondo, Jean Seberg, Daniel Boulanger, Jean-Pierre Melville.
Director: Jean-Luc Godard.

Director Jean-Luc Godard, in his feature debut, appeared briefly as the man in dark glasses who points out Jean-Paul Belmondo (in his first major screen role) to the police. Scripting the film a day at a time from François Truffaut's basic idea, Godard recorded no sound and used few lights on his sets, shouting instructions to actors as filming proceeded—and dubbing in all the voices later. Jean Seberg, performing without makeup, at first regarded the film as hardly more than a peculiar trifle of her career, an effort she likened to making home movies. Offended at first by Godard's apparent misogyny, she walked off the set on the first day but soon returned. Jean Pierre Melville, playing the celebrity novelist Parvulesco, based his character on Vladimir Nabokov. Godard dedicated the film, which became an influential New Wave classic, to Monogram Pictures in tribute to all its cheap gangster thrillers of the Thirties and Forties—films that were highly regarded by French filmmakers. An updated remake in 1983 starred Richard Gere.

BRIDE OF FRANKENSTEIN. 1935. Filmed January–March 1935; Universal Studios, Universal City.
Cast: Boris Karloff, Colin Clive, Ernest Thesiger, Elsa Lanchester, Valerie Hobson, E. E. Clive.
Director: James Whale.

Second of the original classic horror trio (coming between *Frankenstein*, in 1931, and *Son of Frankenstein*, in 1939), *Bride* claimed its own share of horrific behind-the-scenes episodes. Boris Karloff strongly disagreed with the film's attempts to humanize the monster he played, convinced that it would destroy interest in the character. He injured himself in the burning windmill scene, bruising ribs and dislocating a hip, and required infrared back treatments for weeks after. He laughingly recalled the scene in the water beneath the windmill; in early takes, air entered the rubber suit he wore beneath his costume, forcing him to balloon to the surface "like an obscene water lily." Wearing his sixty-two-pound costume caused him to lose twenty pounds, and he habitually reclined between scenes. Trussed up in yards of bandages for her title role, Elsa Lanchester was propped up and hand-fed at lunchtime. At one point, her similarly bound stand-in, suffering a claustrophobic attack, fell into screaming hysteria on the set. Lanchester described her bride's hairdo (inspired by portraits of Queen Nefertiti) as four spikelike braids held by a wired horsehair cage, topped with her own brushed-over hair, plus two white hairpieces on the sides. She lost her voice after several days of screaming. For her hisses, she imitated the swans in London's Regent's Park, and she adapted her jerky movements from Brigitte Helm's performance in the silent classic *Metropolis* (1926). Ernest Thesiger, as personally unpleasant a man off-camera as he looked, busied himself with expert needlepoint between takes, while cinematographer John

Mescall, quite constantly drunk, seemed to function well that way. James Whale had originally wanted Brigitte Helm or Louise Brooks for the title role and Claude Rains for Thesiger's part. After making this film, Whale lost interest in the character and never directed another horror picture. Screenwriter John L. Balderston denounced the finished film, vowing that he had intended the script to be played as satire rather than horror. Portions of footage from the movie later appeared in *The Ghost of Frankenstein* (1942) and *House of Dracula* (1945).

THE BRIDGE ON THE RIVER KWAI. 1957. Filmed October 1956–May 1957; Ceylon: Colombo; Kitulgala.
Cast: William Holden, Alec Guinness, Jack Hawkins, Sessue Hayakawa, James Donald.
Director: David Lean.

Both Alec Guinness and William Holden somewhat dreaded working with David Lean, whose long preparations for scenes and many retakes had antagonized Guinness on the set of *Oliver Twist* (1948); but both actors later enthused about their roles, and Holden's contract provisions netted him a fortune. Producer Sam Spiegel had sought Humphrey Bogart, then Sir Laurence Olivier, for Guinness's role, and Cary Grant for Holden's (Grant later regretted his refusal of the part). At Jack Hawkins's suggestion, location shooting occurred in the more accessible country of Ceylon rather than in Burma, where the story (based on real events in 1942) was set. A reluctant Ceylonese government permitted the production only after receiving assurances that the Japanese in the film would not be portrayed as sadistic captors and that *Bridge* would be antiwar rather than anti-Japanese. Powerful Hollywood columnist Hedda Hopper had tried to scare Holden out of appearing in the film because screenwriters Carl Foreman and Michael Wilson had been blacklisted by the studios. Holden told her to shove it, but Columbia Studios, not so brave, falsely credited Pierre Boulle, author of the original novel, as sole writer (Boulle neither read nor wrote English). Holden's offscreen fascination with fireworks almost led to premature burning of the all-important bridge, which had taken nine months to construct. During one of his pyrotechnic displays, fire balloons drifted toward the span, causing a panicked

Spiegel to lay down some new rules. The actual bridge explosion didn't come off the first time; owing to a mix-up of signals, the sixty-five-year-old locomotive (formerly owned by a maharaja) ended up toppled over a hillside. The film won Academy Awards for best picture, for Lean as director, and for Guinness as best actor, among others. The widows of Foreman and Wilson finally received the writers' Oscars in 1985. And the film proved enormously successful in Japan.

BROADCAST NEWS. 1987. Filmed 1987; Washington, D.C. 20th Century-Fox Studios, Los Angeles.
Cast: William Hurt, Albert Brooks, Holly Hunter, Robert Prosky, Lois Chiles, Joan Cusack.
Director: James L. Brooks.

James Brooks, once a CBS newswriter, cast Holly Hunter at the last minute after a long search for a suitable actress to play Jane Craig. Among those previously considered were Debra Winger—who would probably have landed the role if she hadn't been pregnant—and Kathleen Turner. Both Hunter and Albert Brooks (no relation to the director) researched their roles at the CBS Network News bureau in Washington. Hunter began her day by rubbing her hands in newsprint because she had noticed that TV studio people always had dirty hands. Jack Nicholson's bit role as a pompous network anchorman was reportedly modeled on Chet Huntley. The picture, a smash hit, received seven Academy Award nominations, but finally, no Oscar.

BUS STOP. 1956. Filmed March–May 1956; Phoenix, Arizona. Sun Valley, Idaho. 20th Century-Fox Studios, Los Angeles.
Cast: Marilyn Monroe, Don Murray, Betty Field, Arthur O'Connell, Eileen Heckart, Hope Lange, Hans Conried.
Director: Joshua Logan.

On the basis of this comedy, incredulous critics decided that Marilyn Monroe—in her first performance after studying at the Actor's Studio with Lee Strasberg—was, after all, an actress. Kim Stanley, who had played the role on stage, had wanted to recreate it on film. Though Monroe usually arrived on time, in contrast to her later habitual tardiness on sets, her constant inability to remember lines required take after take.

And her behavior toward other cast members and the crew, when not utterly aloof, often became rude and insulting. At one point, Don Murray hotly demanded (but never got) an apology from her. In the café scene, where she lashes him with the train of her gown, she cut his face in several places. (She had wanted Rock Hudson for the lead role, but Hudson declined.) The love scene between them in the diner contained an item unnoticed until director Josh Logan spotted it in the rushes: a thin thread of saliva as Monroe removes her hand from her mouth. The studio cut this shot, saying it would offend viewers, but Logan insisted on restoring it, declaring it the most beautifully intimate scene in the film. Monroe's flustered appearance when she runs toward the bus station in Phoenix was not faked; moments before, as the evening lighting he wanted was fast fading, Logan had literally hauled her from her room, where she had dallied too long before the mirror. Frightened, she ran, and Logan got his shot. Instead of dubbing Monroe's voice for her rendition of "That Old Black Magic," Logan filmed the sequence live with two cameras and a hidden orchestra—he didn't think she could handle the lip-synching from a studio playback. In the bus sequences, where she constantly fluffed lines and hesitated, Logan finally let the camera run on for take after take without stopping, then rescued her good takes from the mass of prints. Listen for Monroe's genuine stammer in the scene where she lies to Murray about planning to meet him later—Monroe often stammered when she lied, even from a script.

BUTCH CASSIDY AND THE SUNDANCE KID. 1969.
Filmed spring 1969; Utah: Grafton; St. George. Colorado: Durango; Silverton. Mexico: Taxco; Cuernavaca. California: Century Ranch, Malibu; 20th Century-Fox Studios, Los Angeles.
Cast: Paul Newman, Robert Redford, Katharine Ross, Strother Martin, Cloris Leachman.
Director: George Roy Hill.

Ever since the Lone Ranger and Tonto galloped together, male bonding has proven decent box office, and this Western became one of the decentest buddy moneymakers of all. Steve McQueen had wanted to play the Sundance Kid and the studio wanted Warren Beatty, but Paul Newman had enough clout to be able to choose for himself, and the role made Robert Redford a superstar. Though the two had never met previously, they became good friends. Newman himself was reluctant at first because he didn't think he could play comedy. The film borrowed rather obviously in spots from François Truffaut's *Jules and Jim* (1961). George Roy Hill explained the freeze-frame ending by saying he had "no stomach for real violence." He attributed the idea of leaving the characters mythically intact to a back injury (he worked from a stretcher during much of the filming) that gave him time to think. Screenwriter William Goldman thought the film suffered from "a case of the cutes," but he won an Academy Award, as did Conrad Hall for cinematography, Burt Bacharach for best musical score—and Bacharach with Hal David for best song ("Raindrops Keep Fallin' on My Head").

C

CABARET. 1972. Filmed February–July 1971; Munich, West Germany. West Berlin.

Cast: Liza Minnelli, Michael York, Joel Grey, Marisa Berenson, Helmut Griem.

Director: Bob Fosse.

Bob Fosse attempted to pattern his lighting effects after those found in the artworks of German painters George Grosz and Otto Dix. To get his actors in the mood for filming a scene, he played a recording of Marlene Dietrich's "Falling in Love Again." He included real drag queens among the garish extras enlisted for the nightclub scenes, and many of the women deplored the requirement of growing hair under their arms. Liza Minnelli, who won an Academy Award for best actress after losing the Broadway role in *Cabaret* to Jill Haworth, rummaged in German thrift shops for her seedy wardrobe (not including the slinky black dress she wore in her New York nightclub act). She modeled her look as Sally Bowles after the early screen appearances of actresses Louise Brooks and Lya De Putti. Minnelli felt uneasy in Munich, reporting several local expressions of anti-Semitism stirred by the film's recreation of prewar Germany. (So rousing was the scene of the young German singing "Tomorrow Belongs to Me" that it was cut from the film's German version.) Seven other Academy Awards included one for Fosse, for Joel Grey as best supporting actor, and for Geoffrey Unsworth's cinematography.

THE CAINE MUTINY. 1954. Filmed spring 1954; Pearl Harbor, Hawaii. California: San Francisco; Yosemite National Park; Columbia Studios, Los Angeles.

Cast: Humphrey Bogart, José Ferrer, Van Johnson, Fred MacMurray, Robert Francis, Tom Tully, E. G. Marshall, Lee Marvin.

Director: Edward Dmytryk.

Clearly stated at the outset was the disclaimer: "There has never been a mutiny in the United States Navy." In relieved exchange for this epigraph, the service lent all ships, personnel, and materials desired, including the two destroyer minesweepers that would function as the U.S.S. *Caine*. Shipboard scenes were filmed outside Pearl Harbor (except for the typhoon sequence, which was a studio creation). The target-towing sequence, when the ship supposedly cuts its own towline, almost resulted in a disastrous collision with the steel target platform. Scenes on the aircraft carrier *Kearsarge* were chaotic. The frenzied dash that resulted when director Edward Dmytryk instructed all personnel to start running from opposite ends of the ship to their final positions produced one broken leg and assorted other injuries. Humphrey Bogart had wanted to play Captain Queeg since he read Herman Wouk's original novel in 1951, and he took a smaller salary than usual to land the role. But no genuine Annapolis man, protested the film's naval adviser, would break and butter toast in fragments like Bogart did in the strawberry scene: angered, Bogart said he did it in order to reveal Queeg's mental agitation. Producer Stanley Kramer finally settled the matter by trimming the crusts, thereby reducing the toast in size. Van Johnson refused to dye his red hair dark for his role or cover his dented forehead, the result of a near-fatal auto crash in 1943. Robert Francis, playing Ensign Keith, was a promising Hollywood newcomer who died in a plane crash a year later. Donna Lee Hickey, playing May Wynn, retained the latter name as her own in her subsequent two films. Dmytryk believed that the story could have supported a long film, and he professed disappointment in the final truncated version. Sidelight: British actor Maurice Micklewhite took his screen name, Michael Caine, from a theatre marquee advertising this film.

CAMELOT. 1967. Filmed summer–autumn 1966; Spain: Coca; Segovia. Warner Bros. Studios, Burbank.
Cast: Richard Harris, Vanessa Redgrave, David Hemmings, Franco Nero, Lionel Jeffries, Estelle Winwood.
Director: Joshua Logan.

Count how many times you see the color red in this Arthurian musical. Josh Logan wanted the pageantry to look unlike any Hollywood medieval epic ever filmed so he tried not to use the scarlet cloth so typical of most. Since there was no need for historical accuracy in portraying a legendary kingdom, he gave designer John Truscott free rein in creating a variety of strange objects, costumes, and settings. Costumes, not including 361 suits of armor, numbered some 3,500, each given a hand-loomed appearance and home-dyed color. The rainy-green color of the acreage surrounding Camelot (actually Coca Castle) was accomplished by spraying watercolor paint on a brown summer landscape; and the English fog was achieved by giant wind machines blowing clouds of chemical mist over the scenery. Logan filmed key prologue and epilogue scenes in Spain. Joyous Gard, the castle of Sir Lancelot (played by Franco Nero in rubber armor), was actually the famed Alcazar in Segovia. At the other end of the world, Camelot's dense forest stood on Stage 8 of Warner Bros.-Seven Arts Studios, draped in ten tons of artificial snow. Filming was interrupted when Richard Harris fell in his shower and cut his head. When executive Jack Warner accused him of malingering and ordered him back to the set, Harris stayed home awaiting Warner's apology; it took seven days. But there were also moments of hilarity. Behind a screen, Harris physically prepared for his bathtub scene, in which he gets scrubbed by Vanessa Redgrave as Guinevere: he emerged nude with an awesome erection. Redgrave badgered the director to let her sing "Take Me to the Fair" in French, but Logan squelched the idea and used the only take of the song in English that she consented to sing. Genuine romance blossomed between Redgrave and Nero, who met on the set and thereafter lived together and produced a child. Tom and Sue Logan, the director's children, played the farm boy and goose girl in the first scene of the movie filmed.

CAPTAIN BLOOD. 1935. Filmed August–October 1935; California: Laguna Beach; Warner Bros. Studios, Los Angeles.
Cast: Errol Flynn, Olivia de Havilland, Basil Rathbone, Lionel Atwill, Guy Kibbee.
Director: Michael Curtiz.

Devised as a vehicle for Robert Donat and Jean Muir, the leads fell to Errol Flynn and nineteen-year-old Olivia de Havilland when Donat's health prevented his travel to Hollywood from Britain. The film made major stars of both relative unknowns. Flynn owed this breakout starring role to his first wife, flamboyant French actress Lili Damita, who finagled the part for him from studio chief Jack Warner. It became the first of three teamings for Flynn and Basil Rathbone and the first of eight for Flynn and de Havilland. She promptly fell in love with her costar, and Flynn alternately fascinated and repelled her for several years. Their relationship never developed into full-blown romance, mainly because of Flynn's boorish approaches. The cast found the studio sound stage insufferably hot, and Flynn often ruined takes by snatching off his wig and mopping his face. When abrasive director Michael Curtiz, whom Flynn thoroughly despised, got into obscene yelling matches with his star, the shaken de Havilland fled to her dressing room with hands clapped over her ears. The sword duel on Laguna Beach between Flynn and Rathbone came to life only when the gentle Rathbone, egged on by Curtiz, taunted Flynn about how much larger a weekly salary he (Rathbone) was getting. At one point, Rathbone's sword accidentally grazed Flynn's face, causing a small scar; Flynn never forgave the director for having removed the tiny protective knob on the sword's end. All of Flynn's best moments in the film resulted from his transferred hatred for the martinet Curtiz, who relentlessly dragged the actor through ten or more takes of some scenes. Flynn collapsed from a recurrence of malaria during a shipboard scene, and he got hauled on the carpet once for being drunk on the set. No full-size ships were used—small-scale replicas in the studio tank measured only eighteen feet long with sixteen-foot masts. A few action scenes used footage from previous films, including *The Divine Lady* (1929). Until Flynn's stardom, Damita had been much better known than her husband, and she liked it that way, but the success of *Captain Blood* changed things, and the couple soon separated. Almost three decades later, their only son, Sean Flynn, starred in *The Son of Captain Blood* (1962).

CARNAL KNOWLEDGE. 1971. Filmed winter–spring 1971; New York City. Panorama Studios, Vancouver, British Columbia, Canada

Cast: Jack Nicholson, Arthur Garfunkel, Candice Bergen, Ann-Margret, Rita Moreno.

Director: Mike Nichols.

Mike Nichols was said to have based the casting of his actors on his feelings of their basic similarity to the film's characters. Jack Nicholson later found himself contending in real life with hostile reactions aimed at Jonathan, the character he played but with whom he never personally identified. Ann-Margret, whose role of Bobbie Templeton was shot sequentially, said she easily dissolved into required tears whenever Nichols silently placed his hand on her head just before a shot, an act she associated with her father. She gained ten pounds for her role, and dwelling in the mood of her character made her distraught. The role became, she reported, her most demanding in films; and though she worshiped Nicholson as an actor, his intense believability could frighten her. Candice Bergen cited this film as the one she was "always proudest to be in," stating that her performance had increased her sense of self-respect. Only Georgia banned the film as pornographic.

CASABLANCA. 1942. Filmed May–July 1942; California: Van Nuys Airport, Van Nuys; Warner Bros. Studios, Burbank.

Cast: Humphrey Bogart, Ingrid Bergman, Claude Rains, Paul Henreid, Conrad Veidt, Dooley Wilson, S. Z. Sakall, Sydney Greenstreet, Peter Lorre.

Director: Michael Curtiz.

Among players considered for the cast at various times were George Raft (who wanted the lead but was turned down); Ann Sheridan and Hedy Lamarr for Ingrid Bergman's role; Ronald Reagan, Philip Dorn, and Joseph Cotten for Paul Henreid's; Clarence Muse for Dooley Wilson's; and Otto Preminger for Conrad Veidt's. Because of script difficulties and delays, most of *Casablanca* was filmed in the same sequence you see on screen (in contrast to most movies, in which all scenes of a particular setup are filmed at once regardless of story sequence). The studio-created fog of the final scene could have symbolized the production problems of the entire film, for everyone performed in the dark on a daily basis. Lines of script were usually only minutes or hours old when spoken, and the mystified director and cast could only guess at motivations and destinies of the characters. Bogart's violent battles with his third wife, actress Mayo Methot, had become staple items of Hollywood gossip. Methot telephoned him constantly on the set, accused him of having an affair with Bergman (he never did, then or later—his distant politeness, in fact, intimidated her). Wilson, who had never learned to play the piano, faked his keyboard fingering in the film to match studio musician Elliot Carpenter's prerecorded playing. The song "As Time Goes By," which the film made an instant hit, was hardly new; composed in 1931, it came close to being edited out. Music director Max Steiner strongly objected to its inclusion, but because Bergman had already cut her hair for her upcoming role in *For Whom the Bell Tolls*, crucial *Casablanca* scenes without the songs could not be refilmed. In the climactic airport scene, shot mostly on an indoor set and using artificial fog and small airplane models to lend distance perspective, Rains, Bogart, and Henreid walked off when volatile director Curtiz cussed out a bit player. After letting Curtiz beg and apologize for two hours, the actors returned and finished the scene on the first take. Appropriate for a story of international setting, some thirty-four nationalities were represented among cast and bit players. The film was rush-released to coincide with the Allied capture of Casablanca in November 1942. It won three Academy Awards: for best picture, writing, and direction. *You Must Remember This: The Filming of Casablanca* (1980), by Charles Francisco, provides a fascinating, detailed account.

THE CAT AND THE CANARY. 1939. Filmed summer 1939; Paramount Studios, Los Angeles.

Cast: Bob Hope, Paulette Goddard, Gale Sondergaard, Elizabeth Patterson, George Zucco.

Director: Elliott Nugent.

This was Bob Hope's first major starring role, the one he regarded as the turning point in his career. Paramount had viewed his prospects dimly, so it was do-or-die time for him. Charlie Chaplin, married to Paulette Goddard at the time, saw

Hope's rushes and told him he was "one of the best timers of comedy I have ever seen," an accolade that set the young comic up for success. This film was the second of three remakes of the comedy thriller based on John Willard's 1922 stage play.

CAT BALLOU. 1965. Filmed November–December 1964; Canyon City, Colorado. Columbia Ranch, Burbank.
Cast: Jane Fonda, Lee Marvin, Michael Callan, Dwayne Hickman, Nat King Cole, Stubby Kaye, Tom Nardini, John Marley, Burt Mustin.
Director: Elliot Silverstein.

This satire on Hollywood Westerns was turned down by twenty-four directors before Elliot Silverstein agreed to tackle it. Even then he endured constant interference from anxious studio executives. Kirk Douglas had refused the dual-performance leading role that went to Lee Marvin. Not until the eighth take of the scene where he tries and fails to hit the broad side of a barn did Marvin establish to his satisfaction the charactor of broken-down gunslinger Kid Shelleen; the first seven he played for comedy, but the last for sympathy, and that's when Silverstein knew he had a print. The movie made a star of Marvin, who won an Academy Award as best actor. It was also Jane Fonda's first big success. But there were sad notes. Nat King Cole, in his last screen appearance, knew he was being exploited in the odd-couple teaming of a black man with a fat man (Stubby Kaye) for the film's running-ballad commentary; but he went along with it in order to record the title song and sell records. Commuting by plane from Lake Tahoe, where he was appearing in stage shows throughout the filming, Cole exhausted himself, steadily lost weight, and died of cancer two months later. Also during the filming, veteran character actor Jay C. Flippen, playing Sheriff Cardigan, developed an infection in his right leg, resulting in gangrene and eventual amputation; he continued to act, however, until his death in 1971.

CAT ON A HOT TIN ROOF. 1958. Filmed March–May 1958; MGM Studios, Culver City.
Cast: Elizabeth Taylor, Paul Newman, Burl Ives, Jack Carson, Judith Anderson, Madeleine Sherwood.
Director: Richard Brooks.

Grace Kelly was first offered Elizabeth Taylor's role but married Prince Rainier instead. During the filming, Taylor's husband, flamboyant producer Michael Todd, died in an airplane crash. Shattered with grief, Taylor nevertheless insisted on resuming work. For her first scene, the birthday party sequence, Burl Ives conspired with director Richard Brooks to have lots of real food placed on the table and to film several retakes, giving Taylor an excuse to eat—which she did, ravenously. Tennessee Williams, who wrote the original play, thought Taylor gave the best performance of any cast member. He disliked the film as a whole, however, because it gutted the key element of homosexuality in Paul Newman's role, obscuring his motivations. Ives recreated his Broadway stage role of Big Daddy, though also in a much diluted form.

CATCH 22. 1970. Filmed January–August 1969; Guaymas, Mexico. Rome. Paramount Studios, Los Angeles.

Cast: Alan Arkin, Martin Balsam, Richard Benjamin, Art Garfunkel, Jack Gilford, Buck Henry, Bob Newhart, Anthony Perkins, Paula Prentiss, Jon Voight, Orson Welles.

Director: Mike Nichols.

Orson Welles himself had intended to make a movie from Joseph Heller's novel but couldn't obtain the screen rights. On the set, his domineering presence intimidated everybody, but he seemed ill-prepared for his own part of General Dreedle; Mike Nichols had to coach him meticulously, and in the end Welles pronounced the film "dreadful." The four-month location shooting in Mexico, where set designers built an entire air base, was by all accounts a tense, grueling period. Nichols fired actor Stacy Keach, originally cast to play Martin Balsam's role of Colonel Cathcart. And Bob Newhart at one point seemed on the verge of a nervous breakdown; so eager was he to leave after finishing his scenes, he hired a taxicab to drive him to Arizona. The B-25 bomber squadron consisted of eighteen resurrected junk aircraft, piloted by veteran military fliers. The film's opening scene of all bombers taking off at once was not only a dangerous maneuver staged for the camera but evoked much derisive comment from the vets; such a mass launch was never performed in real life. Still, the aerial footage of planes was probably some of the best ever filmed.

Buck Henry, who wrote the screenplay, appeared as Lieutenant Colonel Korn.

CHAMPION. 1949. Filmed winter 1948–49; Los Angeles.
Cast: Kirk Douglas, Arthur Kennedy, Marilyn Maxwell, Paul Stewart, Ruth Roman.
Director: Mark Robson.

Against all advice, Kirk Douglas turned down a $50,000 part in *The Great Sinner* to accept the lead role in *Champion* for only $15,000. Carl Foreman's screenplay fascinated him, and he knew that producer Stanley Kramer, though still virtually unknown, made quality films. With no previous boxing experience, the thirty-two-year-old actor trained daily for six weeks in order to give a convincing ring performance. Doubles hired to stand in for him during fight sequences were never used. In one scene, which Mark Robson left in the picture, Douglas was actually knocked out as he bounced off the ropes into the fists of a boxer playing a bit part; most of his ring partners were former prizefighters, untrained to pull any punches. This film made Douglas a major star and also became Robson's first large success. In contrast to most fight films, this one did not glorify the contest. (It was Kramer who directed the major boxing sequences.) Shirley MacLaine once told Douglas that his scenes with Marilyn Maxwell in this film had inspired her as a child to become an actress; she repeated the dialogue at home with her brother, Warren Beatty.

CHARADE. 1963. Filmed December 1962–January 1963; France: Megève, French Alps; exteriors and Studios de Boulogne, Paris.
Cast: Cary Grant, Audrey Hepburn, Walter Matthau, James Coburn, George Kennedy.
Director: Stanley Donen.

For Cary Grant, who turned fifty-nine while making *Charade*, it was his seventieth film appearance. The twenty-five-year age difference between himself and Audrey Hepburn made him reluctant to take on the role until script changes allowed the couple to face the problem squarely by using the age gap as a running joke. The Paris sequences occurred almost entirely outdoors, with the climactic scene being filmed among pillars of the Comédie Française. Hepburn carried nostalgic memories of performing in the same Paris studio—

which contained the same furniture—she had used when filming *Love in the Afternoon* (1957) with Gary Cooper. *Charade* has been called Grant's last best effort; he made only two more pictures: *Father Goose* (1964) and *Walk, Don't Run* (1966).

CHARIOTS OF FIRE. 1981. Filmed 1981; England. Paris.
Cast: Ben Cross, Ian Charleson, Ian Holm, John Gielgud, Lindsay Anderson, Nigel Davenport, Patrick Magee, Nigel Havers, Nicholas Farrell.
Director: Hugh Hudson.

This was Hugh Hudson's first feature film as well as the first screen appearance of lead actors Ben Cross and Ian Charleson. Their roles required them to be runners, which neither had been before shooting commenced. Both actors intensively researched the two 1924 Olympic athletes they embodied. Charleson, who played Scottish missionary-athlete Eric Liddell, studied the Bible and ran five miles each morning around London's Hyde Park. The letters of 1924 Olympics participant Aubrey Montague provided the basis for the film's narration, with many of his own phrases left intact. Producer David Puttnam attributed the film's success to the long-dead Liddell watching from on high. Modestly budgeted, *Chariots* won four Academy Awards—for best picture, screenplay, musical score, and costume design.

CHINATOWN. 1974. Filmed autumn 1973; California: Mojave Desert; San Bernardino; Hollywood Reservoir and Paramount Studios, Los Angeles.
Cast: Jack Nicholson, Faye Dunaway, John Huston, John Hillerman, Perry Lopez, Diane Ladd.
Director: Roman Polanski.

Faye Dunaway and Roman Polanski clashed frequently on the set. Dunaway disliked the director's rigid methods, while Polanski tired of his star's dissatisfaction with her dialogue and delays while she reapplied makeup between takes. During her scene in the restaurant with Jack Nicholson, a major blowup ensued when Polanski suddenly yanked out an unruly strand of her hair. Ali MacGraw was originally scheduled for the Dunaway role, but the breakup of her marriage to the film's producer, Robert Evans, canceled her out; and Jane Fonda had refused the role. Polanski himself appears as the hood with the knife who slits Nicholson's nose; he used a hinge-tipped knife with a concealed tube and bulb for "blood." Nicholson dreaded the hazardous reservoir scene in which a torrent of water sweeps him into a wire-mesh fence; he hit the fence so hard that his shoes left a dent in the mesh, and he was glad that Polanski managed to capture the scene in one take. Polanski and scriptwriter Robert Towne disagreed on a suitable ending. Polanski wrote the version he favored the night before he filmed it. *Chinatown* made a major box-office star of Nicholson, but only Towne's screenplay received an Academy Award.

CITIZEN KANE. 1941. Filmed June–December 1940; RKO Studios. Culver City.

Cast: Orson Welles, Joseph Cotton, Dorothy Comingore, Everett Sloane, Paul Stewart, Ray Collins, Agnes Moorehead, George Coulouris, Ruth Warrick.

Director: Orson Welles.

Called *the* Great American Film, *Citizen Kane* has inspired vast amounts of hindsight, attention, and analysis. Probably no film has been so influential in the creation of modern cinematic style. In its premiere engagements, though, it was a box office failure; and because twenty-four-year-old Orson Welles had stepped on so many toes, his first film all but finished his Hollywood prospects. The biggest toe he stepped on was that of powerful newspaper publisher William Randolph Hearst, on whom Welles audaciously modeled his role of Charles Foster Kane (though early drafts of the script, originally titled *American*, contained much more Hearst material than the final version). A furious Hearst reacted by banning all mention of the film, including advertising, in his newspapers, successfully intimidating studio executives and an industry dependent upon publicity. Hearst's pal Louis B. Mayer, chief of MGM, even tried to buy up the film negative in order to burn it—and Welles had to threaten a lawsuit just to get RKO to release the film. Innovative techniques included cameraman Gregg Toland's use of deep-focus lenses, in which both close and distant views remain in focus on the screen, as well as numerous optical effects achieved by multiple exposures and lab processing. Notice the rarity of facial close-ups; the Mercury Theater players that Welles assembled for his cast were stage actors; their style of theatrical gestures and mannerisms were unsuited to studio intercutting of close-ups. Welles drove his actors hard, sometimes demanding more than a hundred takes of a single scene. Erskine Sanford, playing a newspaper editor, suffered a breakdown under the pressure of repeated takes. This was Joseph Cotten's screen debut. Playing Jedediah Leland, he modeled the part on two well-known show biz personalities: his own agent, Leland Hayward, and producer Jed Harris. For Cotten's drunken dialogue scene, Welles kept him up for twenty-four hours straight, filming through the night until he felt that Cotten was properly exhausted. But Welles drove himself equally hard. In scenes where he played Kane as an old man, the coated contact lenses he wore in order to age his eyes caused him much pain. He cut his wrist on furniture during the violent scene where he demolishes Dorothy Comingore's bedroom, and he fell ten feet down the steps as he pursued Ray Collins (playing Boss Gettys), injuring his ankle. Comingore was pregnant at the time, requiring all of Toland's camera artistry to hide her condition. Most of the sound track was recorded on the actual sets, though a few touches were dubbed in later. Heavy secrecy shrouded the filming because of the Hearst connection. The 1941 Academy Awards audience loudly booed the film's nine nominations—it won its only Oscar for the screenplay by Herman J. Mankiewicz and Welles. Welles became and, for all practical purposes, remained a Hollywood outcast, honored in time by white-tie tributes but seldom by solid employment. The rosebud-painted sled, cryptic center of so much scholarly speculation, turned up several years ago and is now owned by Steven Spielberg, who bought it for $55,000. And William Randolph Hearst III said in 1985 that he had enjoyed the film and that Welles could visit his grandfather's San Simeon estate anytime he pleased—"on my tab."

CITY LIGHTS. 1931. Filmed December 1928–October 1930; Charles Chaplin Studio, Los Angeles.
Cast: Charles Chaplin, Virginia Cherrill, Harry Myers.
Director: Charles Chaplin.

Chaplin's first sound film, made during the stock market crash and early days of the Great Depression, contained music and sound effects but no voices. Though spoken dialogue had largely supplanted silent-film captions in movies by this time, Chaplin (essentially a pantomime artist) resisted the trend to sound as long as he could; thus making this film was an extreme gamble for him. The film's only script was in his head. He also rehearsed each scene by shooting it, a costly method because he typically required hundreds of revised takes before working out a scene to his satisfaction. (The street-corner shot in which Virginia Cherrill sells the flower to Chaplin was about the three-hundredth take.) A perfectionist, Chaplin directed his cast by acting out each role, however minor, himself—so that all the performances were essentially his own. Twenty-year-old Cherrill (who became Cary Grant's first wife in 1934) had never acted before. Chaplin had wanted someone completely inexperienced for the blind flower-girl role, but Cherrill's busy night life and casual attitude on the set irritated him. He fired her at one point, but brought her back (at a much increased salary) when faced with the prospect of refilming all her scenes with actress Georgia Hale. Most of the production occurred on a small, T-shaped set in Chaplin's own studio. Look for young Jean Harlow, then an unknown who called herself Jean Pope, as an extra in the café scene. Chaplin even composed the film's music (by humming to arrangers who wrote down the notes). He finally considered *City Lights* the best of all his films.

CLEOPATRA. 1963. Filmed September 1960–March 1963; Italy: Cinecittà Studios, Rome; Anzio; Ischia, Bay of Naples. Edkou, Egypt. Almería, Spain. Pinewood Studios, Iver Heath, England.
Cast: Elizabeth Taylor, Richard Burton, Rex Harrison, Hume Cronyn, Martin Landau, Roddy McDowall.
Directors: Rouben Mamoulian, Joseph L. Mankiewicz.

Most of the principal photography occurred in Rome, not far from the real Forum where several of the movie's more spectacular scenes were set. *Cleopatra* was originally conceived as a modest vehicle for Joan Collins on the 20th Century-Fox lot in 1958. Ambitions for it swelled rapidly, but incredible studio mismanagement (Wall Street bankers had replaced experienced film executives in the front offices) made this the most expensive production in history ($40 million). Its on-again, off-again scheduling, its costly stars and sets—and foremost, the publicly budding romance between Taylor and Burton (both married to others at the time)—drew more attention, for a change, than studio publicity flacks really wanted.

Its staggering logistics combined with salacious offscreen speculation on its costars' love lives made the filming almost a better show than the film itself (according to some critics, infinitely better). Taylor's precarious health caused many delays as she checked in and out of hospitals for various ailments, and she lost weight as filming progressed. She devised her own unique eye makeup. Probably her biggest moment was entering Rome seated atop the giant sphinx, surrounded by 7,000 Italian extras. She was moved to tears when the mob spontaneously surged forward, cheering not Cleopatra but her. The "asp" that finally "killed" her was actually a harmless Sardinian garden snake. Burton seemed to revel in the publicity; for him, the movie (i.e., making it) meant major stardom. He owed his role of Mark Antony to Joseph Mankiewicz over the bitter opposition of Fox executive Spyros Skouras. Rex Harrison copiously researched his favorite role of Julius Caesar. When it looked as if the movie's opening scene of the Battle of Pharsalia would not be filmed, he offered to pay for it out of his own pocket. (This sequence, almost the last finished, was finally made in Spain.) The Alexandrian palaces arose as studio constructions at Anzio; while Cleopatra's barge and the Battle of Actium were filmed in the Bay of Naples. Burton and Taylor didn't divorce their spouses and marry until some time later, but *Cleopatra* made them the most sought-after, highest-paid acting couple in movie history. The film took four Academy Awards—for special effects, costumes, set design, and Leon Shamroy's cinematography. Producer Walter Wanger wrote *My Life with Cleopatra* (1963).

A CLOCKWORK ORANGE. 1971. Filmed September 1970–March 1971; England: Oxfordshire; Radlett; Thames Embankment and London area (exteriors); Elstree Studios, Borehamwood; Pinewood Studios, Iver Heath.

Cast: Malcolm McDowell, Patrick Magee, Adrienne Corri, Anthony Sharp, Warren Clarke.

Director: Stanley Kubrick.

According to Stanley Kubrick, the only nonsatirical view in this controversial film about a near-future world full of violence comes in the prison chaplain's words about the need for human choice. Both Kubrick and Malcolm McDowell strongly denied that the film reflected a fascist outlook; but for many viewers, Kubrick's amoral line between satire and sympathy seemed obscure at best. During rehearsals, McDowell improvised his "Singin' in the Rain" bit while kicking the stunt man doubling for Patrick Magee—a sequence that took two days to film. Interactions between Alex (McDowell) and his "civilized" self as represented by Mr. Alexander (Magee) provided only one of the film's many symbolic levels of complexity. In the bizarre duel between McDowell and the Cat Woman (played by Miriam Karlin), Kubrick hand-held the camera himself through take after take as the actors circled each other and finally collapsed from exhaustion.

CLOSE ENCOUNTERS OF THE THIRD KIND. 1977. (*The Special Edition*, 1980.) Filmed May 1976–May 1977; Bombay, India. Devil's Tower National Monument, Wyoming. Mobile, Alabama. California: Mojave Desert; Burbank Studios, Burbank.

Cast: Richard Dreyfuss, François Truffaut, Teri Garr, Melinda Dillon, Cary Guffey, Bob Balaban, Roberts Blossom.

Director: Steven Spielberg.

Special effects outweighed actors' performances in this high-tech fantasy of alien arrival on Earth. The blend of enormous sets with laboratory tricks, matte paintings, and carefully filmed miniatures produced spectacular visual results. Most of the crucial scenes—including the box canyon UFO base, the Crescendo Summit roadway in Indiana, and the cliffside notch at Devil's Tower—were filmed inside a huge World War II dirigible hangar in Mobile, reputedly the largest indoor movie set ever constructed. A house in Mobile was bought and used for domestic scenes. The only portion of the mother ship spacecraft built on the set was its base, a stationary 40,000-pound steel construction with a mirrored, spotlighted "hatch" that opened as a ramp. Everything above this portion was a meticulously crafted miniature, joined by optical processing to the portion on the set. Since the airborne UFOs were also optically added, the astonished actors looking upward had to strain their imaginations as they stared at hangar beams and rafters. Legendary French director François Truffaut—insecure of his English, which he constantly rehearsed with Bob Balaban—joined the cast because he said he wanted the experience of acting in someone else's movie. His half-worshipped, half-intimidating presence on the set made him the real star among the cast. (In a 1982 interview, he revealed that Spielberg had confided to him that "out of this crew of 250, you and I are the only ones who haven't taken any drugs.") The spacecraft aliens consisted of carefully drilled, rubber-suited, six-year-old girls, who ruined several of their takes by erupting suddenly into disco steps; but the close-up extraterrestrial figure was a complex mechanical doll connected by cables to a system of levers that enabled numerous movements. Because of a cool reception from local residents and government caretakers at the actual Devil's Tower in Wyoming, the *Encounters* crew concluded that this would hardly be the place to welcome any real aliens to Earth. The Mojave Desert sequence, which appears first in the movie, was the last filmed. Spielberg clamped the entire, year-long production under tight security wraps, rigidly controlling access to sets and script—and because so much of the action seen by the audience was invisible to the actors at the time, the company operated on little else than faith in the director's visualizations. *Close Encounters* won a single Academy Award, for Vilmos Zsigmond's cinematography. Balaban's *Close Encounters of the Third Kind Diary* (1978) provides an interesting, day-by-day account of the proceedings.

CLUNY BROWN. 1946. Filmed winter 1945–46; 20th Century-Fox Studios, Los Angeles.

Cast: Jennifer Jones, Charles Boyer, Richard Haydn, Una O'Connor, Peter Lawford, Helen Walker, C. Aubrey Smith.

Director: Ernst Lubitsch.

Master of light, sophisticated romantic comedies, Ernst Lubitsch capped his career with this film based on Margery Sharp's novel. Jennifer Jones, in the title role, gave probably the best performance of her career. Charles Boyer entered the production directly from the set of *Confidential Agent*, which he felt was an inferior picture. Eager to work with a good screenplay and a class director, he may also have been influenced by the fact that novelist Sharp was one of his wife's favorite authors. Box office reception disappointed Lubitsch, who concluded that the comedy was *too* sophisticated for its time, its satire too rich.

COAL MINER'S DAUGHTER. 1980. Filmed summer–autumn 1979, Kentucky. Tennessee.
Cast: Sissy Spacek, Tommy Lee Jones, Beverly D'Angelo, Levon Helm, Ernest Tubb.
Director: Michael Apted.

Despite minor quibbles, "the film done us proud," declared country singer Loretta Lynn, on whose autobiography the screenplay was based; both she and her husband were profoundly moved on first viewing. Sissy Spacek was Lynn's choice to play herself, though the actress wasn't much interested in the part until she read Lynn's book. With only a brief background of folk-rock singing, Spacek insisted on doing all the vocalizing herself, and she performed most of her twelve songs live on the set, not mouthing to predubbed recordings, as is usual. She spent hours listening to tapes of Lynn, practicing Lynn's hill-country speech patterns, and working with the singer's backup musicians. To play Lynn as a thirteen-year-old, thirty-year-old Spacek dropped five pounds and bound her bosom: for Lynn at forty, she added a body pad and size-C bra. Tommy Lee Jones acknowledged a few clashes of temperament with his costar but concluded that such difficulties suited the roles they played. Lynn herself visited the sets several times; her only criticism came when she found wood instead of coal beneath the Butcher Hollow cabin set. The 1980 best actress Academy Award went to Spacek.

THE COLOR PURPLE. 1985. Filmed May–July 1985; Anson County, North Carolina. California: Newhall; Universal Studios, Universal City.
Cast: Whoopi Goldberg, Danny Glover, Adolph Caesar, Margaret Avery, Oprah Winfrey, Akosua Busia.
Director: Steven Spielberg.

Director Spielberg, in his first film about real people instead of killer sharks or gentle extraterrestrials, regarded *Color* as his greatest gamble and challenge. Four of his seven main cast members had never appeared on screen before. Whoopi Goldberg, playing Celie, originally sought the part of Sofia, played by Oprah Winfrey; and Margaret Avery played blues singer Shug Avery. Goldberg had suggested singer Tina Turner for this role, but Turner refused, saying the part hit "too close to home." Their roles required both Avery and Winfrey to put on many pounds. Akosua Busia, daughter of an Ashanti chief who was also a prime minister of Ghana, played Nettie. During the three-day filming of the climactic dinner-table sequence, Winfrey said she kept thinking about civil-rights activist Fannie Lou Hamer as she listened to the dialogue. The first scene filmed—the juke joint, on a humid, tightly congested Universal sound stage—seemed inauspicious to the new actors, but matters improved on location. An African village arose in Newhall, while Spielberg chose the North Carolina location for its natural scenery. For winter sequences, trees were defoliated, and special blowers scattered a fluxlike, biodegradable snow over the ground. Crews spread tons of reddish earth on the town streets to recreate Georgia red clay. While the NAACP furiously protested this film's "perpetuation of stereotypes," *Color* was nominated for eleven Academy Awards—but finally took none.

COMING HOME. 1978. Filmed January–May 1977; California: Rancho Los Amigos Hospital, Downey; Los Angeles.

Cast: Jane Fonda, Jon Voight, Bruce Dern, Robert Carradine, Penelope Milford, Robert Ginty, David Clennon.

Director: Hal Ashby.

Historically important because of the early attention it courageously focused on the problems of Vietnam veterans, this film aroused ample controversy. Some of the genuinely paraplegic extras in the film at first hesitated to work with outspoken peace activist Jane Fonda; her politics, however, ceased to be a problem once production began. More important, the U.S. Veterans Administration refused all cooperation, its chief medical director labeling the script a tissue of lies. Though writer Nancy Dowd received screen credit for her original screenplay, the shooting script was the work of Waldo Salt (who spent $50,000 of his own money in taping interviews with wounded vets and developing the story) and Robert C. Jones. Much of the screenplay underwent revisions as shooting progressed; the final confrontation scene between Fonda, Jon Voight, and Bruce Dern was improvised by the three over the weekend prior to filming it. For Voight, *Coming Home* became a labor of love, though he denied any political motives in making it. Sylvester Stallone and Jack Nicholson had both turned down his role as a paraplegic vet, and Voight himself had originally been slated to play the Marine captain role that finally went to Dern. Voight spent five weeks learning to play basketball from a wheelchair, residing in the paraplegic ward of Rancho Los Amigos during production. Important to all the performers was the decision to face squarely the problem of sex between a paraplegic and an able-bodied person—how to portray it sensitively, yet accurately. Fonda was extremely reluctant to play her love scene in the nude—director Ashby cleared the set of all but himself and a cameraman for the sequence (which also used a body double for a few shots). Fonda won her second Academy Award for best actress, Voight won for best actor, and the screenwriters also took an Oscar. But the final word belonged to the hospitalized vets who worked with the cast; they praised the film.

COOL HAND LUKE. 1967. Filmed autumn 1966; California: Stockton; Warner Bros. Studios, Burbank.
Cast: Paul Newman, George Kennedy, J. D. Cannon, Strother Martin, Jo Van Fleet, Robert Drivas, Wayne Rogers.
Director: Stuart Rosenberg.

Paul Newman's weeks of preparation for his role of convict Lucas Jackson included taking guitar lessons and walking and running in shackles. Framing a sequence of ineffable sadness, Luke's song, "I Don't Care If It Rains or Freezes," was a jingle from a company that made plastic religious ornaments. Because Stuart Rosenberg had changed some of the lyrics at the last minute, Newman forgot a line on camera and looked off-camera toward Rosenberg, who motioned him to go on with the song. Newman, angry with himself for fluffing it, began weeping as he completed the song, and there were no more takes. Rosenberg wanted the film to end as Luke dies and is carried away, but the studio insisted on filming an epitaph featuring his cell mates. Donn Pearce, author of the original novel and coauthor of the screenplay, was a former safecracker who knew whereof he wrote; he played the role of Sailor in the chain gang. George Kennedy won an Academy Award for best supporting actor.

THE COTTON CLUB. 1984. Filmed January–March 1984; New York City: Manhattan; Prospect Hall, Brooklyn; Astoria Studios, Queens.
Cast: Richard Gere, Gregory Hines, Diane Lane, Lonette

McKee, James Remar, Allen Garfield, Fred Gwynne, Gwen Verdon, Bob Hoskins, Joe Dallesandro.
Director: Francis Ford Coppola.

Al Pacino had turned down Richard Gere's role, as had Sylvester Stallone. Gregory Hines eagerly accepted the part refused by Richard Pryor, and Lonette McKee based her character indirectly on Lena Horne. Owing to screenplay problems, Francis Coppola took over direction at producer Robert Evans's request after the film was already in production. More than thirty drafts of the script were hammered out even as filming proceeded, leading to much confusion and tension on the set. Dissensions mounted as Evans and Coppola squabbled over casting, concept, and the runaway budget. Both Coppola and Gere—the latter dissatisfied with the constantly revised script and reluctant to improvise on the set—walked out at one juncture. Because of Coppola's off-the-cuff procedures, other cast members, seldom able to anticipate when they would be called in front of the camera, also grew restive. Finally the film's chief financial backer hired a Las Vegas watchdog, Joey Cusumano, to linger on the set. Nicknamed "my favorite gangster" by cast and crew, Cusumano's sinister presence damped frictions, but he got so interested in the goings-on that he later went into acting himself. Diane Lane, in the meantime, became genuinely infatuated with her screen lover, Gere. Coppola filmed the Dutch Schultz shooting episode (which actually occurred in Newark in 1935, several years later than the film's time frame) in a real bar and grill on East 23rd Street in Manhattan. Despite the liberties this picture took with history and the many hassles involved in getting it made, its care for authentic period settings and musical performances brought it much acclaim. Designer Richard Sylbert studied photos of the original Cotton Club in Harlem and interviewed many dancers who had performed there. Some of them, visiting the set, said they felt keen thrills of recognition. The film also provided much-needed employment for a host of actors and crew in a movie industry that still hires few black talents for major productions.

THE COUNT OF MONTE CRISTO. 1934. Filmed summer 1934; Reliance Pictures Studio, Los Angeles.
Cast: Robert Donat, Elissa Landi, Louis Calhern, Sidney Blackmer, Raymond Walburn, William Farnum.

Director: Rowland V. Lee.

Robert Donat's Hollywood sojourn for this swashbuckler became an exhausting five-week experience, full of seventeen-hour days and the pervading sense of unreality that often plagued many foreign actors in the film colony. His lead role had been written for Fredric March, who then became unavailable. Never physically strong, Donat found himself desperately fatigued by the time he returned to London. How much of his exhaustion may have owed to a tentative affair with his Austrian-Italian costar Elissa Landi remained unspoken; but he was especially grateful that for his underwater escape scene, a body double plunged into the studio tank for him. Three French film versions of the Dumas novel were produced between 1942 and 1961. A 1976 American remake starred Richard Chamberlain.

THE COUNTRY GIRL. 1954. Filmed March–April 1954; Paramount Studios, Los Angeles.

Cast: Bing Crosby, Grace Kelly, William Holden, Anthony Ross, Gene Reynolds.

Director: George Seaton.

Gossip columnist Hedda Hopper had maliciously whispered in Bing Crosby's ear that Grace Kelly was a nymphomaniac eager to claim his body, so Crosby initially opposed her for the title role that she eagerly sought, saying that Kelly was too glamorous and inexperienced for the part. (Jennifer Jones was originally scheduled, but dropped out when she became pregnant.) But Crosby at fifty-three also had serious qualms about his own abilities for this heavy drama. Nervous in any part that required more of him than crooning to nuns or trading quips with Bob Hope, he became hypersensitive about his toupee, at one point demanding to use the same one he'd worn two decades before in *College Humor* (1933). Director Seaton, however, refused to let him be Der Bingle for the role of Frank Elgin. At Crosby's urgent request, Seaton wrote a full biography of the character for Crosby to study. Before shooting his Boston jail-cell scene, Crosby stayed up all night, enlisting two of his sons to walk him around and keep him awake. His properly dissipated appearance next morning horrified his elderly mother, who walked away from the set convinced that her Bing had been drinking again. Hedda Hopper notwithstanding, both Crosby and William Holden became vastly smitten with Kelly, and both dated her; she and Holden had had a brief romantic fling just beforehand while starring in *The Bridges at Toko-Ri* (1954). Kelly, at twenty-four, won an Academy Award for best actress but later said she could have done much better in the role if she'd been five years older. Seaton also won an Oscar for his adaptation of Clifford Odets's original playscript.

THE COURT JESTER. 1956. Filmed summer–autumn 1955; Paramount Studios, Los Angeles.
Cast: Danny Kaye, Glynis Johns, Basil Rathbone, Cecil Parker, Mildred Natwick, Angela Lansbury, Robert Middleton.
Directors: Norman Panama, Melvin Frank.

Melvin Frank claimed that Danny Kaye was hard to work with—that he was, in fact, suffering from a serious mental depression while playing the title role. If so, it seemed hardly to affect his ultimate performance, but he did enter psychoanalysis immediately upon completion of the film. A part of his costuming that he hated was the uncomfortable symmetricals (i.e., "leg falsies") that he wore over his calves to improve the appearance of his legs. Sylvia Fine, Kaye's wife and partner who wrote his patter songs, delivered her material late, which caused further tensions. Since Kaye had never handled a rapier in his life, he took fencing lessons from sixty-four-year-old Basil Rathbone, veteran cinema swordsman, who was paid extra for offering instruction. Kaye caught on fast, ultimately besting Rathbone to the point where the latter had to be doubled in several long shots. The film used a few left-over routines created for a previous Kaye comedy, *Knock on Wood* (1954).

THE CREATURE FROM THE BLACK LAGOON. 1954. Filmed autumn 1953; Silver Springs, Florida. Universal-International Studios, Universal City.
Cast: Richard Carlson, Julie Adams, Richard Denning, Antonio Moreno.
Director: Jack Arnold.

In a picture that set many a stereotype, the creature itself, a sort of prehistoric *merman*, became the granddaddy monster for dozens of creature features that emerged in the Fifties and Sixties. Beneath all those fangs and scales, two stunt men played the title role—swimming champ Ricou Browning in underwater shots, and Ben Chapman, a larger man, on land. Browning was noted for being able to hold his breath for up to four minutes underwater, a skill he used repeatedly (along with trips to an off-camera air hose), since no aqualungs or bubbles were allowed. The foam-latex suits and masks worn by both actors were costly creations of studio makeup artists. Because the costume was so buoyant, Browning also had to wear lead weights. Producer William Alland suggested that the gill man's appearance be roughly modeled on nobody less than Oscar, the Academy Award figurine. Underwater sequences occurred at Silver Springs, chosen for the clarity of its water. The movie was one of those few mid-Fifties pictures filmed in the widely heralded but shortlived 3-D process. *Creature*'s popularity virtually rescued Universal-International from bankruptcy. Less popular sequels, using the same rubber suits, included *Revenge of the Creature* (1955) and *The Creature Walks Among Us* (1956). Browning appeared, in one form or another, in many later subsurfacers as well.

CRIES AND WHISPERS (VISKINGAR OCH ROP). 1973.
Filmed 1972; Taxinge-Näsby, Sweden.
Cast: Harriet Andersson, Kari Sylwan, Ingrid Thulin, Liv Ullmann, Erland Josephson.
Director: Ingmar Bergman.

Ingmar Bergman imagined the soul, he said, as "a moist red membrane"; and shades of red, portraying souls in anguish, dominate *Cries and Whispers*, Bergman's most ambitious attempt to put a dream state on film. Some critics maintain that the three sisters represented aspects of the director's own mother. Harriet Andersson's death scene was the first sequence filmed because the bright lights needed were only on brief loan. (After Bergman said "Cut!," the "dead" woman jerked upright and shouted "Booo!" The frequent levity on Bergman sets perhaps served to counteract the material of his morose visions.) Erland Josephson, a familiar face in Bergman features, was primarily a stage performer until his work in this picture. Filming in a rented manor near Stockholm (the house was one in which Bergman had once lived, a place that carried profound associations for him), the entire cast deferred their earnings, since Bergman was broke and hadn't sold the film in advance. *Cries and Whispers* won the

New York Film Critics Circle award for best picture; and Liv Ullmann won the same award for best actress. Its only Academy Award went for Sven Nykvist's cinematography.

"CROCODILE" DUNDEE. 1986. Filmed summer 1985; Australia: McKinlay, Queensland; Kakadu National Park. New York City.
Cast: Paul Hogan, Linda Kozlowski, John Meillon, Mark Blum.
Director: Peter Faiman.

"A simple little film," was how Paul Hogan described the savvy-bumpkin-in-the-big-city blockbuster that, for the first time in history, reaped the year's biggest box office gross for a film that wasn't American made. This film was Hogan's screen debut (as well as his story and screenplay) after a career of hustling commercials and jokes on Australian TV. Australians seemed to take national pride in Hogan's laconic cartoon version of themselves; and American audiences, always tickled by wise rube characters, also made a brief fetish of Dundee's Aussie slang. Though actual crocodiles abounded in the rugged Kakadu National Park area, insurance brokers prohibited their use because they were so dangerous; so the only croc we see up close is a hydraulic, rubber-latex model moving on an underwater rail. American actress Linda Kozlowski, playing Sue Charlton (after Morgan Fairchild had been considered for the role), was cast because Hogan wanted an authentic New Yorker in the part. Fueling show biz scandal, the two costars engaged in a highly publicized affair that threatened Hogan's marriage of three decades. Hogan marveled at the cooperation of movie-wise Manhattan authorities in filming scenes there, in contrast to the general consternation of officials in Australia whenever a filming company appeared. Two Hollywood studios turned down the American distribution rights before Paramount marketed the film and broke the bank (but not before inserting quotation marks in the title to make sure, said Hogan, that Americans "wouldn't think it was a swamp movie"). A year after the filming and despite his superb physical condition, Hogan suffered a mild cerebral hemorrhage that temporarily sidelined him. He went on to make a 1988 sequel, *"Crocodile" Dundee II*, but swore that would be the last of Dundee. We'll see.

CROSSFIRE. 1947. Filmed February–March 1947; RKO Studios, Culver City.
Cast: Robert Young, Robert Mitchum, Robert Ryan, Gloria Grahame, Paul Kelly, Sam Levene.
Director: Edward Dmytryk.

Influential in its frank treatment of anti-Semitism, this modestly budgeted film followed closely on the heels of *Gentleman's Agreement*, with its similar theme, and is generally ranked as director Dmytryk's best. Later in 1947, he was called before the infamous House Un-American Activities Committee, became one of the victimized Hollywood Ten, and was fired by RKO in November. In 1950, he went to prison, along with some of Hollywood's brightest writers and directors as the blacklist ushered in a dark age for creative talent. On the *Crossfire* set, said Dmytryk, Robert Young, Robert Ryan, and Robert Mitchum competed for low-decibel dialogue in a movie full of shouting. The genesis for *Crossfire* was Richard Brooks's novel, *The Brick Foxhole*. John Paxton's adaptation was Oscar-nominated, but lost to George Seaton's *Miracle on 34th Street* screenplay.

THE CRUEL SEA. 1953. Filmed summer–autumn 1952; England: Plymouth; Plymouth Sound; English Channel.
Cast: Jack Hawkins, Donald Sinden, Stanley Baker, Denholm Elliott, Virginia McKenna.
Director: Charles Frend.

Donald Sinden's character, Lockhart, represented the author of the autobiographical novel on which this film was based, Nicholas Monsarrat. The corvette *Compass Rose* in the movie was actually *The Coreopsis* from Malta, formerly used by the Greek navy. Manning it was a crew of English merchant seamen; and crouched on the compass platform, whispering instructions for Jack Hawkins to repeat in the voice pipe, was retired Royal Navy Captain Jackie Broome. The craft, after being "sunk" in the film, ended up at a Newcastle scrap yard. Hawkins's later command ship, the frigate *Porchester Castle*, was actually a Royal Navy vessel that came with its own crew. The filmmakers found a North Sea winter hard to recreate during midsummer in the English Channel. Plastic icicles and glitter dust whitened the front half of the ship as the cast sweltered in heavy Arctic clothing. Plymouth

Race, where seven turbulent currents converge, provided the necessary rough seas. Hawkins, horribly seasick, said he barely got through these scenes. His weeping emotion after the depth charges had been planted among the floating sailors came spontaneously on the first take in his scene with Sinden; director Charles Frend, demanding a stiffer upper lip from Hawkins, made several retakes, but the first take was the one he chose after all. So enthusiastic were the navy extras about moviemaking that many of them competed for the grimy, uncomfortable job of playing the German U-boat sailors floating in the oil-slicked sea. The film boosted Hawkins's career; he said he was never again out of work. Even Nicholas Monsarrat liked the picture.

CRY FREEDOM. 1987. Filmed July–November 1986; Zimbabwe: Harare; Gweru; Shurugwi; Bulawayo; Mutare; Macheke River; Zambezi River. Diani Beach, Mombasa, Kenya. Shepperton Studios, Shepperton, England.

Cast: Kevin Kline, Denzel Washington, Juanita Waterman, Penelope Wilton, Sophie Mgcina, John Thaw, Zakes Mokae.

Director: Richard Attenborough.

This true account of black activist Steven Biko's martyrdom by the Nazilike regime of white South Africa evoked hysterical attacks and sinister threats from that violent, discredited nation even as filming progressed in neighboring Zimbabwe. The news media distortions from South Africa—along with strong encouragement from Biko's own widow and mother—solidified Sir Richard Attenborough's resolve to press on despite many problems; and a constant bodyguard was placed around him to insure his safety. He recruited many white South African exiles to play South African soldiers and police. American actor Denzel Washington, chosen to play Biko after hundreds of actors had been considered, gained weight for his role, studied tapes of Biko's speeches, and wore elevated shoes to increase his physical resemblance to the man. Kevin Kline, playing editor Donald Woods, worked hard on perfecting his South African dialect, while the real Woods, an exile from his homeland, stood on the sidelines, advising on every detail of filming. The picture was, of course, banned by a South African government that remained fearful and oppressive of its majority population. Woods's book *Filming with Attenborough: The Making of Cry Freedom* (1987) details each episode of this dangerous venture that became in itself part of the anti-apartheid struggle.

THE CURSE OF FRANKENSTEIN. 1957. Filmed October–November 1956; Bray Studios, London.
Cast: Peter Cushing, Christopher Lee, Hazel Court, Robert Urquhart.
Director: Terence Fisher.

This Hammer Films production was the first of many teamings for Peter Cushing and Christopher Lee, both of whom became major horror film stars as a result. (Lee's first complaint: "I haven't got any lines!" Cushing: "You're lucky. I've read the script.") Since Boris Karloff's makeup for the classic 1931 *Frankenstein* was a copyrighted recipe, Lee was forced to create a different monster, wearing a getup as painful as Karloff's original. Stiffly wrapped in bandages, Lee could hardly move his head; between scenes, he had to suck his nourishment through a straw. The scene that required him to steam as he lay in his acid bath almost did him in. Gallons of hot water were poured over him, producing lots of steam but also soaking through the bandages and chilling him to the bone. (The set was a small, cold grotto beneath the producer's office.) Though not a heavy drinker, he said he consumed a half-bottle of brandy during the episode. *Curse* established a new horror trend after studios had concentrated for more than a decade on making science fiction films.

D

DARK VICTORY. 1939. Filmed October–December 1938; Warner Bros. Studios, Burbank.
Cast: Bette Davis, George Brent, Geraldine Fitzgerald, Humphrey Bogart, Ronald Reagan.
Director: Edmund Goulding.

One of cinema's classic soap operas (almost as much so offscreen as on), this film went for the tear ducts and big bucks in proven, methodical ways. Neither Bette Davis nor George Brent were first choices. The studio had intended to star Kay Francis, but she refused to play a dying woman; and Spencer Tracy, whom Davis wanted to play opposite her, was unavailable. Davis described this period as "a most vulnerable" time in her life. Upset by the recent collapse of her first marriage (to bandleader Harmon Nelson), she was further devastated shortly after filming began by the sudden marriage of her lover, the director William Wyler, to actress Margaret Tallichet. Davis decided to walk off the picture, after having fought for her role in it for several years, fearing she was headed for a nervous breakdown; but studio executive Hal Wallis persuaded her to stay by convincing her to vent her feelings in the role of Judith Traherne. Davis promptly began a rebound affair with Brent, a relationship that lasted about a year, but she continued to brood over Wyler. Especially difficult for her was the bulb-planting sequence near the end. Knowing that tears weren't right for the scene, Davis said her empathy with the character was such that she nevertheless kept crying during takes. Edmund Goulding patiently directed retakes of the scene until she was able to give a dry-eyed performance. This was Irish actress Geraldine Fitzgerald's first American film; she played Ann, a part added to the script by Goulding. Ronald Reagan, uncomfortable playing the less-than-macho Alex, fought with Goulding over the latter's desire to make Alex a sexually ambivalent character. He disliked the director personally and thought himself badly handled in the role. Though Davis lauded Bogart (still playing character parts at this time) on his portrayal of the Irish stable hand, his broguish appearance strikes many viewers familiar with his later classics as odd, to say the least. The film began a trend toward unhappy endings. *Stolen Hours* was a 1963 remake.

DARLING. 1965. Filmed August–December 1964; France. Italy: Florence; Capri. England: Skindles, Maidenhead; London locales; Shepperton Studios, Shepperton.
Cast: Julie Christie, Dirk Bogarde, Laurence Harvey, Roland Curram, Alex Scott, Pauline Yates.
Director: John Schlesinger.

After an initial lack of interest, Julie Christie overcame a bad case of jitters to play the leading role of Diana in this drama that brought her international stardom. Despite the reluctance of financial backers who thought the project unpromising and Christie ugly, the film was made on a shoestring budget and a killer schedule after producer Joseph Janni mortgaged everything he owned. Fourteen-hour-days and seven-day-weeks completely wore out Christie, who dozed on the set at every opportunity. Her long-dreaded nude scene caught her at her lowest ebb; hard-driving but sympathetic director John Schlesinger, however, accomplished the complex tracking shot in one take. Gregory Peck had turned down the male lead role before Schlesinger enlisted Dirk Bogarde, who claimed that Christie taught him more about ad-libbing than anyone else in the business. Laurence Harvey performed without salary, convinced that the film's success would make his percentage deal profitable. (It did.) Yet the only way Schlesinger could complete the picture was by selling Christie's contract to director David Lean, who was casting for *Doctor Zhivago* (1965) even as the *Darling* production edged toward bankruptcy. So it was a sweet evening for all concerned when Christie won the Academy Award for best actress. Frederic Raphael also won for his acidly satiric screenplay.

DAVID COPPERFIELD. 1935. Filmed summer 1935; Canterbury, England. California: Malibu; MGM Studios, Culver City.

Cast: Freddie Bartholomew, Frank Lawton, W. C. Fields, Roland Young, Edna May Oliver, Basil Rathbone, Maureen O'Sullivan, Jessie Ralph, Lionel Barrymore, Lewis Stone, Herbert Mundin, Elsa Lanchester, Una O'Connor, Hugh Walpole, Arthur Treacher.

Director: George Cukor.

The kindly Basil Rathbone, cast as vicious Mr. Murdstone, recalled how difficult it was for him to show no emotion on his face while thrashing the young Freddie Bartholomew as directed. "When it was over," he said, "I rushed over to Freddie and took him in my arms and kissed him." Bartholomew, however, was well protected by sheets of foam rubber under his trousers. Consequently he was far from the tears that George Cukor finally coaxed from him. When Maureen O'Sullivan (playing Dora) also couldn't cry during her deathbed scene, Cukor sat on the bed out of camera range and twisted her feet until the pain brought tears. Charles Laughton, originally cast as Mr. Micawber, withdrew during rehearsal, saying he couldn't get into the part, and W. C. Fields replaced him. Cukor marveled that for the first time in Fields's career he followed the script (though he did try, unsuccessfully, to insert his juggling routine into the film). Consuming two fifths of whiskey daily and unable to memorize lengthy dialogue, Fields spoke from large-print cue cards. Except for the Dickens nostalgia of producer David O. Selznick, the film would never have been made over the skeptical opposition of studio chief Louis B. Mayer, who had also failed to convince Selznick that Jackie Cooper should play the title role.

THE DAWN PATROL. 1938. Filmed summer 1938; California: Warner Bros. Studio Ranch, Calabasas; Warner Bros. Studios, Burbank.
Cast: Errol Flynn, Basil Rathbone, David Niven, Melville Cooper, Donald Crisp, Barry Fitzgerald.
Director: Edmund Goulding.

Much of the script and all of the aerial footage for this release was lifted from the 1930 version of *The Dawn Patrol* directed by Howard Hawks. Otherwise filmed largely in sequence with an all-British, all-male cast, it was timed to coincide with a rising feeling of imminent war in Europe. Errol Flynn begged off the project—he had just completed *The Sisters* (1938), and his sinus condition was flaring up—but the studio insisted. For David Niven, Flynn's pal and paying house guest at the time, the film meant major stardom. Niven's old school chum Peter Willes, who played Hollister, complained that Niven snubbed him during production. Niven later advised him, he said, never to sleep with leading ladies until after the retakes were finished. Carl Esmond played von Mueller, a role based on the famed Red Baron, German air ace Manfred von Richtofen.

A DAY AT THE RACES. 1937. Filmed September 1936–April 1937; California: Santa Anita Racetrack, Arcadia; MGM Studios, Culver City.
Cast: Groucho, Chico, and Harpo Marx, Allan Jones, Maureen O'Sullivan, Margaret Dumont.
Director: Sam Wood.

This most instantly popular of all the Marx brothers' farces labored to life through eighteen separate scripts and a more-than-usual amount of Marxian shenanigans. Irving Thalberg, MGM executive and the Marxes' chief guiding benefactor in Hollywood, died during production. Owing to his loss, they believed, the quality of their scripts fell ever after; Groucho essentially lost interest, and the brothers never again matched the comic heights of this and their previous films. Groucho said he fell in love with costar Maureen O'Sullivan—the latter admitted that she found him sexy and might have been interested if not for his incessant machine-gun chatter (and the fact that both of them were married). Covering himself, director Sam Wood typically required two dozen retakes of a scene, angering Groucho because the first or second take was often the one finally used. Look for occasional shots of Harpo and Chico just standing still—those are "laughter breaks," predetermined by clocking audience reactions during the Marxes' road show of *Races* long before they made the movie. Groucho started out as Dr. Quackenbush but changed his character's name to Dr. Hackenbush after scores of potentially furious Dr. Quackenbushes turned up in phone directories across the U.S. Look for thirteen-year-old Dorothy Dandridge, making her screen debut in a bit part. The Marxes took huge delight in the fact that this film was banned in the Republic of Latvia on the grounds of being "worthless."

DAY FOR NIGHT (LA NUIT AMÉRICAINE). 1973. Filmed September–December 1972; Victorine Studios, Nice, France.

Cast: Jacqueline Bisset, Valentina Cortese, Alexandra Stewart, Jean-Pierre Aumont, Jean-Pierre Léaud, François Truffaut.

Director: François Truffaut.

François Truffaut wanted to show how movies are made, so he coscripted and directed this affectionate, intriguing film, casting himself as the director. The title refers to the practice of photographing night scenes in daylight by the use of special lens filters. Truffaut determined to use only true incidents from his own moviemaking experience (though the hearing aid he wore was entirely symbolic). The death of the Jean-Pierre Aumont character, for example, was inspired by the auto crash that killed actress Françoise Dorléac after the filming of *The Soft Skin* (1964). Jacqueline Bisset's role was partially based on Julie Christie, who had acted in *Fahrenheit*

451 (1967). Allowing his cast wide latitude to improvise, Truffaut continued writing and revising scenes up to the last shot; often the actors didn't know whether they were rehearsing or actually performing on camera. English novelist Graham Greene played the bit part of an insurance broker. Truffaut's favorite line in the movie, a direction to a crowd of extras: "Don't talk about cinema!"—again, a memory from his own youth, when he had performed as an extra in a crowd scene. *Day for Night* won an Academy Award for best foreign film.

THE DAY THE EARTH STOOD STILL. 1951. Filmed spring 1951; Washington, D.C. 20th Century-Fox Studios, Los Angeles.

Cast: Michael Rennie, Patricia Neal, Hugh Marlowe, Sam Jaffe, Billy Gray.

Director: Robert Wise.

Its pacifist message during the peak of 1951 cold-war hysteria heralded a new genre of peaceful-alien films, even attracting veteran news broadcasters Elmer Davis, Gabriel Heatter, H. V. Kaltenborn, and Drew Pearson for brief cameos. (George Reeves, also playing a newscaster, began his role as TV's Superman later that year.) Spencer Tracy and Claude Rains were considered for the alien's role, but the relatively unknown British actor Michael Rennie, in his first American film, seemed more desirable for the part. The spacecraft on the studio back lot was a 100-foot-high, 25-foot-wide mock-up consisting of a plaster-of-Paris shell and a solid ramp. For Patricia Neal, the chief problem (aside from keeping a straight face at times) was learning the alien words "klaatu barada nikto" (which became a familiar code phrase among science-fiction devotees). Another problem for her was the studio gossip surrounding her ongoing love affair with the married Gary Cooper. Actor J. Lockard "Lock" Martin, standing seven-foot-seven, played Rennie's bodyguard robot Gort in a foam-rubber suit. Despite his towering height, Martin wasn't strong enough to lift and carry Neal unaided. His movements were accompanied by notes of an electronic musical instrument called the theremin. The death ray streaking from Gort's visor was realized by animation processing. The cult status of this Robert Wise production engendered many spinoffs, including a 1970s rock group called Klaatu.

DAYS OF WINE AND ROSES. 1962. Filmed spring 1962; California: San Francisco; Warner Bros. Studios, Burbank.

Cast: Jack Lemmon, Lee Remick, Charles Bickford, Jack Klugman, Jack Albertson.

Director: Blake Edwards.

Cliff Robertson had starred in J. P. Miller's *Playhouse 90* teleplay, but for the movie adaptation, producer Martin Manulis insisted on Jack Lemmon, who threw himself heart and soul into the part of the alcoholic husband. Lemmon and Lee Remick attended meetings of Alcoholics Anonymous, and Lemmon visited drunk tanks and alcoholic treatment centers on his own. After the final take of the protagonist in his straitjacket, director Blake Edwards had to enlist help to calm down the actor, who couldn't bring himself out of the intense mental anguish of the scene. Lemmon shot pool between scenes to keep up his emotional level—and he remained a casual drinker himself throughout the filming. For Edwards too, who said he often went home with migraines and threw up, the intensity of the production generated acute stress. He said he owed the downbeat ending to a call-girl friend of studio executive Jack Warner. Warner had wanted Edwards to film a happy ending, but the woman strongly disagreed, and Warner gave in. An Academy Award went to the title song, composed by Henry Mancini and Johnny Mercer.

DEAD END. 1937. Filmed May–July 1937; Samuel Goldwyn Studios, Los Angeles.

Cast: Joel McCrea, Sylvia Sidney, Humphrey Bogart, Wendy Barrie, Claire Trevor, Allen Jenkins, Marjorie Main, Ward Bond, the Dead End Kids.

Director: William Wyler.

This melodrama introduced the Dead End Kids (later, in various incarnations, the Little Tough Guys, East Side Kids, and Bowery Boys), a group of rowdy adolescent stage actors from Brooklyn. On their arrival in Hollywood to make this film, they went a bit berserk with their cars and new status. (Leo Gorcey received four traffic tickets in eighteen days.) On the set, they loudly complained about the script, which expurgated many lines of the original Broadway play in which they had performed since 1935, and they disparagingly compared their screen colleagues with their former stage peers. William

Wyler had wanted to film on location in New York City, but Samuel Goldwyn overruled him. Humphrey Bogart's marital problems with Mary Philips at this time led to his liaison with another actress, Mayo Methot, whom he married a year later. Both Goldwyn and Wyler had sought George Raft for Bogart's part, but Raft had an aversion to roles where he wound up as a corpse. Bogart cherished his scene with Marjorie Main, playing his mother, as one of his best in films. Despite hours of practice, however, he couldn't master the technique of stabbing an orange peel with a penknife until Wyler showed him how. The success of *Dead End* opened the Hollywood floodgates on slice-of-life dramas of social realism.

DEATH ON THE NILE. 1978. Filmed autumn 1977; Egypt: Nile River; Aswān: Abu Simbel; Luxor; Cairo. Pinewood Studios, Iver Heath, England.

Cast: Peter Ustinov, David Niven, Bette Davis, Angela Lansbury, Mia Farrow, George Kennedy, Maggie Smith, Jack Warden, Lois Chiles, Olivia Hussey, Simon MacCorkindale, Jon Finch.

Director: John Guillermin.

During the filming of this Agatha Christie thriller, David Niven's daughter Kristina suffered a near-fatal car crash, and to Peter Ustinov the experience made his old friend "for the first time seem very frail." Both actors were terrified of Bette Davis and her reputation for towering rages. One morning after a night on the town, the two crept to the set not knowing their lines and prepared for the worst. Davis confessed instead that she had lain awake all night trying to "learn this bloody script because they said you were both such professionals." Olivia Hussey drove Davis wild by playing East Indian chants on her dressing room stereo at dawn; when Davis protested, Hussey got mad and never spoke to her again. Notice the shoes: Davis's were made from the scales of twenty-six python skins; while first murder victim Lois Chiles's footwear, borrowed from a private collection, had diamond heels. Daily filming began at 6 A.M. in Egypt because of intense daytime heat. Cast and crew spent four weeks on the steamer *Karnak* along two hundred miles of the Nile between Aswān and Cairo. Ustinov reprised his role as detective Hercule Poirot in *Evil Under the Sun* (1982). An Academy Award went to costumer Anthony Powell.

THE DEER HUNTER. 1978. Filmed June–December 1977; Ohio: Mingo Junction; Struthers, U. S. Steel Company and St. Theodosius Russian Orthodox Church, Cleveland. West Virginia: Weirton; Follansbee. Pennsylvania: McKeesport; Pittsburgh. Mount Baker, Washington. Thailand: Bangkok; River Kwai.

Cast: Robert De Niro, Christopher Walken, John Cazale, John Savage, Meryl Streep, George Dzundza.

Director: Michael Cimino.

Robert De Niro, who called this indictment of war the most physically exhausting film he ever made, lived incognito among steelworkers for several weeks to help prepare himself for his role. He and John Savage did their own stunts, including the hazardous plunge into the swift Kwai from a hovering helicopter. The aircraft accidentally snagged itself on a bridge strut and almost went down before a crew member climbed out and released the snared cable; this scary episode remained in the final cut. The EMI producion company, anxious about insurance, almost canceled out the day before filming began because of John Cazale's terminal bone cancer. Playing the role of Stan, his condition gradually worsened until he could barely speak his lines; he died nine months later at age forty-two. His live-in companion Meryl Streep (who remained with him until his death) said she found her role difficult because the character she played was totally unlike herself. A real-life steelworker in Gary, Indiana, Chuck Aspegren, played Axel. The steel town of Clairton in the movie consisted of location scenes from eight different towns, most of them in Ohio. Fierce summer temperatures raged during the fall and winter town sequences. For the Appalachian hunting scenes in Washington's Cascade Range, Michael Cimino had two wild deer shipped in from a New Jersey game preserve. All Vietnam scenes were staged in Thailand, using no professional actors except the principals. Bangkok, under military curfew, required all cinematography to be done at night. The entire crew sickened from tropical diseases, and nervous Thai censors hovered constantly. On the River Kwai sequences, bodyguards were posted against dangerous smuggler traffic, and the company physician carried twenty-seven types of snake venom antidotes. Cimino said he never intended the film as a direct political statement, but it fueled plenty of controversy from Vietnam hawks and doves alike. It also won five Academy

Awards: for best picture, director Cimino, supporting actor Christopher Walken, cinematographer Nestor Almendros, and the sound editing team.

THE DEFIANT ONES. 1958. Filmed February–March 1958; Kern River area, California.
Cast: Tony Curtis, Sidney Poitier, Theodore Bikel, Lon Chaney, Jr., Cara Williams, Carl "Alfalfa" Switzer.
Director: Stanley Kramer.

The Defiant Ones was a groundbreaking treatment of racial themes, a film that, upon its initial release, met a hostile reception in Southern states. It established Sidney Poitier as a major star—his role, he said, was the most physically demanding of his career. Poitier liked Tony Curtis and found him easy to work with, and he credited him for insisting upon Poitier's costar billing. Poitier also brought Ivan Dixon, then an unknown bit player, to serve as his occasional stand-in. Carl Switzer performed in his final screen role as Angus; a former child star in the *Our Gang* comedies of the 1930s, he died the following year. Extremes of cold, wind, and rain (as extreme as it gets, anyhow, in southern California) made the location work sufficiently unpleasant so the actors didn't have to fake discomfort. Look for the facial close-up beneath the opening credits—that's Nedrick Young, coauthor of the screenplay under the pseudonym of Nathan E. Douglas; he had been blacklisted in 1953 for invoking the Fifth Amendment before the House Un-American Activities Committee and couldn't work under his own name. Along with cowriter Harold Jacob Smith, Young shared one of the film's two Academy Awards; cinematographer Sam Leavitt won the other.

DELIVERANCE. 1972. Filmed summer 1971; Georgia: Tallulah Falls; Chattooga River.
Cast: Burt Reynolds, Jon Voight, Ronny Cox, Ned Beatty, James Dickey, Herbert "Cowboy" Coward.
Director: John Boorman.

Burt Reynolds, who begged for the part of Lewis, said that the wild river in northern Georgia almost killed him and the other actors at least ten times. Author James Dickey (who also played the sheriff) gave Reynolds a copy of Eugen Herrigel's *Zen in the Art of Archery* to read, and Reynolds marveled that as long as he stayed in character, his canoe seemingly couldn't tip over and his arrows invariably went straight. He and Jon Voight both did many of their own stunts, though a double performed Voight's cliff-climbing sequence with a safety net stretched below. Reynolds used a pork bone tied around his leg for shots of his compound fracture. Hazardous footing on the cliffs and slopes, where director John Boorman set up his cameras, challenged crew as well as cast, but no serious injuries occurred. The toothless "Cowboy" Coward, playing the hillbilly rapist, was an illiterate veteran of Wild West shows. (When Boorman told him what he was expected to do, he replied, "Well, that's all right. I done a lot worse than that.") Billy McKinney, another of the mountain men, was actually a Los Angeles tree surgeon. All dialogue and sound effects were looped (i.e., dubbed later in the studio), while Boorman's Moog Synthesizer created the roar of the river.

THE DESERT FOX. 1951. Filmed spring–summer 1951; California: Borrego Springs; 20th Century-Fox Studios, Los Angeles.
Cast: James Mason, Jessica Tandy, Cedric Hardwicke, Luther Adler, Everett Sloane, Leo G. Carroll, George Macready, Richard Boone, Desmond Young.
Director: Henry Hathaway.

Desmond Young, author of the original book, played himself, but his voice was dubbed by Michael Rennie. James Mason's role as the German field marshal Rommel, revitalized his career. He researched the role thoroughly, watching old newsreels, and he played Rommel again in *The Desert Rats* (1953). *The Desert Fox*, probably the first movie to precede credit titles with an action sequence, aroused much controversy. Some English critics deplored its heroic view of Rommel; while West Germans were divided between those who regarded Rommel as a Johnny-come-lately in his opposition to Hitler and diehard Nazis who considered him a traitor. The Communist *Daily Worker* labeled screenwriter Nunnally Johnson a Fascist for scripting both this film and *Night People* (1954). Most of the battle scenes were staged in the California desert, but a few of them used spliced-in shots from the 1942 British documentary *Desert Victory*, showing actual fighting in North Africa.

DESPERATELY SEEKING SUSAN. 1985. Filmed autumn 1984; New York: Manhasset, Long Island; New York City.

Cast: Rosanna Arquette, Aidan Quinn, Madonna, Laurie Metcalf, Steven Wright, Anne Carlisle.

Director: Susan Seidelman.

Produced, written, and directed by women, this comedy coincided with the meteoric rise of rock singer Madonna, who won her part after some two hundred others had auditioned for it. Her offscreen popularity created problems between her and the nominal star, Rosanna Arquette, who considered Madonna's glitzy fame inconvenient at best, distractive at worst. She resented, for example, the gratuitous insertion into the film of Madonna's song "Into the Groove." Creative turmoil reigned on the sets, as director Susan Seidelman and her cast debated the believability quotient of Arquette's amnesia. Despite the strains of competing egos, however, the principals were nothing if not professionals, and nobody went home permanently mad.

DESTRY RIDES AGAIN. 1939. Filmed autumn 1938; Universal Studios, Universal City.

Cast: Marlene Dietrich, James Stewart, Brian Donlevy, Charles Winninger, Una Merkel, Billy Gilbert.

Director: George Marshall.

Marlene Dietrich's career had all but faded when producer Joe Pasternak offered her the role of Frenchie in this classic Western comedy. In doing so, he countered the studio bosses, who considered Dietrich box office poison and wanted Paulette Goddard for the part. The result was a major comeback for Dietrich, firmly establishing her at age thirty-eight on a star pedestal. She bemusedly reflected that it took a knock-down-and-drag-out brawl, not a love scene, to boost her to the top. The big barroom fight sequence between her and Una Merkel was filmed without rehearsal. (Then James Stewart dumped gallons of water on both of them for numerous takes.) Dietrich, entranced with her costar, said she had never enjoyed working in Hollywood as much as she did when working with bachelor Stewart. But off-camera, Stewart seemed more interested at the time in reading Flash Gordon comics—at least until the sultry Dietrich had a life-size Flash Gordon doll made for him, then locked the three of them together in

Stewart's dressing room for an unusual ménage à trois. This film was a remake of a 1932 Tom Mix Western; later versions were entitled *Frenchy* (1950) and *Destry* (1954). Dietrich's song "See What the Boys in the Back Room Will Have" became one of her standard themes.

DIAL M FOR MURDER. 1954. Filmed July–September 1953; Warner Bros. Studios, Burbank.
Cast: Ray Milland, Grace Kelly, Robert Cummings, John Williams, Anthony Dawson.
Director: Alfred Hitchcock.

Ordered to limit his camera freedom to accommodate the 3-D technique then in vogue, Hitchcock—bored by the fad—found the whole production tedious. He said he directed *Dial M for Murder* only to fulfill his studio contract, preferring to talk on the set about his upcoming *Rear Window*, also starring Grace Kelly. Kelly's offscreen affair with Ray Milland threatened to wreck Milland's marriage before things cooled down. The finger seen dialing the phone at the beginning was a huge, wooden construction created for benefit of the 3-D cameras. Look for Hitchcock's usual cameo appearance, this time in a quickly shown photograph.

THE DIARY OF ANNE FRANK. 1959. Filmed spring–summer 1958; Amsterdam, Netherlands (backgrounds). 20th Century-Fox Studios, Los Angeles.
Cast: Millie Perkins, Joseph Schildkraut, Shelley Winters, Ed Wynn, Richard Beymer, Lou Jacobi, Diane Baker.
Director: George Stevens.

Millie Perkins, a twenty-year-old model, was cast in her first screen role after George Stevens had conducted a long search for the right actress to play Anne Frank. Veteran actor Joseph Schildkraut, on the other hand, had performed his role of Otto Frank more than a thousand times in the Broadway stage version. Stevens brought the real Otto Frank, Anne's father, from Europe to advise the cast and crew on technical matters, and Stevens himself also visited and researched the Frank hideaway in Amsterdam. In the studio, he built a cutaway, four-story duplicate of that apartment house and shot most of the movie in sequence. To pressurize his cast, he alternately turned up the studio heat or froze the set with air conditioners going full blast. He also played recorded Nazi crowd scenes and posted ghetto pictures near the set. For the air-raid scene when the building is shaken by bombs, he had the Frank hideaway reconstructed on wooden pillars and steel locomotive springs; when the crew pulled out the supports, the entire room dropped six inches and bounced. After particularly tense scenes, Stevens would play the nonsense song "Purple People Eater." Shelley Winters, as Mrs. Van Daan, won the first of her two Academy Awards for best supporting actress. William C. Mellor's cinematography also took an Oscar.

DINNER AT EIGHT. 1933. Filmed March–April 1933; MGM Studios, Culver City.

Cast: Marie Dressler, John Barrymore, Lionel Barrymore, Jean Harlow, Wallace Beery, Billie Burke, Roland Young.

Director: George Cukor.

Veteran comic actress Marie Dressler, who died the next year, patterned her role of Carlotta Vance after the eccentric British stage actress Mrs. Patrick Campbell. George Cukor gave John Barrymore wide latitude in his part (which bore more than slight resemblance to Barrymore's own persona) of the has-been matinee idol. Barrymore improvised many of his mannerisms, his actors' club lingo, and the details of his death scene. Note how he favors his left, Great Profile side. Wallace Beery considered Jean Harlow, the least experienced cast member, a real-life tramp and treated her like one; and Harlow cordially hated Beery offscreen as well as on. This mutual antagonism no doubt helped their performances as the battling spouses. In her braless white dresses, Harlow caused a sensation. Her all-white bedroom set also became an influential design element of the 1930s Hollywood *Moderne* style. With its all-star cast, this comedy-drama proved one of MGM's biggest money-makers of the Depression period.

THE DIRTY DOZEN. 1967. Filmed 1966; Elstree Studios, Borehamwood, England.

Cast: Lee Marvin. Ernest Borgnine, Charles Bronson, Jim Brown, John Cassavetes, George Kennedy, Trini Lopez, Donald Sutherland, Telly Savalas, Robert Ryan, Clint Walker, Ralph Meeker, Richard Jaeckel.

Director: Robert Aldrich.

Trini Lopez (playing Jimenez) died off quickly in this violent war adventure; his agent wanted more money, so director Robert Aldrich hastily wrote him out of the script. John Wayne had been offered the lead but withdrew to make *The Green Berets*; Jack Palance turned down the psycho part that went to Telly Savalas. Lee Marvin's legendary drinking bouts occasionally interfered with the shooting schedule, to the particular annoyance of Charles Bronson, who liked to get on with the job. Bob Phillips, who played Morgan, became Marvin's bodyguard and drinking partner for the duration. Jim Brown actually ran for his life in the explosive climactic sequence; no available stunt double could run as fast as the former pro football star. A host of imitations followed, including a 1985 TV-movie sequel with Marvin, Ernest Borgnine, and Richard Jaeckel reprising their original roles.

DIRTY HARRY. 1971. Filmed spring 1971; California: San Francisco; Warner Bros. Studios, Burbank.
Cast: Clint Eastwood, Harry Guardino, Reni Santoni, Andy Robinson, John Vernon, John Mitchum.
Director: Don Siegel.

Clint Eastwood not only originated his violent detective character Harry Callahan in this revenge drama but also inspired entire platoons of holier-than-thou, dirty-cop imitators. John Wayne, Frank Sinatra, and Paul Newman (who suggested Eastwood) all rejected the opportunity to limn the title role, originally scripted as much less superhuman. To the horror of studio bosses, Eastwood performed his own hazardous stunts, most notably jumping from a bridge onto the roof of a moving bus. At the end, when he chucked his badge into a pond (director Don Siegel insisted on this touch, to Eastwood's reluctance), nobody was giving a thought to sequels. (There have been four to date.) Eastwood later mused that "a bit of elastic" had attached to the badge—"it sprang right back into his hand." While Eastwood has always denied the fascist implications of his vigilante movies, a chilling outcome of this one was that a local Philippine police department actually requested a print for use as a training film. Siegel appeared in a bit part as a man running down the street.

THE DISCREET CHARM OF THE BOURGEOISIE (LE CHARME DISCRET DE LA BOURGEOISIE). 1972. Filmed May–July 1972; Paris.

Cast: Fernando Rey, Stéphane Audran, Jean-Pierre Cassel, Delphine Seyrig, Michel Piccoli, Bulle Ogier.
Director Luis Buñuel.

You'll miss the point of this surrealistic fantasy unless you submit to having your leg pulled by the masterful joker Luis Buñuel. The director reported that he agonized for months over a proper title; not until he named it, he said, did the scenes he had filmed seem to come together into a congruent shape. His cast enthusiastically brought many kinds of food and drink to the set for use in the many dinner-table scenes. The movie won an Academy Award for best foreign film, despite the fact that Buñuel had scandalized Hollywood (never hard to do despite its high tolerance for scandal among its own); he had perversely quipped that, since he had bribed the Academy with $25,000, the Oscar would come as no surprise. In a more serious mood, he stated that this film—together with *The Milky Way* (1969) and *The Phantom of Liberty* (1974)—formed part of a loose trilogy. His favorite characters in the film? The cockroaches.

DOCTOR JEKYLL AND MR. HYDE. 1932. Filmed autumn 1931; Paramount Studios, Los Angeles.
Cast: Fredric March, Miriam Hopkins, Rose Hobart, Edgar Norton.
Director: Rouben Mamoulian.

This adaptation of Robert Louis Stevenson's classic tale is generally acclaimed as the best of many that have been made over the years. Rouben Mamoulian liked to emphasize that his concept of Hyde was not as a monster, but as an exuberant, Neanderthal-like, primitive man who only gradually becomes corrupted. Fredric March (known heretofore as a light comedian) wore different layers of makeup (created by Wally Westmore); each layer was sensitive to different lens filters, thereby allowing March to accomplish his intricate transformations from Jekyll to Hyde. Applying the Hyde makeup was a four-hour task. This dual role brought March his first Oscar for best actor. To achieve the effect of the whirling laboratory, cinematographer Karl Struss tied himself to the camera, then had himself spun around. The heartbeat sounds of the transformation scene were Mamoulian's own; he raced up and down stairs for two minutes before having a recording made.

DR. JEKYLL AND MR. HYDE. 1941. Filmed February–March 1941; MGM Studios, Culver City.
Cast: Spencer Tracy, Ingrid Bergman, Lana Turner, Donald Crisp, Ian Hunter, C. Aubrey Smith, Barton MacLane.
Director: Victor Fleming.

Spencer Tracy, assigned to the dual lead role against his wishes (Robert Donat was originally slated), was unhappy playing parts too far removed from his own persona, and the critics crucified him on this one—less for his own performance, probably, than for daring to create an entirely different sort of Jekyll-Hyde than Fredric March had defined a decade earlier. Tracy had proposed to studio bosses that Katharine Hepburn be assigned to play both female parts opposite him, but Ingrid Bergman and Lana Turner were chosen instead. At Bergman's pleading, the roles were switched so that she could play the barmaid floozy (a radical innovation in her good-girl typecasting) and Turner the fiancée. Bergman fell in love with director Victor Fleming, as Tracy did with Bergman, but neither platonic affair lasted beyond the filming. We see a genuinely hysterical Bergman in her scene where, distraught, she confronts the vicious Hyde; Fleming had just slapped her face, repeatedly and hard, after she had complained that she couldn't do the scene. Fleming achieved the same effects with a dry-eyed Turner, twisting her arm to make her cry in a scene with Tracy, who thought the director's methods a bit radical. The staircase scene, in which Tracy races up the steps carrying Bergman, was actually accomplished by a sling hoisting the actress, with Tracy (who had complained of a hernia) hanging on. During the umpteenth rehearsal for this scene, the rope broke, Bergman fell against Tracy, and both rolled head over heels down the stairs. Lying in a heap at the bottom, the two stars roared helplessly with laughter.

DR. NO. 1962. Filmed January-March 1962; Jamaica: Kingston; Port Royal; Laughing Water Estate, Ocho Rios; Blue Mountains; Dunn's River Falls; North Shore. Pinewood Studios, Iver Heath, England.
Cast: Sean Connery, Ursula Andress, Jack Lord, Joseph Wiseman, Bernard Lee, Lois Maxwell.
Director: Terence Young.

First and one of the best of the James Bond spy thrillers, *Dr. No* boosted Scots actor Sean Connery to fame but also typecast him in a role he found increasingly confining as he continued to portray Agent 007 in six more hugely successful films over two decades. Ian Fleming, author of the original novels, had wanted a craggier face than Connery's for the spy, suggesting actor-composer Hoagy Carmichael. Other early possibilities included Patrick McGoohan (who reputedly turned down the role on moral grounds), Richard Johnson, and Roger Moore (who, in later Bond films, did replace Connery). Director Terence Young put rugged ex-laborer Connery through a crash course of the social niceties required of James Bond, sending him to his own tailor and working to upgrade his country accent. Swiss actress Ursula Andress was cast as Honeychile Ryder because, said producer Harry Saltzman, she came "beautiful and cheap"—but Connery liked her best of all his Bond costars. Noel Coward had refused the title role, which went to Joseph Wiseman, but some of the background shots were filmed on the Jamaican estates of Coward and Fleming. Bernard Lee and Lois Maxwell (as M and Miss Moneypenny) were the most durable performers of the series —they appeared in eleven consecutive Bond films.

DR. STRANGELOVE, OR: HOW I LEARNED TO STOP WORRYING AND LOVE THE BOMB. 1964. Filmed January–April 1963; England: IBM Corporation, London; Shepperton Studios, Shepperton.

Cast: Peter Sellers, George C. Scott, Sterling Hayden, Keenan Wynn, Slim Pickens, Peter Bull, James Earl Jones.

Director: Stanley Kubrick.

Playing three characters in this first-ever nuclear comedy, Peter Sellers was also scheduled to play a fourth, the physically active role of Major Kong; an ankle injury, however, resulted in this part being assigned to Slim Pickens. As the title character, Sellers may have borrowed his assortment of compulsive tics and mannerisms from Dr. Rotwang in *Metropolis*, the 1926 German silent; Stanley Kubrick attributed the inspiration for Strangelove's accent to physicist Edward Teller. (Sellers and Kubrick both denied any intentional parody of Henry Kissinger, who hadn't yet become well known.) George C. Scott described his flamboyant role of Gen. Buck Turgidson as his best in films. The only woman in the film, Tracy Reed playing a nubile Pentagon secretary, was the daughter of British director Sir Carol Reed. Because the U.S. Air Force refused any assistance in technical details, designers recreated the B-52 mock-ups and models from photographs. Background air sequences were filmed over the Arctic. Kubrick gave all his performers (especially Sellers) wide latitude for their own bits of business and ad-libs. He originally envisioned a custard-pie fight finale between the opposing diplomats, but he decided against it. As cold-war satire, the film elicited strong criticism from superpatriots.

DOCTOR ZHIVAGO. 1965. Filmed December 1964–October 1965; Spain: Soria; Canillas; CEA Studios, Madrid. Finland: Joensuu; Lake Phyaselka. Kicking Horse Pass, Calgary, Alberta, Canada.

Cast: Omar Sharif, Julie Christie, Geraldine Chaplin, Tom Courtenay, Rod Steiger, Rita Tushingham, Alec Guinness, Ralph Richardson.

Director: David Lean.

Omar Sharif, in the title role, had his eyes taped back to give him more of a Russian face. Both he and Julie Christie remained singularly unimpressed with each other. The continental Sharif, who usually expected to fall in love with his female leads as a matter of course, professed horror at seeing his uninhibited English costar eat fried-egg sandwiches—"totally unromantic" and "rather unfeminine," he sniffed. Sharif directed his own seven-year-old son Tarek in the role of Zhivago as a boy. Christie, who owed her casting to David Lean's admiration for her in *Billy Liar* and *Darling*, believed her own performance as Lara a failure. Her low self-confidence and raw-edge emotions on the set weren't helped by the high-powered Lean, who shouted and harassed her into learning the ropes of a major production; she later credited him with teaching her discipline on the set. Lean had first considered, then rejected, Sophia Loren for the role. In a scene where Christie slaps Rod Steiger (playing Komorovsky), Method actor Steiger spontaneously belted her back, an unscripted move that Lean left in. Though he wanted to make the film in the Soviet Union, Lean decided on Spain because he feared too much official interference in Russia. The many extras included Spanish army soldiers (by dictator Francisco Franco's special permission), villagers from the pueblo of El Molar, and Finnish Laplanders, who portrayed the Siberian refugees.

The ten-acre, precisely detailed Moscow set arose at Canillas, using thousands of daffodils imported from the Netherlands for the spring scene; the long train and snowy landscape scenes were filmed in Finland. Neither Rita Tushingham nor Sir Alec Guinness had read Boris Pasternak's novel before joining the cast, but they leapt at the chance to work with Lean. This was Geraldine Chaplin's first major film appearance. The film won three Academy Awards, but none for acting and direction. Its box office success, though, bailed out MGM from severe financial straits.

LA DOLCE VITA. 1960. Filmed March–August 1959; Italy: Fregene; Passo Corese; exterior scenes and Cinecittà Studios, Rome.
Cast: Marcello Mastroianni, Anita Ekberg, Anouk Aimée, Alain Cuny, Yvonne Furneaux, Lex Barker, Annibale Ninchi.
Director: Federico Fellini.

Fellini tried without success to land several big-name performers for this film: Henry Fonda for the part of Steiner, which went to Alain Cuny; Maurice Chevalier, in the role taken by Annibale Ninchi; and Silvana Mangano for the role accepted by Anouk Aimée. For the lead, the director told Marcello Mastroianni that he needed a face with no personality in it, "like yours." Instead of a script, Fellini sent him a rude cartoon, and the actor accepted the part. Of the six principal actors, only Mastroianni spoke Italian during production. Anita Ekberg and Lex Barker spoke English, while Aimée and Yvonne Furneaux used French. Swedish actress Ekberg intimidated Mastroianni on their first encounter by her distracted air; she reminded him, he said, of a German soldier who had once shoved him onto a truck. "What a night!" he recalled of their fountain scene. "Was cold. She didn't feel nothing. Well, she's Swedish. I was drunk with vodka." Fellini flirted outrageously with Ekberg to get the performance he wanted. For the more inhibited Aimée, he danced crazy jigs and made faces at her behind the camera; putting her on a constant edge of laughter again gave him the character he sought. This film launched the word *paparazzi* into the world, a slang term identifying the aggressive mobs of photographers who hound the famous. Much of the visionary miracle scene was improvised on the spot in the Tivoli Gardens. Fellini disliked the final scene of the bloated fish (actually made of plaster) but maintained it anyway. The film won the prestigious Palme d'Or prize at Cannes but evoked huge controversy from the Italian press and government; missing the satiric point entirely, the Vatican blasted it for its "glamorized" hedonism.

DRACULA. 1931. Filmed September–November 1930; Universal Studios, Universal City.
Cast: Bela Lugosi, Helen Chandler, David Manners, Dwight Frye, Edward Van Sloan.
Director: Tod Browning.

A publicity gimmick at this movie's premiere engagements was to station nurses in theatre lobbies. Lew Ayres was first cast for the role that went to David Manners. By some accounts, Lon Chaney, Sr., had been preparing to play the title role when he died. With an imperfect handle on English, forty-nine-year-old, Hungarian-born Bela Lugosi had performed Count Dracula on Broadway from 1927 to 1930, and the film role typecast him as a sinister character forever after. Far from objecting, however, he made the most of the persona, not only in films (remaining distant and aloof on the set) but also offscreen, where he affected the cape and courtly manners of the Count. After the film's release, Lugosi claimed that 97 percent of his fan mail came from women who cited a "strange attraction" toward him. But the only money Lugosi ever made from this picture was $500 for seven weeks work. Each showing or revival of the film reminded him that, under a different financial arrangement, he could have been a wealthy man. (He died in near-poverty in 1956, regretful that he was never offered the chance to do a superior remake of the film.) Cinematographer Karl Freund aimed twin pencil-spotlights into Lugosi's eyes to enhance his hypnotic stare; note that one of the lights, however, consistently shines a bit off the mark. The expensive giant sets built for Dracula's Transylvanian castle and Carfax Abbey continued to be used in Universal films for a decade. That eighteen-foot spider web on Dracula's staircase was rubber cement shot from a rotary gun. The Albert Hall sequence was filmed on Universal's famed Phantom stage, where Lon Chaney's 1925 silent classic *The Phantom of the Opera* had been produced. And those distant mountains in the opening scenes are actually the Rockies, not the Alps.

DUCK SOUP. 1933. Filmed summer 1933; California: Arden Villa, Pasadena; Paramount Studios, Los Angeles.
Cast: Groucho, Harpo, Chico, and Zeppo Marx, Margaret Dumont, Louis Calhern, Raquel Torres, Edgar Kennedy.
Director: Leo McCarey.

Some Marx fans believe this wild satire to be the brothers' best. Groucho thought that Leo McCarey was the only first-class director the group ever had. Zeppo bowed out of acting after this film. *Duck Soup* is set in "Freedonia," but when town fathers of the real Fredonia, New York, loudly objected to the name being used, Groucho advised the mayor to change his town's name: "It is hurting our picture." Despite its classic status, the film was not a commercial success—probably its satire needled a bit too sharply for the times as nations industriously prepared for another war. Benito Mussolini banned the film in Italy, taking Groucho's role of dictator Rufus T. Firefly as a direct personal insult. This news made the Marxes ecstatic. *Duck Soup* was the only Marx film in which all four brothers performed musically together.

E

E.T., THE EXTRATERRESTRIAL. 1982. Filmed September 1981–February 1982; California: Northridge; Tajunga; Crescent City; Laird International Studios, Culver City.
Cast: Dee Wallace, Henry Thomas, Peter Coyote, Robert MacNaughton, Drew Barrymore.
Director: Steven Spielberg.

The biggest financial blockbuster in movie history began under the working title *E.T. and Me*. Steven Spielberg indulged wholeheartedly in one of his favorite topics: suburban childhood. He seldom raised his camera lens more than four feet, eight inches from the floor, in order to reflect the child's-eye view of Henry Thomas. This film also provided a visual catalogue of special effects and state-of-the-art gimmickry. The gentle, wizened alien—the type of electronically controlled surrogate that Spielberg often seemed to prefer over living actors—actually consisted of three creatures of varying complexity: a mechanical doll bolted to the floor; an intricate electronic robot with eighty-six separate points of movement and forty facial expressions on four interchangeable heads; and a padded suit worn over a midget actor. Pencil spotlights sparkled the eyes (a technique first devised for *Dracula*, 1931). The alien plants in the spaceship greenhouse, in addition to handmade models and exotic African species, included blooms of polyester blown over inflated condoms. This was the second film for both ten-year-old Henry Thomas and six-year-old Drew Barrymore, granddaughter of John Barrymore. (When asked if she thought E.T. was a real creature or a mechanical device, she sensibly replied, "Both.") M&M candies *could* have been E.T.'s favorite morsel, but that distinction fell to Reese's Pieces after the M&M company refused use of its label. Plenty of other commercial interests, however, reaped bonanzas from franchise deals. Four Academy Awards certified the box office success.

EAST OF EDEN. 1955. Filmed May–August 1954; California: Mendocino; Salinas; Warner Bros. Studios, Burbank.

Cast: James Dean, Raymond Massey, Julie Harris, Burl Ives, Jo Van Fleet, Richard Davalos, Albert Dekker.

Director: Elia Kazan.

"Jesus Christ, he *is* Cal!" exclaimed novelist John Steinbeck upon meeting James Dean. But Dean's first starring role (as young loner, Cal Trask) caused difficulties for his more experienced acting colleagues. He came to Hollywood with a big publicity buildup and lost no time in marking himself as a rigidly intense Method actor who tried to stay in character even offscreen. Complicating the filming, accomplished largely in sequence, was Dean's carelessness about such nuts-and-bolts factors as knowing his lines, adhering to cues and marks, and not making people wait for him. Dean severely antagonized the veteran Raymond Massey, most memorably in the Bible-reading scene. For Massey's close-up, Dean read a scriptural passage offscreen, loading it with profanities and obscenities; when the enraged Massey stormed off the set, Elia Kazan apologetically claimed that he had put Dean up to it in order to evoke the reaction he wanted from Massey, and Dean also apologized. Later, during the reconciliation scenes, the two actors warmed up to each other. On camera, Dean reportedly improvised details of the scene in which he tearfully tries to stuff money into Massey's coat, and the shock registering on Massey's face was quite genuine. (A bemused Kazan admitted that his first choice for Cal had been Marlon Brando.)

EASTER PARADE. 1948. Filmed November 1947–February 1948; MGM Studios, Culver City.
Cast: Judy Garland, Fred Astaire, Peter Lawford, Ann Miller, Clinton Sundberg, Jules Munshin.
Director: Charles Walters.

It was almost a parade of invalids. Her psychiatrist suggested that Judy Garland's husband, Vincente Minnelli, shouldn't direct her, as scheduled; so a crushed Minnelli withdrew in favor of Charles Walters. Garland had just returned from several weeks in a sanitarium, her nerves still shaky—she often appeared late on the set, and her weight and physical appearance fluctuated alarmingly from scene to scene. Gene Kelly, slated for the male lead, broke his ankle playing softball two days before the start date. Semiretired Fred Astaire agreed to replace him (even though he had not danced for two years) because he wanted to work with Garland, who adored him. Even Garland's feather-shedding gown in the "Beautiful Faces" number—a pet peeve of the forty-eight-year-old Astaire, who detested feathers, bangles, and any sort of loose, hazardous objects in his partners' raiment—couldn't deter their mutual admiration. Astaire synchronized all his drumming movements with the prerecorded sounds in his opening "Drum Crazy" number. Ann Miller, a replacement for the injured Cyd Charisse, performed with a bad back, doping herself on pain killers and taping her torso (her injuries had resulted from a fall down a flight of steps while pregnant, and she lost her baby). To avoid towering over Astaire, she flattened her hairdo and wore ballet shoes in their duet scenes. "A Couple of Swells" became a highlight of Garland's famed 1950s stage show.

EASY RIDER. 1969. Filmed spring 1969; California. Arizona. Texas. New Mexico: Taos; Las Vegas. Louisiana: Morganza; New Orleans.
Cast: Peter Fonda, Dennis Hopper, Jack Nicholson, Karen Black, Robert Walker.

Director: Dennis Hopper.

This counterculture classic of the late Sixties—the flip side of *Alice's Restaurant*—was Jack Nicholson's big break. Rip Torn had been scheduled for the supporting role of the jail-bird-lawyer, but he fought with Dennis Hopper over the script, and Bruce Dern also turned it down. Hopper, who wanted a real Texan, was initially opposed to Nicholson. Nicholson said he drew from Lyndon B. Johnson's Texas good-ole-boy style for his performance—and he hated the haircut. The acting careers of both Hopper and Peter Fonda were at a standstill when they made this picture; Hopper was about ready to teach school. The New Orleans cemetery scene, in which Fonda climbs into the statue's lap and questions it as his surrogate mother, hit him extremely hard emotionally (his own mother had committed suicide when he was a child); he wanted the scene removed, but Hopper insisted on leaving it in. Inspiration for the movie came to Fonda in a Toronto hotel room. Filmed on the road, the picture utilized many townspeople of various localities, some of whom were initially hostile to the grubby trio of actors. Hopper won the Cannes Film Festival award for direction.

8½. 1963. Filmed May 1962–January 1963; Italy: Filacciano; Fiumicino; Tivoli; Viterbo; Cecchignola military reservation, EUR Buildings, Cinecittà Studios, Titanus-Appia Studios, and Scalera Studios, Rome.
Cast: Marcello Mastroianni, Claudia Cardinale, Anouk Aimée, Sandra Milo.
Director: Federico Fellini.

Usually the story idea comes first—but in this case, Federico Fellini labored to find or create a script for the express purpose of making a movie. He finally decided to make a film about that difficulty itself, his own creative block. For a title, he gave it an opus number, his own 8½th movie (its original title: *I Confess*). Fellini thrives on improvisation, and his cast members (many of them nonactors) often received their lines on a sheet of paper moments before filming a scene; only Marcello Mastroianni was allowed to read the full script. The latter didn't like losing weight for his role as Guido, while Sandra Milo, playing Carla, had to put on ten pounds. Unfamiliar with her lines in a restaurant scene with Mastroianni, Milo consumed sixteen chicken legs during retakes. Saraghina, the fat prostitute dancing on the beach, was American opera singer Edra Gale, whom Fellini cast after a long, fruitless search. "I am Guido," said Fellini, whose doting female entourage often resembled the film's harem scene. Full of chaotic genius, fantasy, and folly, *8 ½* won Academy Awards for best foreign film and for costume design.

ELMER GANTRY. 1960. Filmed spring 1960; California: Columbia Studios, Los Angeles; Columbia Ranch, Burbank; MGM Studios, Culver City.
Cast: Burt Lancaster, Jean Simmons, Dean Jagger, Arthur Kennedy, Shirley Jones, Patti Page.
Director: Richard Brooks.

Burt Lancaster, after almost fifteen years of interest in making a movie from Sinclair Lewis's novel, patterned his mannerisms and demeanor in the title role on director John Huston—though Lancaster also derived character bits from the flamboyant, real-life evangelist Billy Sunday. To the actor's annoyance and disgust, his original final line ("See you in hell, brother") was censored by the Catholic Legion of Decency and removed, but surprisingly few dissenting voices were heard from the Protestant church establishment. Jean Simmons based her part on Aimee Semple McPherson, another famous revivalist. Lewis himself had advised Richard Brooks to read all the negative reviews of the novel before making the movie. For playing audiences of true believers, Brooks scoured Long Beach for elderly folk who often attended Baptist tent meetings; he then bussed them to the studio tent mock-up. Many of the devout believed they were actually in church and joined wholeheartedly in the singing and emotionalism. Academy Awards went to Lancaster as best actor, to Shirley Jones as best supporting actress, and to Brooks for writing the screenplay.

ENTER THE DRAGON. 1973. Filmed February–May 1973; Hong Kong.
Cast: Bruce Lee, John Saxon, Jim Kelly, Shih Kien, Bob Wall.
Director: Robert Clouse.

Probably the best of all the chop-socky movies and the first aimed primarily toward an American audience, this film was also martial artist Bruce Lee's last, released a few days after his sudden death at age thirty-three. Lee, high-strung and nervous about his most ambitious screen effort, endlessly rehearsed his kung fu routines. He damaged his hands as well as his ego during the fight with Bob Wall (playing the villain Oharra), when the latter came at him with broken bottles (real glass, not Hollywood breakaways); a miscalculated blow resulted in severe cuts that laid him off for a week. He was also accidentally bitten by a devenomed cobra in one scene. Lee's motions were so fast that some of his flying-kick sequences had to be filmed in slow motion so as not to look faked. An unhappy man who always kept himself aloof on the set, he operated at a pitch of high-wired intensity that never let up for a second. Chinese craftsmen and laborers hand-built all sets and props, and language problems between Chinese and American cast and crew were constant. All sound was post-dubbed. A huge box office success, the film even broke records in Japan, traditionally the worst market for Chinese movies. Lee himself, however, saw little long-term future for kung fu films and seemed eager to expand his acting horizons at the time of his death.

EXODUS. 1960. Filmed March–July 1960; Israel: Haifa; Acre; Caesarea; Jerusalem; Kafr Kanna; Atlit. Cyprus: Nicosia; Famagusta; Kyrenia Mountains.
Cast: Paul Newman, Eva Marie Saint, Ralph Richardson, Peter Lawford, Lee J. Cobb, Sal Mineo, John Derek.
Director: Otto Preminger.

Creating the state of Israel on film seemed only a little less tremendous a task than the actual event. "Otto, let my people go," said satirist Mort Sahl as he watched the film's 220-minute preview. Director Preminger believed the film came much closer to historical truth than had the original novel by Leon Uris, who publicly declared that Preminger had ruined his book. After thirteen years of being blacklisted, screenwriter Dalton Trumbo was credited under his own name (at Preminger's courageous insistence after Kirk Douglas had taken the initial step by resuscitating Trumbo as screenwriter for *Spartacus*). Most scenes were filmed in locations where the original events had occurred, and the production stirred furious criticisms from political moderates and terrorists alike for various reasons; both Preminger and Paul Newman received death threats. Preminger's autocratic style also stirred resentments. He clashed frequently with Newman and with Lee J. Cobb—whom he verbally browbeat in a shouting match concerning Cobb's final balcony scene in the public square. To get a dozen Israeli tots to cry in a scene where an Arab attack is imminent, Preminger told them their mothers had deserted them and would never return. Israeli statesman Meyer Weisgal played the part of David Ben-Gurion in exchange for $1 million for the Weizmann Institute of Science. This was fourteen-year-old Jill Haworth's screen debut; she became enamored of Sal Mineo, her screen lover. Almost the only genuine Jew in the entire lineup of show folk was Preminger himself. Ernest Gold won an Academy Award for his musical score.

THE EXORCIST. 1973. Filmed August–November 1972; Baghdad, Iraq. Georgetown University, Washington, D.C. New York City: Goldwater Memorial Hospital, Welfare Island; New York University Medical Center.

Cast: Ellen Burstyn, Max von Sydow, Jason Miller, Linda Blair, Lee J. Cobb, Jack MacGowran.

Director: William Friedkin.

Based on a supposedly actual case of demon possession, this enormously popular shocker cast twelve-year-old Linda Blair, in her first substantial screen role, as the possessed child. Her work-day included two hours of latex-foam makeup, coupled with the wearing of painful contact lenses. Some of Blair's more repellent scenes, however, don't contain her at all; that's Eileen Smith, for example, doing at least some of the vomiting (by means of an ingenious device involving mouth tubing, a squeeze bulb on her back, and green pea soup—plus optical printing); Blair's revolving head is a dummy copy; and husky-voiced actress Mercedes McCambridge speaks the demon part (she swallowed eighteen raw eggs with a pulpy apple to produce her violent gagging sounds). Recorded cries of pigs being driven to slaughter produced the exorcised scream of the demon. The bedroom set in the exorcism scene was a virtual refrigerator, a room built inside an insulated "cocoon" and chilled to −20 degrees to produce splendid breath trails. Among the nonprofessional actors in the cast were three actual priests; playwright Jason Miller; and Vasiliki Maliaros (whom William Friedkin found in a Manhattan Greek restaurant—she played Jason Miller's mother). Revered Irish actor Jack MacGowran, a murder victim in the film, died before production was completed. William Peter Blatty won an Oscar for his screenplay, which spawned a veritable devil's rash of inferior imitations.

F

FAHRENHEIT 451. 1967. Filmed January–April 1966; Châteauneuf-sur-Loire, France. England: Roehampton; Black Park; Pinewood Studios, Iver Heath.
Cast: Oskar Werner, Julie Christie, Cyril Cusack, Anton Diffring, Jeremy Spenser.
Director: François Truffaut.

François Truffaut's first color film and first English-language feature adhered rigidly to the script (not his usual procedure) because Truffaut himself spoke little English. Oskar Werner, at odds with the director from the outset over the interpretation of his character, Montag, wanted to emphasize the brutal, fascist elements of the man, while Truffaut's conception was milder. As a result, much of Werner's footage was edited out, and Truffaut also frequently used a stand-in for Werner. In some successive shots, for example, Montag appears crop-headed and helmeted, then with normal-length hair. Julie Christie, playing dual roles, came to the production exhausted from her American promotion tour for *Doctor Zhivago*, but her energy returned as filming progressed. Ray Bradbury, author of the original novel, called the final snow scene one of the most beautiful in the history of cinema; Truffaut wrote it into the script when snow unexpectedly fell at Pinewood Studios.

FAREWELL, MY LOVELY. 1975. Filmed March–April 1975; California: Long Beach; Los Angeles.
Cast: Robert Mitchum, Charlotte Rampling, John Ireland, Sylvia Miles, Anthony Zerbe.
Director: Dick Richards.

In the first of two films playing Raymond Chandler's detective Philip Marlow (the second was *The Big Sleep*, 1978), Robert Mitchum reprised Dick Powell's role in *Murder, My Sweet* (1944). Novice director Dick Richards annoyed old pro Mitchum with his constant screenplay revisions; finally Mitchum told him flat-out to "stick to the script." Charlotte Rampling signed on mainly for the opportunity to work with Mitchum, whose leading ladies almost unanimously worshipped him—including Sylvia Miles, who repeated an Oscar nomination for her supporting performance here. Sylvester Stallone appeared in the small role of Jonnie just before hitting major stardom in *Rocky*.

A FAREWELL TO ARMS. 1932. Filmed summer 1932; Paramount Studios, Los Angeles.
Cast: Helen Hayes, Gary Cooper, Adolphe Menjou, Mary Philips.
Director: Frank Borzage.

Ernest Hemingway hated director Frank Borzage's film treatment, but he liked Gary Cooper's performance; later they became friends and hunting buddies. Originally written for Fredric March and Claudette Colbert, the screenplay gutted most of the elements that distinguished Hemingway's novel. Stage actress Helen Hayes (replacing a bitterly disappointed Eleanor Boardman) and Cooper formed a mutual admiration society. The fifteen-inch difference in their heights violated the strict tape measures of traditional Hollywood pairings, but Hayes said she would have kicked over the traces of her marriage in an instant had Cooper so much as hinted an interest. (He never did.) Mary Philips was a stage actress married to a young actor whose career was going nowhere at the time: Humphrey Bogart. (She divorced him in 1938.) Two different endings—one happy, one sad—were filmed so each exhibitor would have a choice; the video version kills off Hayes in the sad, brave fade-out that most viewers preferred.

FATAL ATTRACTION. 1987. Filmed September 1986–July 1987; Mount Kisco, New York. Paramount Studios, Los Angeles.
Cast: Glenn Close, Michael Douglas, Anne Archer, Ellen Hamilton Latzen, Stuart Pankin.
Director: Adrian Lyne.

This postfeminist revenge thriller about the perils of adultery (though ultimately an antifeminist film, despite the angry denials of its makers) marked some sort of psychological watershed in the adversary drama of the sexes, yuppie version; it stroked some darkly attractive feminine fantasies while giving many men a bad case of shudders. Often compared to an Alfred Hitchcock berserker, it owed much more to Clint Eastwood's *Play Misty for Me* (1971). Debra Winger had refused Glenn Close's key role of Alex, and Barbara Hershey was unavailable. Close consulted three psychoanalysts in constructing a plausible history for her psychotic character. She valued the role as a significant breakthrough in her career and also credited it with liberating her own personal style of dress. The extremely manipulative final sequence was filmed and inserted seven months after the original Hitchcockian climax had been filmed; preview audiences had turned thumbs down on the first ending, though that sequence was retained for Japanese audiences, who found it much more authentic and satisfyingly fatalistic.

FIDDLER ON THE ROOF. 1971. Filmed August 1970–January 1971; Yugoslavia: Lakenik, Mala Gorica. Pinewood Studios, Iver Heath, England.

Cast: Topol, Norma Crane, Leonard Frey, Molly Picon, Michael Glaser.

Director: Norman Jewison.

Playing Tevye, the dairyman, Israeli actor Chaim Topol enjoyed his biggest film role; he had performed the part on the London stage in the 1967–68 season. The mythical Ukrainian village of Anatevka—actually two small Yugoslavian villages combined—arose near Zagreb. Leonard Frey (playing Motel the tailor) reported that the location "got to be like a prison." Norma Crane, playing Golda, died of cancer shortly after the film's completion. Robert Boyle designed the village synagogue after studying plans of many actual ones in the Ukraine. To achieve a period effect, he avoided primary colors in costuming and sets—director Norman Jewison said he aimed for the colors of surrealist painter Marc Chagall—and cinematographer Oswald Morris capped his lens with a woman's nylon stocking to accent the earth tones. Music of the fiddler himself (British actor Tutle Lemkow) was dubbed by violinist Isaac Stern. The film (directed not by a Jew but a Methodist) won Academy Awards for cinematography and music adaptation.

THE FLIGHT OF THE PHOENIX. 1965. Filmed April–August 1965; Yuma, Arizona. 20th Century-Fox Studios, Los Angeles.

Cast: James Stewart, Richard Attenborough, Peter Finch, Hardy Kruger, Ernest Borgnine, Ian Bannen, Dan Duryea, George Kennedy.

Director: Robert Aldrich.

Movie critics thought better of this airplane-crash-in-the-desert melodrama than James Stewart did. Richard Attenborough, struggling even then to begin the production that would result in *Gandhi* in 1982, joined this cast for purely monetary reasons. Buttercup Valley near Yuma, the desert location scene, became the site of tragedy on July 8, 1965; veteran stunt pilot Paul Mantz, doubling for Stewart in flying the rickety, single-engine *Phoenix*, crashed while landing the plane after repeated attempts to bring it down close to the camera. He was killed instantly.

THE FLY. 1958. Filmed spring 1958; 20th Century-Fox Studios, Los Angeles.

Cast: Vincent Price, David Hedison, Herbert Marshall, Patricia Owens.

Director: Kurt Neumann.

"We kept laughing ourselves sick," recalled Vincent Price of the scene where he and Herbert Marshall examine the spider's web for the trapped, half-human fly. Finally the only way they could get a decent take was by standing back to back. Al (later David) Hedison said that trying to act inside the large plastic fly's head he wore was "like playing a piano with boxing gloves." Director Kurt Neumann (who came to Hollywood from Germany in the mid-Twenties) died soon after completion of the film. Two sequels—*The Return of the Fly* (1959) and *Curse of the Fly* (1964)—never gained the box office popularity of the first, though David Cronenberg's 1986 remake of *The Fly* was both a critical and popular success.

FLYING DOWN TO RIO. 1933. Filmed summer 1933; Rio de Janeiro, Brazil (backgrounds). California: Malibu Beach; RKO Studios, Los Angeles.

Cast: Dolores Del Rio, Gene Raymond, Fred Astaire, Ginger Rogers, Raul Roulien.

Director: Thornton Freeland.

Astaire's second film, his first of ten with Ginger Rogers, rescued the Depression-hit RKO Studios from bankruptcy. "The Carioca" dance they performed became a nationwide craze. Astaire's role reflected the stage persona he developed over years of dancing in Broadway shows with his sister Adele—and Rogers, in a film notable for its brash sexual references, dressed more daringly than in any later movie she made. Brazilian tenor Raul Roulien, on the other hand, was never again seen in a Hollywood film. Merian C. Cooper had an ulterior motive in producing this film; as a director of the fledgling Pan American Airways and eager to promote air travel, he saw to it that dozens of PAA Sikorsky clippers were made available to the production, though no cast member actually flew to Rio (or got off the ground, for that matter). The finale number, for example, took place inside a hangar, using wind machines and planes suspended from the ceiling. The musical score was composer Vincent Youmans's last.

FOLLOW THE FLEET. 1936. Filmed November–December 1935; RKO Studios, Culver City.
Cast: Fred Astaire, Ginger Rogers, Randolph Scott, Harriet Hilliard, Betty Grable, Lucille Ball, Tony Martin.
Director: Mark Sandrich.

Astaire's running gag in this musical, his bugle-call greeting to Ginger Rogers, sprang from an offscreen joke during rehearsals for their earlier *Roberta*; he would herald his arrival on stage by piano bugle notes. In their number "Let's Face the Music," one of Rogers's heavy beaded sleeves caught him in the jaw and eye as she spun, knocking him groggy for an instant; despite twenty more takes of the routine, however, this first take is the one we see. Astaire got tossed around by the sailors in this film, antics unusual for him—he generally shied away from tumbling exercises. With little experience in punch-pulling fight scenes, he bloodied Randolph Scott, to his own profound chagrin and Scott's studied nonchalance. Harriet Hilliard (who married Ozzie Nelson and became one of TV's best-known mothers in *Ozzie and Harriet*) made her film debut here, substituting for the unavailable Irene Dunne. She wore a brunette wig so as not to distract from blonde Rogers. Her song "Get Thee Behind Me, Satan" was a number left over from *Top Hat* (1935). Lucille Ball played her biggest role to date—and two decades later bought the entire RKO studio, which became Desilu, for producing *I Love Lucy*.

FOREIGN CORRESPONDENT. 1940. Filmed March–July 1940; the Netherlands (windmill exteriors and car chase). Samuel Goldwyn Studios, Los Angeles.
Cast: Joel McCrea, Laraine Day, Herbert Marshall, George Sanders, Albert Basserman, Edmund Gwenn, Robert Benchley.
Director: Alfred Hitchcock.

Originally titled *Personal History* after Vincent Sheean's memoir, this was Hitchcock's first Hollywood film after his arrival from England. Neither Joel McCrea nor Laraine Day exactly suited him for the lead roles—he found McCrea too leisurely in the part that Gary Cooper had turned down (and later regretted that he had); and Day wasn't the big name he had hoped for. He admired classical actor Albert Basserman (playing Van Meer), who had fled Nazi Germany in 1933, but the veteran performer knew little English and had to speak his lines phonetically. Famed humorist Robert Benchley wrote his own dialogue. Producer Walter Wanger wanted this picture to reflect daily news headlines, and he constantly badgered Hitchcock to adjust the script accordingly. The director largely ignored him—except for changing the ending at the last moment. That ending accurately predicted the bombing of London, which occurred only five days after the scene was filmed. The Hollywood production code at the time prohibited any mention of Germany and references to American war preparations. Hitchcock's costly, elaborate studio sets included a ten-acre city square in "Amsterdam," three hundred linnets (house finches) for the windmill interiors, and an enormous water tank for the airplane crash into the sea (an underwater track made sure that the airplane wing floated properly). Look for Hitchcock's usual cameo appearance: a newspaper-reading pedestrian passing McCrea on the street.

FORT APACHE. 1948. Filmed June–July 1947; Utah: Monument Valley; Mexican Hat. RKO Studios, Los Angeles.
Cast: Henry Fonda, John Wayne, Shirley Temple, Ward Bond, John Agar, Victor McLaglen.

Director: John Ford.

Searing heat, high winds, and desert storms plagued filming schedules. Instead of waiting for clear, bright weather, as called for in the script, John Ford proceeded to shoot the scene—judged one of his most realistic—in which seven hundred Mormon extras, representing cavalry troops, ride downhill in the rain. Shirley Temple and John Agar, playing lovers in Agar's first film, were real-life spouses at the time. His inexperience and awkwardness on horseback brought savage derision from Ford, who called him "Mr. Temple"—which, in turn, brought Agar consolation from no less a Ford crony than John Wayne, himself worried about his most complex role in years. Never brimming with human kindness, Ford also looked for ways to highlight Ward Bond's ample posterior; in several scenes, he angled the camera to catch Bond's rear instead of a normal over-the-shoulder shot. Such was Ford's perverse sense of humor.

THE FORTUNE COOKIE. 1966. Filmed October 1965–January 1966; Cleveland Browns Stadium, Cleveland, Ohio. Samuel Goldwyn Studios, Los Angeles.
Cast: Jack Lemmon, Walter Matthau, Ron Rich, Cliff Osmond, Lurene Tuttle.
Director: Billy Wilder.

Check in hand, Walter Matthau races up the stairs to Lemmon's apartment. Between that scene and the one in which he opens the door, Matthau suffered a near-fatal heart attack, spent seven weeks recovering, and dropped almost forty pounds. "Act heavier," Billy Wilder directed him after production resumed. Matthau and Jack Lemmon, who had never met, began a close, enduring friendship on the set. Wilder, a stickler for hewing exactly to the script (in this case, his own and I. A. L. Diamond's), nevertheless created several scenes of this bitter comedy just before filming them. He said that inspiration for the film came to him after seeing a football player fall on a line-side spectator. Critics marveled at Lemmon's ability to play straight man for a change. An Academy Award went to Matthau as best supporting actor.

42ND STREET. 1933. Filmed September–November 1932; Warner Bros. Studios, Burbank.
Cast: Warner Baxter, Bebe Daniels, George Brent, Una

Merkel, Ruby Keeler, Dick Powell, Ginger Rogers, Ned Sparks.
Director: Lloyd Bacon.

This prototype of all putting-on-a-show movies—source of many hoary show biz clichés that fueled Hollywood musicals forevermore—highlighted Busby Berkeley's innovative choreography. A former army drill instructor, he reportedly auditioned five thousand chorines, narrowing the choice to those with the prettiest faces, then weeding them down to best ankles and shapeliest knees. He placed his hundred finalists on a rigorous training program of strict diets and regular sleeping hours, later claiming that, thanks to the regimen, the 1932 Hollywood influenza epidemic never touched one of them. Warner Baxter's role of impresario was apparently based on Broadway producer Flo Ziegfeld, who had died two months before filming began. Ruby Keeler, rather graceless but full of charm, made her film debut here, apparently assigned the lead role through the influence of her husband's, Al Jolson, friendship with studio chief Jack Warner; her sisters Helen and Gertrude Keeler also joined the cast. Bebe Daniels was trying for a comeback in her once-thriving film career, while Ginger Rogers, Dick Powell, George Brent, and Una Merkel were still on the brink of stardom. Keeler and Powell ultimately made seven musicals together. Sexist as all get-out, Berkeley's routines triggered scores of subsequent musicals; and this feature by itself—a box office smash in the depths of the Great Depression—rescued Warner Bros. from imminent bankruptcy.

THE FOUNTAINHEAD. 1949. Filmed winter–spring 1949; California: Fresno; Warner Bros. Studios, Burbank.
Cast: Gary Cooper, Patricia Neal, Raymond Massey, Kent Smith, Henry Hull, Ray Collins.
Director: King Vidor.

Ayn Rand's novel about a maverick architect, based on Frank Lloyd Wright, provided forty-eight-year-old Gary Cooper with his most challenging role in years. Critics, however, thought him miscast, and the film did little to revive his flagging career. Director King Vidor would have preferred Humphrey Bogart or James Cagney for the part; and Rand wanted Greta Garbo for the female lead, but she turned it down. Barbara Stanwyck, however, severed her contract with the studio in her disappointment over not being cast. Cooper and twenty-two-year-old Patricia Neal (this was only her second picture) promptly fell in love and entered an affair that survived well beyond the completion of the film. The situation led to some awkwardness on the set, since Cooper was married (and somehow stayed married despite everything). Rand herself wrote the screenplay.

THE 400 BLOWS (LES QUATRE CENTS COUPS). 1959. Filmed November 1958–January 1959; France: Honfleur; Paris.

Cast: Jean-Pierre Léaud, Patrick Auffray, Claire Maurier, Albert Rémy.

Director: François Truffaut.

The French idiomatic expression for raising hell in protest against authority is *les quatre cent coups*. François Truffaut used that as the title for his feature debut—based mainly on his own childhood. It was also fourteen-year-old Jean-Pierre Léaud's first film; as he grew up, he continued to portray Truffaut's alter ego, Antoine Doinel, in four subsequent films. Relying heavily on improvisation, Truffaut filmed mostly in well-known Paris locations—Clichy, Pigalle, the Champs Élysées, and the Luxembourg Gardens. At the latter spot, he filmed the children's reactions to the Punch and Judy show with a hidden camera, partly because he found that directing children was so difficult; he resolved never again to use kids in any film (a vow he repeatedly broke). Adult roles went to little-known actors who agreed to work for deferred pay—but look for Jeanne Moreau in a bit part as a woman with a dog. Truffaut himself appeared in the amusement park sequence, as a man on the rotor ride. Most of the dialogue was postdubbed. An immediate success and an influential landmark of the French New Wave, this movie won Truffaut the best director award at the 1959 Cannes Film Festival. He considered it the best of all his films.

FRANKENSTEIN. 1931. Filmed August–September 1931; Universal Studios, Universal City.

Cast: Boris Karloff, Colin Clive, Mae Clarke, John Boles, Edward Van Sloan, Frederick Kerr, Dwight Frye.

Director: James Whale.

Planning for this most famous horror film of them all

(Boris Karloff also thought it his own best film) began with different principals envisioned for its main roles. Bela Lugosi, offered the monster role, turned it down because he liked neither the script nor the requisite heavy makeup. (John Carradine also refused the part.) The studio wanted Leslie Howard for the role of Dr. Frankenstein, but James Whale insisted on Colin Clive. Karloff's forty-eight pounds of makeup and accessories—including his elevated, twelve-pound boots, steel struts inside two pairs of trousers, a double-quilted suit, rubber facial features, and boltlike electrical plugs on the sides of his neck (which left him with scars long after the film was finished)—were creations of makeup artist Jack Pierce, requiring almost four hours daily to apply. Hot studio lights caused him much discomfort beneath his layers; extensive massages and heat-lamp treatments after each day's shooting became part of his routine, especially after he strained his back while carrying Clive in the windmill scene. (Eventually he required a spinal operation to mend the damage.) An iron girder served as his stand-in during rehearsals. Karloff copied the hand gestures of Lon Chaney, Sr., in *The Trap*, a 1922 silent thriller. Mae Clarke was the actress who received the sadistic grapefruit treatment from James Cagney in *The Public Enemy* that same year. Her *Frankenstein* assignment almost went to Bette Davis, whom Whale finally decided was "too aggressive" for the part. John Boles, a popular singer heretofore, broke into dramatic roles with this film. Whale filmed mostly in continuity, using village scenes from the set of *All Quiet on the Western Front*; the same village was also seen in several *Frankenstein* sequels. Long-missing footage that was cut from the theatrical version (to Karloff's intense disgust) has been restored in the video release.

THE FRENCH CONNECTION. 1971. Filmed December 1970–February 1971; Marseilles, France. Washington, D.C. New York City.

Cast: Gene Hackman, Fernando Rey, Roy Scheider, Tony LoBianco, Marcel Bozzuffi.

Director: William Friedkin.

Its tough cops and car chases spawned a host of imitations. Real-life detectives Eddie Egan and Sonny Grosso, the prototypes on whose exploits the film was based, did not play themselves but appeared in small roles as Simonson and

Klein. The New York Police Department, unhappy with its image as reflected by scenarist Ernest Tidyman and director William Friedkin, fired Egan only seven hours before he was to have signed his retirement papers; he went on to play small parts in TV and other films. For Gene Hackman, the movie meant stardom and leading roles after years of character parts. Columnist Jimmy Breslin had been considered for the role of Popeye Doyle, while Egan had envisioned himself being portrayed by Rod Taylor. Hackman spent two weeks in a squad car with Egan to gain a feel for his role. The incredible chase scenes took five weeks to film, often with Hackman himself driving a car that held cameras attached to the back seat and front fenders. Despite a soundtrack that seemed deliberately botched (as if to somehow increase its authenticity), the film won Academy Awards for best picture, best director, Hackman as best actor, and for screenplay and editing.

THE FRENCH LIEUTENANT'S WOMAN. 1981. Filmed spring 1980; England: Lyme Regis; Twickenham Studios, Twickenham.

Cast: Meryl Streep, Jeremy Irons, Leo McKern, Hilton McRae, Patience Collier, Lynsey Baxter, Penelope Wilton.

Director: Karel Reisz.

For this adaptation of his novel, John Fowles at first wanted Vanessa Redgrave for the dual key roles of Sarah and Anna. Meryl Streep regarded this as her first attempt at truly serious filmmaking, and she approached her characters fearfully—partly because she identified strongly with Sarah's obsession for lost love (her own longtime lover, actor John Cazale, had died of cancer in 1978); and also because she didn't think herself beautiful enough for the part. She studied the novels of Jane Austen and George Eliot, immersing herself in Victoriana while also nursing her young son. Her perfectionism on the set somewhat daunted costar Jeremy Irons, appearing in his first major film and also playing dual roles. He later claimed (and Streep denied) that they had had a brief, intense love affair that ended "when the cameras stopped." Proud Lyme Regis townsfolk polished up their streets and buildings for the camera crew, but director Karel Reisz wanted the Dorset town to look natural, so he ordered the work undone. Local citizens balked at removal of their TV roof antennas, however; the studio finally provided them with temporary portable ones so that filming of a Victorian skyline could proceed.

FRIENDLY PERSUASION. 1956. September–December 1955; California: Rowland V. Lee Ranch, Chatsworth; Sacramento River, Chico; Republic Studios, Los Angeles.
Cast: Gary Cooper, Dorothy McGuire, Anthony Perkins, Marjorie Main, Richard Eyer, Robert Middleton, Walter Catlett.
Director: William Wyler.

Originally planned by Frank Capra as a vehicle for Bing Crosby and Jean Arthur, this story of southern Indiana Quakers was not a production that Gary Cooper begged to join. "My life hasn't been very Quaker-like," he told the novel's author, Jessamyn West. But his unfamiliar role of pacifist farmer resulted in one of his best performances. In preparation for their roles, West took both Cooper and Dorothy McGuire to a Quaker meetinghouse in Pasadena to expose them to some real Friendship. Cooper gave special help in mutual scenes to novice film actor Anthony Perkins, who was dating Cooper's daughter at the time. And Samantha the pet goose, it can now be told, was not one bird but a whole flock of look-alikes. West and William Wyler argued vehemently over the outcome of Cooper's temptation to pick up a gun in the movie; they finally reached a compromise satisfactory to both. West's journal of the production (*To See the Dream*, 1956) details her simultaneous joys and traumas in helping Wyler (and screenwriter Michael Wilson) convert her novel into film. *Friendly Persuasion* won the prestigious Palme d'Or award at Cannes.

FROM HERE TO ETERNITY. 1953. Filmed March–June 1953; Schofield Army Barracks, Honolulu. Columbia Studios. Los Angeles.
Cast: Burt Lancaster, Deborah Kerr, Frank Sinatra, Donna Reed, Montgomery Clift, Ernest Borgnine.
Director: Fred Zinnemann.

James Jones deeply resented Hollywood's sanitized treatment of his antimilitary novel. "Columbia Pictures ass-kissed the army," he charged, so they could film the exteriors at

Schofield Barracks. Jones insisted on Montgomery Clift for the role of Prewitt despite studio chief Harry Cohn's preference for Aldo Ray or John Derek. Method actor Clift trained rigorously by jogging and learning to play the bugle (though the actual bugle calls in the film were dubbed) and to box; but since he couldn't master how to throw a proper punch, Fred Zinnemann had to use trick shots. Edmond O'Brien had been originally slated for Burt Lancaster's role, and Joan Crawford for Deborah Kerr's. The fight scene between Clift and Ernest Borgnine required twelve hours to rehearse and film. They used plastic knives, but their painfully real falls bruised them from head to foot. Offscreen, Clift, Jones, and Frank Sinatra became close drinking buddies. Clift worshiped Sinatra, spent much time coaching him in the role of Maggio, and also imitated Jones's mannerisms in his own part of Prewitt. Sinatra literally begged for his role, which had first been proposed for Eli Wallach, offering himself at bargain salary in hopes the film would restore his faltering career (which it did) during the period when his marriage to Ava Gardner was breaking up. Sinatra's death scene was filmed with a very intoxicated Clift almost unable to articulate his sole line of dialogue. The film won eight Academy Awards: for best picture, supporting players Sinatra and Donna Reed (a part that Shelley Winters had refused), Zinnemann, writer Dalton Trumbo, and cinematographer Burnett Guffey, among others. Clift, who had eagerly hoped for an Oscar, was crushed. Curiously, while the army okayed the film for showing to troops, the U.S. Navy banned it as "derogatory to a sister service." Later films, notably *The End* and *Airplane!*, parodied the erotic beach scene between Lancaster and Kerr.

FROM RUSSIA WITH LOVE. 1963. Filmed April–August 1963; Istanbul. Madrid. Crinan, Scotland. Pinewood Studios, Iver Heath, England.

Cast: Sean Connery, Daniela Bianchi, Pedro Armendariz, Lotte Lenya, Robert Shaw, Bernard Lee.

Director: Terence Young.

Sean Connery's second James Bond adventure cast him opposite Italian actress Daniela Bianchi, whose voice was dubbed by British Shakespearean actress Barbara Jefford. Frequent Bond director Terence Young liked to live well on his sets, and the champagne flowed freely. But during location shooting in Scotland, Bianchi suffered facial bruises in a car accident, while Young crashed in a helicopter off the coast, also receiving minor injuries. Robert Shaw added muscle, weight, and blond hair color for the assassin's role of Red Grant. Mexican character actor Pedro Armendariz, in his last screen role, was dying of cancer at the time and committed suicide a short time afterward. This was Lotte Lenya's third film of five (her first was in 1931); the Austrian singer-actress, famed for her stage interpretations of Bertolt Brecht and her husband Kurt Weill's songs, played enemy agent Rosa Klebb purely for kicks. Connery's spontaneous throwaway lines added wit to an enormously popular film.

THE FRONT PAGE. 1931. Filmed autumn–winter 1930; United Artists Studios, Los Angeles.
Cast: Adolphe Menjou, Pat O'Brien, Mary Brian, Edward Everett Horton, Walter Catlett, Mae Clarke.
Director: Lewis Milestone.

Adolphe Menjou swore that his four six-minute-long scenes were the toughest takes of his career. Louis Wolheim had originally been cast in the role based on legendary *Chicago Tribune* editor Walter Howey; but Wolheim died of a stroke just as filming began, and Menjou replaced him. Menjou's final line—"The s.o.b. stole my watch!"—finally passed muster when he came up with the idea of bumping against his typewriter, thus masking his censorable words with the carriage bell. Lewis Milestone had hoped for James Cagney or Clark Gable to play fast-talking reporter Hildy Johnson, but producer Howard Hughes insisted on Pat O'Brien, mistakenly believing that the actor had played the role on stage. O'Brien actually had minimal experience with the play and none with the role, but by the time Milestone discovered the mix-up, O'Brien was well into the film—his first—and stayed to make Hollywood movies for the next half century. Signs on the mostly one-set production warned studio janitors not to clean or sweep the increasingly dirty press room, which also held a crap table and bar at one end for refreshment of the actors. Milestone himself played a bit part as a reporter in one crowd scene. The film spawned a host of newspaper movies and ultimately three remakes: *His Girl Friday* (1940), *The Front Page* (1974), and *Switching Channels* (1988).

FUNNY GIRL. 1968. Filmed May–August 1967; New York City. California: Santa Monica Pier, Santa Monica; Los Angeles; Columbia Studios, Burbank.

Cast: Barbra Streisand, Omar Sharif, Kay Medford, Anne Francis, Walter Pidgeon, Frank Faylen, Gerald Mohr.

Director: William Wyler.

Barbra Streisand's film debut as Fanny Brice won her an Oscar for best actress. She had honed the performance to perfection by playing the title character on Broadway for two years. Her demanding perfectionism on the set made her a rigorous lady to work with; but her legendary feuds with William Wyler (directing his first and only musical) finally led to mutual admiration and respect. She wanted only her left profile photographed, and her problems with lip-synching her songs led Wyler to reverse the usual process and synchronize sound to the picture after filming (except for her finale "My Man," performed live). Streisand's favorite number, the "Swan Lake" ballet, had been rehearsed for weeks but was largely cut from the film, appearing only as a brief montage. Married to Elliott Gould at the time, she fell in love with costar Omar Sharif; but their intense, highly publicized affair lasted only the length of the filming. (She and Gould separated in 1969.) The Arab-Israeli Six-day War, which broke out just after production started, brought Egyptian actor Sharif sharp criticism from Cairo newspapers (both Brice and Streisand, as well as his own character, were Jewish), a tempest he ignored. Wyler had wanted Frank Sinatra to costar, but Streisand wouldn't take second billing, and a costarring deal with David Janssen also fell through. Anne Francis, playing a Ziegfeld Follies girl, came away bitter after much of her part was cut, charging that her performance had been judged too competitive with Streisand's; she even wanted her name removed from the screen credits. Composer Jule Styne, who wrote most of the music, was also unhappy with the film's second-half abundance of Brice's self-pity. But box office receipts and Streisand's electrifying performance finally transcended all these problems. The sequel *Funny Lady*, also starring Streisand and Sharif, appeared in 1975.

A FUNNY THING HAPPENED ON THE WAY TO THE FORUM. 1966. Filmed spring–summer 1966; CEA Studios, Madrid.

Cast: Zero Mostel, Phil Silvers, Jack Gilford, Michael Crawford, Michael Hordern, Leon Greene, Annette Andre, Buster Keaton.
Director: Richard Lester.

This was the dying Buster Keaton's final American film. All of his running scenes and long shots were doubled by British stuntman Mick Dillon. Director Richard Lester thought Keaton the best screen comedian bar none, an opinion shared by many others, though his best work had occurred decades earlier. Phil Silvers went through the film blind in his left eye because of a cataract, causing him to miss his chalk marks, bump into furniture, and seethe with frustration. Lester had persuaded him to play Lycus the procurer without his trademark glasses, which didn't help matters. At one point, paralyzed with fear, Silvers had to be physically rescued from a high parapet off which, in a bit of trick photography, he "jumps." Lester fought constantly with producer Melvin Frank over a screenplay that Lester largely rewrote on the set.

FURY. 1936. Filmed February–April 1936; MGM Studios, Culver City.
Cast: Spencer Tracy, Sylvia Sidney, Bruce Cabot, Walter Abel, Edward Ellis, Walter Brennan.
Director: Fritz Lang.

Mob psychology fascinated Fritz Lang. In this film (originally titled *Mob Rule*), based on an actual 1933 lynching of two kidnappers in San Jose, the director explored the sudden transition in a crowd from good humor to hate and violence. A recent German emigré, Lang was disliked by both studio and cast for his autocratic style, his monocle, and his refusal to adjust to the Hollywood system of making films. MGM frankly wanted to get rid of him, even tried to subvert this picture's box office chances in order to have an excuse for firing him. It didn't work out quite that way. As word-of-mouth publicity built, the film exploded into a huge success, astounding the studio and making a major star of Spencer Tracy. Feelings were tense on the set. Incensed because of Lang's blithe disregard for union rules such as scheduling of noon breaks, Tracy himself led a mutinous cast and crew off the set one day at lunchtime. (How much of Lang's behavior was deliberate, in order to anger Tracy sufficiently for his role, remains uncertain.) Hostility toward the director turned murderous during the filming of the mob storming the jail. Lang insisted on throwing the smoke pots himself in the sequence; one of them hit Bruce Cabot (playing Kirby Dawson) in the head, and the enraged actor went for Lang's throat. Restrained by crew members, Cabot was informed that studio electricians were planning an "accident" to take care of Lang —a heavy overhead lamp would be rigged to fall on him. To the credit of saner minds, this never happened. The entire episode provided keen illustration of how a movie's subject matter can permeate the atmosphere of a set, overlapping from screenplay to all-too-real emotional involvement. The film, Lang's favorite American effort, remains one of his classics.

G

GANDHI. 1982. Filmed November 1980–May 1981; India: Sikanderpura Ghasi; Rashtrapi Bhavan; Porbandar; Patna; Udaipur; Bombay; Delhi. England: Staines; Shepperton Studios, Shepperton.
Cast: Ben Kingsley, Candice Bergen, Edward Fox, John Gielgud, Trevor Howard, John Mills, Martin Sheen.
Director: Richard Attenborough.

Sir Richard Attenborough had been trying to bring *Gandhi* to the screen for two decades, accepting numerous character acting jobs through the years to help build the project financially. For him, as well as for many of the cast, the film became a labor of love. Martin Sheen, for example, donated his entire salary, for playing the newsman Walker, to charity. Ben Kingsley, thirty-six years old and half-Indian himself, prepared meticulously for the title role. He went on a vegetarian diet, lost seventeen pounds, practiced Yoga daily, learned to spin thread, studied everything by and about Gandhi, and visited every major Gandhi locale. Actors who had turned down the role included Dirk Bogarde, Peter Finch, Anthony Hopkins, Albert Finney, Sir Alec Guinness, and Tom Courtenay. Gandhi's assassination scene was filmed at Birla House, where it had actually occurred in 1948. (The crew went shoeless in this holy spot.) Harsh Nayar, who played the assassin Godse, deliberately never spoke with Kingsley beforehand. Gandhi's funeral, using 250,000 extras, was staged on January 31, 1981—thirty-three years to the day from the actual event. *Gandhi* won eight Academy Awards, including best picture, for Kingsley as best actor, for John Briley's screenplay, and for Attenborough's direction. Attenborough's book *In Search of Gandhi* (1982) provides interesting details.

GASLIGHT. 1944. Filmed winter 1943–44; MGM Studios, Culver City.
Cast: Ingrid Bergman, Charles Boyer, Joseph Cotten, Angela Lansbury, May Whitty.
Director: George Cukor.

Ingrid Bergman had just finished making *For Whom the Bell Tolls*, and she jumped at the chance to costar with Charles Boyer. But her studio "owner," David O. Selznick, almost botched the loan-out deal to MGM by insisting that she receive top billing. Bergman cried and begged Selznick to back off, and he finally did. For her role of the victimized wife of sinister Boyer, she studied hospitalized mental patients, adopting habits and quirks from one particular woman suffering from a nervous breakdown. Viewing the rushes, she said she looked far too healthy for the part. Because Bergman stood several inches taller than her costar, Boyer perched on a wooden box in the railroad station scene, as he also did when the couple again costarred in *Arch of Triumph* (1948). This scene was the first one filmed—the two barely knew each other, and Bergman always dreaded beginning a new picture by passionately embracing a stranger. Boyer had a hard time concentrating on work: his only child, a son Michael, was born during the production. When he wasn't calling home, he was treating cast and crew to champagne. This was Angela Lansbury's screen (and acting) debut. As Nancy the maid, she wore high platform shoes in order to tower threateningly over Bergman. Her defiant act of lighting a cigarette in one scene had to await, by law, her eighteenth birthday, which was celebrated on the set. Bergman won her first Academy Award as best actress for her performance.

GENTLEMAN JIM. 1942. Filmed May–July 1942; Warner Bros. Studios. Burbank.
Cast: Errol Flynn, Alexis Smith, Jack Carson, Alan Hale, Minor Watson, Ward Bond.

Director: Raoul Walsh.

Despite his glowing appearance in this fictionalized biography of boxer James J. Corbett, Errol Flynn was in wretched health. Even the wartime army wouldn't take him. His heart and lungs were in such bad shape that doctors gave him only two years to live. (Hardly modifying his lifestyle, however, he lived until 1959.) His illnesses frequently interrupted this production, and he suffered a mild heart attack on the set, requiring much time off. Raoul Walsh filmed all the boxing scenes last in case Flynn collapsed or received a black eye. Flynn trained six weeks for these scenes with welterweight champion Mushy Callahan. While he rarely used a stunt double in the ring, he could only spar for a minute at a time before becoming exhausted, to the intense frustration of Walsh and Ward Bond (who played John L. Sullivan). Flynn's ring partners before Bond in the film included six professional wrestlers; he liked to relate how, for sport between takes, he egged one behemoth against another and soon had them all tossing each other around. With fighter Jack Loper, however, he ran into trouble. Loper couldn't pull his punches, and though he begged forgiveness each time, he kept decking Flynn in spite of himself. The Joe Choynski fight scene occurred on the ship stage of *The Sea Hawk*, which Flynn had made in 1940. One of his lines—"I'm no gentleman"—evoked snickers from movie audiences; the actor had just been charged in a notorious rape case when *Gentleman Jim* was released. (He was ultimately cleared.) As the most strenuous film of Flynn's swashbuckling career, it remained one of his favorites.

GENTLEMAN'S AGREEMENT. 1947. Filmed summer 1947; New York City. Darien, Connecticut. 20th Century-Fox Studios, Los Angeles.

Cast: Gregory Peck, Dorothy McGuire, John Garfield, Celeste Holm, Anne Revere, June Havoc.

Director: Elia Kazan.

"Why rock the boat?" asked MGM's Louis B. Mayer and Hollywood mogul Samuel Goldwyn when they heard that Darryl F. Zanuck's studio was about to address the problem of anti-Semitism in a picture. Mayer, Goldwyn, and other Jewish studio executives feared this adaptation of Laura Z. Hobson's novel would be viewed as self-serving propaganda. As mild an assault on bigotry as the film seems today, it was Hollywood's first major attack on a closet problem and required much courage to produce—especially since neither Zanuck nor Elia Kazan nor Gregory Peck were themselves Jewish. (John Garfield was the only principal cast member who was.) Peck's agent tried to talk him out of starring, but the actor strongly believed in the timeliness of the message, as did the rest of the cast. Garfield and Anne Revere would face bigotry of another sort in the coming months as they became victims of the political witch hunt gearing up to gut the film colony's best creative resources; the government didn't like their friends and past associates. The movie's success astonished Hollywood. It won Academy Awards for best picture, for Kazan as director, and for best supporting actress Celeste Holm.

GHOSTBUSTERS. 1984. Filmed October 1983–February 1984; New York City. California: exteriors and Entertainment Effects Group Studio, Los Angeles; Burbank Studios, TBS-Columbia Ranch, Burbank.

Cast: Bill Murray, Dan Aykroyd, Sigourney Weaver, Harold Ramis, Rick Moranis, Annie Potts, Ernie Hudson.

Director: Ivan Reitman.

This was another much-ado put-on in which special effects wizardry became the real show. Performers Dan Aykroyd and Harold Ramis wrote the screenplay, not so much for actors to act as for platoons of bright young studio technicians to strut their stuff. Aykroyd, who originally intended lead roles for himself and his friend John Belushi, was a serious student of parapsychology (though one might never know it from the film). Although Belushi died before filming began, it was later suggested that the Onionhead ghost character bore certain strong similarities to Belushi's role of Bluto in *National Lampoon's Animal House*. Rick Moranis helped tailor his own nerdish character of Louis, a part originally slated for John Candy. Sets were intricate combinations of Manhattan and Los Angeles locales, studio recreations, matte paintings, and miniatures; while action sequences used various elements of animation, optical composites, and stop-motion techniques integrated with mechanical replicas, foam-latex ghosts, and genuine warm bodies. A 1959 Cadillac ambulance became the Ectomobile, while the gooey ectoslime was a chemical thickening agent. The real star was Stay-Puft Man, the giant marshmallow form (actually Billy Bryan in a foam-latex costume) that plodded through miniature Manhattan streets like a King Kong mutant. The cartoon owners of Casper the Friendly Ghost were perturbed, however, at the film's ghost logo (likewise friendly) and filed a large, unfriendly lawsuit to prevent its use. A court dismissed the charges in 1986, making the world safe for big box office munchkin ghosts. Don Shay's book, *Making Ghostbusters* (1985), details every ectoplasmic nuance of the film.

GIANT. 1956. Filmed May–October 1955; Marfa, Texas. Warner Bros. Studios, Burbank.
Cast: Elizabeth Taylor, Rock Hudson, James Dean, Mercedes McCambridge, Carroll Baker, Dennis Hopper.
Director: George Stevens.

Three days after James Dean finished his own work in this contemporary Western, he died in a highway crash and catapulted himself into cult status. (The studio had banned him from racing his sports car for the duration of filming.) Dean's role had been turned down by Alan Ladd, and many critics thought the young actor miscast. He liked Elizabeth Taylor and Mercedes McCambridge, but his endless complaints and suggestions annoyed Rock Hudson and director George Stevens. Because Dean's voice in his climactic "last supper" monologue proved inaudible, Nick Adams postdubbed it after Dean's death. Taylor, already distraught over the impending breakup of her marriage to Michael Wilding, was devastated at Dean's sudden death and furious at Stevens for making her report for a scene the day after. Verging on hysteria, she held her emotions in check just long enough for the director to aim the camera over the back of her head in one brief scene. She collapsed the next day and spent the next two weeks in a hospital, stalling completion of the film. *Giant* proved an important turning point in her career, however. Stevens had wanted Grace Kelly for the role, thought twenty-three-year-old Taylor too young. He gave Hudson his choice of costars, finally, and the two formed a lifelong friendship on the set. William Holden had coveted Hudson's role, which required the actor to age twenty-five years. In his later scenes, Hudson wore a fifty-pound belt to help him simulate age—though working with the demanding Stevens, he said, became "an aging process in itself." Even so, Hudson named *Giant*, as his personal favorite of his own films. Notice McCambridge's beat-up Stetson hat, loaned to her by no less a cowboy than Gary Cooper. Cooper wouldn't hear of her using a new hat for the part, vouchsafing that this one had been suitably "peed on a lot" by horses. Dean admired it so much that, according to McCambridge, he tried to steal it from her for his own scenes. The ranch manor was an artful façade construction, built on the Warner lot and carted to the Texas location, where cast and crew sweltered in 120-degree heat. Stevens won an Academy Award for direction.

GIGI. 1958. Filmed August–October 1957, February 1958; France: Montfort-l'Amaury; Musée Jacquemart-André, Palais de Glace, and Bois de Boulogne, Paris. California: Venice Beach; MGM Studios, Culver City.
Cast: Leslie Caron, Louis Jourdan, Maurice Chevalier, Hermione Gingold, Jacques Bergerac, Eva Gabor, Isabel Jeans.
Director: Vincente Minnelli.

Leslie Caron had performed in a nonmusical stage version of Colette's story in Paris, and the 1948 French adaptation of *Gigi* was also nonmusical. For this film, Caron's singing voice was dubbed by Betty Wand. Director Minnelli wanted Ina Claire, who refused, for the role of Tante Alicia (played by Isabel Jeans). A reluctant Louis Jourdan didn't want a singing role, almost walked out during prerecording sessions, but was finally convinced to stay. Much of the picture centered in the actual Maxim's, the fashionable place to be seen in 1890s Paris. The restaurant closed up for three days, allowing MGM to redecorate the interior as it looked a century ago. The hot interior, heavy costumes, and endless retakes exhausted everybody. Also reconstructed was the old Palais de Glace interior for the ice-skating scenes. Jacques Bergerac had been cast before somebody realized that he couldn't skate; so he and Eva Gabor were pulled around the ice on a small wooden sled. For veteran international star Maurice Chevalier, who celebrated his seventieth birthday on the studio set, the musical represented a return to Hollywood favor after years of ostracism for having once signed a pacifist manifesto—an act he made clear that he never regretted. He won a special Oscar for his "contributions to the world of entertainment." Nine other

Academy Awards also went to *Gigi*, including best picture. In France, however, the film was not a hit; putting Colette to music was, to Parisians, like watering down champagne.

GILDA. 1946. Filmed autumn 1945; Columbia Studios, Los Angeles.
Cast: Rita Hayworth, Glenn Ford, George Macready, Steven Geray, Joseph Calleia.
Director: Charles Vidor.

This is the movie that made Rita Hayworth a superstar. Haphazardly scripted, with players often receiving a page or two on the very day of filming, *Gilda* abounds with sexual implications and suggestiveness, every nuance of which was thoroughly discussed on the set. Glenn Ford wouldn't reveal what Charles Vidor told his cast to think about before filming a scene, only that his whispered instructions were "marvelous images to hold." Hayworth's songs were dubbed by Anita Ellis. For their big fight scene, Ford was told not to fake it when he hit his costar, and he stunned her; when she hit him four times in a later scene, she knocked out two of his teeth. Despite this violence, the two fell in love with each other (at the time Hayworth was separated and soon to be divorced from Orson Welles)—and while the affair didn't last long, their friendship remained close for thirty-five years. They delighted to "talk dirty" in her dressing room, where they knew that studio mogul Harry Cohn had planted a hidden microphone to spy on them. Ford and Hayworth were later reteamed in *The Loves of Carmen* (1948), *Affair in Trinidad* (1952), and *The Money Trap* (1966).

THE GLENN MILLER STORY. 1954. Filmed autumn 1953; California: Santa Monica Pier, Santa Monica; Universal-International Studios, Universal City.
Cast: James Stewart, June Allyson, Harry Morgan, Charles Drake, Frances Langford, Louis Armstrong, Gene Krupa.
Director: Anthony Mann.

James Stewart just "wasn't as good-looking as my son," said Glenn Miller's mother, but she thought he was otherwise okay enacting the popular trombonist-bandleader. Despite numerous inaccuracies in the screenplay, the music was the main thing. Stewart himself provided none of that. His trombone coach was Joe Yuki; most trombone solos in the film were dubbed by studio musician Murray McEachern, though Yuki dubbed for Stewart's jam-session scene. June Allyson accepted the part of Miller's brave, self-sacrificing wife solely on Stewart's request before seeing the script. They had previously costarred in *The Stratton Story* (1949) and would hitch up again for *Strategic Air Command* (1955). Some thirty years after he saw this film, former RAF navigator Fred Shaw checked his World War II logbooks and revealed that Miller's untimely death in 1944 over the English Channel was probably accidental; it occurred when Shaw's plane jettisoned its bombs, blowing Miller's low-flying aircraft into the sea.

THE GODFATHER. 1972. March–July 1971; Sicily. New York: Guggenheim Estate, Sands Point; New York City (Brooklyn, Manhattan, Staten Island); Filmways Studio, Bronx.

Cast: Marlon Brando, Al Pacino, James Caan, Richard Castellano, Robert Duvall, Diane Keaton, Sterling Hayden, Richard Conte, Al Martino.

Director: Francis Ford Coppola.

Marlon Brando believed this Mafia drama made an important statement about the American corporate mind. Ironically, in order to make the film in New York, producer Albert S. Ruddy had to meet mob leader Anthony Columbo, agreeing not to use the words *Mafia* or *Cosa Nostra* in the sound track in exchange for Columbo's noninterference. Ruddy and Francis Ford Coppola had wanted Sir Laurence Olivier for the chief role of Don Corleone. But novelist Mario Puzo, who cowrote the screenplay with Coppola, held out for Brando, despite the fact that Paramount Studios wanted nothing to do with the difficult actor. Brando, however, came as near begging for this role as for any in his career, and his behavior proved exemplary. Worshiped by the other, mostly younger cast members (Brando was forty-seven), he enjoyed an easy camaraderie with them. Brando patterned his voice after real-life mobster Frank Costello's wheeze but had to redub some of his passages to clarify his mumbling. He wore flesh-colored earplugs to aid his concentration. Mafiosi flacks, who watched street filming from the sidelines, offered sober criticism of Brando's clothing, saying he should wear an Italian block hat and diamond belt buckle and tie clasp. Real-life godfather Joseph Columbo was "hit" and seriously wounded at a rally during the production, adding a contemporary fillip to the proceedings. Burt Reynolds had wanted the role of Sonny, but Brando nixed him and James Caan got the part. So studious was Caan's research in hanging about with gangland types and imitating their styles that, at one point, FBI undercover agents mistook him for one of the boys. Vic Damone turned down the crooner role that finally went to Al Martino. With Coppola's strong backing, Al Pacino won out over Rod Steiger for the key role of Michael Corleone. Diane Keaton, then an unknown in her second film role, said she felt miscast and inconsequential as Kay Adams, Pacino's girlfriend. Coppola's sister, Talia Shire, made her film debut here as Connie Corleone. The film won three Academy Awards: for best picture, for Brando as best actor, and for screenplay adaptation.

THE GODFATHER, PART II. 1974. Filmed winter 1973–74; Santo Domingo, Dominican Republic. Sicily. Nevada: Las Vegas; Lake Tahoe. Washington, D.C. Los Angeles.

Cast: Al Pacino, Robert Duvall, Diane Keaton, Robert De Niro, John Cazale, Talia Shire, Lee Strasberg, Troy Donahue, Harry Dean Stanton.

Director: Francis Ford Coppola.

Coppola, granted more authority by Paramount in directing this sequel as a result of his success with *The Godfather*, assumed that Marlon Brando would again star; but Brando had made his social statement in the original picture and by this time was on the outs again with Paramount. Actors Studio director Lee Strasberg made his screen debut as gangster Hyman Roth, a part loosely based on real-life don Meyer Lansky. Coppola had wanted to cast Elia Kazan in this role; but Al Pacino, Strasberg's former student, conspired to bring Coppola and the seventy-three-year-old teacher together "accidentally," persuading each to try out the other. Strasberg, true to his Method, spent weeks beforehand living out the part of the frail but tough mobster he would portray. Pacino himself, continuing his role of Michael Corleone, worked himself to physical exhaustion during production. Industrialist Henry J. Kaiser's former estate at Lake Tahoe served as the Corleone estate. *Part II* won six Oscars, including best picture, director, and supporting actor (Robert De Niro). For video presentation, Coppola reedited the two films into one seven-hour package (variously titled *The Godfather Epic* or *The Godfather Saga*).

GOING MY WAY. 1944. Filmed August 1943–February 1944; Paramount Studios, Los Angeles.
Cast: Bing Crosby, Barry Fitzgerald, Risë Stevens, Frank McHugh, Gene Lockhart, William Frawley.
Director: Leo McCarey.

Studio executives were so worried about Catholic church reaction to this sentimental comedy (originally titled *The Padre*) that they shelved it for six months after its completion. They needn't have feared; one of its most devoted fans was Pope Pius XII, who kept a print for personal viewing. Producer-director Leo McCarey threw his own life savings into the production, audaciously casting as priests a well-known crooner (who was, at least, Roman Catholic) and an Irish Lutheran character actor mainly noted for playing drunken old rogues. Production began without a complete script, McCarey and his "priests" improvising scenes as they went along. Bing Crosby modeled his role of Father O'Malley on one of his tutors at Gonzaga University. (Two priests at St. Monica's Church in Santa Monica had inspired McCarey's screenplay.) McCarey despaired at times of teaching Barry Fitzgerald, a 1936 emigrant from Dublin's famed Abbey Theater, not to genuflect backwards. Fitzgerald had to anglicize his genuine brogue just to be understood—then, during playbacks, he said he couldn't understand himself. Bing's song "Swinging on a Star," one of his big hits, was inspired when composer Jimmy Van Heusen heard the crooner admonish one of his sons: "What do you want to be—a mule?" Crosby reprised his priestly role in *The Bells of St. Mary's* (1945) and *Say One for Me* (1959). *Going My Way* won seven Academy Awards, among them best picture, best actor (Crosby), and best supporting actor (Fitzgerald).

GOLD DIGGERS OF 1933. 1933. Filmed spring 1933; Warner Bros. Studios, Los Angeles.
Cast: Dick Powell, Ruby Keeler, Joan Blondell, Warren

William, Ginger Rogers, Aline MacMahon, Guy Kibbee.

Director: Mervyn Le Roy.

Between the filmed beginning and end of Busby Berkeley's elaborate "Shadow Waltz" production number, earthquake tremors jolted the circular staircase set and the lights went out. The choreographer ordered the sixty frightened women to sit down where they were and not move; the sequence was finished that night after the repair of a ramp. The illuminated violins in the same number represented a recent advance in technology, neon gas for commercial lighting. Each woman carried batteries and dangled unseen wires. Ginger Rogers's pig-Latin rendition of "We're in the Money" was her own creation, used for the opening number after Berkeley noticed her improvising with the song at a piano. Berkeley himself briefly appeared—thanks to a studio inventory shutdown that made extras unavailable—as a stagehand callboy. Singer Marian Anderson dubbed Joan Blondell's songs. Following hard on the melodic trail of *42nd Street*, *Gold Diggers* helped establish the film musical as a new medium during the bluest period of the Great Depression. This film's brave singing and audacious dialogue helped uplift a nation sadly wrecked in economy and morale. It was remade in 1951 as *Painting the Clouds with Sunshine*.

GONE WITH THE WIND. 1939. Filmed December 1938–August 1939; California: Old Laskey Mesa, San Fernando Valley; RKO Studios, Culver City.

Cast: Clark Gable, Vivien Leigh, Olivia de Havilland, Leslie Howard, Thomas Mitchell, Hattie McDaniel, Butterfly McQueen, Victor Jory, Evelyn Keyes, Jane Darwell, Ward Bond.

Directors: George Cukor, Victor Fleming.

The hype for it began long before a camera turned or a script page emerged. Producer David O. Selznick's publicity blitz, aimed toward "discovery" of an actress to play Scarlett O'Hara, finally narrowed to two quite familiar faces: Bette Davis and Paulette Goddard. Neither was finally chosen; the decision came suddenly when Selznick's agent brother, Myron, introduced to him the British actress Vivien Leigh, a relative unknown in the United States. No such contest surrounded the selection of Clark Gable as Rhett Butler. From the start, Gable was slated to play Butler—though the actor felt the role lay beyond his talents. Intimidated by a part that required more complex self-exploration than any of his previous (or later) roles, he strongly protested the scene that required him to cry after hearing of Scarlett's miscarriage. Shedding tears, he believed, would risk his carefully nurtured macho image. He even threatened to walk off the picture and give up his career. Only by subtle handling could director Victor Fleming persuade him to rehearse the scene both with and without tears; then Fleming used the weeping scene after assuring Gable that it would enhance, not destroy, his image. British actor Leslie Howard took little interest in the film, agreeing to join the cast only because Selznick promised him he could produce *Intermezzo* (1939). At age forty-six, Howard believed himself miscast as the twenty-eight-year-old Ashley Wilkes, and he steadfastly refused even to read Margaret Mitchell's novel. Scripting was chaotic; Selznick hired and fired writers with impatient abandon (F. Scott Fitzgerald, among others, was an eventual script doctor), and the actors often received their dialogue only at the last moment. The cast broke into factions when Selznick unceremoniously sacked initial director George Cukor (perhaps at Gable's instigation) in favor of Fleming, who was considered a man's director. Leigh and Olivia de Havilland strenuously objected to this replacement, to no avail; so they proceeded on their own to get secret coaching for their roles from Cukor throughout the rest of the filming. The burning of Atlanta, the first sequence filmed even before the cast was finalized, consumed several old sets that had been patched with false fronts on the RKO lot; these included remnants from *King Kong*, *The Garden of Allah*, *The Last of the Mohicans*, and *Little Lord Fauntleroy*. Trivia: Evelyn Keyes, playing Suellen, was the only cast member who had actually lived in Atlanta; twenty-eight-year-old Butterfly McQueen, playing Prissy, didn't like playing a slave, but the money helped her through U.C.L.A., and years later she made a part-time career of reminiscing to audiences about the film; look for TV's first Superman, George Reeves, as Stuart Tarleton in the opening scene at Tara (the screen credits mistakenly listed him as Brent Tarleton); Eddie Anderson, Jack Benny's longtime sidekick, appears as Uncle Peter; the white horse ridden by Thomas Mitchell later became the

Lone Ranger's Silver. The film won ten Academy Awards—among them best picture, Leigh as best actress, Hattie McDaniel as best supporting actress (the first Oscar awarded to a black person), and Fleming as best director. Gavin Lambert's book *GWTW* (1973) provides a detailed account of the filming.

THE GOOD EARTH. 1937. Filmed February 1936–January 1937; China (backgrounds): Shanghai; Soochow; Nanjing; Peiping; Foochow. Utah. California: Chatsworth; MGM Studios, Los Angeles.

Cast: Paul Muni, Luise Rainer, Walter Connolly, Tilly Losch, Jessie Ralph, Charley Grapewin, Keye Luke.

Director: Sidney Franklin.

Irving Thalberg had wanted to produce Pearl Buck's novel ever since the 1931 publication, and this was his last effort; he died during production. He convinced a reluctant Paul Muni, who at age forty thought himself too old, to play the chief role of Wang Lung; but once decided, Muni entered the project with characteristic intensity, losing weight, immersing himself in the daily life of Los Angeles's Chinatown, and experimenting with makeup to become as convincingly Chinese as possible. While Thalberg employed many Chinese extras for speaking roles, most of the major cast members were non-Asians. A team of researchers and photographers scoured China, with the friendly cooperation of the Nationalist government, for authentic background shots, shipping eighteen tons of properties (including entire farmhouses) back to MGM for the film. Designers carefully reproduced a Chinese agricultural landscape near Chatsworth, where director Sidney Franklin shot most of the action exteriors. Skillfully intercut montages of genuine locust swarms in Utah plus studio special effects created the locust-plague scenes. Austrian actress Luise Rainer won an Academy Award (her second) for best actress, as did Karl Freund for cinematography. Pearl Buck, who received only a nominal sum, never complained until years later, when MGM ignored her plea for a sizeable donation to help Amerasian children.

GOOD MORNING, VIETNAM. 1987. Filmed summer 1987; Thailand: Phuket; Bangkok.

Cast: Robin Williams, Forest Whitaker, Tung Thanh Tran,

Chintara Sukapatana, Bruno Kirby, Robert Wuhl, J. T. Walsh.
Director: Barry Levinson.

Humor's knife cuts sharpest. In a decade's roster of cinematic Vietnam honesty, this film's underlying commentary about the rending national experience made some of the more solemn efforts look bland by contrast. *Good Morning* was also lauded as the first film in which Robin Williams's unique verbal comedy style was given free rein. His monologues as disc jockey Adrian Cronauer, largely unscripted, formed examples of what Williams called his "Zen lock," a pouring-forth of extemporized, free-association comedy that could be edited but never restrained. Barry Levinson often had his camera running when Williams was only warming up. (His role was loosely based on experiences of the real-life Cronauer.) Thai actors and extras played most of the "Vietnamese" roles.

GOODBYE MR. CHIPS. 1939. Filmed summer 1938; Denham Studios, Denham, England.
Cast: Robert Donat, Greer Garson, Paul Henreid, Lyn Harding, Terry Kilburn, John Mills.
Director: Sam Wood.

Robert Donat's shy schoolmaster role almost went to Charles Laughton. For Donat, Chips was entirely unlike the romantic heroes his audience had grown to expect; accepting the role meant a career risk. He modeled his speech and mannerisms after his wife's uncle, eminent English architect C. F. A. Voysey. This was Greer Garson's film debut as well as Austrian actor Paul Henreid's first English-language film (playing a German schoolmaster, he was billed as Paul von Hernried). Note the lettering on the Austrian railroad coach in the train station scene; Henreid pointed out to director Wood that the name of the state-owned railroad was incorrect for the time period, but Wood chose to ignore the error—to his sorrow, for hundreds of moviegoers wrote in to correct him. Donat won an Academy Award for best actor, and the film proved his greatest popular success.

THE GRADUATE. 1967. Filmed March–August 1967; Los Angeles.
Cast: Dustin Hoffman, Anne Bancroft, Katharine Ross, William Daniels, Murray Hamilton.

Director: Mike Nichols.

Producer Laurence Turman found Robert Redford too self-assured for the role of Benjamin Braddock, so he cast an awkward, nervous unknown. And the role made Dustin Hoffman a star. Playing a character very similar to his own at the time (except for age—he turned thirty just after filming was completed), Hoffman fretted over Mike Nichols's wish that he not *act* but simply *be* as uncomfortable as he actually felt. The bedroom seduction scene between Hoffman and Anne Bancroft (playing Mrs. Robinson) proved difficult for both performers. Sensitive to Bancroft's modesty before scenes of undress became relatively common in movies, Nichols cleared the set and erected partition screens for her scantily clad sequences. (Doris Day had turned down the part because it offended her sense of values.) The film's theme of youthful rebellion against a materialistic adult world and its portrayal of a budding generation gap reflected (and anticipated) the temper of the times. Young people, strongly identifying with the confusion that Hoffman projected, attended the film in droves, making it a blockbuster hit. Nichols won an Academy Award as best director, but his cynical final assessment also proved an accurate forecast of the yuppie Eighties: "I think Benjamin will end up like his parents."

GRAND HOTEL. 1932. Filmed January–February 1932; MGM Studios, Culver City.

Cast: Greta Garbo, John Barrymore, Lionel Barrymore, Joan Crawford, Wallace Beery, Jean Hersholt, Lewis Stone.

Director: Edmund Goulding.

Grand Hotel represented a grand experiment in casting for MGM as the first all-star film. Edmund Goulding took pains to ensure that the Berlin hotel scenes were meticulously authentic, down to the last detail of uniform and decor. Unlike filming procedure in most productions, the set-bound action enabled him to shoot in chronological sequence, duplicating the stage play. Greta Garbo had wanted her former lover, John Gilbert, to play opposite her, but Gilbert's career was fast fading, and producer Irving Thalberg's switch to John Barrymore (after considering Clark Gable and Robert Montgomery) spelled the end of Gilbert's career. Some jockeying among the cast occurred at the outset. Jean Hersholt wanted Wallace

Beery's role, which Beery himself had irascibly resisted because it didn't fit his lovable lug image. But Thalberg insisted, and Hersholt accepted a lesser part. Goulding desired Buster Keaton for Lionel Barrymore's role, but again Thalberg intervened. The Barrymores always enjoyed acting together, each reveling in the other's scene-stealing attempts. Joan Crawford almost turned down her role, fearing she would get lost among all the heavyweight stars. To reduce chances of temperamental outbursts among all these monumental egos, Goulding filmed his players individually whenever possible—in many close-up dialogue shots, the performer was actually addressing a blank wall. Still, "the upstaging was historic," Crawford reported. Off-camera, she said, she maintained an awestruck distance from Garbo; John Barrymore, giggling and profane, ignored her; Beery treated her as boorishly as his role's character; but she liked Lionel Barrymore, who coached her during rehearsals. The film received an Academy Award for best picture. *Weekend at the Waldorf* was a 1945 remake.

GRAND ILLUSION (LA GRANDE ILLUSION). 1937.
Filmed January–April 1937; France: Neuf-Brisach; Haut-Koenigsberg; Colmar; Tobis and Éclair Studios, Epinay-sur-Seine.
Cast: Jean Gabin, Pierre Fresnay, Erich von Stroheim, Marcel Dalio, Julien Carette, Dita Parlo.
Director: Jean Renoir.

The provocative thesis of this classic antiwar film—that soldiers of warring powers have more in common with each other than with the governments they supposedly serve—was hardly gauged to fetch applause from nations eagerly gearing up for another World War. Strong foes united, at least, in mutual condemnation of the film, while President Roosevelt (as a neutral) recommended that "everyone who believes in democracy" should see it. Erich von Stroheim's portrayal of the Prussian commandant von Rauffenstein was probably the Austrian actor-director's best screen role. With Jean Renoir's admiring approval, he vastly enlarged what was originally a small part, adding such touches as his corset and neck brace (appliances obtained after some incredible bureaucratic hassling from a medical shop in Colmar) to increase his character's rigidity. Note the potted geranium plant in the commandant's chapel living quarters; von Stroheim used this geranium image in many of his films as a symbol of hope and life. Among the curious responses evoked from the Allied-Axis powers of the time, German propaganda minister Joseph Goebbels called von Stroheim's commandant a caricature. Yet an expurgated version of the film was widely shown for a time in Nazi Germany, though Mussolini banned it outright in Italy. Conversely, upon its reissue in 1946, some critics on the Allied side attacked the picture for being pro-German and anti-Semitic. Only the capture of a hidden negative in Munich after the war rescued the film from total oblivion. The fact that chauvinistic politicians all over the globe hated *Grand Illusion* seemed sufficient assurance that Renoir had indeed created a masterpiece.

THE GRAPES OF WRATH. 1940. Filmed September–November 1939; McAlester, Oklahoma. California: Arvin-Lamont-Bakersfield area; San Fernando Valley; Needles; 20th Century-Fox Studios, Los Angeles.
Cast: Henry Fonda, Jane Darwell, John Carradine, Charley Grapewin, John Qualen.
Director: John Ford.

By over-rehearsing it, "you'll leave the performance in the locker room," warned John Ford, justifying his practice of filming each scene fresh and seldom more than once. Thus the moving farewell between Henry Fonda and Jane Darwell, though meticulously rehearsed by the two, was completed in a single take. The match in Fonda's hand that lights up Darwell's face in the scene was actually a small electric light with wires running up Fonda's arm. When the scene was in the can, Fonda reported, Ford stood silently, then left the set—a sure sign that the director was pleased. Strong opposition from banks and big-farm interests, the villains of John Steinbeck's novel, caused Fox studio chief Darryl F. Zanuck to take unprecedented security measures during production, which proceeded under the cover title *Highway 66*. Armed guards stood at the studio door, and Zanuck had the scripts collected every night. He had wanted Don Ameche or Tyrone Power for Fonda's role, which established the latter as a major star. Actress Beulah Bondi remained bitter about not receiving the part of Ma Joad, which went to contract player Darwell. Zanuck himself wrote Darwell's moving speech in the farewell scene. The studio, Ford, and performers alike bent over backwards to assure moviegoers that the film was apolitical and not intended as a social document. Steinbeck, nevertheless, was pleased at the result. The film won an Academy Award for Darwell as best supporting actress, and for Ford's direction.

THE GREAT DICTATOR. 1940. Filmed September 1939–March 1940; California: Malibu Lake; Charles Chaplin Studios, Los Angeles.
Cast: Charles Chaplin, Jack Oakie, Paulette Goddard, Reginald Gardiner, Henry Daniell, Billy Gilbert.
Director: Charles Chaplin.

Chaplin's ultimate satire of totalitarianism—his first all-sound movie—was all the more remarkable because, at the time he made it, nobody knew what the outcome of Hitler-Mussolini noises in Europe would be. In hindsight, Chaplin said he unknowingly erred in making his dictator, Adenoid Hynkel, a harmless nincompoop instead of the monster that Hitler proved to be. (The great comic actor was placed on Hitler's murder list.) His second role, the Jewish barber, was Chaplin's final display of his famed little tramp character. From imploring him not to make a controversial, censorable film, United Artists, the distributor, did a radical turnabout when England declared war, nagging Chaplin to hurry *The Great Dictator* to completion. Jack Oakie's character, first named Benzino Gasolini in an obvious parody of the Italian *duce*, was changed to Napaloni because the Axis alliance still looked uncertain at the time. Chaplin brought a chef on the set to fatten up his already chubby codictator. By all accounts, Chaplin was a demanding slavedriver, pushing himself hardest of all. Tension and arguments on the set struck the death blow to his failing marriage with Paulette Goddard, who said he embarrassed her in front of cast and crew. He found huge fault with stage actor Henry Daniell's measured speech, accusing the bewildered Daniell, who played Garbitsch (i.e., Goebbels), of trying to sabotage the part. Reginald Gardiner, playing the pilot, noted a striking difference in Chaplin's own personality depending on his role for any given day. As the barber, he was warm and outgoing; as the uniformed Hynkel, his offscreen manner became severe and abrupt. Chaplin entirely improvised his gibberish speech as the dictator. (Grape-nuts cereal on a tray over a vibrator produced the noise of crowd scenes.) Many critics observed that his long, final harangue about world peace was a colossal self-indulgence that ruined the film's pacing, providing a textbook example of why stars should not direct their own films.

THE GREAT ESCAPE. 1963. Filmed summer 1962; West Germany: Geiselgasteig; Munich.
Cast: Steve McQueen, James Garner, Richard Attenborough, James Donald, Charles Bronson, Donald Pleasence, James Coburn, David McCallum.
Director: John Sturges.

Steve McQueen's own passion for motorcyle racing resulted in an emphasis on chase scenes that weren't in the original story; but all of the hazardous riding was done by stuntmen, notably Bud Ekins, who had taught McQueen to ride professionally. (For bike buffs: the actor's wartime BMW cycle in the film was actually a disguised TTS Special 650 Triumph.) In one chase sequence, McQueen even doubled as a German motorcyclist chasing himself—cycle freaks claim they can distinguish him from the Nazis by his riding style. Despite his spectacular interest in high speed (he collected more than forty speeding tickets in his Mercedes from German cops on location), McQueen was not too swift a professional on the set. He became incensed at his friend James Garner, convincing himself that the latter was trying to "steal" the picture with producer-director John Sturges's complicity. (Garner established his smiling con-man persona with this picture.) So infantile and paranoid was his behavior that Sturges threatened to fire him. McQueen could hardly bear to watch the film, even though it made him a major star. Charles Bronson had mixed feelings about his role as a miner digging the escape tunnel—for he actually was a former coal miner, having escaped from a background of dire poverty to pursue a theatrical career. On the set one day, he told David McCallum that he was going to steal McCallum's wife, actress Jill Ireland. Eventually he did, and married her. The script, based on an actual POW breakout in 1943 wartime Germany, underwent constant revisions during filming, with Sturges doing his utmost to tailor the lines to his cast. Four German actors in this film had been POWs in the United States. *The Great Escape* was a reworking of a 1958 British picture called *Breakout*, in which Richard Attenborough had also performed.

THE GREEN PASTURES. 1936. Filmed January–March 1936; Warner Bros. Studios, Burbank,
Cast: Rex Ingram, Oscar Polk, Eddie Anderson, Frank Wilson, Abraham Gleaves, Hall Johnson Choir.
Directors: William Keighley, Marc Connelly.

A racist film, it nevertheless marked a sympathetic if patronizing appreciation of black culture and folk traditions at the time it was made, and as such represented an advance for Hollywood. Rex Ingram, a fine actor, played three roles (Hezdrel, De Lawd, and Adam). Eddie Anderson, of course, played Jack Benny's sidekick, Rochester, for many years. Abraham Gleaves, playing the archangel, had been a Pullman porter on the *Santa Fe Chief*. But most of the nonprofessional cast came straight from Central Avenue in Los Angeles. A white actor from Louisiana, in fact, was imported to coach the cast in bayou accents. Codirector Marc Connelly, author of the original stage play, wanted to shoot on location in the South and out-of-doors, but he was overruled; the entire production, a virtual stencil of his play, occurred on indoor studio sets. As mild as this film seems today, it evoked plenty of controversy, especially in the South, where most exhibitors boycotted it.

GUESS WHO'S COMING TO DINNER. 1967. Filmed February–May 1967; Columbia Studios, Los Angeles.
Cast: Spencer Tracy, Sidney Poitier, Katharine Hepburn, Katharine Houghton, Cecil Kellaway, Beah Richards.
Director Stanley Kramer.

This comedy-drama about events leading up to an interracial marriage seems teapot-tempestuousness now—and even seemed so at the time—but Hollywood folk (if hardly anybody else) held self-congratulation marathons over it. What still matters, perhaps, is that Spencer Tracy, obviously dying and knowing it, felt the film important enough to give it literally his last ounce of energy. Aside from that—and the fact that Stanley Kramer and Tracy both liked ambitious message films and made several together—this picture's main interest today is historical, since it was the ninth teaming of Tracy and

Katharine Hepburn, as well as Tracy's last of seventy-four films. Kramer refused to make it without him, but because insurance companies handling the contract deemed Tracy a bad health risk, he along with Hepburn and Kramer put up the money—in effect performing for nothing. Tracy could only work a few hours each morning, and all scenes that didn't require him were photographed late in the day. His long, climactic speech, shot over three mornings (but its climax delivered faultlessly in one take) evoked considerable emotion on the set, especially from Hepburn; spontaneous applause, a rarity on movie sets, broke out as he completed it. The drive-in scene between Tracy and Hepburn was the final sequence filmed. Too weary to attend the wrap-up party but jubilant because he had survived the job, Tracy went home. He died there of heart disease fifteen days later. Sidney Poitier, almost paralyzed by nervousness in his scenes with the two veteran players, finally chose to play his close-up scenes to empty chairs. Kramer was unhappy with Katharine Houghton, Hepburn's niece, who was making her film debut but treating Kramer's publicity men as if she were a star. The film won two Academy Awards: for Hepburn as best actress and for William Rose's screenplay. White supremacists picketed the movie in the South, while left-wing groups condemned it as a tokenist effort in the North, and many blacks disliked the film. As Poitier said later, however, "Hollywood was incapable of anything more drastic in 1967."

GUNFIGHT AT THE OK CORRAL. 1957. Filmed spring 1956; Arizona: Old Tucson; Elgin; Phoenix. Paramount Studios, Los Angeles.

Cast: Burt Lancaster, Kirk Douglas, Rhonda Fleming, Jo Van Fleet, John Ireland, Earl Holliman, Dennis Hopper, DeForest Kelley, Lee Van Cleef, Jack Elam.

Director: John Sturges.

The story isn't exactly the way it happened on October 26, 1881, date of the famed Earp-Clanton shoot-out in Tombstone. The real gunfight lasted only thirty seconds in contrast to the five minutes on screen. But as one of the first postwar big Westerns, the film revitalized the genre. Kirk Douglas and Burt Lancaster teamed in several films—large egos both, they remained good friends but also wary professional rivals in their mutual appearances. In this film they rewrote most of their own dialogue. Because they kept bursting into howling laughter over their machismo, multiple retakes were required of the sequence in which they subdue a whole saloonful of rowdy baddies. To key up for her scenes, Jo Van Fleet demanded that Douglas slap her, hard, just before she went in front of the camera. Though hesitant, Douglas obliged her. Lancaster agreed to appear here only in exchange for producer Hal Wallis's promise to give him the lead role in *The Rainmaker* (1956). Many scenes were filmed in Old Tucson, the adobe village that had been erected for *Arizona* (1941), later used for location filming in *Rio Bravo* (1959) and *El Dorado* (1966) plus the TV series *High Chaparral*. The gunfight, which took four days to film, was meticulously choreographed, with each move plotted on a map. Wallis aimed, he said, for the dry-brown, burned-out look of Frederic Remington paintings.

GUNGA DIN. 1939. Filmed June–October 1938; California: Chatsworth; Lake Sherwood; Lone Pine; RKO Ranch, Encino; RKO Studios, Los Angeles; RKO-Pathé Studios, Culver City.
Cast: Cary Grant, Victor McLaglen, Douglas Fairbanks, Jr., Sam Jaffe, Eduardo Ciannelli, Joan Fontaine.
Director: George Stevens.

This remains one of the great adventure films despite its underlying racism and patronizing colonial attitudes. One of Cary Grant's favorites, it was also RKO's most expensive production to that date, employing some nine hundred brown-painted extras for the climactic battle scene on the slopes of Mount Whitney. Grant and Douglas Fairbanks, Jr. switched roles, at Grant's request, before cinematography began; as Archibald Cutter in the movie, Grant also managed to use his own real first name. George Stevens embellished much of the script on location, while also allowing Grant to improvise many of his scenes. Grant liked the film because it gave him the chance to emulate the strenuous athletics of his own screen idol, Douglas Fairbanks, father of his costar. Victor McLaglen said his role of MacChesney was also his own favorite in films. Sam Jaffe patterned his title role upon Sabu, the popular Indian actor. Location work in the Sierras was an ordeal, with temperatures soaring to 115 degrees. *The Lives of a Ben-*

gal Lancer (1935) and *The Charge of the Light Brigade* (1936) were also filmed in the same area. India understandably banned the film on its first release. *Soldiers Three* (1951) was a virtual remake.

THE GUNS OF NAVARONE. 1961. Filmed March–November 1960; Isle of Rhodes. Shepperton Studios, Shepperton, England.

Cast: Gregory Peck, David Niven, Anthony Quinn, Anthony Quayle, Irene Papas, James Darren, James Robertson Justice, Stanley Baker, Richard Harris.

Director: J. Lee Thompson.

This production set the style for a trend, that of all-star international casts ganging up to make action-adventure epics. The assembled big names were wary of one another at first but tension and rivalries eased as filming progressed. On location at Rhodes, the fifty-five-foot boat *Maria* was rented from local fishermen. More than a thousand Greek soldiers impersonated German troops. The storm at sea, simulated in a huge water tank at Shepperton, almost cost David Niven his life. With only three days of filming left, he cut his lip in the tank and was stricken with septicemia. After being hospitalized for a month, he returned to complete his scenes with Gregory Peck, but he suffered a relapse that lasted seven weeks. Before this, brandy had flowed freely as the actors worked nine hours a day in the freezing-cold water. Niven (no teetotaler himself) expressed awed admiration for Peck's drinking capacity under such duress. Producer Carl Foreman had wanted Kenneth More for Niven's role; this film gave Niven what was probably his final top-quality part. The film won an Academy Award for special effects. *Force 10 From Navarone* (1978) was an inferior sequel.

GUYS AND DOLLS. 1955. Filmed spring 1955; Samuel Goldwyn Studios, Los Angeles.

Cast: Marlon Brando, Jean Simmons, Frank Sinatra, Vivian Blaine, Stubby Kaye, Sheldon Leonard.

Director: Joseph L. Mankiewicz.

An oddly miscast film, with the dominant singing role going to Marlon Brando instead of Frank Sinatra, this was Joseph L. Mankiewicz's first and only attempt at directing a musical. Sinatra boiled with rage throughout. Miffed at being passed over for the role that went to Brando in *On the Waterfront*—and again for Brando's part of Sky Masterson in this film—he barely held his animosity in check for the duration. Their acting styles also clashed; Sinatra grew increasingly impatient with the endless rehearsals and retakes demanded by Brando. In the Mindy's Restaurant scene, where Brando required eight takes while Sinatra sat eating cheesecake, the latter finally stormed off the set. The antipathy became mutual, with Brando even daring to criticize Sinatra's vocal style. Finally they seldom spoke offscreen, using intermediaries to communicate. Ironically, neither actor ended up liking his own performance. Brando took voice lessons and did his own singing. Jean Simmons, who had previously acted with him in *Desirée*, also performed her songs without substitute voice dubbing. Gene Kelly had been another disappointed contender for Brando's role, and Marilyn Monroe for Vivian Blaine's. Years later, Mankiewicz said he found the film "too slow and too talky."

GYPSY. 1962. Filmed winter 1962; Warner Bros. Studios, Burbank.

Cast: Rosalind Russell, Karl Malden, Natalie Wood, Ann Jillian.

Director: Mervyn LeRoy.

Rosalind Russell thought her role of Mama Rose should have gone to Ethel Merman, who originated the part on Broadway, but Merman wasn't asked and Russell was, so she took it. Her singing was dubbed at first by Lisa Kirk, but Russell dubbed in her own voice for most of the songs before the film's release. Actress June Havoc, sister of stripper Gypsy Rose Lee on whose autobiography the musical was based, angrily contested with the studio over the child actress playing herself at age five; Havoc wanted a real five-year-old in the part—and the studio finally awarded her a $125,000 settlement. The real Gypsy Lee herself, often appeared on the set, giving Natalie Wood tips on her stripping routines. Look for Harvey Korman, in his screen debut, as a press agent. The National Legion of Decency rated the film *objectionable* because of its attempt "to rationalize a morally questionable occupation," but that didn't keep audiences away. In fact, it may have augmented the box office take.

H

HAMLET. 1948. Filmed May–December 1947; Denham Studios, Denham, England.

Cast: Laurence Olivier, Eileen Herlie, Jean Simmons, Basil Sydney, Felix Aylmer, Peter Cushing, Stanley Holloway, Anthony Quayle.

Director: Laurence Olivier.

Olivier and his team of Old Vic players created what many critics believe to be the best Shakespearean performance on celluloid. His aim, said Olivier, was to make the film as the Bard himself might have done. He closed the set to avoid distraction from onlookers, and fellow cast members said he became more and more dictatorial as filming progressed. Part of this attitude may have resulted from his own problems on the set. He reinjured his right knee, first hurt during the making of *Henry V* (1944), in a sword fight with Laertes (played by Terence Morgan). Then he injured an ankle leaping onto the battlements of Elsinore. Also, studio chief J. Arthur Rank had insisted on casting a young actress for the part of Ophelia; Olivier's wife, thirty-three-year-old Vivien Leigh, was bitterly disappointed that she hadn't been chosen and became convinced that Olivier was having an affair (which he vehemently denied) with his eighteen-year-old Ophelia, Jean Simmons. Friends marked this period as the beginning of Leigh's increasing emotional instability. Olivier saved his most spectacular stunt—his flying leap onto Claudius (Basil Sydney) from a parapet—until the final day of production. Olivier jumped without injury (for once), but Sydney's stand-in for the scene, professional strongman George Crawford, was knocked out and lost two front teeth. (There was only one take of the scene.) The only actors who wore their own hair in the film were Olivier and Peter Cushing (playing Osric). Olivier turned forty and also received his knighthood during the filming. Neither Simmons nor Stanley Holloway had ever played Shakespeare before—indeed, Simmons had never even read a Shakespeare play, but Olivier believed that her very unfamiliarity with the lines brought vivid freshness to them. Anthony

Quayle made his screen debut as Marcellus. Listen for Christopher Lee (you won't see him) shouting the single word "Lights!" in his third film (of seemingly hundreds). *Hamlet* took the first Academy Award for best picture granted to a non-American production. Oscars also went to Olivier as best actor and for art direction and costumes.

HANNAH AND HER SISTERS. 1986. Filmed 1985; Jersey City, New Jersey. New York City.
Cast: Woody Allen, Michael Caine, Mia Farrow, Barbara Hershey, Dianne Wiest, Carrie Fisher, Max von Sydow, Maureen O'Sullivan, Lloyd Nolan, Tony Roberts.
Director: Woody Allen.

In many of his movies, Woody Allen plays intricate variations on his favorite theme of worried man (usually portrayed by himself). *Hannah*, however, focused to a larger extent on another favorite subject—women—in the context of sibling emotions and rivalries. Allen encouraged Mia Farrow, Barbara Hershey, and Dianne Wiest, playing the three sisters, to overlap their dialogue naturally, to improvise audible responses in the course of conversation (a style disliked by most directors since it interferes with conventional editing). He also inserted many details of his beloved Manhattan architecture. Family relationships extended beyond the roles: Farrow, Allen's longtime companion, is the daughter of veteran actress Maureen O'Sullivan and the late director John Farrow: and Carrie Fisher is the daughter of Debbie Reynolds and Eddie Fisher. Note the physician advising Allen that his sperm count is too low; not a professional actor, Benno C. Schmidt, Jr., was the president of Yale University at the time. The Marx brothers film clip toward the end came from *Duck Soup*. Veteran character actor Lloyd Nolan made his final screen appearance in *Hannah*; battling lung cancer, he died before the film's release. *Hannah* won Academy Awards for Allen's screenplay, for Michael Caine as best supporting actor, and for Wiest as best supporting actress.

A HARD DAY'S NIGHT. 1964. Filmed March–April 1964; England: London; Twickenham Film Studios, Twickenham; and on trains through rural England.
Cast: The Beatles (John Lennon, Paul McCartney, George Harrison, Ringo Starr), Wilfrid Brambell, Victor Spinetti, Anna Quayle.

Director: Richard Lester.

The Beatles' first and probably best film was made as a semidocumentary day-in-the-life comedy at the dawn of their spectacular careers. Richard Lester admitted that he directed the comedy to take advantage of what everybody assumed would be the group's short-lived popularity, and he made it primarily for English audiences, with no idea it would prove a classic. Lester had to work fast to film the London street scenes, getting two takes at most before mobs of adoring fans would descend. Those crowds, and the police trying to control them, forced Lester to improvise certain location scenes rapidly—most notably the press reception, filmed inside London's La Scala Theatre. The film's title, a last-minute decision, came from Ringo Starr's description of an all-night recording session, and John Lennon immediately composed the song to fit the title. Lester decided at the outset that the Beatles were unlikely to sit still long enough to memorize lines of dialogue, so he directed them by speaking a line himself, then had them repeat it back on camera. "I think it a bit silly," Lester said of the film in 1970; of the two Beatles pictures he directed, he much preferred *Help!* (1965).

HAROLD AND MAUDE. 1972. Filmed January–May 1972; California: San Francisco; Redwood City; Oyster Point; Oakland; Palo Alto; Daly City; Cabot.

Cast: Ruth Gordon, Bud Cort, Vivian Pickles, Cyril Cusack.

Director: Hal Ashby.

This black-comedy cult classic would have cast John Rubinstein as the demented male lead—the part was written for him—if director Ashby had had his way. Instead, Harold became Bud Cort's enduring claim to fame. For veteran actress-screenwriter Ruth Gordon, who specialized in dotty old ladies, the part of flower-child-granny Maude was a lark, albeit a somewhat tiresome one—as Ashby carted his company all over California's Bay Area for location shots. Gordon's pink scarf, worn in a car scene with Cort, was a memento of her death scene in *What Ever Happened to Aunt Alice?* (1969).

HARPER. 1966. Filmed summer 1965; Warner Bros. Studios, Burbank.

Cast: Paul Newman, Lauren Bacall, Julie Harris, Arthur

Hill, Janet Leigh, Pamela Tiffin, Robert Wagner, Shelley Winters, Strother Martin.
Director: Jack Smight.

Paul Newman's film titles beginning with the letter H—including *The Hustler* (1961) and *Hud* (1963)—had proved highly successful, so Ross MacDonald's fictional detective Lew Archer became Lew Harper for Newman's sake. Frank Sinatra had turned down the role. Newman patterned the character on Humphrey Bogart and a personal political hero, Robert F. Kennedy. Screenwriter William Goldman recalled that, in the close-up scene where Robert Wagner listens to Newman insult his girlfriend, Wagner began crying spontaneously. Newman was delighted, but his surprise at this unscripted action caused him to botch his own lines. This scene, and Newman's genuine astonishment, were left intact in the final cut. Less successful was the sequel, *The Drowning Pool*, which Newman made ten years later.

HEAVEN CAN WAIT. 1978. Filmed summer 1977; Paramount Studios, Los Angeles.
Cast: Warren Beatty, Julie Christie, James Mason, Charles Grodin, Dyan Cannon, Buck Henry, Jack Warden.
Directors: Warren Beatty, Buck Henry.

This remake of *Here Comes Mr. Jordan* (1941) was Warren Beatty's first effort as a director. He also cowrote the script (with Elaine May) and produced the film. Not intending at first to play the lead himself, he asked Muhammed Ali to play the reincarnated prize fighter. When Ali declined, Beatty rewrote the part as a Los Angeles Rams quarterback, then trained strenuously to make himself a believable athlete. Cary Grant and Senator Eugene McCarthy were others considered early on for James Mason's role as Mr. Jordan. Ex-lovers Beatty and Julie Christie, just good friends again by the time filming began, had previously costarred in *McCabe and Mrs. Miller* (1971) and *Shampoo* (1975).

HELLO, DOLLY! 1969. Filmed April–August 1968; New York: Garrison; Poughkeepsie; Cold Springs. 20th Century-Fox Studios, Los Angeles.
Cast: Barbra Streisand, Walter Matthau, Michael Craw-

ford, Marianne McAndrew, Tommy Tune, E. J. Peaker, Louis Armstrong.
Director: Gene Kelly.

Elizabeth Taylor and Julie Andrews were among those considered for the role of fortyish matchmaker Dolly Levi. The studio wanted Carol Channing, who had played Dolly on Broadway for eighteen months, but finally decided that her personality was too large for the screen. Barbra Streisand entered the role enthusiastically but soon recognized that she was miscast; at twenty-four, she was considerably too young for the part. Director Gene Kelly seemed unable to help her as she floundered, modeling Dolly alternately on Mae West, Fanny Brice, and her own superstar persona, losing confidence in Kelly and herself as a result. Also her abrasive manners on the set won her no friends. Walter Matthau, especially, became increasingly annoyed at her behavior, developing psychosomatic pains and ailments over the daily confrontations. Their feud escalated to the point where he was calling her "Miss Ptomaine," while she labeled him "Old Sewermouth." Adding to the stress was the New York heat and humidity and the assassination of Robert F. Kennedy, which occurred during the filming, weighing heavily on the cast and crew of a lighthearted musical. One of the best things about it was the set design. A fifteen-acre, sixty-building complex that condensed a stretch of Manhattan's Fifth Avenue arose in the studio entrance drive—a set to be used again in *The Great White Hope* (1970), *Up the Sandbox* (1972), and *Nickelodeon* (1976), as well as in many TV commercials. Designers modernized the scenic Hudson River town of Garrison to represent Yonkers in the 1890s, adding gingerbread touches to its 1840s structures. *Dolly* bombed at the box office, and Streisand assessed the film as the biggest mistake of her career.

HELP! 1965. Filmed February–April 1965; Obertauren, Austria. Nassau, Bahama Islands. England: Salisbury Plain; Twickenham Film Studios, Twickenham.
Cast: The Beatles (John Lennon, Paul McCartney, George Harrison, Ringo Starr), Leo McKern, Eleanor Bron, Victor Spinetti.
Director: Richard Lester.

The Beatles' second cinematic lark was gauged for an international, rather than exclusively British, audience—in contrast to *A Hard Day's Night*. The working title was *Eight Arms to Hold You*. According to John Lennon, the Fab Four remained constantly high on marijuana during production, and he perceived that his life seemed to be falling apart. The Lennon-McCartney title song was literally a cry for help, he said. Bothered by his own increased weight and eating and drinking habits, Lennon called this his "fat Elvis period." He hated the Bahamas location, with its stark contrasts between opulence and dire poverty, and he thought the film story ludicrous. In the Austrian Alps location, Lester put the Liverpool lads on skis and told them to ski. Somehow they learned in a few hours' time.

HENRY V. 1944. Filmed June 1943–February 1944; Powerscourt Estate, Ennis Kerry, Ireland. England: Denham Studios, Denham; Pinewood Studios, Iver Heath.
Cast: Laurence Olivier, Robert Newton, Leslie Banks, Esmond Knight, Renée Asherson, George Robey, Leo Genn, Ernest Thesiger, Max Adrian, Felix Aylmer.
Director: Laurence Olivier.

England needed a patriotic propaganda film to help rally a unified Britain in wartime, and producer-director Laurence Olivier's adaptation of this Shakespeare play proved ideal for the purpose. He wanted Hollywood veteran William Wyler to direct, but Wyler thought Olivier himself should do it, and *Henry V* thus became the latter's directorial debut, for which he was released from military duties. Olivier envisioned Vivien Leigh, then his wife, for the French princess role, but David O. Selznick, who owned her contract, balked, saying the tiny part would devalue her Scarlett O'Hara image; so Renée Asherson, wife of actor Robert Donat, was cast. England was under constant aerial bombardment throughout the production. During the Battle of Agincourt sequence—completed in six weeks at Powerscourt Estate in Ireland, where battle scenes for *Barry Lyndon* would also be filmed in 1974—Olivier badly strained his right knee when he fell from a horse. Realistic props, in scarce supply, were largely handcrafted: chain mail consisted of knitted, spray-painted twine; weapons were metal-painted wood; and gold tiaras of papier-mâché rested lightly on crowned heads. The film, released in the U.S. in 1946, suffered cutting by the movie industry's prudish production code office, which felt that Americans weren't ready for Shakespeare's *damns* and *bastards*. Boston exhibitors censored it further. Olivier, however, won an honorary Academy Award for his triple-threat achievement.

HERE COMES MR. JORDAN. 1941. Filmed spring 1941; Columbia Studios, Los Angeles.
Cast: Robert Montgomery, Evelyn Keyes, Claude Rains, James Gleason, Edward Everett Horton, Rita Johnson, Donald McBride.
Director: Alexander Hall.

"What the hell does heaven look like?" barked studio chief Harry Cohn to his set designers. The answer, to Cohn's apparent satisfaction, turned out to be fog atop dry ice to simulate a location somewhere above the clouds. Evelyn Keyes complained that the studio tried to make her into a blond replica of Rita Hayworth for this film, padding her figure and adding hairpieces "including one of Otto Kruger's old toupees pasted to my forehead." Robert Montgomery frowned on Keyes's sexually free lifestyle, specifically her liaison with the still-married director Charles Vidor. (The couple later married.) After she told Montgomery to mind his own business, she said, he never spoke to her again—but by then, most of the filming was completed. Harry Segall's original play, on which the film was based, won an Academy Award; and Warren Beatty remade the film in 1978 as *Heaven Can Wait*.

HIGH NOON. 1952. Filmed September–October 1951; California: Calabasas Park Golf Club, Calabasas; Iverson Ranch, Chatsworth; Tuolumne City; Warnerville; Columbia; Columbia Ranch, Burbank; Motion Picture Center Studios, Los Angeles.
Cast: Gary Cooper, Grace Kelly, Thomas Mitchell, Lloyd Bridges, Katy Jurado, Otto Kruger, Lon Chaney, Jr., Harry Morgan.
Director: Fred Zinnemann.

Gary Cooper's career was badly sagging when he made this Western, and his health was also wretched. He was beset with stomach ulcers and lower back troubles, and an old hip injury flared up and impaired his walk. No less a shambles was his emotional life; separated from his wife, he was slowly ending a love affair with actress Patricia Neal. At age fifty and looking it, he required almost no makeup for his role of beleaguered Will Kane (changed from Will Doane because Mexican actress Katy Jurado had trouble pronouncing Doane). Gregory Peck had refused the role, feeling he could not match his performance in *The Gunfighter* (1950). Grace Kelly, a twenty-two-year-old novice actress in her first major role, disparaged her own performance; yet it was precisely her inexperience that director Fred Zinnemann sought—and the number of close-ups he gave Kelly infuriated Jurado. Screenwriter Carl Foreman strongly identified with Will Kane as lone man in town. Called before the House Un-American Activities Committee during the filming to answer questions about his past associations, he was soon ostracized from the movie industry and spent the rest of his life under the blacklist shadow; his widow received his belated Academy Award for *The Bridge on the River Kwai* in 1985. John Wayne was one of those who deplored the film as a basically unpatriotic Western. At preview time, the film bombed, disappointing the audience with its slow-moving action. Then famed editor Elmo Williams went to work on it, and to him goes the credit for turning *High Noon* into a film classic. Look for Lee Van Cleef, future spaghetti-Western star, as a harmonica-tooting baddie. Cooper won an Academy Award as best actor (his second), quickly rejuvenating his career; the musical scoring and title song also won Oscars.

HIGH SIERRA. 1941. Filmed July–September 1940; California: Lone Pine; Arrowhead Springs; Warner Bros. Studios, Burbank.

Cast: Humphrey Bogart, Ida Lupino, Alan Curtis, Arthur Kennedy, Joan Leslie, Henry Hull, Henry Travers.

Director: Raoul Walsh.

This was Humphrey Bogart's breakthrough film, the one that made him a top-billed star after years of playing subordinate roles and B-film leads. He grabbed for the part of killer Roy Earle after several well-known actors—including George Raft (who refused to play a role that required him to die at the end), Paul Muni, and James Cagney—had turned it down. Location photography on the scenic slopes of Mount Whitney was strenuous for Bogie, who loved his civilized comforts and complained loudly about roughing it. Costar Ida Lupino alleged that he verbally abused her during the filming, certainly an unusual accusation against him. Among the first of films to treat a villain as romantic antihero, *High Sierra* also invented many of the bits that, with repetition over the decades, became gangster movie clichés. It was remade as *Colorado Territory* (1949, also directed by Raoul Walsh) and as *I Died a Thousand Times* (1955).

HIROSHIMA, MON AMOUR. 1959. Filmed August–December 1958; Japan: Hiroshima (exteriors); Tokyo (interiors). France: Autun and Nevers (exteriors); Paris (interiors).
Cast: Emmanuelle Riva, Eiji Okada, Stella Dassas, Bernard Fresson.
Director: Alain Resnais.

What James Joyce did for literature, filmmaker Alain Resnais did for cinema in this revolutionary, stream-of-consciousness vanguard of the French New Wave. The story—a love affair in postwar Hiroshima—is nothing; the way it is told, everything. The director's original intention was to make a straightforward documentary about Hiroshima twelve years after the atomic bomb fell. Complexities of that project changed his focus, however, and the result was this stark drama about the impossibility of aiming an objective camera on the city and its people. He wanted it to be a woman's film, he said; the screenwriter was noted French novelist Marguerite Duras. Resnais inserted actual newsreel footage of Hiroshima after the blast into the mosaic of time sequences. This was stage actress Emmanuelle Riva's screen debut; she moved on to a thriving career in French movies but has never appeared in an English-language film.

HIS GIRL FRIDAY. 1940. Filmed summer–autumn 1939; Columbia Studios, Los Angeles.
Cast: Cary Grant, Rosalind Russell, Ralph Bellamy, Ernest Truex, Roscoe Karns, Helen Mack, Billy Gilbert.
Director: Howard Hawks.

This remake of *The Front Page*, substituting a female lead in the previously male role of Hildy Johnson, was Howard Hawks's own inspiration. Unlike most remakes, it is probably superior to the original. Hawks, one of the first directors to shoot naturalistic, overlapping dialogue and plenty of fast-paced improvisation, gave his cast free rein, savoring their throw-away lines and spontaneous business, even using microphones on the newsroom set to pick up background voices. Rosalind Russell had been far from his first choice to play Hildy—some of Hollywood's biggest names, including Ginger Rogers, Irene Dunne, Jean Arthur, Claudette Colbert, and Carole Lombard, had turned down the role—but he later realized that she was just right. Russell worried about her sagging jowls; a makeup man solved the problem by painting a dark mark along her jaw line, which became a shadow in the high key-lighting, giving her face a firm, youthful appearance. Cary Grant, between marriages at the time, dated Russell and introduced her to producer Frederick Brisson, her future husband. Cary Grant moments to watch for: his line about Archie Leach cutting his throat—that name was Grant's own, and he tossed it into his films whenever he could get by with it; and his spontaneous, surprised line "Is she going to do that?" directed to Hawks off-camera and referring to one of Russell's improvised antics—the director left it in.

HOBSON'S CHOICE. 1954. Filmed summer 1953; Shepperton Studios, Shepperton, England.
Cast: Charles Laughton, John Mills, Brenda De Banzie, Daphne Anderson, Prunella Scales.
Director: David Lean.

Lean's last black-and-white film was to have starred Robert Donat as Willy Mossop; but Donat, always in precarious health, suffered a severe asthma attack and John Mills was brought in at the last moment. The redoubtable Charles Laughton, however, took a dim view of the substitution and thought Mills miscast. Laughton hated playing drunk scenes and also developed a dislike toward Brenda De Banzie, who played his shrewd daughter. Despite such grumpiness on the set, however, the movie ranked as one of the most successful English comedies; it played to packed houses on both sides of the Atlantic.

HOLIDAY INN. 1942. Filmed winter–spring 1942; Paramount Studios, Los Angeles.
Cast: Bing Crosby, Fred Astaire, Marjorie Reynolds, Virginia Dale, Walter Abel, Louise Beavers.
Director: Mark Sandrich.

The musical comedy that introduced Irving Berlin's "White Christmas" also gave its title to the national chain of motels. Ironically, in view of Bing Crosby's later identification with the tune, he initially tried to get out of singing it because, being a devout Catholic, he feared it would further commercialize the holiday. Berlin, who also conceived the idea for the film, had composed "White Christmas" in 1939, then laid it aside until resurrecting it here. The song's huge success as a nostalgic reminder of home fires during the darkest period of World War II caught both him and Crosby by surprise. Crosby virtually adopted it as a personal Yuletide anthem, singing it in two subsequent films—*Blue Skies* (1946) and *White Christmas* (1954)—as well as in his annual TV specials. Fred Astaire, in his frenzied jitterbug dance with Marjorie Reynolds, was supposed to look inebriated, so he downed two stiff shots of bourbon before each take. There were seven takes; "the last one was the best," he reported. For his notable firecracker dance on an electrically wired stage, Astaire rehearsed endlessly, making thirty-eight takes over three days; the intricate sequence is reputedly the fastest dance number ever filmed. Astaire began the film weighing 140 pounds, ended it at 126. An Academy Award went to Berlin for his best-known song.

HOUSE OF WAX. 1953. Filmed autumn–winter 1952; Warner Bros. Studios, Burbank.
Cast: Vincent Price, Frank Lovejoy, Phyllis Kirk, Carolyn Jones, Paul Picerni.
Director: André de Toth.

This remake of *The Mystery of the Wax Museum* (1933) rejuvenated Vincent Price's career, more or less typecasting him in hammy horror pictures thenceforth. Look for Charles Bronson (screen credited as Charles Buchinski, his real name), playing Igor. A box office smash, this film was mainly noted for its new 3-D gimmickry. Asking an unusual degree of viewer participation, the film required audiences to wear specially provided Polaroid glasses. This wasn't the first 3-D feature (that was *Bwana Devil*, in 1952) or the last, but it was more profitable than any of the others. Ironically, director André de Toth had lost the use of one eye, making him one of the film's few viewers who couldn't appreciate the 3-D effects. Another notable milestone concerned the picture's incorporation of an early stereophonic soundtrack, unnoticed in the video version but a marvel for moviegoers back in 1953.

HOW TO MARRY A MILLIONAIRE. 1953. Filmed spring 1953; 20th Century-Fox Studios, Los Angeles.
Cast: Betty Grable, Marilyn Monroe, Lauren Bacall, William Powell, Cameron Mitchell, David Wayne, Fred Clark, Rory Calhoun.
Director: Jean Negulesco.

Lauren Bacall, Marilyn Monroe, and Betty Grable came on as the Fifties version of material girls—and probably only during that decade could the old gold diggers' theme have received this cynically sexist a workout. Grable, in her last big film, easily related to Bacall, who had never done comedy, and to the totally insecure Monroe (who idolized Grable, imitating her walk and talk). Studio chief Darryl F. Zanuck criticized Grable's hair style as outmoded and a ploy to upstage the others—but Grable was never the hysterical type and continued to wear her hair as she pleased. While Monroe's constant tardiness and frequent trouble with dialogue annoyed her costars, since it necessitated extra work, they recognized her innate lack of self-confidence and went out of their way to befriend her. Screenwriter Nunnally Johnson, not so kind in his opinions, called Monroe "an arrogant little tail switcher." Monroe depended heavily on her personal acting coach, Natasha Lytess, who stood on the sidelines and, to the fury of director Jean Negulesco, advised the actress on whether or not a take was satisfactory. In preparation for their roles, Bacall added pounds, while Grable and Monroe had to diet them off. This was the first motion picture in Cinemascope, though *The Robe* introduced the process by its release earlier in 1953.

HUD. 1963. Filmed summer–autumn 1962; Claude, Texas. Griffith Park and Paramount Studios, Los Angeles.
Cast: Paul Newman, Melvyn Douglas, Patricia Neal, Brandon de Wilde, John Ashley.
Director: Martin Ritt.

Weeks before filming began, Paul Newman worked on a Texas cattle ranch, acquiring genuine calluses and a cowboy's lope in preparation for his title role. Patricia Neal, grieving the death of her seven-year-old daughter some months before, desperately needed a lift in her career and seized the chance to join the cast as Alma, the earthy, work-worn housekeeper. The Bannon Ranch in the film was actually a place called the Henderson Ranch, located near Claude, that had lain unoccupied for a decade. Notice cameraman James Wong Howe's lighting of faces: strong and undiffused for Neal, dark contrasts for Newman, shadow-cut for Melvyn Douglas, brightly lit for Brandon de Wilde—in order to emphasize the characters' inner qualities. Howe won his second Academy Award for cinematography, while Neal took an Oscar for best actress and Douglas for best supporting actor.

THE HUNCHBACK OF NOTRE DAME. 1939. Filmed summer 1939; California: RKO Ranch, Encino; RKO Studios, Los Angeles.

Cast: Charles Laughton, Maureen O'Hara, Edmond O'Brien, Cedric Hardwicke, Thomas Mitchell, George Zucco.

Director: William Dieterle.

Charles Laughton, in perhaps his greatest screen role, liked playing Victor Hugo's hunchback for several reasons. For one, the portly actor didn't have to diet or squeeze himself into corsets. Also, Quasimodo offered him chances to pantomime, which pleased him. His makeup rivaled the elaborate medieval Paris set itself (adapted in 1945 for use in *The Body Snatcher*) for meticulous attention to detail. Sponge rubber covered the left side of his face, masking his eye and creating a lower eye socket, giving his countenance its twisted, malformed appearance. His hump consisted of an aluminum frame packed with foam rubber. He was actually whipped in the public square sequence; one day he was lashed for sixteen takes. Record summer heat compounded his suffering from pain and heavy makeup. A moving moment occurred following the sequence when Quasimodo rings the bells in the tower for the gypsy girl Esmeralda (played by Maureen O'Hara). It was the day, filled with intense emotion and anguish for all the British residents in Hollywood, when England went to war against Germany. After the sequence ended for the camera, Laughton continued ringing the bells with almost frenzied abandon, and everyone knew why. Edmond O'Brien as Gringoire the poet and Walter Hampden as the archbishop made their film debuts here. Laughton and his wife, Elsa Lanchester, had launched O'Hara in her film career earlier that year with *Jamaica Inn*, and Laughton always prided himself on having discovered her. The 1956 remake starred Anthony Quinn and Gina Lollobrigida.

THE HUSTLER. 1961. Filmed spring 1961; Ames Billiard Academy, New York City. Exteriors and 20th Century-Fox Studios, Los Angeles.
Cast: Paul Newman, Piper Laurie, George C. Scott, Jackie Gleason, Murray Hamilton, Myron McCormick.
Director: Robert Rossen.

Stroke of Luck and *Sin of Angels* were its original titles. The role of pool shark Fast Eddie Felson made Paul Newman an overnight star, and the film remained one of his personal favorites. He practiced pool obsessively, being coached by old pro Willie Mosconi, whose hands substituted for Newman's in most of the close-up cue work. Piper Laurie, whose career was definitely on the slide, spent her off-camera time on the set remote and silent, deeply depressed over her prospects—and this downbeat melodrama didn't help her. Robert Rossen believed *The Hustler* to be his best directing effort, however, and it won Academy Awards for cinematography and art direction. An angry Newman thought the picture could have taken even more Oscars if the studio's marketing strategy hadn't aimed for the quick buck. He finally won his own Oscar for *The Color of Money*, the 1986 sequel wherein he again played Fast Eddie.

I

I AM A FUGITIVE FROM A CHAIN GANG. 1932. Filmed July–September 1932; California: Los Angeles; Chatsworth; Pasadena; Warner Bros. Studios, Burbank.
Cast: Paul Muni, Glenda Farrell, Preston Foster, Helen Vinson. Allen Jenkins.
Director: Mervyn LeRoy.

Robert E. Burns, author of the original autobiography, was still a fugitive from Georgia (his 1920 crime: stealing $5.29 in order to eat) and feared extradition when he came to Hollywood to help work on the screenplay. Studio personnel kept him hidden under a phony name on the studio lot. James Cagney would probably have been chosen for the leading role if he hadn't been temporarily suspended for scrapping with studio bosses. The rock quarry scene was filmed in extreme summer heat at Chatsworth, where Paul Muni characteristically refused to have a double substitute for him. Mervyn LeRoy said he achieved the final blackout scene by accident; when a fuse blew on the klieg lights during rehearsal, he liked the effect and so duplicated the dimout during actual filming. The bridge explosion scene was filmed entirely in miniature. LeRoy considered this his most important picture, arguably America's first filmed social drama. Though *Fugitive* focused a glaring spotlight on the Georgia penal system, resulting in quick reform, Georgia officials threatened LeRoy and studio executives with arrest or worse if they ever set foot in the state. The film also became a hit in the Soviet Union. What of Burns? He continued to dodge his pursuers until 1945, when his sentence was finally commuted to time served; he died a decade later.

IMITATION OF LIFE. 1959. Filmed August–October 1958; California: Hollywood Methodist Church, Los Angeles; Universal-International Studios, Universal City.
Cast: Lana Turner, John Gavin, Juanita Moore, Susan Kohner, Robert Alda, Sandra Dee, Dan O'Herlihy.
Director: Douglas Sirk.

Remake of a 1934 film based on Fannie Hurst's novel, this classic tearjerker was Douglas Sirk's last directorial achievement before his retirement. Lana Turner joined the cast reluctantly and in shaky emotional condition. This was her first screen effort after the traumatic episode in which her fourteen-year-old daughter, Cheryl Crane, had slain Turner's petty-mobster lover, Johnny Stompanato, the previous April. During filming of the church funeral finale, she became hysterical and left the set. She credited her hairdresser, Patti Westmore, with convincing her to resume her pew seat and finish the sequence. The tragedy did not hurt her at the box office. *Imitation* proved not only the biggest commercial success of Turner's career; it also rescued her financially. Gospel singer Mahalia Jackson made a rare film appearance to sing the 23rd Psalm.

IN COLD BLOOD. 1967. Filmed March–June 1967; Kansas: Kansas City; Holcomb; Garden City.
Cast: Robert Blake, Scott Wilson, John Forsythe, Paul Stewart, Jeff Corey.
Director: Richard Brooks.

Truman Capote said that Robert Blake's physical resemblance to murderer Perry Smith was uncanny. Incredibly, Columbia Studios wanted Paul Newman and Steve McQueen for the leading roles of the two murderers. In order to heighten the actors' sense of here and now, Richard Brooks discouraged them from reading Capote's so-called nonfiction novel during production; he also withheld the complete script from the cast. Most locations were authentic; the Kansas farmhouse shown was the actual Clutter family residence where the 1959 murders occurred; and the trial was reenacted in the Finney County Court House in Garden City, using the same people for the jury who had convicted the pair. Perry Smith's real father played himself, and Holcomb citizens became crowd extras. Capote worked closely with Brooks and was pleased with the movie's faithfulness to his best-selling book.

IN THE HEAT OF THE NIGHT. 1967. Filmed spring 1967; Sparta, Illinois, Tennessee.
Cast: Sidney Poitier, Rod Steiger, Warren Oates, Lee Grant, Quentin Dean.
Director: Norman Jewison.

Rod Steiger remained completely immersed in his character of tough Southern police chief Bill Gillespie, speaking in the same cadence offscreen as well as on, chewing gum constantly, shambling around in oversized chukka boots. Norman Jewison wanted to see more of Steiger's belly over his belt, so the already chubby actor said he was glad to eat additional desserts for the sake of art. The two leading actors had never worked together before but were old friends, and each became the other's best publicist when the picture was released. Sidney Poitier went on to make two routine sequels in his role of detective Virgil Tibbs: *They Call Me MISTER Tibbs!* (1970) and *The Organization* (1971). Five Academy Awards went to

In the Heat—for best picture, to Steiger as best actor, and to Sterling Silliphant's screenplay, among others.

IN WHICH WE SERVE. 1945. Filmed February–June 1942; Denham Studios, Denham, England.
Cast: Noel Coward, Bernard Miles, John Mills, Richard Attenborough, Celia Johnson, Michael Wilding.
Directors: Noel Coward, David Lean.

Britain's most notable and effective propaganda film of World War II was almost scuttled at the start by wary officials who believed it would lower rather than raise morale. No less an official than Lord Louis Mountbatten intervened to rescue the project. The film was based on the torpedo sinking of *HMS Kelly*, commanded by Mountbatten, early in the war. Though Noel Coward (who also wrote the screenplay) always maintained that he never intended to portray the officer he hero-worshiped, the inference was clear. (He even wore Mountbatten's old cap in some scenes.) For Coward, a specialist in drawing room comedy, this radical shift of style derived from his patriotic desire to enlist his talents for the war effort. He paid meticulous attention to shipboard details. The full-size destroyer replica used was the biggest set ever built in a British studio, a model that could list sixteen degrees in either direction. (Many of the extras became seasick.) Britain's royal family witnessed the filming of Coward's Dunkirk speech, standing offstage during the three short takes required. But Coward also incurred the lasting wrath of his old enemy, English press mogul Lord Beaverbrook, by his shot of an edition of the *Daily Express* floating in the harbor; the newspaper's headlines trumpeted NO WAR THIS YEAR just after England's declaration of war. The strafing gunfire that "wounded" John Mills in the water used creative special effects. A row of condoms was attached to a length of hollow tubing and placed just below the water surface; suddenly inflated and burst by compressed air, they nicely simulated a spatter of bullets. Mills said he was reasonably certain of being the only actor in history who could claim he was "shot in the arm by a French letter." Coward's most chilling memory, however, was of the last scene filmed. Standing on his shipboard bridge mockup, he is inundated by hundreds of gallons of water. The torrent struck him in the back from tanks outside camera range, tossing him helplessly as the bridge capsized under him. This was Richard Attenborough's screen debut and David Lean's first directing job. It also marked the first screen appearance of actress Juliet Mills, the eleven-week-old daughter of John Mills; in the true spirit of typecasting, she was Mills's infant child in a domestic scene. Coward recruited Leslie Howard, himself a later casualty of the war, to speak the familiar lines of prayer at the end of the film—a prayer repeated on wartime naval vessels throughout the world. Perhaps not entirely coincidentally, Lean, Coward, Mills, and Attenborough all received knighthoods later in their careers.

THE INFORMER. 1935. Filmed February–April 1935; RKO Studios, Los Angeles.
Cast: Victor McLaglen, Heather Angel, Preston Foster, Joseph Sawyer, Wallace Ford.
Director: John Ford.

John Ford directed his first acknowledged masterpiece only after five studios turned down the film as "not commercial material"; finally a reluctant RKO backed it. Victor McLaglen, a former British heavyweight boxing champion, also became the subject of a Hollywood legend through this movie. It was said that Ford kept him constantly off-balance (and thus in character) by getting him drunk, changing his schedules, verbally abusing him on and off the set, and filming scenes when he told McLaglen he was only rehearsing. McLaglen lost weight and sleep under Ford's sadistic regimen. For the crucial rebel court scene, goes the story, Ford reduced the actor to a trembling wreck; he promised him the day off, then brought him in early and extremely hung over, insisting that he spit out his lines. McLaglen supposedly threatened a dozen times to quit acting—*after* he had killed Ford. How much of this gamesmanship actually occurred remains uncertain. McLaglen always denied that Ford had tricked a performance from him, but Ford kept his own counsel (also using McLaglen in several of his later films). What remains certain is that Ford deeply believed in this project and, with Dudley Nichols, labored intensely over the script. The drama won Academy Awards for McLaglen as best actor, Ford as best director, Max Steiner's music, and Nichols's screenplay. *Uptight* (1968) was an inferior remake.

INHERIT THE WIND. 1960. Filmed autumn 1959; Universal-International Studios, Universal City.
Cast: Spencer Tracy, Fredric March, Gene Kelly, Florence Eldridge, Harry Morgan, Dick York.
Director: Stanley Kramer.

Based on the 1925 Scopes Monkey Trial, with Spencer Tracy and Fredric March playing protagonists modeled respectively on Clarence Darrow and William Jennings Bryan, this film was an adaptation of the Jerome Lawrence-Robert E. Lee stage play. March, made up to resemble Bryan, said he found it hard not to go "overboard" in his own performance, which was much more flamboyant than Tracy's. Part of his preparation involved studying newsreels of Bryan to pick up gestures and mannerisms. Though March's theatrical background was much more extensive than Tracy's, he marveled at Tracy's capacity for memorizing long speeches—especially his eleven-minute summation to the jury, completed in one astounding take. Florence Eldridge, March's wife, also played his spouse in the film. Stanley Kramer, noted for his message dramas, staged the courtroom battle in continuity, photographing speeches in their entirety rather than in short takes. Observers on the set enjoyed the rare spectacle of the two veteran actors trying to outperform each other in their own unique ways, March with his vigorous fanning, Tracy with his ten-second pauses and pulls at his nose. Gene Kelly, who felt himself outclassed in this company, performed in one of his few nonmusical roles.

INTERIORS. 1978. Filmed autumn 1977; New York: Southampton and Larchmont, Long Island; Westchester County; New York City.
Cast: Kristin Griffith, Mary Beth Hurt, Richard Jordan, Diane Keaton, E. G. Marshall, Geraldine Page, Maureen Stapleton, Sam Waterston.
Director: Woody Allen.

For many comedy artists, curiously, the height of ambition is to create something serious, and director Allen is no exception. His first film in which he didn't also star was also his first to disallow humor, made in homage to (and imitation of) his hero, Swedish director Ingmar Bergman. Renting a thirty-room mansion in Southampton, he completely redesigned its interior, paying meticulous attention to details of furnishing, color, and shape. (The house owners later complained that things weren't put back exactly right, as per agreement.) Decor, Allen maintained, was "almost as important as plot or characters." Diane Keaton's residence in the film was the former home of poet Phyllis McGinley in Larchmont. It was Keaton who suggested the film's title.

INVASION OF THE BODY SNATCHERS. 1956. Filmed 1956; California: Sierra Madre; Bronson Canyon and Allied Artists Studios, Los Angeles.
Cast: Kevin McCarthy, Dana Wynter, Larry Gates, King Donovan, Carolyn Jones.
Director: Don Siegel.

With a working title of *Sleep No More*, this film received almost stone silence from critics on its release, but it has since become a science fiction sleeper. Many viewers likened the insidious spread of the pod people to the menace of Communism that so frightened Americans in the Fifties; but for director Don Siegel, the broader, more dangerous theme was that of unthinking social conformity. Siegel deliberately avoided the use of special-effects gimmickry. The studio, fearful of making audiences think *too* hard, forced him to add the brief prologue and epilogue scenes after he had finished principal photography. Look for Charlie, the town meter reader, a small speaking part—that's future filmmaker Sam Peckinpah. This picture brought Kevin McCarthy his most famous role, one he briefly reprised in a bit part when the film was remade under the same title in 1978.

IT HAPPENED ONE NIGHT. 1934. Filmed November–December 1933; California: Sunland; RKO Ranch, Encino: Columbia Studios, Los Angeles.
Cast: Clark Gable, Claudette Colbert, Walter Connolly, Roscoe Karns, Alan Hale.
Director: Frank Capra.

This comedy was one of Hollywood's first productions to go outside the studio complex for location scenes. Louis B. Mayer had refused the story for MGM because he thought it didn't give the tycoon father (played by Walter Connolly) the proper respect that a captain of industry should command. Robert Montgomery was envisioned for the male lead but he refused the part, as did female lead possibilities Myrna Loy,

Miriam Hopkins, Constance Bennett, and Margaret Sullavan. Bette Davis wanted the costarring role, but Warner Bros. refused to loan her out. A loan deal that did work out between Mayer and Columbia's Harry Cohn assigned Clark Gable the starring role as punishment for "goldbricking" at MGM (he had apparently laid off for a long, secret siege of dental work). Frank Capra wasn't overjoyed to get him, especially after Gable arrived loudly drunk for their first meeting. Claudette Colbert also proved difficult, arguing over Capra's impromptu rehearsals and casual style, also balking at the various scenes of undress her role required. She refused to expose her leg in the hitchhiking scene (filmed on a country road in Sunland), then angrily agreed to do it when Capra brought in a chorus-girl replacement for the scene. Despite these initial problems, the costars became good friends, and the filming turned into something of a lark. The last thing anybody expected was a runaway hit. Its success launched a whole genre of screwball comedies that made huge stars of Irene Dunne, Carole Lombard, and Lucille Ball, among others. Gable's clothes—his Norfolk jacket, V-neck sweater, snap-brim hat, and trenchcoat (the "lucky coat," which he wore in many subsequent films)—also became fads of 1930s apparel. At the same time, men's underwear manufacturers complained that Gable's bare chest had grievously hurt their business. When Gable munched a raw carrot, he unknowingly gave birth to the most famous carrot muncher of all; cartoonist Bob Clampett received inspiration for creating Bugs Bunny from that scene. Five Academy Awards: best picture, Gable as best actor, Colbert as best actress, Capra for direction, and Robert Riskin for screenplay. Two remakes—*Eve Knew Her Apples* (1944) and *You Can't Run Away From It* (1956)—proved less successful.

IT'S A MAD MAD MAD MAD WORLD. 1963. Filmed spring–summer 1962; California: Mojave Desert; Long Beach; Oxnard; Santa Monica; Malibu; San Pedro; Palos Verdes; Thousand Oaks; Camarillo; Santa Rosa; Tustin; Santa Ana; San Diego; Kernville; Palm Springs; Universal Studios, Universal City; Revue Studios, Los Angeles.

Cast: Spencer Tracy and scores of comedy stars in cameo appearances.

Director: Stanley Kramer.

It was a Mel Brooks romp that predated Mel Brooks. By bringing together all the foremost comics of the day for a wild chase movie *à la* Keystone Kops, Stanley Kramer thought he could "make a comedy to end all comedies." Instead, he demonstrated that, in comedy, more doesn't necessarily equal merrier. With such a troup of grandstanders trying to outdo one other, some of the best comedy bits occurred just after Kramer shouted "Cut!" to end a scene. Spencer Tracy, ill and wan (this was his next-to-last film), was replaced by doubles in all his scenes except close-ups; a stuntman in a rubber Spencer Tracy mask performed the veteran star's strenuous action bits. Other performers suffering problems on the set included Phil Silvers, who pulled a groin muscle while running into the loft building; he had to be carried off; a nonswimmer, he also had to be carried ashore by studio frogmen when he drove the car into the Kern River. Sid Caesar, also doing an ABC-TV show at the time, later admitted that, in his constant alcoholic fog of those days, he walked through his scenes on pure instinct. This film marked the last screen appearances of Jimmy Durante and ZaSu Pitts.

IT'S A WONDERFUL LIFE. 1946. Filmed April–July 1946; California: RKO Ranch, Encino; Beverly Hills High School and RKO Studios, Los Angeles.
Cast: James Stewart, Donna Reed, Lionel Barrymore, Gloria Grahame, Henry Travers, Beulah Bondi, Thomas Mitchell, H. B. Warner.
Director: Frank Capra.

Its unabashed sentimentality has made it a Christmas favorite, but the film's popularity came late. It lost money at the box office, and not until its copyright was allowed to expire in 1974 did its consequent TV exposure gain it a huge audience. At loose ends with his career stalled just after his World War II army discharge, James Stewart gratefully accepted Frank Capra's offer of the role of George Bailey, a part in a long-shelved script that RKO had originally bought for Cary Grant. Jean Arthur spurned the costarring role that went to Donna Reed. As Mary Hatch, requiring her to age from eighteen to forty, Reed worked harder than in any previous assignment. Lionel Barrymore, reveling in skinflint characters, accepted his part without reading the script. Jimmy the Raven, the bird on Thomas Mitchell's desk, had been a staple Capra "character" in all his movies since *You Can't Take It With You* (1938). The town of Bedford Falls, including tons of chemical snow, shaved ice, and gypsum to simulate snow, arose on the RKO Ranch. Himself, a recent army dischargee, Capra began the production with many qualms, fearing failure after his own five-year absence from Hollywood. Both he and Stewart have claimed the film (at least since its rejuvenation into classic status) as their favorite. Jeanine Basinger's *The It's a Wonderful Life Book* (1986) details many interesting aspects of the production.

IVAN THE TERRIBLE. Part I. 1947. Filmed April 1943–June 1944; Alma-Ata Film Studio, Alma-Ata, U.S.S.R. Part II, 1959. Filmed September–December 1945; U.S.S.R.: Alma-Ata; Mosfilm Studios, Moscow.
Cast: Nikolai Cherkassov, Ludmila Tselikovskaya, Serafina Birman, Piotr Kadochnikor.
Director: Sergei Eisenstein.

Ponderous, sweeping, and exquisite in its grandeur, Sergei Eisenstein's *Ivan the Terrible* became a metaphorical reaffirmation for Mother Russia during that nation's darkest days of World War II. Nazi invaders were smashing toward Moscow as Part I began filming, necessitating evacuation of the production to the Kazakhstan region. Eisenstein paid meticulous attention to details of costuming, makeup, and historical authenticity in his recreation of the sixteenth-century founding of the modern Russian state. Nikolai Cherkassov, somberly playing the title role, endured plenty of personal hardships, sweltering in padded costume and hot armor during filming of the attack on Kazan Fortress (actually a plywood facade mounted on a precipice). His mourning posture beside the czarina's coffin required him to assume fiendishly cramped positions because of the set's crowded decor. By the time Part II finished, Cherkassov bordered on nervous collapse, so intense was Eisenstein's discipline. The director won patriotic honors in the Soviet Union for Part I but suffered humiliating disgrace for Part II, which Joseph Stalin banned as "antihistorical" and "antiartistic." Soviet underground consensus was that Part II's bloodthirsty Ivan reflected much too directly upon Stalin himself. Eisenstein dutifully made his confessions and apologies.

Idolized in other nations as perhaps the world's foremost filmmaker, but abused and neglected by his own beloved country, he died at age fifty in 1948. The Soviet ban on Part II was lifted three years after Stalin's death.

J

JAWS. 1975. Filmed May–November 1974; Coastal waters, Australia. Massachusetts: Menemsha; Edgartown, Martha's Vineyard. California: Santa Catalina Island; Universal Studios, Universal City.

Cast: Roy Scheider, Robert Shaw, Richard Dreyfuss, Lorraine Gary, Murray Hamilton, Peter Benchley.

Director: Steven Spielberg.

One of the biggest moneymakers in cinema history (number one until *Star Wars*), *Jaws* was coscripted by Peter Benchley, author of the original novel, and Carl Gottlieb, who later wrote an entertaining account of the production (*The Jaws Log*, 1975). Both also briefly appeared in the movie, Benchley as a TV interviewer and Gottlieb as newspaper publisher Meadows. Location photography at sea off Martha's Vineyard was a five-month ordeal governed by vagaries of weather, tourist influx, mechanical problems with three studio-created sharks, and finally a wiped-out cast and crew. Charlton Heston had wanted to play the lead role of Brody, but the producers chose to cast non-superstars instead. (None of the cast were bankable at the time, though several became so as a result of this picture.) The part of Quint had been slated for veteran character actor Sterling Hayden, but tax problems kept him from working in the U.S. The part went to British actor Robert Shaw, who based his crusty portrayal on an actual Yankee oldtimer living on the island. Footage of great white sharks, filmed by an underwater team off Australia's Great Barrier Reef, were skillfully intercut with Steven Spielberg's big toy ones. So realistically were the latter built and so precisely operated that distinguishing them from the real ones is virtually impossible. The main mechanical shark, a 25-foot-long, one-ton monster nicknamed Bruce, was connected to a submerged sea sled operated by scuba divers and tubing. Two other half-sharks, open on left and right sides, respectively, were tethered from a long control platform on the ocean floor; a dolly arm, hydraulic pistons, and compressed-air hoses enabled their movement for a seventy-foot distance near the water surface. Each shark (representing just the one behemoth in the movie) consisted of neoprene foam and polyurethane "skin" over a steel skeleton, with flexible joints and hinges. The scene in which the shark violently tips the *Orca* from below resulted in actual, unintended sinking of the vessel, with cameras and exposed film ending thirty feet down. Retrieved, flushed with fresh water, and immediately processed, the film survived its briny bath. That sequence, filmed as the *Orca* sank, remained in the finished picture. *Jaws* won three Academy Awards. Three sequels—*Jaws 2* (1978) *Jaws 3-D* (1983), and *Jaws, the Revenge* (1987) followed.

JEZEBEL. 1938. Filmed October 1937–January 1938. Warner Bros. Studios, Burbank.

Cast: Bette Davis, Henry Fonda, George Brent, Fay Bainter, Donald Crisp, Margaret Lindsay.

Director: William Wyler.

Bette Davis credited this historical drama as the beginning of her "box office years as a prestige star." Her role of Julia Marsden somewhat resembled that of Scarlett O'Hara in *Gone With the Wind*, which began shooting after the completion of *Jezebel*. The part may have been offered to Davis in consolation for her bitter disappointment at not being cast as Scarlett; Miriam Hopkins, who had played *Jezebel* on Broadway, was rankled at being bypassed for the movie, and Tallulah Bankhead also sought the role. William Wyler, whom Davis always praised as her best director, was a painstaking craftsman whose endless retakes infuriated cost-conscious studio chiefs. During this production he and Davis began a romantic affair that lasted about a year. Her fear of its exposure led to various health problems; afflicted with colds and bronchitis, she lost weight and finished the picture in a state of nervous exhaustion. She wasn't the only paranoid one. Studio chief Hal Wallis suspected that Wyler was vindictively demanding an excessive number of retakes from Henry Fonda because both Wyler and Fonda were ex-husbands of actress Margaret Sullavan, and both were also clients of her third husband, agent Leland Hayward. (Fonda himself never made this charge.) Though Wallis had originally wanted Jeffrey Lynn for Fonda's role of Pres Dillard, Davis herself chose Fonda to costar with her. An offscreen event of the time was the birth of Fonda's daughter, Jane. Fonda's absence from the set during the birth required Davis to film many of her close-up reaction shots alone, a difficult feat. Despite all the soap-operatic events occurring off screen, the film won Davis her second Academy Award as best actress; and Fay Bainter also took an Oscar for best supporting actress.

JOHNNY BELINDA. 1948. Filmed autumn 1947; California: Mendocino; Warner Bros. Studios, Burbank.

Cast: Jane Wyman, Lew Ayres, Charles Bickford, Agnes Moorehead, Stephen McNally, Jan Sterling, Alan Napier.

Director: Jean Negulesco.

For her role as deaf mute Belinda McDonald, Jane Wyman went to great lengths to assure an authentic performance. She studied signing and lipreading with experts, observed behavioral traits of the handicapped, and on the set wore plastic earplugs. Wyman's offscreen life at this time was beset with personal problems. After the deeply affecting death of a prematurely born daughter in June 1947, her marriage with Ronald Reagan, increasingly distracted by politics, was cracking up. (They divorced in 1948.) Also, Lew Ayres was unhappy with the casting of Wyman, having preferred Teresa Wright for the part. As the heroine of this weeper, Wyman found that her tears came almost *too* easily. Her efforts paid off; she won an Academy Award for best actress. In her first film role, Jan Sterling played Stella—after almost losing out to Janis Paige.

JUDGMENT AT NUREMBERG. 1961. Filmed spring 1961; West Berlin (exteriors). Revue Studios, Los Angeles.

Cast: Spencer Tracy, Burt Lancaster, Richard Widmark, Marlene Dietrich, Maximilian Schell, Judy Garland, Montgomery Clift, William Shatner, Edward Binns, Werner Klemperer.

Director: Stanley Kramer.

Spencer Tracy pronounced this Stanley Kramer production the finest picture of his career, despite his disappointment when Sir Laurence Olivier dropped out of the cast to be replaced by Burt Lancaster. Marlene Dietrich selected her own clothes for her last major screen role, a part she felt keenly eager to play and one she accepted before seeing the script. Playing a straight dramatic role, Judy Garland came to the film beset with weight, drug, and psychological problems, finding a sympathetic friend in the likewise shaky Montgomery Clift. Trembling and twitching, the sad emotional and physical wreck that Clift had become was able to perform his scene as a war crimes witness only by Tracy's gentle guidance. Kramer made four takes of Clift's seven-minute sequence on the witness stand, and on each take the actor's final words and breakdown came out differently. On the last take, as his audience on the set strained with him, observers said that the pathos of his own condition seemed to merge completely with the character's; and when Kramer said "Cut," the entire courtroom broke into waves of applause. Clift drank openly and constantly on the set when he wasn't on camera, weeping copiously when he watched Garland do her own witness scene. The entire courtroom set, a close duplication of the actual Nuremberg chambers, was portable, built on wheels for movement on the premium-space sound stage. German reaction to this film was mostly hostile or silent but drew more interest after the 1984 *Holocaust* TV series. Austrian actor Maximilian Schell received an Academy Award as best actor, and Abby Mann took an Oscar for his screenplay.

JULES AND JIM (JULES ET JIM). 1962. Filmed April–June 1961; France: Alsace; St. Paul de Vence; Paris.
Cast: Jeanne Moreau, Oskar Werner, Henri Serre, Marie Dubois, Vanna Urbino.
Director: François Truffaut.

"A perfect hymn to love, and perhaps even to life," was what François Truffaut tried to transpose to the screen from Henri-Pierre Roché's novel. The Catholic Legion of Decency called it an immoral film, concerning as it does a sexual ménage à trois spanning twenty years; but most viewers saw it as the lyrical expression that Truffaut intended. The film became his best-loved feature and secured his international reputation. Jeanne Moreau, in probably the best role of her career, also achieved major stardom, and the film remained her favorite. Truffaut's self-styled "album of old photographs" won many international awards.

K

KEY LARGO. 1948. Filmed winter 1947–48; Warner Bros. Studios, Burbank.
Cast: Humphrey Bogart, Lauren Bacall, Edward G. Robinson, Lionel Barrymore, Claire Trevor, Thomas Gomez.
Director: John Huston.

Lauren Bacall and Humphrey Bogart were almost three years into their marriage. Edward G. Robinson, playing his umpteenth gangster role as Rocco (intended as a composite of Lucky Luciano and Al Capone), joined the cast somewhat reluctantly; according to John Huston, the actor disliked his hoodlum screen image and seemed eager to compensate for it by becoming an art collector of impeccable taste. Huston described Robinson in his introductory bathtub appearance as "like a crustacean with its shell off." Lionel Barrymore, wheelchair-bound and suffering almost constant arthritic pain, disguised the anathema he felt toward the late President Roosevelt in his scripted speech defending FDR; Huston said he loved the way the veteran actor gritted his teeth all through the scene. Bacall, though, remembered Barrymore's unconscious moans of pain on the set. Note Bogie's scenes aboard the *Santana*, named for his own yacht. Exterior hurricane shots came from stock footage of the later-released *Night Unto Night* (1949). Claire Trevor, playing Rocco's drunken moll, won an Academy Award as best supporting actress; her role was modeled on Gay Orlova, Luciano's mistress.

THE KILLERS. 1946. Filmed April–June 1946; Universal-International Studios, Universal City.
Cast: Burt Lancaster, Ava Gardner, Edmond O'Brien, Albert Dekker, Sam Levene, Donald McBride.
Director: Robert Siodmak.

Former circus acrobat Burt Lancaster's screen debut at age thirty-two was as a "dumb Swede"; he was third choice after the unavailable Wayne Morris and Sonny Tufts. Though Ava Gardner had made some twenty-one films in the preceding four years, her role as Kitty Collins was also her first important dramatic part. She worked on her big scene, as Kitty faces arrest, for days as director Robert Siodmak alternately cajoled, threatened, and frightened her into near hysteria. By the time the scene was ready to film, her genuine terror of the director made her breakdown only half simulated. This film was also radio actor William Conrad's screen debut. Recognize the music? It later became the theme of the popular *Dragnet* TV series. Ernest Hemingway, who wrote the original story, also contributed to the screenplay, as did John Huston, though both remained uncredited. A 1964 remake featured Ronald Reagan's last screen appearance.

THE KILLING FIELDS. 1984. Filmed March 1983–August 1984; Thailand: Khao-i-Dang refugee camp; Bangkok. Toronto. Camp Pendleton Marine Base, Oceanside, California.

Cast: Sam Waterston, Haing S. Ngor, John Malkovich, Craig T. Nelson, Athol Fugard, Julian Sands, Bill Paterson.

Director: Roland Joffe.

Based on appalling fact, the Cambodian genocide of 1973, this true-life tale of a friendship paired Sam Waterston, playing *New York Times* reporter Sydney Schanberg, with Dr. Haing S. Ngor, a Cambodian physician who had never previously acted. Ngor, playing news photographer Dith Pran, had himself been a refugee from the Communist Khmer Rouge, which succeeded in eliminating a large part of the country's population. He had narrowly escaped the country in 1979, leaving almost all of his relatives, as well as his fiancée, there. Waterston spent a week with Schanberg, but Ngor never met Dith Pran until filming was completed. One day Ngor ran off the set in terror; in the scene where a girl soldier pulls up his solitary tomato plant, her flat, dead eyes—so familiar to Ngor after years of torture and imprisonment by this vicious children's army—convinced him that the actress actually belonged to the Khmer Rouge. Director Joffe reassured him that the girl was Thai, hired for the bit part. The choice of Ngor for the role came after Joffe conducted hundreds of interviews with Cambodian refugees in America. Khmer Rouge work camps were authentically recreated, using Thai actors and extras, from refugee accounts and Yugoslavian newsreels of the actual camps. The mass grave scene used plastic and latex bones created for the film by a local Thai doctor and his students. Ngor won an Academy Award for best supporting actor, and Chris Menges won for cinematography. Spalding Gray's book *Swimming to Cambodia* (1985) and the 1987 film based upon it gave an intriguing account of his own involvement as a bit player with the production.

KIND HEARTS AND CORONETS. 1949. Filmed winter 1949; Pinewood Studios, Iver Heath, England.
Cast: Dennis Price, Valerie Hobson, Joan Greenwood, Alec Guinness, Audrey Fildes, Arthur Lowe.
Director: Robert Hamer.

This satirical black comedy brought Alec Guinness major character-actor stardom; a master of disguises, he played eight roles—all members of the ill-fated d'Ascoyne family (though he was originally scheduled to play only four of them). In his balloon ascent scene as Lady Agatha, however, he was doubled by a Belgian balloon expert. Expert and balloon rose and sailed out of sight, finally landing in a Thames estuary fifty miles away. The film's final shot came about because of U.S. censors, who refused to release the movie for American distribution unless it was made clear that the murderer (played by Dennis Price) would be punished—thus destroying director Hamer's fine ambivalent riddle at the end. *They All Died Laughing* (1964) was a near-remake coscripted by Hamer.

THE KING AND I. 1956. Filmed August–December 1955; 20th Century-Fox Studios, Los Angeles.
Cast: Deborah Kerr, Yul Brynner, Rita Moreno, Martin Benson, Terry Saunders, Alan Mowbray.
Director: Walter Lang.

His role as King Monghut of Siam, only his second film appearance, made Yul Brynner a major star. Not only had he played the king for four years on Broadway before making the film—a musical remake of *Anna and the King of Siam* (1946)—but he continued to perform the role in stage revivals for the rest of his life. Understandably possessive about the production, Brynner wanted to direct the film version, and he wanted Marlon Brando for the male lead. Brando turned it down, however, and Brynner consented to star, adding dozens of subtle nuances to his stage role. His definite ideas about how the picture should be directed and acted brought him into constant conflict with producer Charles Brackett and director Walter Lang, and he threatened several times to walk off the set. Usually, however, he got his way, and the film largely reflected his own slant on Ernest Lehman's screenplay. Though Dinah Shore had sought the part of Anna, Brynner insisted on Deborah Kerr, who took voice lessons for her songs. (Marni Nixon, however, dubbed her high notes as well as all of "Hello Young Lovers.") Kerr believed that Brynner's precise direction (in all but name) turned a run-of-the-mill film into a great one. Brynner won an Academy Award for best actor and went on to perform in other films, but he will always be identified most strongly with this one role.

KING KONG. 1933. Filmed June 1932–February 1933; California: San Pedro; Bronson Canyon and Shrine Auditorium, Los Angeles; RKO-Pathé Studios, Culver City.
Cast: Fay Wray, Bruce Cabot, Robert Armstrong, Victor Wong, Frank Reicher.
Directors: Merian C. Cooper, Ernest B. Schoedsack.

Producer-codirector Merian C. Cooper promised Fay Wray at the outset "the tallest, darkest leading man in Hollywood." The great ape really wasn't that tall—only eighteen inches, to be exact. But in the detailed miniature sets that were merged and composited with glass paintings, rear-projection backgrounds, stop-motion animation sequences, wooden puppets, and full-size actors, Kong became the fearsome granddaddy of all movie monsters, wreaking havoc but also eliciting empathy. This Kong's flesh and bone consisted of rabbit fur, which covered molded sponge rubber on an aluminum frame. In the jungle scenes, the basic scale ratio for its size was one inch to one foot; but the city scenes required a somewhat larger Kong that stood twenty-four inches tall on the same scale so as not to be dwarfed by the skyscrapers. While Kong in his entirety was thus a monkey-size doll, the parts of him that would engage with human actors were built on a massive scale. These included a foot, lower leg, and giant furry paw—the latter a cranelike device about eight feet long in which Wray would writhe sexily and be lifted ten feet over the studio floor for her scene atop the Empire State Building. A huge head-and-shoulders portion made of rubber and bearskin for close-ups held three men; they operated a compressed air device that could produce facial expressions on the monster—surpassing, some said, the capacities of many a professional actor. While this film's special effects look primitive when compared with Steven Spielberg gadgetry, *King Kong* pioneered the basic machinery and techniques that modern filmmakers, with the aid of electronics, have only refined. Scenes of the four biplanes that finally bring down Kong consisted of naval aircraft hired for the occasion, intercut with model planes in miniature projection. The codirectors played the pilots in the plane mock-up that kills Kong. (The flight commander of the real Curtiss trainer aircraft died in a crash only a few weeks after the scene was filmed.) Most of the sound was postdubbed; Wray screamed herself hoarse for a day in the sound studio, and the many animal sounds were either actual or human imitated, recorded at various speeds, then played backwards. Wray always discounted the many horror and adventure films she made in favor of her earlier work for serious directors, but her role here remains her best known. Although she was a natural brunette and usually appeared so, her wig in this film gave her a blonde image for the rest of her career. At the same time she filmed *King Kong*, she was hopping between sound stages and making wardrobe changes to star in two other highly rated films, *Doctor X* and *The Most Dangerous Game*; the latter used some of the same jungle sets as *King Kong*. The set of the Skull Island ruins was a remnant from Cecil B. DeMille's *The King of Kings* (1927), reused for *She* (1935). This set went up in a blaze of glory as part of burning Atlanta in *Gone With the Wind*. Orville Goldner and George E. Turner's book *The Making of King Kong* (1975) details aspects of the entire production. *Son of Kong* (1933) was the only direct sequel among many inferior rip-offs in the following decades. A 1976 remake of *King Kong* was itself followed by *King Kong Lives* (1986).

KING SOLOMON'S MINES. 1950. Filmed winter 1949–50; Kenya: Machakos; Lake Naivasha; Meru; Isiolo. Murchison (Kabalega) Falls, Uganda. Kigali, Rwanda. Elstree Studios (interiors), Borehamwood, England. Death Valley, California.

Cast: Stewart Granger, Deborah Kerr, Richard Carlson, Hugo Haas, Lowell Gilmore.

Directors: Compton Bennett, Andrew Marton.

This remake of the 1938 English production was filmed in some of the same locales as *The African Queen.* It also encountered some similar production problems. While the leading players stayed relatively healthy, jungle dysentery so ravaged the company that even the cast had to pitch in for manual labor on occasion. The variety of location scenes amounted to a travel tour of East Africa, with the production spanning several countries and tribal cultures. At one point, five hundred Masai tribesmen who were performing traditional war rituals for the camera got so fired up that they began hurling spears in earnest, seven of which lodged in a camera case. Other excitable peoples included the Meru, who chased Stewart Granger, Deborah Kerr, and Richard Carlson in one sequence that became altogether too realistic for the likes of screen artists. Giant, dignified Watusi villagers in Burundi, by contrast, remained aloof from the visitors. The costars' love scene atop Murchison Falls occurred in blinding sunlight, the heat increased by giant Technicolor reflectors, while dysentery-afflicted technicians groaned on the sidelines. Granger, performing his first starring role in an American film, had little use for British codirector Compton Bennett, especially after Bennett told him that Errol Flynn had been first choice for the male lead. For Granger and Kerr, however, the filming provided a pleasant reunion after a brief but mutually intense love affair in 1944. Both were now married to others; Kerr's husband was exceedingly present in the mostly male company. In the scene where Granger grabs the cobra behind its head, we see a leading man about to faint. (To encourage its threatening behavior, the snake had not been devenomed, but Granger had been assured that its mouth was safely taped. After the take, however, he learned that the tape had come off, whereupon he grew very giddy.) Excess jungle footage from this film appeared in *Watusi* (1959), *Tarzan, the Ape Man* (1959), and *Trader Horn* (1973), among others. Critics excoriated the 1985 remake of this film.

KING'S ROW. 1941. Filmed August–October 1941; Warner Bros. Studios, Burbank.

Cast: Robert Cummings, Ann Sheridan, Ronald Reagan, Claude Rains, Betty Field, Charles Coburn, Judith Anderson, Maria Ouspenskaya.

Director: Sam Wood.

This is the film that Ronald Reagan always cited as his best, a line from which he used to title his autobiography (*Where's the Rest of Me?*, 1965). Certainly the role of playboy Drake McHugh, who awakes to find his legs amputated, was the most challenging of his screen career, and this melodrama made him a major star. In his book he described his intense anxiety at playing the key scene of grisly discovery, believing he had neither the experience nor talent to simply act it. Before the actual take, he spent a terror-stricken hour in the bed where he "wakes," his legs stiffly supported by a box below the mattress in which leg-holes had been cut. In genuine panic at the crucial moment of discovery, he screamed "Randy!"—whereupon Ann Sheridan (playing Randy) burst through the door to respond even though she wasn't in the scene. Sam Wood filmed the scene in one take with no prior rehearsal. Bette Davis had badly wanted the role of Cassandra, but the studio rejected both her and Olivia de Havilland; Ida Lupino, the actress Warner Bros. *did* want, turned down the part, and it finally went to Betty Field. The studio had also preferred Tyrone Power over Robert Cummings (who was concurrently filming *It Started with Eve*), and Reagan was seventh choice for his role. Hollywood censor Joseph J. Breen, whose office gutted the screenplay based on Henry Bellamann's best-selling novel, called the entire sanitized effort a "definite disservice" to the motion picture industry, one likely to bring down "the condemnation of decent people everywhere." Instead it won three Academy Award nominations.

KISS OF THE SPIDER WOMAN. 1985. Filmed October 1983–February 1984; São Paulo, Brazil.
Cast: William Hurt, Raul Julia, Sonia Braga, José Lewgoy.
Director: Hector Babenco.

Brazilian director Hector Babenco's first English-language film was so precariously financed that all the actors deferred their salaries and worked for expenses only. Burt Lancaster had been cast as Molina (ultimately played by William Hurt), but heart surgery forced his withdrawal. Babenco thought that Hurt, who had actively pursued the role, was too handsome and well-built for the part as written; but then he changed his concept of the character. Raul Julia had also sought the same role but settled for the part of the revolutionary, Valentin. At one point during rehearsals, the two switched roles as an exercise, and Hurt was shocked to discover that Julia's Molina seemed better than his own; a thorough professional, Hurt proposed that they exchange roles, but Babenco nixed the change. While Hurt explored the homosexual dives of São Paulo in researching his part, Julia studied books by South American revolutionaries and talked with former political prisoners. "There are no fat revolutionaries," Julia concluded and thereupon dieted off thirty pounds. The film became a surprising commercial success, and Hurt won the Academy and Cannes awards for best actor.

KITTY FOYLE. 1940. Filmed summer 1940; RKO Studios, Los Angeles.
Cast: Ginger Rogers, Dennis Morgan, James Craig, Eduardo Ciannelli, Gladys Cooper, Ernest Cossart.
Director: Sam Wood.

The screenplay diluted Christopher Morley's feminist novel into conventional Hollywood sweet-and-sour; but Ginger Rogers, playing the title role with darkened hair in her fortieth movie, won an Academy Award as best actress. Her straight dramatic role was a career gamble after years of phenomenal success as Fred Astaire's dancing partner, and she was reluctant at first to tackle it. But the film represented her long-sought goal to act as well as dance, and her subsequent career continued to reflect her versatility. British actress Gladys Cooper, eager for a film job after a long hiatus, was cast as the mother-in-law after director Wood saw her perform in Noel Coward's *The Astonished Heart* on stage. She found the studios and her own tiny dressing room at RKO uncomfortable, but she was too grateful for the work to complain.

KNIFE IN THE WATER. 1962. Filmed summer 1962; Poland: Mazurian lakes; Kamera Studios, Warsaw.
Cast: Leon Niemczyk, Jolanta Umecka, Zygmunt Malanowicz.
Director: Roman Polanski.

In his first feature film, Roman Polanski used mainly nonprofessional actors—only Leon Niemczyk was experienced—and regretted it. He discovered Jolanta Umecka, who played the wife, at a Warsaw swimming pool; but he became intensely exasperated with her when he found her unable to remember her dialogue and scripted actions. Her lackadaisical attitude tested his patience repeatedly. After many takes of the scene where she was supposed to be startled to see Zygmunt Malanowicz reappear, Polanski finally fired a flare pistol behind her to get her to react. But some observers reported that Polanski's behavior was sadistic, that he had an affair with Umecka, then cruelly shared the intimate details with his cronies. In any case, Umecka's anxiety apparently gave her a ravenous appetite for sweets, and her consequent increase in weight further antagonized the director. Polanski badly wanted to play Malanowicz's role of the hitchhiker himself, but the producers objected. He did, however, dub the actor's voice with his own (Umecka's voice was also postdubbed by another actress). The Polish government banned *Knife in the Water*. One result of that action was to bring recognition to Polanski as a brilliant, innovative director from the international film community.

KRAMER VS. KRAMER. 1979. Filmed June–December 1978; New York City: exteriors and Camera Mart's Stage 54.

Cast: Dustin Hoffman, Meryl Streep, Justin Henry, Jane Alexander, JoBeth Williams, Howard Duff.

Director: Robert Benton.

Enormous personal problems of quite conventional people became hugely popular in films of the Seventies and Eighties. This one put a high, slick sheen on an old reliable soap opera formula, artfully slanted to address problems (i.e., child custody battles) unique to this generation. Dustin Hoffman's contract gave him control over every phase of production, including scripting, casting, and editing. Meryl Streep had originally auditioned for the part of Phyllis (played by JoBeth Williams) because the studio had wanted Kate Jackson for Joanna, the costarring role that finally went to Streep. The costars battled over some of Streep's dialogue, notably in the restaurant scene where she tells Hoffman that she will seek custody of their son. Streep wanted to rewrite her lines while Hoffman, convinced and enraged that she was trying to upstage him, resisted. She also rewrote her own dialogue for her courtroom scene. Seven-year-old Justin Henry related well to both stars, and Hoffman lavished praise on him for his intelligence and ability. Before each scene, Hoffman would discuss it with him so that Henry understood what it was about; then, instead of memorizing dialogue, Henry would use his own words. For his big crying scene, the young actor thought of his dog dying, and only one take was required. Academy Awards went for best picture, to Hoffman as best actor, to Streep as best supporting actress, and to Robert Benton for direction and screenplay.

L

THE LADY FROM SHANGHAI. 1948. Filmed October 1946–February 1947; Acapulco, Mexico. California: Sausalito; Chinatown, San Francisco; Century Ranch, Malibu.

Cast: Orson Welles, Rita Hayworth, Everett Sloane, Glenn Anders.

Director: Orson Welles.

No character from Shanghai, lady or gentleman, ever appears in this film. Orson Welles began with only a title, dreamed up on a spur of the moment to coax money from Columbia's Harry Cohn, then proceeded to build a screenplay that had little to do with the title. Ida Lupino was originally intended for the female lead, but Welles preferred Rita Hayworth, his wife at the time; though separated, the couple amicably reunited for the duration of filming. Columbia publicity staged a glitzy photo session before production began, showing Hayworth being shorn of her famed russet tresses for the film, in which she appeared blonde and short-haired. Welles hated shooting the type of close-ups that studios demanded in any movie featuring top stars; but since Hayworth had been loaned by 20th Century-Fox under those stipulations, he was forced to comply. Storms during the hurricane season, insects, and torrid heat plagued the production in Acapulco. The yacht *Circe* on which many scenes were filmed was actually the *Zaca*, owned and loaned by Errol Flynn, who constantly hovered on the set to watch over his boat (he even briefly appeared in one scene outside a cantina). Welles's financial problems resulted in his losing control of the film's subsequent production details. The studio cut and rearranged entire sequences. Welles angrily declared the final musical scoring more suitable for a Disney cartoon than a serious thriller. Despite powerful scenes that remained in the finished version (notably the final shootout filmed in the San Francisco Fun House hall of mirrors), Welles considered his movie ruined by studio interference. Glenn Anders, here playing a villainous lawyer, parodied later New York governor and U.S. vice president Nelson Rockefeller, an old Welles enemy, by addressing everybody as "fella." And Hayworth, who celebrated her twenty-eighth birthday in Acapulco and divorced Welles later in 1947, played the only death scene of her career.

THE LADY VANISHES. 1938. Filmed October–December 1937; Islington Studios, London.

Cast: Margaret Lockwood, Paul Lukas, Michael Redgrave, May Whitty.

Director: Alfred Hitchcock.

Hitchcock's most famous English thriller was originally slated for another director; this is probably the only film he made that was not written either by or for him. Michael Redgrave, in his first starring screen appearance, only reluctantly accepted the role of Gilbert. Performing nightly in the London theatre throughout the filming, he shared the common disdain of English stage actors for movies. His insistence on careful rehearsals annoyed Hitchcock, and he found the whole project boring—until veteran actor Paul Lukas reminded him one day that this performance, unlike his stage acting, was "all going in the can" for posterity. From that moment Redgrave started to give it his best. Watching the film for the first time fifteen years later, he said he immediately detected the moment when his attitude changed. Dame May Whitty, whom Hitchcock thought too sedate as Miss Foy, received a rude jolt in her first scene when the director shouted, "Stop! That's terrible." Shocked out of her serenity, she then proceeded to give him the performance he wanted. Basil Radford and Naunton Wayne, playing the oblivious Charters and Caldicott on the train, established their long-term partnership in this film and went on to make many cozy English comedies. Hitchcock's own cameo appearance comes as a man waiting at a London railroad station. The entire production was filmed on one sound stage, using a single railroad coach; rear projection and miniatures accounted for all the apparent location scenes.

THE LADYKILLERS. 1955. Filmed summer 1955; Ealing Studios, London.

Cast: Alec Guinness, Peter Sellers, Katie Johnson, Cecil Parker, Frankie Howerd, Herbert Lom.

Director: Alexander Mackendrick.

Alec Guinness never trusted movie property men who assured him that certain hazardous sequences were perfectly safe. In one scene, on the edge of a sixty-foot-high wall, the wooden rail he was holding snapped, and he fell—not down, fortunately, but backward. This black farce, a prototypical Ealing comedy, was Peter Sellers's first notable film. It also marked the true beginning of his varied acting career. Primarily a zany radio comic up to this time, he worshiped Guinness and resolved to emulate him in becoming a versatile character actor. He later also imitated his hero by playing multiple roles in several films (e.g., *The Mouse that Roared* and *Dr. Strangelove*). Sellers and Herbert Lom teamed again later in the Pink Panther series.

THE LAST DETAIL. 1973. Filmed winter 1972–73; Toronto. Washington, D.C. New York City. Burbank Studios, Burbank.

Cast: Jack Nicholson, Randy Quaid, Otis Young, Michael Moriarty, Carol Kane.

Director: Hal Ashby.

Imagine! A film about sailors who booze, whore, and talk dirty. The dialogue, loaded with profanity and thus quite realistic in a service comedy, nevertheless made U. S. Navy officialdom blanch with horror and refuse all cooperation. Hal Ashby had wanted Rupert Crosse for the part of Mulhall (played by Otis Young in his first starring role), but Crosse's terminal illness prevented his casting. "It isn't exactly a recruiting film," laconically observed Jack Nicholson, who relished playing naval petty officer "Bad Ass" Buddusky. That partially explained, no doubt, why Chief Justice Warren Burger personally banned the company from shooting a drunk scene on the steps of the Supreme Court building in Washington.

THE LAST EMPEROR. 1987. Filmed summer–autumn 1986; Manchuria. China: Tientsin; Imperial Palace and Beijing Film Studios, Beijing. Rome.

Cast: John Lone, Joan Chen, Peter O'Toole, Ying Ruocheng, Victor Wong, Dennis Dun, Ryuichi Sakamoto.
Director: Bernardo Bertolucci.

Giving an Academy Award to an Italian Communist director would have been unthinkable in the Hollywood that Ronald Reagan knew—but eight other Oscars, including the one for best picture, also went to Bertolucci's colorful epic about Pu Yi, China's last emperor. Four actors played the emperor at different ages, including three-year-old Richard Wu from New York City and American actor John Lone as the adult Pu Yi. Joan Chen, as the empress, was China's most popular film actress. She had little sympathy for the real Pu Yi, calling him "cold-blooded." Ying Ruocheng, China's vice minister of culture and a veteran actor, played the prison governor. After the picture's release, he underwent close questioning and criticism from the government about Bertolucci's apparent violation of a historical preservation law: Bertolucci had filmed inside Beijing's Imperial Palace, where Chinese emperors had reigned for some five hundred years. The dark, ornate interiors were filmed with natural lighting to protect the ancient paint. This was the first Western production allowed inside the walls of China's Forbidden City. The director also aroused the antagonism of gay activists by ignoring the well-established fact of Pu Yi's homosexuality. Employing some 19,000 extras (including two thousand soldiers of the People's Liberation Army) who wore fake pigtails and authentic costumes made in Italy, China, and London, Berlotucci filmed mostly in sequence, using a studio in Rome for prison interiors. This wasn't the film that the director had originally wanted to make in China, but authorities had refused him permission to film André Malraux's *Man's Fate*.

LAST TANGO IN PARIS. 1972. Filmed January–March 1972; Paris.
Cast: Marlon Brando, Maria Schneider, Massimo Girotti, Jean-Pierre Léaud, Catherine Allegret.
Director: Bernardo Bertolucci.

According to Bernardo Bertolucci, Marlon Brando revealed more of himself emotionally in *Last Tango* than in any film of his career—most notably in the soliloquy to Maria Schneider about his childhood and past. Brando almost entirely ad-libbed this scene, which was filmed in one take. Neither of the costars had been Bertolucci's first choices—he had sought Jean-Louis Trintignant for the male lead and Dominique Sanda, then Catherine Deneuve for the part that went to nineteen-year-old German actress Schneider in her first major screen appearance. The graphic sex scenes between the costars attracted most attention, of course; never before had an actor of Brando's stature simulated sexual intercourse on film. For her partner, who displayed a gallantly paternal attitude offscreen, Schneider said she felt no sexual attraction. Brando wore no makeup and either couldn't or wouldn't memorize dialogue, reading instead from cue cards and notes hidden in props on the set. Bertolucci believed this procedure was a deliberate technique Brando used to increase his sense of risk and spontaneity. In what the Italian director labeled a "drastic act," Italy banned the film as obscene. *Last Tango*'s significance lay in its joining of two hitherto exclusive film genres—starry-eyed romance and outright pornography (or love and lust), showing their complex interdependence.

THE LAST TEMPTATION OF CHRIST. 1988. Filmed autumn–winter 1987–88; Morocco.

Cast: Willem Dafoe, Harvey Keitel, Barbara Hershey, Harry Dean Stanton, David Bowie.

Director: Martin Scorsese.

Its unorthodox version of the life and death of Jesus enraged conservative Christian believers, whose righteous anger publicized the movie far more effectively than any studio effort could have (though some wags suggested that Martin Scorsese had hired Fundamentalist imposters for the purpose). The film was a long time coming. Barbara Hershey, who played Mary Magdalene, had given Scorsese a copy of the Nikos Kazantzakis novel in 1972. A decade later, Scorsese was ready to begin filming, but Paramount Studios backed out of the agreement in 1983 after being pressured by evangelicals, just weeks before filming was to start. (Aidan Quinn had been cast as Jesus in that aborted effort.) The new start in 1987 resulted chiefly from screenwriter Paul Schrader's threat to direct the film himself if Scorsese didn't get moving. Scorsese said he didn't want to make a standard religious picture "where a bunch of wonderful English actors read beautiful words." Instead, for most of the major roles, he cast Americans who spoke a variety of U.S. dialects—while Satan and the Romans spoke BBC English, an option similar to William Wyler's in *Ben-Hur*. One rock star, Sting, was replaced by another, David Bowie, in the role of Pontius Pilate. The budget for *Last Temptation* was pinchpenny, with the entire cast working for union scale. For Willem Dafoe, who played Jesus, the crucifixion sequence was especially demanding physically; he could only be suspended on the cross for about a minute at a time before starting to asphyxiate, and the entire sequence required three days to film. Citing the faded careers of actors who had previously played Jesus, Dafoe's friends warned him that he was gambling his future, but he eagerly took the risk. Later, as everyone involved with making the picture strenuously fended off the organized attacks (mainly from people who had never viewed it), many objective critics finally declared the film a profoundly religious work and Scorsese's masterpiece.

LAURA. 1944. Filmed April–July 1944; 20th Century-Fox Studios, Los Angeles.

Cast: Dana Andrews, Gene Tierney, Clifton Webb, Vincent Price, Judith Anderson.

Directors: Rouben Mamoulian, Otto Preminger.

Originally intended as a B-picture, this troubled effort shifted to A status overnight when studio chief Darryl F. Zanuck took over as its producer. Zanuck disliked Otto Preminger and kept him from the plum directing job as long as he could; but circumstances finally forced him to depose Rouben Mamoulian and assign the volatile Austrian as the only able director available (though Mamoulian always claimed, over Preminger's loud objection, that the final film was mainly his product). Casting was a problem, too. Zanuck wanted Jennifer Jones for the title role, but she declined, as did Hedy Lamarr. Though Gene Tierney accepted the role only reluctantly and felt she gave a lackluster performance, the part became the best-remembered one of her quarter-century film career. Laird Cregar was Zanuck's choice for acerbic Waldo Lydecker, played finally by Clifton Webb, with Preminger's support over Zanuck's stern disapproval. Webb's first major screen role, a part modeled on drama critic Alexander Woollcott, typecast him as waspish characters for the rest of his life. Except for Webb (who suffered a nervous breakdown after filming), Preminger dealt throughout with a hostile cast—especially Judith

Anderson, who resented Mamoulian's replacement. A further thorn was Vera Caspary, author of the novel, who loathed the script and objected to the numerous revisions made in her story. One of the picture's most durable legacies was its theme song "Laura," composed over one weekend by David Raskin. (Preminger had originally wanted to use Duke Ellington's "Sophisticated Lady.") For all of Preminger's problems in pulling the film together, it hit big at the box office and remains arguably his best work. Moreover, it furthered the careers of everybody involved, including cinematographer Joseph La Shelle, who won an Academy Award.

LAWRENCE OF ARABIA. 1962. Filmed May 1961–October 1962; Saudi Arabia. Jordan: Jebel Tubeiq; Aqaba. Spain: Almería; Sevilla. Ouarzazate, Morocco. Hammersmith Studios. London.

Cast: Peter O'Toole, Alec Guinness, Anthony Quinn, Jack Hawkins, José Ferrer, Anthony Quayle, Claude Rains, Arthur Kennedy, Omar Sharif.

Director: David Lean.

You haven't really seen this film unless you've seen it projected in a full-scale cinema. Few pictures suffer more from the cropping ratio imposed by the TV screen; on video, you're only viewing about thirty percent of the Super Panavision frame that director Lean intended you to see. Peter O'Toole won the title role over Marlon Brando, Albert Finney, Anthony Perkins, and Sir Alec Guinness. Former British foreign minister Anthony Nutting helped O'Toole research the enigmatic T. E. Lawrence. With his hair dyed blond (and an operation that amended his nose), O'Toole, who stood almost a foot taller than Lawrence, also had to surmount his own image as a wild Irish pub brawler to convince Lean that he could stay the course. He very nearly didn't. Lean pushed him to the limits of his physical endurance; O'Toole's long list of injuries included two concussions and assorted sprains, bruises, burns, and torn ligaments. Camels bit him and threw him, but he finally mastered how to ride the animal by adding a layer of sponge rubber under the saddle blanket to ease his battered backside—an innovation that the Bedouin tribesmen on the desert location eagerly adopted. In England during the last scene filmed (but the opening scene in the movie), O'Toole almost repeated Lawrence's fatal motorcycle accident when a towing bar from the camera car snapped and sent the trailer-mounted cycle careening toward a ditch. But it was the ever-present desert sun that affected the actor most; he vowed never to subject himself to it again. When filming was finally finished, he retired to a London hospital to relax. He said he never watched the entire picture until two decades later, then found himself highly impressed. The film also made Omar Sharif, in his first English-language role, a major star. For Jack Hawkins, the role of General Allenby carried mixed blessings. Allenby's family strongly criticized his performance as a "distorted" version of Allenby's dealings with the Arabs, a criticism that Hawkins admitted had merit. All of the city scenes—Damascus, Cairo, Jerusalem—were filmed on sets in Spain. To play Moslem women, several hundred Egyptian Christians were imported, since no actual Moslem woman could allow her face to be exposed for the camera. Most of the Bedouin extras had never seen a movie screen and couldn't grasp the idea of playacting, so Lean filmed them behaving in their normal fashion. The film won seven Academy Awards—for best picture, Lean as best director, and Frederick A. Young's cinematography, among others.

LENNY. 1974. Filmed January–July 1974; Miami, Florida.
Cast: Dustin Hoffman, Valerie Perrine, Jan Miner, Stanley Beck, Gary Morton.
Director: Bob Fosse.

Before portraying stand-up comedian Lenny Bruce, Dustin Hoffman researched the role thoroughly, listening to Bruce's recordings, watching films (including *The Lenny Bruce Performance Film*, showing the performer in one of his final concerts the year before his 1966 death), and talking to people who knew Bruce intimately. Filming conditions were often uncomfortable. In one hotel room love scene, Hoffman and Valerie Perrine sweltered in 105-degree heat, an unforgettable ordeal for both. While many critics felt that his mimicry of Bruce's mannerisms and his monologue reenactments were uncannily precise, perfectionist Hoffman himself considered the film "a flawed work." Former Las Vegas show girl Perrine was cast as Bruce's wife, Honey, after everybody thought that actress-singer Joey Heatherton was a shoo-in for the part. In the course of the production, Perrine, who brought her background as a stripper to the role, met the real-life Honey Bruce.

She worried for weeks beforehand about her graphic lesbian scene. When the time came to film it, she admitted that she performed with no erotic feelings whatever. Director Bob Fosse used mild shock tactics on her to produce tears—Gary Morton, playing the so-called Mr. Entertainment, patterned his role on Milton Berle. The film was a huge critical and financial success, winning several Academy nominations but no Awards.

LIFEBOAT. 1944. Filmed July–November 1943; 20th Century-Fox Studios, Los Angeles.
Cast: Tallulah Bankhead, John Hodiak, Walter Slezak, Canada Lee, Henry Hull, Mary Anderson, Heather Angel, William Bendix.
Director: Alfred Hitchcock.

Hitchcock sought the technical challenge of filming a story in the smallest confined space possible. The one set consisted of a small boat in a large studio water tank, backed up by rear-projection scenes of Florida seas and skies. The director's close-up camera work anticipated TV studio techniques. The cast, repeatedly drenched by spray from wind machines and from falling into water slicked with crude oil, underwent strenuous weeks of filming this World War II propaganda story, which pitted the Allies against an arrogant Nazi in the microcosmic world of the boat. Hitchcock cast Tallulah Bankhead in what was probably her best screen role because he wanted to use "the most oblique, incongruous" character imaginable in such a situation. She learned her German lines phonetically. Constantly soaked, at one point she caused a studio furor by discarding her underclothing on the set; even the redoubtable Hitchcock backed away from confronting her on that, deferring the problem to the makeup department. Bankhead also suffered two bouts of pneumonia that left her weak and wobbly during the final third of the picture. She seemed to believe (or pretended she did) that Austrian actor Walter Slezak, who played the Nazi, really was a Nazi. Though the bewildered character actor, actually a fervent anti-Nazi, protested that he was only playing a part, her behavior toward him became verbally and physically abusive. Hitchcock made his typical cameo appearance as before-and-after profile views in a newspaper ad for reducing pills; the timing was right, since the portly director had just dropped a hundred pounds on one of his periodic crash diets. He deeply offended author John Steinbeck, who wrote the original story, by changing some of its elements. Steinbeck protested what he felt were slurs against organized labor and the use of a "stock comedy Negro" (Canada Lee). He requested that his name be removed from the credits. (It wasn't.) Several prominent critics also objected to Hitchcock's treatment of the Nazi as a three-dimensional character; revealing the lifeboat occupants' common humanity, they felt, wasn't a good propaganda tactic during wartime.

LILIES OF THE FIELD. 1963. Filmed November–December 1962; Tucson, Arizona.
Cast: Sidney Poitier, Lilia Skala, Lisa Mann, Isa Crino, Stanley Adams.
Director: Ralph Nelson.

Ralph Nelson put up his own house as collateral in order to finance this production, made on a pinchpenny budget at an abandoned farm near Tucson. All of the five professional actors took union scale and deferred percentages for salary, and Nelson hired local Mexican construction workers as extras. He filmed the picture in a record fourteen days. Having done so, he was stumped for a commercially acceptable title. Among the suggestions he turned down: *Piety in the Sky, The Amen Man*, and *The Mischief Maker*. His Italian distributor, wanting to be helpful, chimed in with *Mother of Mine, I've Run Out of Bricks*. This was Viennese stage actress Lilia Skala's screen debut. Sidney Poitier won an Academy Award as best actor, the first ever given to a black male. Believing that this film "did more for integration than the Washington March," he accepted his Oscar with the heartfelt words: "It's been a long journey to this moment."

LIMELIGHT. 1952. Filmed November 1951–January 1952; London (background exteriors). California: Universal-International Studios, Universal City; Charles Chaplin Studios and Paramount Studios, Los Angeles.
Cast: Charles Chaplin, Claire Bloom, Buster Keaton, Sydney Chaplin, Nigel Bruce, Norman Lloyd.
Director: Charles Chaplin.

Some of the same people who welcomed an elderly Charlie

Chaplin back to Hollywood in 1971 to receive a belated Academy Award for his contributions to their industry had given him the cold shoulder during the McCarthy witch-hunt period when he made *Limelight*. During that time, only worshipful talents such as Claire Bloom and Buster Keaton had remained grateful for the chance to work with him. Chaplin began scripting this film, originally titled *Footlights*, in 1948. He employed many of his own large family in bit parts: his eldest sons Sydney (as the composer Neville) and Charles, Jr. (as a clown); his younger children Geraldine (in her screen debut), Michael, and Josephine as street urchins: and his half brother Wheeler Dryden as a doctor. Chaplin's method of direction was to act out each nuance of each role for his performers to imitate exactly—thus his casts became extensions of himself in a way that few other directors would desire or attempt. One exception, to whom Chaplin gave free rein was fifty-seven-year-old Keaton. Thanks to TV exposure, Keaton was just emerging at this time from years of obscurity. So great was his admiration for Chaplin that he said he would have worked in this picture for nothing; but off-camera, he typically kept to himself. A delighted guest on the set who observed the two old masters performing together was film critic James Agee, who heralded an appreciative rediscovery of their talents. For twenty-year-old Bloom, whom Chaplin brought from England, her costarring role meant overnight stardom. She recalled Chaplin's frequent monologues on and off the set about the London of his poverty-scarred boyhood, a painfully nostalgic subject for him. Rehearsing the scene in which she discovers that she can walk again—one she dreaded because of her inability to weep on cue—Chaplin exploded in fury, completely shattering her; he then steered her, still weeping, to the set where his forewarned camera crew filmed the scene in one take (an unusual instance because Chaplin seldom filmed *anything* in one take). Ballerina Melissa Hayden skillfully doubled for Bloom in the ballet scenes. Bloom's favorite scene was the one following the ballet, in which she and Chaplin do a gentle patter and a few dance steps together. Sydney Chaplin, with whom Bloom had a brief romance, wickedly satirized his father's authoritarian style offstage—but confronted with him on the set, he became a very meek, obliging boy. All musical episodes were filmed on the stage at Universal Studios, where Lon Chaney, Sr., had made *The Phantom of the Opera* in 1925. Because of Chaplin's liberal politics, RKO chairman Howard Hughes tried to get *Limelight* banned; Los Angeles exhibitors canceled showings when the American Legion threatened to picket; and FBI chief J. Edgar Hoover, terrified of the Little Tramp, went after him with all the governmental resources he could muster. Banished from the U.S. as an undesirable alien after he had gone to London for the film's premiere, Chaplin met a huge, adoring public in his native country. *Limelight* won an Academy Award for Chaplin's music—in 1972, when the film was first commercially released in Los Angeles.

THE LION IN WINTER. 1968. Filmed January–May 1968; France: Arles; Victorine Studios, Nice. Wales. Ireland: Bray Studios, Dublin; Ardmore Studios, Kilbride.
Cast: Peter O'Toole, Katharine Hepburn, Jane Merrow, John Castle, Timothy Dalton, Anthony Hopkins.
Director: Anthony Harvey.

Nobody like the redoubtable Katharine Hepburn had ever hit Peter O'Toole, quite a free-swinging spirit himself. She literally did hit him at times, pummeling him in not-always-mock exasperation. They each said terrible things to and about each other, unsuccessfully masking the deep affection that grew between them on the set. He likened her to "a bloody poultice" that "pulls a performance out of you" and respected not a bit the twenty-three-year age difference between them. After sufficiently savage bluster, he usually meekly complied with his costar's slightest whim. For Hepburn, making this picture was much-needed therapy, her first work after the 1967 death of her longtime companion, Spencer Tracy. O'Toole was reacquainting himself with Henry II, the monarch he had first embodied in *Becket* (1964), an older, wiser king whom the actor consciously played as a continuous role from the earlier film. In the scene where Henry meets the queen's barge, O'Toole badly pinched a finger that he somehow wedged between the boats. Production halted for several days when Anthony Hopkins, playing Richard Lion-Heart, fell off his horse and injured himself. Hepburn took her third Academy Award as best actress, while James Goldman's screenplay, John Barry's musical score, and the art direction also received Oscars.

LITTLE BIG MAN. 1970. Filmed June 1969–February 1970; Montana: Crow Reservation, Billings; Lame Deer; Custer Battlefield National Monument. Calgary, Alberta. Cinema Center Studios, Los Angeles.

Cast: Dustin Hoffman, Faye Dunaway, Martin Balsam, Richard Mulligan, Chief Dan George, Jeff Corey.

Director: Arthur Penn.

Crow extras dressed as Cheyenne tribespeople for this epic —in which the only nonauthentic Indian was Dustin Hoffman himself, playing 121-year-old survivor Jack Crabb. A fourteen-piece mask that took five hours to apply—including contact-lens cataracts—gave Hoffman his wizened features. To achieve his old man's gravelly voice, he practiced long and hard but finally resorted to screaming himself hoarse before going in front of the camera. Bareback horse riding gave him the most trouble; his short legs made it difficult for him to hold on, and he spent many nights bathing in epsom salts baths to ease the resulting soreness. Once he shot himself while learning to draw rapidly from his holster, inflicting powder burns from the blank cartridge. The main ordeal for cast and crew, however, was the bitter weather. Filming Custer's Oklahoma massacre sequence in frigid cold near Calgary —a sequence that has been called one of the most grueling in motion picture location work—the company endured a wind-chill of sixty below. Camera equipment froze up and had to be thawed repeatedly. Dan George, seventy-one-year-old veteran showman and honorary chief of the Squamish tribe in Canada, seemed to survive it best; as Old Lodgeskins, he wore thermal underwear beneath his deerskin clothing and was not heard to complain. The key role that brought him fame in old age as a character actor had earlier been offered to Sir Laurence Olivier, Paul Scofield, and Richard Boone. Hoffman became fond of the tough old chief, habitually calling him Grandfather. In contrast to the high-priced talent around him, George cleared only $9,000 after taxes for his work in the film. Despite Native American criticism of George's refusal to endorse the militant strategy of the American Indian Movement, this film was one of the first to treat Indians as humans and to reflect accuracy about some unsavory events in U.S. history.

LITTLE CAESAR. 1930. Filmed July–August 1930; Warner Bros. Studios, Burbank.

Cast: Edward G. Robinson, Douglas Fairbanks, Jr., Glenda Farrell, Sidney Blackmer, George E. Stone.

Director: Mervyn LeRoy.

This hugely successful film not only launched an entire genre of gangster epics but also marked the turning point in the careers of both Edward G. Robinson and director Mervyn LeRoy. Originally scheduled for the role of Otero that finally went to George E. Stone, Robinson convinced studio brass to let him play the gangster Rico, a character modeled on Al Capone. The close-up scene in an alley where Robinson fires his revolver required many retakes because he always flinched; LeRoy wanted him "cold and unblinking." The director even taped Robinson's eyelids open, giving him a reptilian stare. LeRoy had wanted Clark Gable for the role of Joe Massara that finally went to Douglas Fairbanks, Jr. Sidney Blackmer's role of Mr. Big was based on Chicago's corrupt mayor, Big Bill Thompson. Those church steps on which William Collier (playing Tony Passa) dies were the same ones on which James Cagney would expire in *The Roaring Twenties* (1939). Some of the extras used in the film, LeRoy came to believe, were real Chicago mobsters sent to spy on the proceedings. Because of the screenplay's subject matter, which seemed to prey on everybody's mood and temperament, LeRoy used tomfoolery and practical jokes on the set to keep things relaxed. One of his favorite ploys was to nail Robinson's ever-present cigar to wooden props on the set and wait for the actor's doubletake when he tried to pick it up.

LIVES OF A BENGAL LANCER. 1935. Filmed summer–autumn 1934; California: Lone Pine; Alabama Hills, Independence; Paramount Ranch and Studios, Los Angeles.

Cast: Gary Cooper, Franchot Tone, Richard Cromwell, Guy Standing, C. Aubrey Smith, Monte Blue.

Director: Henry Hathaway.

Using 1931 background footage filmed in India's Khyber Pass, this picture became Henry Hathaway's first important feature, establishing his reputation. Action scenes were filmed in some of the same locations later used in *Gunga Din* (1939); scenarists also salvaged some of Cecil B. De Mille's leftover sets from *The Crusades* (1935). Hathaway insisted on using authentic uniforms for his British colonials, and his extras included a hundred American Piute Indians as well as Hindu migrant workers from the Napa Valley and ranchers from Inyo

County. Toying with his image by wearing a mustache was Gary Cooper's own idea, a phase in his working life when he apparently wanted to look like Clark Gable; he never repeated the experiment. In its blend of adventure-comedy-drama, however, *Lives* became a peak in the range of his long film career.

LOLITA. 1962. Filmed winter 1962; Elstree Studios, Borehamwood, England.
Cast: James Mason, Shelley Winters, Peter Sellers, Sue Lyon.
Director: Stanley Kubrick.

Even if remade as a film today, Vladimir Nabokov's novel would probably evoke widespread controversy in its treatment of an older man lusting after a teenage nymphet. In order to clear the censors, Stanley Kubrick unwillingly gutted most of Nabokov's outright eroticism, choosing instead to focus on visual metaphors and *doubles entendres* to convey the book's spirit of perverse comedy—but the film still evoked a poor critical reception. Cary Grant indignantly turned down the role that went to James Mason. Sue Lyon, playing the title role in her screen debut (a part first offered to Hayley Mills), was thirteen when filming began. Nabokov thought her too old for the part. Though he generally admired Kubrick's adaptation, he regretted his own waste of time in penning a screenplay that the director radically altered during filming. Kubrick encouraged improvisation on the set, giving Peter Sellers, especially, a free hand to create the character of the shadowy Clare Quilty. As Charlotte, Lolita's sex-starved mother, Shelley Winters gave one of her best screen performances.

LONG DAY'S JOURNEY INTO NIGHT. 1962. Filmed autumn 1961; New York City: City Island, Bronx (exteriors); Production Center Studios, Manhattan.
Cast: Katharine Hepburn, Ralph Richardson, Jason Robards, Jr., Dean Stockwell, Jeanne Barr.
Director: Sidney Lumet.

Lacking her usual boundless self-confidence Katharine Hepburn approached her role of drug-addicted Mary Tyrone with qualms, terrified that she couldn't play a part so unlike her own buoyant nature. But her performance in this adaptation of Eugene O'Neill's autobiographical stage masterpiece was electrifying. Both Hepburn and producer Ely Landau wanted Spencer Tracy for the role of James Tyrone, but Tracy wasn't up to it physically, so Sir Ralph Richardson was chosen. (The British stage actor found O'Neill's speech cadences difficult.) Hepburn later confided that if Tracy had played the role, he would have "pierced the sky" and that her own performance, consequently, would not have seemed so "towering." Young Dean Stockwell, playing Edmund Tyrone, was drinking heavily at the time, and he received Hepburn's solicitous concern on the set; on the first day, when the weather turned cold, she went out and bought him a coat. Sidney Lumet filmed chronologically, first the exterior scenes, then the interiors. All four leading actors received a joint award at the Cannes Film Festival.

THE LONGEST DAY. 1963. Filmed August 1961–March 1962; France: Ste-Mère L'Église; Caen area; Pte. du Hoc; Île de Rey; Boulogne Studios, Paris.

Cast: John Wayne, Robert Mitchum, Henry Fonda, Robert Ryan, Rod Steiger, Robert Wagner.

Directors: Andrew Marton, Ken Annakin, Bernhard Wicki, and (uncredited) Darryl F. Zanuck.

Aside from the box office gimmick of using many familiar Hollywood faces to decorate his D-Day epic, producer Darryl F. Zanuck took pains to make this chronicle accurate. Invasion scenes were reenacted on the same Normandy coasts where they occurred on June 6, 1944 (with the historical markers and monuments hidden by sandbags). Separate directors guided American, British, and German sequences, with cinemogul Zanuck himself as supreme commander of this multifaceted epic. Zanuck even insisted that principal photography occur in the same kind of weather conditions as the real D-Day. He found old Spitfire fighter planes in Belgium and Messerschmitts in Spain; and he had new gliders built in England. Some 23,000 U.S., British, and French troops were donated by their governments for "training exercises" (French extras played the German soldiers); and paratroopers made twenty-one night jumps at Ste-Mère l'Église for filming. At Pte. du Hoc, scene of a bloody Ranger assault in 1944, six hundred live land mines from that battle had to be cleared from the beach before filming could begin. Studio technicians burned off beach vegetation with flamethrowers, and rubber tires burning in smokepots helped simulate battle atmospheres. Because the actual Omaha Beach had changed so much, Zanuck used Île de Rey beaches near La Rochelle for this location sequence. Most of the name cast worked for only the few days' time required for their own scenes. Richard Burton, playing an RAF pilot, changed from a Roman toga, coming fresh from the beleaguered set of *Cleopatra* for his stint. John Wayne, nursing an old grudge against Zanuck, held out for $250,000 for his four days as Lt. Col. Vandervoort (a role first slated for William Holden). Robert Mitchum, who had to keep up with trained GIs in his action scenes, evoked a furor when a reporter quoted derogatory remarks he supposedly made about some of them being afraid to board a landing craft in rough seas (he strenuously denied the story). This production was so expensive ($10 million) at a time when 20th Century-Fox was also throwing millions into *Cleopatra* that studio executives wanted to scuttle it. One man rescued it: studio board member and retired Korean War general James A. Van Fleet, who spoke emotionally in support of Zanuck's project, thereby saving the film from almost certain abandonment before it was finished.

THE LOST WEEKEND. 1945. Filmed October–December 1944: New York City. Paramount Studios, Los Angeles.
Cast: Ray Milland, Jane Wyman, Philip Terry, Howard Da Silva, Doris Dowling, Frank Faylen.
Director: Billy Wilder.

In their mutual opposition to the making of this film, the liquor industry and Prohibition groups found themselves aligned on the same side for once. A lacerating story of a three-day bender, it was one of Hollywood's first social problem films and the first authentic screen treatment of alcoholism. Paramount bigwigs also fought making the picture; only contractual obligations forced the studio to permit Billy Wilder to proceed. After he completed the film, Paramount then stalled its release for a year while mulling a $5-million offer from distillery interests (made through mobster Frank Costello) for prints and negative. Later, making the best of the situation, the liquor industry praised the film as a boon to producers of *better* brands of whiskey, while Prohibitionists lauded the picture as a useful lesson on the evils of drink. Ray Milland, breaking with his romantic-lead image against the advice of friends who told him he was committing professional suicide, gave the best performance of his career. At the beginning, he lacked confidence in both himself and the director. (Wilder had courted José Ferrer for the lead role, accepting Milland only by order from higher-ups.) Milland, who dropped eight pounds to begin filming the horrifying last scenes first, launched himself and the picture in Bellevue Hospital's alcoholic ward. Wilder had wangled permission to film there by showing the hospital director a bogus script; later, when some of his footage showed male nurses brutalizing patients, hospital officials reacted angrily. One of the film's best-remembered sequences—Milland's long walk up Manhattan's Third Avenue to pawn his typewriter for a drink—was filmed in a single day. Cameras hidden in bakery trucks and empty store windows followed his course for blocks. (One old friend who spotted him lurching seedy and unshaven up the street worriedly contacted Milland's wife back in Hollywood.) After the film's long-delayed release, Milland endured months and years of fallout from his role: countless letters from alcoholics and their families, both praising and cursing him; taunting remarks during social occasions; and even street ridicule. The movie struck plenty of raw nerves. (Milland himself was never more than a light, occasional drinker.) Nat's Bar in the film, a studio set, duplicated P. J. Clarke's tavern on New York's Third Avenue. Four Academy Awards—for best picture, Milland as best actor, Wilder as best director, and the screenplay by Charles Brackett and Wilder—went to this unwanted, almost aborted film. Unfortunately Hollywood wasted Milland (see next entry) and never again gave this fine actor material suiting his talents. Look for: Philip Terry (playing Milland's brother), who was Joan Crawford's husband at the time; Lillian Fontaine, mother of Joan Fontaine and Olivia de Havilland, playing Mrs. St. James; and Loretta Young's arm only, handing Milland his hat as he leaves the bar.

LOVE STORY. 1970. Filmed September 1969–March 1970; Massachusetts: Harvard University campus, Cambridge; Boston. New York: Phipps Estate, Old Westbury, Long Island; Paramount Building, Fordham University, City College of New York, Villa Pauline, Mount Sinai Hospital, and Biograph Studios, New York City. Newport-Balboa beach areas, California.

Cast: Ali MacGraw, Ryan O'Neal, John Marley, Ray Milland, Katherine Balfour.
Director: Arthur Hiller.

Banal and saccharine in the opinion of most critics, *Love Story* became the most popular screen tearjerker of all time. Audiences flocked, either to weep or laugh hysterically. Erich Segal, a sober, professorial type who took much flak for displaying his lucrative trash-writing talents, penned the novel after he wrote the screenplay. Did costarring in this film mean *always* having to say you're sorry? Ryan O'Neal, for one, apparently thought so as he sought subsequent roles to "exonerate" himself from having played Oliver Barrett IV (see *Paper Moon*). Ironically, O'Neal had at first refused the part, as had Beau Bridges, Robert Redford, and Michael York. In preparation for their roles, O'Neal learned to ice-skate and Ali MacGraw—whom the crew dubbed Bucky Beaver for her slightly tilted incisors—took harpsichord lessons. The Phipps Estate locale was the same mansion used by Alfred Hitchcock in *North by Northwest* (it also appears frequently in TV commercials). For the office of the Harvard Law School dean, Arthur Hiller used the long-time Manhattan working quarters of Paramount founder Adolph Zukor; and Harvard Club scenes occurred in the huge former office of producer William Fox at the Deluxe Film laboratories. MacGraw performed her harpsichord concerto in the Villa Pauline, conductor Arturo Toscanini's former home in Riverdale, the Bronx; one of the audience extras in this scene was Julie Garfield, daughter of film star John Garfield. Another brief appearance was that of socialite Charlotte Ford Niarchos, daughter of Henry Ford II; she played the hospital receptionist. Ray Milland, as O'Neal's father, appeared for the first time on screen without the toupee he had worn for decades. Francis Lai's musical score won an Academy Award. See Nicholas Meyer's book *The "Love Story" Story* (1971) for details of the filming. O'Neal, apparently cooled off and eager for lots more abuse, appeared in the sequel, *Oliver's Story* (1978).

M

M. 1931. Filmed winter 1931; Berlin: exteriors and Zeppilinhalle; Nero-Film A.G. Verlag Star Film-G.m.b.H. Studios.

Cast: Peter Lorre, Ellen Widmann, Gustav Grundgens, Inge Landgut.

Director: Fritz Lang.

The tortured mind of a compulsive child-murderer, brilliantly revealed by Peter Lorre in his most notable screen performance, was the subject of Fritz Lang's first sound film. This landmark of German expressionism was also one of the first attempts to explore the criminal psyche sympathetically. Lorre's role, while it brought him international fame, also typecast him as a bizarre or psychopathic character, and he tired of replaying variations on the same part. At the same time he performed for Lang's camera by day, he was acting on the Berlin stage by night. Lang, who based this drama on newspaper reports about one Peter Kurten, spent several days in a Berlin mental hospital observing criminal psychopaths, and he employed many thuggish types as extras in the film; indeed, before he completed the picture, twenty-four of them had been arrested for various felonies and criminal acts. The film's original title, *Murderers Among Us*, led to difficulties at the outset. When Lang sought the use of Berlin's old zeppelin hangar for a makeshift studio, Nazi officials refused him permission, and he began to receive threatening letters. He then discovered that those officials believed the production's title referred to the Nazi party; permission was quickly granted when he explained the title's reference to child molesters. (The Nazis valued Lang's reputation. He despised them, however, and left Germany in 1934. Later they cynically lifted Lorre's confession at the end of this film and used it out of context for the anti-Semitic "documentary," *The Eternal Jew*, 1940.) Lang anticipated voice-dubbing of the film into other languages by avoiding or masking close-up shots of characters talking; except for Lorre's, the dubbed English voices were not those of the original performers, but the director himself did Lorre's whistling. Seymour Nebenzal, the producer, also produced an American remake of *M* in 1951.

THE MAGNIFICENT AMBERSONS. 1942. Filmed October 1941–January 1942; California: Los Angeles; RKO Studios, Culver City.

Cast: Joseph Cotten, Anne Baxter, Tim Holt, Agnes Moorehead, Dolores Costello, Ray Collins, Richard Bennett.

Director: Orson Welles.

"A magnificent ruin," in the words of one critic, is what remains of director Welles's follow-up masterpiece to *Citizen Kane*. Studio fixers, convinced that the original version was unreleasable, not only removed some fifty minutes of Welles's footage, took scenes from context and replaced them elsewhere, and added a grotesque happy ending—but they also summarily destroyed, without a word to Welles, all the removed footage so that this film can never be seen as its creator intended. Welles remained bitter to the end of his life about this mutilation (though some critics still rank the film above *Kane*) and about lead-actor Joseph Cotten's apparent complicity in the revisions. Welles's method was to rehearse his cast, then allow them to improvise in their own words during filming, often with numerous retakes. He almost drove Agnes Moorehead, playing emotional Aunt Fanny, to genuine hysteria with his insistence on endless retakes of some of her scenes. Harsh studio makeup of years past had scarred the face of Dolores Costello, wife of John Barrymore, and repairing these ravages became a daily cosmetic problem in her scenes as Isabel Amberson. Veteran stage actor Richard Bennett, father of screen actresses Barbara, Constance, and Joan Bennett, played the role of Major Amberson. Welles himself spoke the ironic narration. In the ballroom sequence, filmed over nine days, Welles perfected a long crane shot that tracked through three rooms as wall partitions ascended on silent, invisible chains to allow camera passage. The exterior snow sequences were actually filmed indoors in the same Los Angeles ice warehouse used in filming *Lost Horizon* (1937) and, later, *The Thing* (1951); mountains of frozen fish were pushed aside for the tons of crushed ice required for sleigh ride scenes, while the 10,000-watt bulbs used for lighting the action constantly popped in the cold. Welles and cinematographer Stanley Cortez created ingenious metaphorical combinations of light and shadow (best seen in the laser disc video version) that are still being studied by filmmakers. Toward the end of production, Welles began simultaneous shooting of *Journey Into Fear* (1942).

THE MAGNIFICENT SEVEN. 1960. Filmed spring–summer 1960; Tepoztlán, Mexico.
Cast: Yul Brynner, Steve McQueen, Eli Wallach, Horst Buchholz, James Coburn, Charles Bronson, Robert Vaughn.
Director: John Sturges.

If Mexican bandits were to be the baddies in this picture, then Mexicans should also play the good guys. So maintained the image-conscious Mexican government when permission was sought to film there. Compromise was achieved by casting German actor Horst Buchholz as a heroic Mexican. This Americanized remake of Akira Kurosawa's classic *The Seven Samurai* (1954) received the blessing of Kurosawa himself, an admirer of John Sturges. Eli Wallach, playing the bandit chief Calvera, was a newcomer to horses and guns, as was Yul Brynner; Wallach had his own informal, thirty-man escort of tough *bandido* types who took him under their guidance and protection during the filming (probably to make sure he gave a suitably authentic performance) and taught him to ride and shoot. Two colossal egos—Brynner and Steve McQueen—clashed repeatedly. Brynner felt that McQueen, an old hand at Hollywood Westerns, was constantly trying to upstage him by gratuitous bits of business, such as fiddling with his hat. Even Sturges called McQueen on his scene-stealing efforts several times; at one point, Brynner himself hired a man to do nothing but keep track of what McQueen was doing with his hat. Despite problems of such magnitude, Sturges said the production progressed without a repeated shot in the whole film. The sixteenth-century chapel in the small village set was a meticulous papier-mâché construction. Elmer Bernstein's musical score was later adapted for Marlboro cigarette TV commercials. Three sequels—*Return of the Seven* (1966), *Guns of the Magnificent Seven* (1969), and *The Magnificent Seven Ride*! (1972)—used mostly different casts and inferior scripting. Brynner later parodied his own gang-leader performance in *Westworld* (1973).

THE MALTESE FALCON. 1941. Filmed June–July 1941; Warner Bros. Studios, Burbank.

Cast: Humphrey Bogart, Mary Astor, Sydney Greenstreet, Elisha Cook, Jr., Peter Lorre.

Director: John Huston.

John Huston's first directing stint proceeded smoothly, ahead of schedule, and exactly as scripted. (Huston got the job in exchange for scripting *High Sierra*.) The result was a Bogart classic. The lead role of Sam Spade was originally offered to George Raft, who turned it down because of his reluctance to work with an untried director. Geraldine Fitzgerald refused Mary Astor's role for the same reason. Portly stage actor Sydney Greenstreet, nervous and insecure in his first screen role, weighed 285 pounds at the time. Careful rehearsals meant that few takes were required of any one scene. One exception, in the nature of a practical joke, was the brief sequence of Captain Jacobi's staggering into Spade's office with a package and falling dead on the floor. For a lark, the director had talked his father, veteran actor Walter Huston, into playing this uncredited bit. Huston *fils* stretched the scene into hours of retakes. This film was actually the second remake of Dashiell Hammett's novel. The original was a 1931 version of the same title; then came *Satan Met a Lady* (1936). *The Black Bird* (1975) was a son-of-Sam-Spade parody. Lee Patrick reprised her role as Sam Spade's secretary in the latter film, and Elisha Cook, Jr., also reappeared in it. Appearing only briefly in the film, the 18-inch falcon statuette was actually one of seven duplicate figurines made as spare props, one of which made headlines in 1974 by being stolen from a Los Angeles art museum.

A MAN FOR ALL SEASONS. 1966. Filmed 1966; England: Beaulieu; Oxfordshire; Shepperton Studios, Shepperton.

Cast: Paul Scofield, Robert Shaw, Wendy Hiller, Orson Welles, Susannah York, John Hurt.

Director: Fred Zinnemann.

In his first major screen appearance, Paul Scofield repeated his stage role as Sir Thomas More. (Playwright Robert Bolt wrote the film adaptation himself.) This historical drama is full of small, authentic touches. Orson Welles, playing Cardinal Wolsey, uses actual sheepskin parchment, a genuine quill pen (rigged to hold more ink, however, than Wolsey's own), and the exact duplicate of Wolsey's own official seal. Welles himself persuaded Fred Zinnemann to allow him to use eye drops to make his pupils look bloodshot. The ax used in the execution scene was an authentic one of the period. Brother and sister Corin and Vanessa Redgrave—the latter uncredited—played William Roper and Anne Boleyn. The Beaulieu River stood in for the Thames, while More's garden scenes were filmed in Oxfordshire. This film won six Academy Awards: for best picture, Scofield as best actor, Zinnemann's direction, Bolt's screenplay, Ted Moore's cinematography, and costume design.

THE MAN WHO KNEW TOO MUCH. 1956. Filmed spring–summer 1955; Marrakech, Morocco. England: Brixton; Albert Hall and American Embassy, London. Paramount Studios, Los Angeles.
Cast: James Stewart, Doris Day, Daniel Gelin, Brenda De Banzie, Bernard Miles, Christopher Olsen.
Director: Alfred Hitchcock.

This was Hitchcock's second time around with this suspenser—the first version, produced in 1934 under the same title, was "the work of a talented amateur," he later stated, while this was "made by a professional." His directorial style, which consisted of strict noninterference with his cast unless mistakes became obvious, became a source of keen anxiety for Doris Day, an actress used to receiving ample suggestions and feedback. She went through most of the experience convinced that Hitchcock's aloof silence meant that he deplored her performance. Considering walking off the picture, she finally confronted him in desperation and was astonished to discover that he had no fault to find, that she would be first to know when he had. Her well-known concern for animal welfare resulted in feeding stations being set up on the Morocco sets for all the sheep, goats, dogs, and horses of the vicinity; so all the animals you see here are well fed. The murder scene in the Marrakech marketplace almost turned into a genuine riot when fights and shoving broke out among the extras; they had been misinformed that unless they were seen on camera they wouldn't be paid. Day's song "Que Sera, Sera," which she introduced in this picture (and which won an Academy Award), became her biggest hit. Day's hysterical reaction to the news of her young son's kidnapping was a scene she completed, after long gearing up, in one take. The film was James Stewart's third (of four) for Hitchcock, a director he worshiped. Hitchcock cast bald, smooth Danish actor Mogens Wieth for the ambassador's role after a casting agency had sent him dozens of small, hairy men it considered stereotypical diplomats. In his trademark cameo appearance, the director is seen from the back as he watches a group of Arabian acrobats.

THE MAN WHO SHOT LIBERTY VALANCE. 1962. Filmed September–November 1961; Paramount Studios, Los Angeles.
Cast: James Stewart, John Wayne, Vera Miles, Lee Marvin, Edmond O'Brien, Andy Devine, John Carradine.
Director: John Ford.

Some critics believed that the pessimistic tone of this Western, one of John Ford's last, reflected the director's own final disillusioned statement on the history of the American West—especially as compared to the vibrancy of his first Western, *The Iron Horse* (1924), and many that followed. In contrast to most of his Westerns, which he filmed in big-sky, majestic-scenery locations, Ford shot this film almost entirely on the studio lot, and the seedy-looking sets show it. A five-month postponement in starting the film, owing to studio delays, angered and frustrated the director. Observers said that he seemingly lost interest in the project before he began it, uncharacteristically cutting corners and overlooking details. He repeated some of the music, the "Ann Rutledge Theme," from one of his earlier pictures (*Young Mr. Lincoln*) primarily because it was one of his favorite tunes. This is the film in which John Wayne addresses James Stewart as Pilgrim, a catchword in every Wayne impersonation since. The film met a poor critical reception. Though Wayne and Stewart would appear together in two more films, this is the only one in which they costarred as leads.

THE MAN WHO WOULD BE KING. 1975. Filmed January–March 1975; Morocco: Atlas Mountains; Marrakech.
Cast: Sean Connery, Michael Caine, Christopher Plummer, Shakira Caine, Saeed Jaffrey.

Director: John Huston.

One of John Huston's best adventure films cast British stars Sean Connery and Michael Caine, two old friends, in the lead roles that Huston years before had envisioned for Clark Gable and Humphrey Bogart. Huston shelved it after their deaths, then wrote a new screenplay of the story for Paul Newman and Robert Redford. Newman liked the script but suggested that Britishers would better serve the roles, and it was he who suggested Connery and Caine. Caine's wife Shakira, Guyanese by birth and a nonactress, was drafted for the tribal princess role of Roxanne, replacing Tessa Dahl, daughter of actress Patricia Neal, because Huston decided at the last minute to use a dark-skinned woman. Incapable of pretending false emotion, Shakira Caine couldn't show fear as she was supposed to in the final scene, so Huston coached her merely to roll back her eyes, showing the whites, as if swooning. Christopher Plummer, playing author Rudyard Kipling, studied every photo and recording of Kipling he could find, totally immersing himself in the part of the English imperialist. In order to film in Morocco, a locale that duplicated the Indian scenario of Kipling's original story, the film company had to deal with pervasive official corruption, handing out constant bribes in order to function. Berber tribespeople from the hills joined the company as extras, loaning their tents and other equipment for certain sequences. For the Khyber Pass scenes, since Berber women could not be photographed, women from Marrakech brothels were recruited. The three old men playing the high priests were local tribesmen discovered by Huston, who could only make them understand what the scene was about, then let them act it out naturally; astonished to see themselves on film, they concluded through a translator to Huston that "we will never die." The business end of making the film—payroll problems—annoyed and embarrassed Huston considerably. Connery and Caine both ended up having to sue Allied Artists to obtain their contractual percentages. The Wall Street types who had achieved control of the studios, Huston decided, "weren't people you'd care to spend long weekends with."

THE MANCHURIAN CANDIDATE. 1962. Filmed January–February 1962; New York City. Los Angeles.

Cast: Frank Sinatra, Laurence Harvey, Janet Leigh, Angela Lansbury, Henry Silva, John McGiver.
Director: John Frankenheimer.

The ironic history of this film had much to do with its depiction of an attempted presidential assassination. United Artists chief Arthur Krim, also a Democratic party official, wanted nothing to do with producing an adaptation of the Richard Condon novel he considered anti-American propaganda. So Frank Sinatra, who had committed to play the lead role, contacted his friend, President Kennedy; the latter called Krim, said he had enjoyed the novel, and encouraged him to go ahead and make the movie. Several years after Kennedy's assassination, this picture, along with *Suddenly* (1954), was pulled from distribution (probably not by Sinatra, as was long alleged) and re-released only in 1988. Condon thought Laurence Harvey especially well cast as the brainwashed hero Shaw. Harvey's total absorption in the complex character extended to plunging himself into Central Park's icy lake instead of using a stuntman. Other location sequences were filmed at Madison Square Garden and at the Olympic Auditorium in Los Angeles. The brainwashing scenes were reportedly created by John Frankenheimer on the spot. "Fat and quite middle-aged looking" was how Angela Lansbury described herself at the time she played Harvey's mother. (She was only three years older than the actor.) Though Sinatra considered this film one of his best, it failed at the box office, and its revival to semiclassic status was no doubt helped by its fifteen-year absence from the screen. First released only thirteen months before JFK's death, it was rumored to be one of his favorite films.

MANHATTAN. 1979. Filmed spring 1978; New York City.
Cast: Woody Allen, Diane Keaton, Michael Murphy, Mariel Hemingway, Anne Byrne, Meryl Streep.
Director: Woody Allen.

Widely regarded as Woody Allen's comic masterpiece, this film was also a sharply observed morality play, using Allen's own, exquisitely photographed Manhattan as its locale. "Woody Allen Comes of Age," pronounced *Time* magazine upon the movie's release. At (and in) the same *Time*, Allen himself remained characteristically unsure. He cast old friends Michael Murphy and Diane Keaton as well as seventeen-year-old Mariel Hemingway, granddaughter of novelist Ernest Hemingway, in her second screen role. Her natural timidity made her love scenes with Allen difficult; to get her to kiss him, he found himself coaxing her like an adolescent youth; but he marveled that despite her limited acting experience, she gave exactly the performance he sought. Meryl Streep, a relative unknown at the time who played Allen's lesbian ex-wife, was one of the few cast members in any Allen picture to come away less than enchanted with the actor-director. She thought him "very self-involved" and accused him of "trivializing his talent," claiming that "on a certain level the film offends me." Feminist writer Susan Braudy charged that Allen had, without permission, borrowed details from her life for elements of the Streep and Keaton roles. The only major award for this classic came from the local New York Film Critics Circle. (They could hardly ignore it.)

MARTY. 1955. Filmed winter 1954–55; Bronx, New York.
Cast: Ernest Borgnine, Betsy Blair, Joe De Santis, Esther Minciotti.
Director: Delbert Mann.

Television was pushing the movie industry hard, even threatening its existence, when *Marty*—perhaps the first crossover example of a TV drama inspiring a screenplay—was made on a shoestring budget. Cast with relative unknowns, this American kitchen-sink drama made a star of Ernest Borgnine, who nevertheless remained unable to advance beyond permanent character-actor status. (Rod Steiger had played the title role on TV.) As the shy schoolteacher, Betsy Blair, wife of Gene Kelly at the time, also never again equaled her performance. In 1959, this became the first American film since World War II to be shown in the Soviet Union. It became enormously popular there. Despite its low budget and the fact that United Artists executives almost canceled the production because of their own anti-TV bias, *Marty* was revolutionary realism (even though playwright Paddy Chayefsky had intended it mainly as a satire of lower middle-class values). The film reaped an armload of awards, including four Oscars: for best picture, Borgnine as best actor, Chayefsky's screenplay, and Delbert Mann's direction.

MARY POPPINS. 1964. Filmed spring 1964; Walt Disney Studios, Burbank.

Cast: Julie Andrews, Dick Van Dyke, David Tomlinson, Glynis Johns, Ed Wynn, Arthur Treacher, Karen Dotrice, Matthew Garber.

Director: Robert Stevenson.

Probably Disney's most successful blend of live action and animation, this musical fantasy also made Julie Andrews, in her screen debut as a flying nanny, an overnight major star. P. L. Travers, whose series of children's books served as inspiration, approved of Julie Andrews for the title role. The many flying bodies were wafted by means of invisible wires; most of the performers used stunt doubles for such scenes, except Dick Van Dyke, who flew on his own. For Andrews, playing the title role became something of a consolation prize for losing the lead in *My Fair Lady* to Audrey Hepburn. *Mary Poppins* not only fostered a sudden new interest in nannies and coined the adjective's adjective—*supercalifragilisticexpialidocious*—but also begat a busy merchandizing industry featuring dolls, housewares, jewelry, books, and recordings, all adding to the Disney coffers. Andrews won an Academy Award as best actress, and Oscars also went for editing, special effects, the musical score, and "Chim-Chim-Cheree" as best song.

M*A*S*H. 1970. Filmed summer 1969; California: Century Ranch, Malibu; 20th Century-Fox Studios, Los Angeles.

Cast: Donald Sutherland, Elliott Gould, Tom Skerritt, Robert Duvall, Sally Kellerman, Jo Ann Pflug, René Auberjonois, Gary Burghoff.

Director: Robert Altman.

A much more savage, iconoclastic film than the eleven-year TV series it spawned, *M*A*S*H* (Mobile Army Surgical Hospital) had original characters who, in the words of one critic, would have "chewed up and spit out" the TV clowns who finally inherited the roles. Only Gary Burghoff, playing Radar O'Reilly, carried over his movie part to the series. Director Robert Altman constantly fought studio chief Richard Zanuck to keep scenes showing the blood and guts of war intact. Fourteen directors had turned down the job, and Altman was convinced that the film finally got made only because the studio was distracted by the making of two priority war-glory films: *Patton* and *Tora! Tora! Tora!*—thereby ignoring what Altman was doing at the studio ranch and back lot. Donald Sutherland and Elliott Gould were already fashionable stars, but the film provided the first big break for Sally Kellerman, cast as Hot Lips Houlihan, when Angie Dickinson refused the part. Kellerman's nude scene, as Sutherland and Gould pull down the tent curtain, was achieved by a bit of trickery. Because of her shyness, Altman arranged for the entire cast to remove their clothing and stand off-camera when the tent came down, thus capturing her extremely genuine look of surprise. Altman encouraged his cast to improvise; some of the scenes that began only as filmed rehearsals ended up in the final print. Though its scenario concerned the Korean War, *M*A*S*H* was made during the Vietnam War and was thus seen as a direct commentary on the latter conflict. The U.S. Army and Air Force initially banned the film from service installations because it reflected unfavorably on the military. Ring Lardner, Jr., author of the screenplay, won an Academy Award, and the film took several international prizes.

MCCABE AND MRS. MILLER. 1971. Filmed May–July 1970; West Vancouver, British Columbia.

Cast: Warren Beatty, Julie Christie, René Auberjonois, Shelley Duvall, Michael Murphy, Keith Carradine, John Schuck, William Devane.

Director: Robert Altman.

This film, with a production title of *The Presbyterian Church Wager*, owed much to script revisions on the set by Robert Altman and Warren Beatty. The powers at Warner Bros. had wanted George C. Scott for the role of John McCabe, but Altman insisted on Beatty, with whom he established almost collaborative direction of the film. Julie Christie, accustomed to firm direction, found it somewhat unnerving to "work with a democratic director." She and Beatty, who were live-in lovers at the time, never bothered to deny the false rumors sweeping the set that they had been secretly married. Altman filmed the picture mainly in sequence, creating many scenes off the cuff and usually shooting eight or nine takes of each because he found that Beatty, unlike most screen performers, improved with each take. The cake eating scene at the whorehouse table was almost entirely improvised after the participants had indulged for some time in real vodka. As the screenplay expanded, the set of the town that arose in West Vancouver also grew. The film's muddy color was Altman's idea; he wanted to emulate the look of an old photograph. Adding to those rusty-brown tones was a shipment of iron ore from Anaconda Mines that Altman ordered dumped on the town site.

MEET ME IN ST. LOUIS. 1944. Filmed December 1943–April 1944: MGM Studios, Culver City.
Cast: Judy Garland, Margaret O'Brien, Lucille Bremer, Mary Astor, Tom Drake, Marjorie Main, June Lockhart, Harry Davenport, Leon Ames.
Director: Vincente Minnelli.

How do you get a child performer to cry on cue? Simple—tell the kid her dog has died. So many film directors have said they used this tactic that the story has become a cliché smacking strongly of studio publicity mills. Vincente Minnelli juiced up his version of the tale with graphic details of the animal's suffering, fetching plenteous tears from seven-year-old Margaret O'Brien, who had achieved a reputation as being one of Hollywood's brattiest kids. One of her mischiefs between takes of the long dinner sequence was to mix up the tableware, requiring the property man to reset everything. Because of the studio caste system, he could only smile and cajole—and, of course, she knew it (and won an Academy Award as outstanding child actress). Judy Garland was twenty-one, already separated from her first husband David Rose, and wanted no more teenager parts—thus her reluctance to play seventeen-year-old Esther Smith in this nostalgic musical. Moreover, she felt uneasy with Minnelli, but studio chief Louis B. Mayer threatened to suspend her if she didn't sign on. Her lack of enthusiasm caused trouble when she ridiculed her role by reading her lines incredulously during rehearsals. The perfectionistic Minnelli refilmed her first work in the picture—the scene where she primps before a mirror with Lucille Bremer—some twenty-five times, finally winning her over as the picture progressed. In time she threw herself into her role heart and soul, as only Garland could. She also began dating Minnelli toward the end of filming, and they married a year later. Garland annoyed many cast members, especially Mary Astor, by chronic tardiness on the set. Her real problem, as few knew at the time, was chronic fatigue owing to a killing schedule of acting and recording aggravated by her increasing pill addiction. Van Johnson had been slated to play John Truett, the part that finally went to Tom Drake. Producer Arthur Freed dubbed in Leon Ames's singing voice for "You and I," while Garland introduced the song "Have Yourself a Merry Little Christmas," which has made this film highly visible on TV during Yuletide. MGM used the St. Louis street set many times over in later films.

MIDNIGHT COWBOY. 1969. Filmed spring–summer 1968: Texas. Florida. New York City.
Cast: Dustin Hoffman, Jon Voight, Sylvia Miles, John McGiver, Brenda Vaccaro, Barnard Hughes.
Director: John Schlesinger.

Dustin Hoffman risked his mint-fresh stardom achieved in *The Graduate* by playing the scuzzy street bum Ratso Rizzo. Friends strongly urged him not to take the role, but Hoffman's subsequent career revealed him as an actor who constantly stretched himself, in contrast to an earlier generation of stars —the Grants, Gables, Crawfords, and Tracys—who essentially and repeatedly played themselves. Hoffman rated this film as one of his best. It also made a major star of Jon Voight, playing Joe Buck, the naive, transplanted Texan. Serious discussions were held during the filming about showing an actual homosexual encounter between the pair, but the final decision left the relationship only implicit. One unlikely person who went on record as a huge admirer of the movie was James Leo Herlihy, who had written the novel. This was British director John Schlesinger's first American film. It won three Academy Awards: for best picture (the only X-rated film ever to win an Oscar, though its rating was later changed to R); for Schlesinger's direction; and for Waldo Salt's screenplay.

A MIDSUMMER NIGHT'S DREAM. 1935. Filmed spring 1935; Warner Bros. Studios, Burbank.
Cast: James Cagney, Dick Powell, Olivia de Havilland, Jean Muir, Mickey Rooney, Ian Hunter, Joe E. Brown, Hugh Herbert, Ross Alexander, Victor Jory.
Directors: Max Reinhardt, William Dieterle.

This comedy remains one of the best movie treatments of the Bard—even though its source was Hollywood, its directors Teutonic, and its cast composed of studio stock players, not prestigious Old Vic artists. James Cagney interrupted his gangster roles reluctantly, to play Bottom. Today that performance is regarded as one of his best, though critics at the time thought he was much too hammy. Dick Powell later confessed that he never really understood the lines he mouthed as Lysander. Joe E. Brown and Hugh Herbert, old circus-burlesque veterans, decided to stick to the low comedy style they knew so well. Notice Jean Muir, a fine actress playing Helene; blacklisting in 1950 ruined her career. At age fourteen, the irrepressible Mickey Rooney (who played Puck) went out and smashed a toboggan against a tree, breaking his leg. This happened midway during the filming; in order to move him in his leg-cast through the forest foliage, hidden stagehands pushed him on a tricycle. In his "up-and-down speech," Rooney had to raise and drop the stiff cast through a hole cut in a platform, doing deep knee-bends with his good leg. The entire movie was filmed on large indoor sets. Note the classic opening credit: "Script by William Shakespeare, Additional Dialogue by Samuel Taylor." The film's cinematography won an Academy Award.

MILDRED PIERCE. 1945. Filmed spring 1945; Warner Bros. Studios, Burbank.
Cast: Joan Crawford, Zachary Scott, Ann Blyth, Jack Carson, Eve Arden, Bruce Bennett.
Director: Michael Curtiz.

The number of tears provoked down through the years by this classic soap opera would sufficiently salt Michigan roads through two heavy winters. Joan Crawford's repertoire of bitch goddesses and masochistic martyrs here achieved its peak. She badly needed a box office comeback after a two-year career hiatus, and she was uncharacteristically willing to bow and scrape a bit to land this title role. (Bette Davis had turned it down.) Michael Curtiz, who took fierce delight in chewing up at least one self-important movie star before breakfast, wanted Barbara Stanwyck for the part and loudly proclaimed that he wouldn't work with Crawford. The decision was made for him, however, and he treated Mommie Dearest roughly on the set, later fawning over her when she won her only Oscar as best actress for her role. Crawford said she had a phobia against slapping or being slapped (though upon occasion, according to Christina Crawford's 1978 biography, she could beat her own children savagely); but the scene in which she slapped sixteen-year-old Ann Blyth, playing the demonic daughter Veda, was extremely traumatic for both actresses. Scripting of scenes proceeded only a day or two in advance of filming them, requiring cast and crew to work under great disadvantages. Novelist James M. Cain reportedly disliked the film version, though he, too, fawned over Crawford. A refreshing face: Butterfly McQueen, six years after appearing in *Gone With the Wind*, played essentially the same role (named Lottie in this film). Why Lana Turner spared us a remake of this film remains a mystery and a blessing.

THE MILKY WAY. 1936. Filmed autumn 1935; Paramount Studios, Los Angeles.

Cast: Harold Lloyd, Adolphe Menjou, Verree Teasdale, Helen Mack, William Gargan, Lionel Stander, Marjorie Gateson.

Director: Leo McCarey.

Ranked as silent-comedy master Harold Lloyd's best sound film, this farce never went far at the box office but has since become one of his must-see classics. Lloyd at age forty-two played timid milkman Burleigh Sullivan, transformed into a cocky prize fighter by con artist Adolphe Menjou as his boxing promoter. Never using stand-ins or doubles, Lloyd bore mute witness to that fact in his missing right thumb and forefinger, result of a 1920 accident on the set of *Haunted Spooks*. Menjou said he ad-libbed in one take the entire scene in which he dwells on Lloyd's "split personality" and urges him to fight in the ring; the scene was a spontaneous idea from Leo McCarey. McCarey wanted a white horse that could "act" for the purpose of pulling the milk wagon. He could only come up with a dark animal, however, so Agnes in the film is a bleached-blond horse with a facial makeup job. The dairy industry did a promotional tie-in with the film ("Bordens—the Milky Way to health"). Ironically, during a production so full of health, Menjou was stricken with a severe ulcer flare-up during filming, and Verree Teasdale suffered an acute colitis attack. Unbilled, Milburn Stone appeared in a brief scene as a reporter. Lionel Stander repeated his dumb sidekick role in a 1946 remake, *The Kid from Brooklyn*.

MIRACLE ON 34TH STREET. 1947. Filmed autumn 1946; New York City.
Cast: Maureen O'Hara, John Payne, Edmund Gwenn, Gene Lockhart, Natalie Wood, William Frawley, Thelma Ritter.
Director: George Seaton.

This perennial Christmas favorite (production title: *It's Only Human*) evoked so little faith from 20th Century-Fox that the studio released it in July rather than December. In 1947 nobody realized what a mighty advertising commercial for Macy's Department Store the film would be. Christmas spirit reigned when the store's chief rival, Gimbel's, took out a full-page ad in *The New York Times* commending the film and congratulating its competitor. Eight-year-old Natalie Wood, who became a top Hollywood star ten years later, was no stranger to movies, this one being about her fourth. Edmund Gwenn, playing Kris Kringle, won an Academy Award as best supporting actor; other winners: director George Seaton for his screenplay and Valentine Davies for original story.

THE MIRACLE WORKER. 1962. Filmed June–August 1961; Middletown, New Jersey (exteriors). Production Center Studios, New York City.
Cast: Anne Bancroft, Patty Duke, Victor Jory, Inga Swenson, Andrew Prine.
Director: Arthur Penn.

Anne Bancroft and Patty Duke had sharply honed their performances of Annie Sullivan and Helen Keller during their long-run Broadway appearance in William Gibson's play. For the film version of the Sullivan role, United Artists wanted to cast a more familiar name, but Arthur Penn insisted on Bancroft, and the part brought her major stardom. This was fifteen-year-old Duke's third film but her first significant screen role. Both actresses became intensely involved with their roles and both worked to exhaustion (Bancroft was hospitalized with pneumonia immediately after production ended). Duke said she dreaded the wrap-up because it meant her final separation from the performing company. She thought the final scene of the movie spoiled its dramatic unity. A sad personal note revealed in Duke's 1987 memoirs: during the period of filming exterior scenes in New Jersey, she became the victim of traumatic sexual abuse from her guardian-manager. In her dining room battle with Bancroft (which occupied five days and three cameras for nine minutes of film), both actresses wore pads beneath their clothing. At one point during the fight, Bancroft began laughing from sheer exhaustion, and that scene was left in. Bancroft erupts in a spontaneous "Shit!" in one outdoor scene when her foot slips into an icy stream; we don't hear it, though, because no mikes were present and the scene was voiced-over later. Much of the film was shot with hand-held cameras by operators seated in wheelchairs. Bancroft won an Academy Award for best actress, as did Duke for best supporting actress. In 1979, Duke played the Sullivan role in a TV movie remake.

THE MISFITS. 1961. Filmed July–November 1960; Nevada: Dayton; Quail Canyon. Paramount Studios, Los Angeles.

Cast: Clark Gable, Marilyn Monroe, Montgomery Clift, Thelma Ritter, Eli Wallach.

Director: John Huston.

Clark Gable's sixty-sixth sound movie was his last; he died twelve days after completing a retake of his final scene with Marilyn Monroe, convinced at age fifty-nine that his work had been his best since *Gone With the Wind*. It was also Monroe's twenty-eighth and final film, the sad climax of her career as she approached the bottom of her long slide toward death from pill addiction and lifelong psychoses. Her habit of showing up on the set hours late or not at all had become an unmanageable problem; and her high-priced colleagues spent most of the months between start and finish of the picture sitting around on desert locations waiting for Monroe to show up. Gable took the situation calmly, at least outwardly; privately he anguished that "it drives me nuts . . . It's stealing." Rejuvenating news came in August that his wife was pregnant. (His son, a child he would never see, was born the following March.) Stuntmen did the most dangerous of his scenes with the wild horses. But Gable himself, who had crash-dieted from 230 to 195 for his part, performed numerous retakes of the strenuous action sequences showing him running and being rope-dragged through the desert. Sensing Monroe's paralyzing lack of self-confidence (especially when working with her childhood idol Gable)—and when drugs didn't make her an absolute zombie on the set—Gable took great pains to put her at ease, as did John Huston and his entire cast. Monroe, in turn, became protective toward Montgomery Clift, another burned-out soul, whose little-boy-lostness aroused the maternal instincts of almost every actress he worked with. He was probably the only one of the entire company who could make Monroe feel somewhat secure, if only by default. Monroe's third marriage, to playwright (and the film's screenwriter) Arthur Miller, had ended in all but name. Cast and crew tried to ignore the painful spectacle when she taunted and humiliated him as he stood on the sidelines. Marilyn affected everybody present with vast, foreboding feelings as she slowly self-destructed, and only by untypical patience was Huston able to coax adequate scenes from her. Despite his constant daily vodka intake, Clift was able to maintain control of his psyche (evidently for the last time in any film he made); he researched his rodeo rider part thoroughly, winning Gable's admiration and respect.

MISSING. 1982. Filmed spring 1981; Mexico: Acapulco; exteriors and Cherebusco Studios, Mexico City.
Cast: Jack Lemmon, Sissy Spacek, John Shea, Melanie Mayron, Janice Rule, David Clennon, Joe Regalbuto.
Director: Costa-Gavras.

The U.S. State Department howled in outrage at the implications drawn by this political thriller. Based on a true incident following the 1973 Chilean coup, it was Greek director Costa-Gavras's first American film. Jack Lemmon, for one, delighted in the bureaucratic reaction. Costa-Gavras himself, a familiar thorn in the flesh of thuggish governments, denied any intention of making an anti-American polemic. Security on location in Mexico was tight, with few of the performers knowing the full story being filmed even as they worked. Since both budget and official cooperation remained in short supply for the politically suspect director, he used military tanks made of cardboard, which he set up on streets and airfield, also employing Mexican policemen and their vehicles for Chilean military forces. He filmed in some thirty locations in and around Mexico City; for Viña del Mar, he used Acapulco locations. American officials filed a $6 million libel suit against the director, further publicizing the picture, which won the director and Donald Stewart Academy Awards for their screenplay

MR. BLANDINGS BUILDS HIS DREAM HOUSE. 1948. Filmed autumn 1947; California: Century Ranch, Malibu; RKO Studios, Los Angeles.
Cast: Cary Grant, Myrna Loy, Melvyn Douglas, Reginald Denny.
Director: H. C. Potter.

Ironic things were happening behind the Norman Rockwell façades of this Cary Grant comedy. Aimed toward ineffably middle-class viewers (who still relate best to it), *Mr. Blandings* is alternately considered hilarious and—well, bland. Myrna Loy recalled the filming experience as "sheer heaven." Presumably she didn't mean to include one ugly off-camera episode involving Melvyn Douglas, an ominous foretaste of Hollywood's blacklist. Douglas's wife, U.S. Congresswoman Helen Gahagan Douglas, became the recipient of covert anti-Semitic remarks about Douglas himself, whose real name was Hesselberg. The racist remarks came from Congressman John Rankin; Melvyn Douglas eloquently challenged the congressman to bring him before the House Un-American Activities Committee in order to clarify the statements, but Rankin backed down. As a result, however, both Loy and Douglas eagerly joined a committee being formed by John Huston and William Wyler to protect First Amendment rights. Cary Grant expressed no interest and never joined the group. Immensely popular with postwar audiences, *Mr. Blandings* was revised for 1986 yuppies as *The Money Pit*.

MISTER ROBERTS. 1955. Filmed September–October 1954; Midway Island. Kaneohe Marine Corps Air Station and Kaneohe Bay, Hawaii. Warner Bros. Studios, Burbank.
Cast: Henry Fonda, James Cagney, William Powell, Jack Lemmon, Betsy Palmer, Ward Bond.
Directors: John Ford, Mervyn LeRoy.

Old pals Henry Fonda and John Ford had differing opinions about embellishing the title role that Fonda had played for seven years on the stage. Their disagreements erupted into physical violence one night in their quarters when the director assaulted the actor and knocked him down. Though Ford later apologized, the episode ended their friendship. James Cagney, too, found Ford barely tolerable. The U.S. Navy strongly faulted the command image conveyed by Cagney. Only after Ford appealed directly to the Chief of Naval Operations did the service agree to lend technical support. This included use of the 172-foot, 250-ton cargo ship USS *Hewell*, on which shipboard scenes were filmed at Midway. Stuntmen earned their wages in this film. In the ship's laundry scene, the semi-toxic substance simulating the billowing soapsuds caused severe skin rash and eye trouble for both Jack Lemmon and his double. The stuntman who drove the motorcycle off the end of the pier in the rowdy drunk scene was far from eager to perform this bit. He drank so much beforehand that he had to be helped on the motorcycle. Then, in a burst of alcoholic bravado, he gunned the machine and soared off the dock about 50 feet further than expected. Ford was about to call for a rescue squad when the man's head finally surfaced; he had, he explained, stayed underwater as long as possible so as not to "ruin the take." This film was William Powell's last before his long retirement. Lemmon won a best supporting actor Oscar for his performance. Accounts differ as to just how much Ford footage ended up in the finished film; Mervyn LeRoy, Ford's replacement, claimed responsibility for directing ninety percent of it. *Ensign Pulver* (1984) was an inferior sequel.

MOBY DICK. 1956. Filmed July 1954–spring 1955. Youghal, Ireland. South Irish Sea. Fishguard, Wales. Madeira, Portugal. Canary Islands. Bikini. England: Shepperton Studios, Shepperton; Elstree Studios, Borehamwood.

Cast: Gregory Peck, Richard Basehart, Leo Genn, Orson Welles, James Robertson Justice, Harry Andrews, Bernard Miles, Friedrich Ledebur.

Director: John Huston.

John Huston insisted that this was the most difficult film he ever directed. Not one but three great white whales, ninety-foot-long creatures made of plastic and rubber stretched over steel frames, played the title role. Electronically controlled and towed by offscreen boats, two of the monsters were eventually lost at sea and bobbed around for years as navigation hazards. The century-old vessel used as the sailing ship *Pequod* had once been a coal carrier and was holding an aquarium museum in Scarborough, England, when Huston discovered it; the vessel had previously served as the *Hispaniola* in Walt Disney's *Treasure Island* (1950). Huston converted it to a three-master, taking great pains to conform every aspect of its structure and rigging to the descriptions in Herman Melville's novel. Authentic touches extended to the whalebone rudder, as well as to Gregory Peck's whalebone peg leg. Huston's quest for realism led to great risk-taking on stormy seas. The vessel's modified superstructure—despite its added engines and expert captaincy by veteran sea dog Alan Villiers—made it the plaything of winds, all but uncontrollable at times. Peck thought himself miscast in the role of Captain Ahab (most critics agreed); he believed himself better suited to Starbuck (played by Leo Genn) and thought that Huston himself would have made the ideal Ahab. (Years before, Huston had intended to cast his father, Walter Huston, as Ahab.) Genn injured his back when he fell twenty feet into a longboat, and Richard Basehart (playing Ishmael) broke his foot jumping into another boat. Peck himself, suffering a severe cold when lashed to the side of the whale replica for the film's final scenes, endured repeated dowsings as the creature rolled over in the sea; close-ups precluded the use of a stuntman for these scenes. Peck's real leg hung through a hole in the side of the beast, while his peg leg lay tied down with the rest of his body. A nervous Orson Welles, playing a cameo role as Father Mapple, completed his sermon in two takes at Elstree Studios. For the New Bedford waterfront, the entire quayside area of Youghal was revamped into a Yankee seaport. Austrian aristocrat Count Friedrich Ledebur, in his first screen appearance, played the cannibal Queequeg with shaven head and elaborate makeup. Huston and screenwriter Ray Bradbury had a serious falling-out as filming progressed; the latter strenuously objected to Huston's credit line as cowriter.

MODERN TIMES. 1936. Filmed October 1934–August 1935; California: Wilmington; Charles Chaplin Studios, Los Angeles.

Cast: Charles Chaplin, Paulette Goddard, Henry Bergman, Chester Conklin.
Director: Charles Chaplin.

Chaplin, essentially a pantomime artist, resisted the advent of sound in movies as long as he could, and this bittersweet comedy represented only a partial concession to modern times in the film industry. Called the last of the great silent features —its soundtrack consists only of Chaplin's musical score, a gibberish ditty he sings, and various sound effects (he made his stomach "rumble" by blowing bubbles into a pail of water)—*Modern Times* also marked the final starring appearance of Chaplin's Little Tramp character (though he encored him in another guise for *The Great Dictator*). This film was Chaplin's emotional response to the dehumanizing economic conditions that had instigated the Great Depression. The genesis was an account he heard about auto assembly-line workers in Detroit. He and Paulette Goddard, not yet married but living together, prepared and rehearsed scenes for some two years before production began, and Chaplin continued to revise scenes on the set through endless takes. Chaplin enlisted his friend, Dr. Cecil Reynolds, an English brain surgeon and amateur actor, to play the parson who visits the jail. While the film enjoyed large success in the U.S., some reviewers labeled it Communist propaganda; Germany and Italy banned it as such, while the Soviets considered it insulting. Tobis Studios in France sued Chaplin for plagiarizing the conveyor-belt sequence from René Clair's *À Nous la Liberté* but dropped the suit when Clair professed himself honored ("I have certainly borrowed enough from *him*").

MONKEY BUSINESS. 1931. Filmed summer 1930; Paramount Studios, Los Angeles.
Cast: Groucho, Harpo, Chico, and Zeppo Marx, Thelma Todd.
Director: Norman Z. McLeod.

The Marx brothers' third film, one of their best, was the first written directly for the screen without long preliminary rehearsals on the vaudeville circuit. Margaret Dumont, the brothers' stately, familiar foil, is absent. Instead, the female lead went to Thelma Todd, a popular comic actress for whom Groucho admitted a burning physical passion; she also appeared in the Marx brothers' next film, *Horse Feathers*. In 1935, she died at age thirty from carbon monoxide poisoning in her garage—whether by suicide or gangland murder remains one of those sordid Tinseltown mysteries that never got resolved. Mourners noted in retrospect that a line addressed to her in this film seemed to foreshadow the tragedy: "We can clean and tighten your brakes, but you'll have to stay in the garage all night." Look for mustached Sam "Frenchie" Marx, father of the zany team; he appears twice as an extra, once wearing a white hat in a group of ship passengers, and once on the dock, apparently waving goodbye to the same shipboard crowd. Such cloning was not, for once, deliberate; it just escaped somebody's notice, and Sam was nothing if not accommodating. It is recorded that British prime minister Winston Churchill watched this farce in 1941 to revive his flagging spirits during a heavy bombardment of London.

MONSIEUR HULOT'S HOLIDAY (LES VACANCES DE MONSIEUR HULOT). 1953. Filmed July 1951–October 1952; France: St. Marc-sur-Mer; Studios de Billancourt, Billancourt.

Cast: Jacques Tati, Nathalie Pascaud, Michelle Rolla, Valentine Camax.

Director: Jacques Tati.

Jacques Tati's pantomimic artistry owed much to the great silent comedy tradition of Charlie Chaplin and Buster Keaton, and he was one of the last cinema masters of the sight gag. He assembled his supporting cast from nonprofessionals, most of them summer visitors and residents of the seaside Brittany resort where he filmed the exteriors. Nathalie Pascaud, playing Martine, was only a social acquaintance; her husband strenuously objected to her participation until Tati cast him in the part of the American businessman. Most of the English voice dubbing was done by that versatile British player of monsters, Christopher Lee. The film won Grand Prize at the Cannes Film Festival.

MONSIEUR VERDOUX. 1947. Filmed April–September 1946; Charles Chaplin Studios, Los Angeles.

Cast: Charles Chaplin, Martha Raye, Isobel Elsom, Mady Correll, Allison Roddan, William Frawley.

Director: Charles Chaplin.

Chaplin's satire became sardonic if not totally black in his treatment of a Bluebeard character based on the French murderer Landru. (The film's original title was, in fact, *Landru*.) Orson Welles apparently suggested the idea, later magnifying the significance of his own contribution against Chaplin's disclaimer. The Breen Office, Hollywood's arbiter of morals at the time, recommended that Chaplin scrap the entire screenplay at the outset; by careful rewriting, however, he was able to get the script okayed. In contrast to Chaplin's lengthy trial-and-error procedures in filming his previous pictures, postwar production costs forced him this time to conform to a more typical studio schedule. Martha Raye, playing Annabella, was one of the few Chaplin costars who could get away with tweaking his rather pompous ego; she audaciously called him "Chuck" on the set, and when personality conflicts built uncontrollably, her clarion voice yelling "Lunch!" quickly alleviated tension. Chaplin wanted to cast his old partner of silent comedy shorts, a stouter Edna Purviance who hadn't acted for two decades, in the role of Madame Grosnay; the part finally went to Isobel Elsom, but Purviance did appear as an extra in the garden party sequence. With inexperienced Marilyn Nash, playing a prostitute, Chaplin worked long and patiently to help her give a convincing performance. Chaplin's larger aim, he said, was to make the film an antiwar comedy; in his anti-establishment zeal, he even claimed at one point that it was meant as a protest against the A-bomb. Except by a few astute critics, the film was not well received.

THE MOUSE THAT ROARED. 1959. Filmed autumn–winter 1958–59; England: Southampton; HMS *Queen Elizabeth*; Maidenhead area; London; Shepperton Studios, Shepperton. New York City.

Cast: Peter Sellers, Jean Seberg, David Kossoff, William Hartnell, Leo McKern.

Director: Jack Arnold.

In this zany comedy Peter Sellers first emulated his hero Alec Guinness by playing multiple roles. It was also his first important starring performance, the occasion of his first screen kiss (from Jean Seberg), and the film that made him widely known to American audiences. This was Seberg's second screen appearance. Director Jack Arnold, best known for his science-fiction thrillers, filmed the Marseilles and New

York harbor sequences in Southampton, also using the fortuitous presence of the *Queen Elizabeth* ocean liner for several scenes. In Manhattan, he filmed the invasion sequences on a Sunday morning, thus accounting for the city's empty streets. *The Mouse on the Moon* was a 1963 sequel.

THE MUMMY. 1932. Filmed autumn 1932; Universal Studios, Universal City.
Cast: Boris Karloff, Zita Johann, David Manners, Arthur Byron, Edward van Sloan.
Director: Karl Freund.

Blame the ancient Egyptian pharaoh Tutankhamen for all the mummy movies. Discovery of his tomb in 1922 was still being discussed when ex–Frankenstein-monster Boris Karloff (the most patient actor ever to face a studio makeup department before dawn) was again wrapped and plastered. Yards of linen and gauze, plus caked clay and fuller's earth, went into his garb for the opening scenes. Later in the movie, he performed a less desiccated role as quietly menacing Ardath Bey (his seamy face produced by liquefied cotton fibers painted on). So entrenched had Karloff become as moviedom's ace monster that he was billed in the credits by surname alone, a distinction heretofore reserved for Greta Garbo. This was Karl Freund's first feature as a director. A widely acclaimed cinematographer of classic films both before and after this debut, he ended his career as a cameraman on TV's *I Love Lucy*. Stock footage of Karloff in his mummy getup was matched with Tom Tyler in one of the film's countless sequels, *The Mummy's Hand* (1940). A 1959 remake of *The Mummy* inspired a whole new pyramid of sequels.

MURDER, MY SWEET. 1944. Filmed spring 1944; RKO Studios, Culver City.
Cast: Dick Powell, Claire Trevor, Anne Shirley, Mike Mazurki, Otto Kruger, Miles Mander.
Director: Edward Dmytryk.

This film noir classic gave a boost to the careers of both Dick Powell and director Edward Dmytryk. Heretofore cast mainly as a playboy-crooner, Powell found his singing juvenile persona increasingly dated, and he eagerly sought the role of Raymond Chandler's hardboiled detective Philip Marlowe.

As a result of his success in the role, RKO killed plans to star Powell in another series of musicals, instead concentrated on polishing his new tough-guy image. Powell's previous image, however, meant scrapping the movie's original title, *Farewell, My Lovely*; audiences, anticipating another airhead Powell musical, stayed away in droves until the picture was retitled. Mike Mazurki, playing Moose Malloy, was supposed to tower over Powell in the story. Unfortunately Powell was only two inches shorter than Mazurki's six-five; so Dmytryk stood Mazurki on a box and Powell in his stockings—and had Powell walk in the curbside gutter—in their one-on-one scenes. Powell was the first screen Marlowe and probably truest to Chandler's conception. (Successors included Humphrey Bogart, Robert Montgomery, George Montgomery, James Garner, Robert Mitchum, and Elliott Gould.) Though Powell never played the detective again, the picture brought him similar tough-guy parts, and he probably never crooned another line in his life. *Murder, My Sweet* was remade under its jinxed first title, *Farewell, My Lovely*, in 1975—by which time everyone knew it was vintage Chandler and that Robert Mitchum was not much of a singer.

MURDER ON THE ORIENT EXPRESS. 1974. Filmed spring 1974; Turkey. France. Elstree Studios, Borehamwood, England.

Cast: Albert Finney, Lauren Bacall, Martin Balsam, Ingrid Bergman, Jacqueline Bisset, Jean-Pierre Cassel, Sean Connery, John Gielgud, Wendy Hiller, Anthony Perkins, Vanessa Redgrave, Rachel Roberts, Richard Widmark, Michael York.

Director: Sidney Lumet.

Probably the best screen adaptation of an Agatha Christie mystery (the Lindbergh kidnapping case had inspired her original 1934 novel), this prestige production brought together some of the screen's most luminous names. For Lauren Bacall, reviving her film career after eight years, it became the chance of a lifetime to perform with Ingrid Bergman, the costar with her late husband, Humphrey Bogart, in *Casablanca*. Bacall said that making the film was the "happiest work experience" of her movie career. Sidney Lumet had wanted Bergman for the Russian dowager princess role, which finally went to Wendy Hiller, but Bergman preferred to play the missionary. Bergman was acting in *The Constant Wife* on the London stage at the same time. Nobody knew that she was studiously procrastinating a biopsy to diagnose the developing cancer that would kill her eight years later. Rachel Roberts, in her role as Hiller's companion, copied Marlon Brando's German accent in *The Young Lions* (1958) for her part. Richard Widmark took the role of the American murder victim for the sole purpose of working with the other performers. Albert Finney's makeup as detective Hercule Poirot changed his appearance drastically. He wore a false nose, padded cheeks, as well as body padding to make him stocky. Bootblack and Vaseline gave him the greasiest hairdo this side of 1954. Original blueprints of Orient Express coaches and a few surviving cars helped recreate a studio mock-up—built on rubber wheels so it could be moved and rocked by the film crew. No attempt was made, however, to duplicate exact details of lavish upholstery and furnishings. Said to be the most financially successful British film ever made, this movie received six Oscar nominations; but only Bergman won, as best supporting actress.

MUTINY ON THE BOUNTY. 1935. Filmed summer 1935; Tahiti (exteriors). California: Santa Catalina Island; MGM Studios, Culver City.

Cast: Charles Laughton, Clark Gable, Franchot Tone, Movita, Dudley Digges.

Director: Frank Lloyd.

Clark Gable invariably had to be bribed, threatened, or coerced into making what turned out to be his best films; he much preferred anchoring his macho image in the security of inferior scripts—and he almost mutinied from this bounteous production before it began. His first problem lay in having to shave off one of his best badges, his mustache; that and wearing all those prissy wigs and knickers! The character of Fletcher Christian was too dandified for him, he felt; but once he was dragged into the part, he enjoyed making the film despite constant bickering with the temperamental Charles Laughton. Laughton wouldn't look him in the eye, he complained, a fatal diversion for a reactor actor, as Gable was. Nor did Laughton come eagerly to the tyrannical Captain

Bligh; but it was the sort of meaty, raving role at which Laughton excelled. He took great pains to research his part (which had almost gone to Wallace Beery), even obtaining exact copies of naval uniforms from Bligh's own surviving London tailor shop. Robert Montgomery had declined the role of Midshipman Byam, which went to Franchot Tone. That actor found himself in the uneasy position of mediating quarrels between the two high-powered costars and between each of them and director Frank Lloyd. Thanks partly to Tone, no major blowups occurred, and filming proceeded smoothly. (Tone was soon to marry actress Joan Crawford, one of "Gable's women" both before this marriage and after it ended.) At a time when rising young actors as well as famed stars liked to sneak into movie crowd scenes as extras, David Niven briefly appeared in a scene aboard the *Bounty*; and it is said that James Cagney also joined a crowd in front of the camera. Most of the filming occurred off Santa Catalina Island, but much background footage as well as some 2,500 natives were filmed in forty Tahitian villages. The two ships HMS *Bounty* and *Pandora* were faithful replicas of the original vessels, and both of them actually sailed to Tahiti and back during filming preparations. *Mutiny* won an Academy Award as best picture. With the possible exception of Rhett Butler, the role of Christian was probably Gable's best screen part. A 1962 remake starred Marlon Brando and Trevor Howard (ironically, Mexican actress Movita Castenada, playing Gable's Tahitian lover, became Brando's second wife in 1960); and *The Bounty* (1984) offered yet another treatment of the story.

MY DARLING CLEMENTINE. 1946. Filmed May–June 1946; Monument Valley, Arizona-Utah. 20th Century-Fox Studios, Los Angeles.

Cast: Henry Fonda, Linda Darnell, Victor Mature, Walter Brennan, Cathy Downs, Tim Holt, Ward Bond, Alan Mowbray, Jane Darwell.

Director: John Ford.

The movies repeatedly made heroes of the two frontier characters Wyatt Earp and Doc Holliday—a couple of dismal losers in real life—and John Ford claimed to have gotten the story of the famed Tombstone gunfight between the Earps and Clantons straight from Earp himself. If so, he revised the scenario considerably from the witnessed event; yet this film's feeling for the Old West showed old mythmaker Ford at his best. This was Henry Fonda's first picture after his 1945 discharge from the wartime navy. The bilious Ford, noted for his crude wit, usually chose at least one scapegoat in his film casts to harass, and Victor Mature (playing Doc Holliday) became the victim here. "Greaseball" and "Liverlips" were some of the milder epithets hurled at the actor known as "the Hunk," a good-natured, brawny fellow with no illusions or pretensions about his acting ability—but whose performance had some style and, in this film, was probably the best of his career. Walter Brennan, playing the vicious Old Man Clanton, didn't take Ford's baiting so lightly; thoroughly fed up, he swore never to act in another Ford picture, and he never did. *Gunfight at the OK Corral* (1957) was another telling of the tale, and Ford himself brought back Earp and Holliday in his *Cheyenne Autumn* (1964).

MY FAIR LADY. 1964. Filmed August–December 1963; Warner Bros. Studios, Burbank.
Cast: Rex Harrison, Audrey Hepburn, Stanley Holloway, Wilfrid Hyde-White, Gladys Cooper, Jeremy Brett, Theodore Bikel.
Director: George Cukor.

Rex Harrison and Julie Andrews had costarred for several years in the Broadway production of this musical based on George Bernard Shaw's *Pygmalion*; but when it came time to cast for the film, the better known Audrey Hepburn replaced Andrews, to the latter's bitter disappointment. The fact that Hepburn couldn't sing (at least not well enough for a film musical) meant that studio vocalist Marni Nixon dubbed almost all of her songs. Among others who deplored the dropping of Andrews was the show's lyricist, Alan J. Lerner, who hated the film from beginning to end. Cary Grant, incredibly, had been offered Harrison's role of Prof. Henry Higgins but quickly refused it, saying Harrison was the only possible choice. Harrison insisted on singing his numbers live instead of predubbing and mouthing the words, as is usually done. George Cukor also gave him immense freedom to "lead the camera," another untypical procedure. In Hepburn's early scenes as Eliza Doolittle, her makeup consisted of expertly applied dirt, an ordeal for which she prepared by dousing herself in perfume "to keep up my morale." She had just finished filming her song "Wouldn't It Be Loverly?" when she received news of John F. Kennedy's assassination, which she announced to a shocked cast and crew. Hepburn's marriage to actor Mel Ferrer was growing stormy at this time also; so between the veiled hostility toward her for replacing Andrews and the emotional trauma of national events—coupled with her personal troubles—her performance was a marvel of concentration. English actor Stanley Holloway, playing Eliza's dustman father, performed here in his first American film. Look for former silent-screen siren Betty Blythe playing a matronly type in evening dress and for veteran character actor Henry Daniell in his final role as Prince Gregor; he died just before the picture's release. The film won an Oscar for best picture; Academy Awards also went to Harrison as best actor and director Cukor, among others.

MY LITTLE CHICKADEE. 1940. Filmed autumn 1939; Universal Studios, Universal City.

Cast: Mae West, W. C. Fields, Joseph Calleia, Dick Foran, Margaret Hamilton, Donald Meek, Fuzzy Knight.

Director: Edward Cline.

Long before filming commenced, this classic of inspired burlesque comedy—one of the all-time great bad movies—underwent months of script changes and rewrites. Universal Pictures envisioned it originally as *The Jaywalkers*, a takeoff on the studio's recent success *Destry Rides Again*. But W. C. Fields had his own ideas, as usual, and he corresponded at length with Mae West about the proposed film, which was renamed at various times *December and Mae* and *The Lady and the Bandit*. After much bickering with the studio, West finally constructed the plot, and she and Fields each wrote their own dialogue, improvising their shared scenes. But their collaboration never really jelled. West entered the project with misgivings over her costar's well-known weakness for the bottle on the set, but none of her threats or cajolery halted his occasional lapses of drunken behavior. Also, she tired of his mincing manner, offscreen as well as on—when, for example, he would plant a kiss on her forehead with thumb and forefinger, addressing her as "my little brood mare." Director

Edward Cline sometimes couldn't keep from cracking up as he watched these two veteran con artists try to top each other in front of the camera; certain scenes had to be delicately edited for sound in order to eliminate his offscreen chokes of laughter. Joseph Calleia's role of the masked bandit was originally offered to Humphrey Bogart. When reviewers favored Fields in the movie after its release, a furious West—upstaged for the first time in her career—had nothing good to say either to or about Fields, and she remained hostile to him for the rest of her life.

MY MAN GODFREY. 1936. Filmed winter 1936; Universal Studios, Universal City.
Cast: William Powell, Carole Lombard, Alice Brady, Gail Patrick, Eugene Pallette, Mischa Auer.
Director: Gregory La Cava.

Probably no Hollywood divorce was ever so amicable as that of William Powell and Carole Lombard; they parted in 1933 after two years of marriage. Even after Lombard and Clark Gable became a hot item and Powell launched into an affair with Jean Harlow, the ex-spouses remained good friends. It was Powell who insisted on casting Lombard for the screwball comedy role that gave her stalled career a huge boost, making her the highest-paid female star in Hollywood. Another personal aspect was the presence of Alice Brady; now in her mid-forties and playing the rich mother, she had enjoyed a brief affair with Gable back in 1930, but said she couldn't remember much about it when Lombard asked her for useful pointers. This mélange of pals worked well together, though Powell gave chief credit for the film's success to Gregory La Cava's direction and his overnight inspirations for dialogue revisions. Powell liked the new challenge that his role of the down-and-outer-turned-butler offered him; and Lombard relished a part that enabled her to showcase her comic talents. As a Depression comedy with sardonic overtones, the film represented one of the fiercest attacks on the superrich that Hollywood ever produced. Look for Jane Wyman in her screen debut; she played a bit role in the party scene. This film inspired *Merrily We Live* (1938) as well as a 1957 remake starring June Allyson and David Niven.

N

NASHVILLE. 1975. Filmed summer 1974; Nashville, Tennessee.

Barbara Baxley, Ned Beatty, Karen Black, Ronee Blakley, Keith Carradine, Geraldine Chaplin, Shelley Duvall, Allen Garfield, Henry Gibson, Scott Glenn, Barbara Harris, Michael Murphy, Lily Tomlin, Keenan Wynn.

Director: Robert Altman.

Often rated one of the best films of the 1970s, *Nashville* was intended, said Robert Altman, as "a metaphor for my personal view of society." As such, it proved one of his most controversial films in a career full of them. He filmed mostly in sequence and recorded everything live, with no postdubbing. He also gave his cast ample space to improvise. (Keenan Wynn, the only veteran actor in the bunch, was also the only one who adhered to his written lines.) Several of the players, including Karen Black, Ronee Blakley, Keith Carradine, and Henry Gibson, wrote some or all of the songs they performed. Susan Anspach had been originally cast as Barbara Jean, the role that went to Blakley in her feature film debut; and Robert Duvall turned down the role of Haven Hamilton that went to Gibson. While Blakley brought little acting experience to her role, her background as a singer-composer, plus an actual childhood episode of being severely burned in a fire, helped her characterization. Allen Garfield, playing her tyrant husband-manager Barnett, had violent arguments with Altman on the set, a situation that almost erupted into fisticuffs between them. He made up his own confrontation scene with Michael Murphy (playing John Triplette), and much of that scene alluded directly to the Garfield-Altman antagonism. Blakley likewise wrote her own nervous breakdown scene that occurs on the Grand Ole Opry stage. Several of the characters suggested (though none were actually patterned on) real-life Opry figures: among them, Blakley as Loretta Lynn, Gibson as Hank Snow or Roy Acuff, Timothy Brown as Charley Pride. The leering men in the stag party scene were members of the Nashville Chamber of Commerce. A Mississippi novelist and political conservative by the name of Thomas Hal Phillip wrote and spoke the sound-truck speech of Replacement Party candidate Hal Phillip Walker, giving the movie its narrative underpinnings. Carradine won an Academy Award for his song "I'm Easy."

NATIONAL LAMPOON'S ANIMAL HOUSE. 1978. Filmed October–November 1977; University of Oregon campus, Eugene.
Cast: John Belushi, Tim Matheson, Peter Riegert, John Vernon, Verna Bloom, Thomas Hulce, Karen Allen, Kevin Bacon, Donald Sutherland.
Director: John Landis.

Chevy Chase had turned down the role of Otter, finally played by Tim Matheson. And about fifty colleges declined the dubious honor of hosting the Faber College location work; finally, the University of Oregon became the production site. Owing to the rapid thirty-day filming schedule, John Landis cultivated panic and hysteria among his rather laid-back players just to get the job done. He fostered a keyed-up sense of rampant anarchy on his sets, yelling and throwing pencils and other small objects at his on-camera actors to keep them hyperactive. One of his many problems was finding actresses willing to perform in the nude scene leered upon by John Belushi from his ladder. Belushi liked to do his own stunts but had to wire his nerves on cocaine for his climactic, Tarzan-style swing down to the street from a rooftop. Tom Hulce, the Delta brother who tries to seduce the mayor's daughter while an angel and devil compete for his ear, kept somewhat classier company a few years later, when he played Mozart in *Amadeus* (1984).

NETWORK. 1976. Filmed April–July 1976; CFTO-TV Studios, Toronto. MGM Building and other locales, New York City. MGM Studios, Culver City.
Cast: Faye Dunaway, William Holden, Peter Finch, Robert Duvall, Ned Beatty, Beatrice Straight.
Director: Sidney Lumet.

This scathing satire of the television news industry succeeded in arousing the hackles of some of TV's most genially pompous millionaire news readers. Peter Finch, performing his last screen role as a network newsman gone berserk (and then cynically used to increase ratings), was first slated for the part of Max Schumacher that finally went to William Holden; and Holden was to have played Finch's role. Finch was actually fourth choice (not including Holden) for the role of Howard Beale; George C. Scott, Glenn Ford, and Henry Fonda had all refused it, and MGM was not enthusiastic about casting a foreigner in the role. An Australian actor who labored to perfect an American TV-bland accent for the part, Finch said he modeled his voice and TV personality on real-life anchorman John Chancellor. Finch and Holden became good friends on the set, but Holden somewhat fearfully approached his own scenes with Faye Dunaway (playing the dead-souled producer, based on a figure well-known to Hollywood insiders). The two had previously clashed while making *The Towering Inferno*, owing to Holden's anger over her habitual late arrivals on the set. This time, however, they related well, though Holden expressed later reservations about their bedroom scene; it was meant, he said, "to be more amusing than it came off." Robert Duvall said he tried to play network executive Frank Hackett like "a vicious President Ford." Office scenes were filmed in New York City, as were several other location sequences, while all broadcasting sequences occurred in a Toronto TV studio. Finch died suddenly just before the Academy Award ceremonies and received the first posthumously awarded Oscar (for best actor). Other winners: Dunaway as best actress, Beatrice Straight as best supporting actress, and Paddy Chayefsky for his screenplay.

NEVER ON SUNDAY. 1960. Filmed spring 1960; Greece: Piraeus; Perema.
Cast: Melina Mercouri, Jules Dassin, Georges Foundas, Titos Vandis, Despo Diamantidou.
Director: Jules Dassin.

Another victim of Hollywood's purge during the Red scare of the 1950s, Jules Dassin made this comedy (originally titled *The Happy Whore*) on a shoestring, casting his lover and future wife, Melina Mercouri, in the lead role of cheerful prostitute Illya. Dassin reluctantly cast himself as the naive American scholar when he couldn't pay enough to get Jack Lemmon, Henry Fonda, or Van Johnson for the part. He injured his back in the scene where he climbs a ladder to reach a dock, causing production to halt for three weeks; this was a severe financial blow, since he made the film without the normal minimal cushion of an insurance policy, a fact that didn't emerge until much later. Mercouri had problems lip-synching her title song with the previously recorded playback for the camera. She had never done this before, and as her timing repeatedly fell off and Dassin refilmed the scene again and again, her frustration mounted. When she finally exploded, a general melee erupted on the set with everybody yelling and slapping each other until the bedlam dissolved into hilarity and kisses. Then she got the scene right. The musical scoring by Manos Hadjidakis was largely off-the-cuff, composed on the spot and played by ear, since none of the musicians read music. His title song received an Academy Award. Mercouri later starred in a Broadway musical adaptation, *Illya, Darling*.

NEW YORK, NEW YORK. 1977. Filmed August 1976–February 1977; MGM Studios, Culver City.
Cast: Robert De Niro, Liza Minnelli, Mary Kay Place, Barry Primus, Lionel Stander.
Director: Martin Scorsese.

Martin Scorsese's nostalgic recollection of the big band era aimed for a harder, more realistic view than any Hollywood musical of those times could have dared. Scorsese created the shooting script by getting his cast to improvise on basic story situations for video cameras. He deliberately filmed on Hollywood sets rather than in New York City itself in order to recreate the romantically artificial look and feel of the New York that movie audiences of the 1940s saw. (Some scenes were filmed on the same sound stage where Judy Garland had filmed *The Pirate*.) Robert De Niro, noted for intense absorption into his roles, learned to play the saxophone for his part from jazz saxophonist Georgie Auld. (Auld also played a bandleader in the movie.) De Niro did not, of course, actually play the instrument in the film—Auld recorded the musical soundtrack earlier—but he learned proper fingering and breathing for all the numbers. In the climactic fight scene between De Niro and Liza Minnelli, the action turned so realistically violent that both performers and Scorsese ended up in a hospital emergency room for minor repairs. De Niro's wife, actress Diahnne Abbott, briefly played a torch singer. Rumors flew that Scorsese and Minnelli were having a torrid love affair during the filming, though both denied it. Both were criticized for trying to turn Minnelli into a Judy Garland look-alike, a charge they even more indignantly denied. Main title footage for the movie came from the 1946 *The Man I Love*, starring Ida Lupino. The video version of this film restored footage deleted from the original release.

A NIGHT AT THE OPERA. 1935. Filmed spring–summer 1935; MGM Studios, Culver City.
Cast: Groucho, Chico, and Harpo Marx, Allan Jones, Kitty Carlisle, Margaret Dumont, Sig Ruman.
Director: Sam Wood.

The sixth, most profitable, and many think the best of the Marx brothers' thirteen romps wasn't always funny on the set. Sam Wood, a humorless, disagreeable director, threatened several times to resign from the production. Groucho, for one, did his considerable best to harass the director into doing so. All three brothers fervently disliked Wood and made him the butt of crude practical jokes heretofore reserved for the stately Margaret Dumont. They mainly criticized his demand for endless retakes of scenes, then his invariable use of the first or second take he had filmed. The brothers auditioned key portions of the script on a vaudeville road tour before filming commenced. Kitty Carlisle, a serious though novice opera singer at the time, was recruited as Allan Jones's love interest. Years after she married playwright Moss Hart, she would call the film her one claim to fame, having had "no idea it would become such a classic." Jones (the father of popular singer Jack Jones) sang the only hit song ever associated with a Marx brothers picture: "Alone" became one of the top favorites of 1936. This was the first Marx film without brother Zeppo.

THE NIGHT OF THE HUNTER. 1955. Filmed spring 1955; California: Rowland V. Lee Ranch, Chatsworth (exteriors); RKO-Pathé Studios, Culver City; Republic Studios, Los Angeles.
Cast: Robert Mitchum, Shelley Winters, Lillian Gish, Billy Chapin, Sally Jane Bruce, Evelyn Varden, Peter Graves, James Gleason.
Director: Charles Laughton.

Arguably Robert Mitchum's best film, and one of the finest suspense movies ever made, *Hunter* was a financial disaster at the box office (despite its inclusion on that prestigious list of films that have been banned in Memphis). *Hunter* was Charles Laughton's first and only effort as a film director; he also condensed and rewrote James Agee's unusable script, though Agee received screenplay credit. Mitchum was filming *Not as a Stranger* at the same time and had to do many of his scenes for Laughton on Sundays and at other odd times. He and Laughton formed a mutual admiration society during their work. Laughton had no great love for children and despised directing them in this film, often ignoring the pair of youngsters who played the hunted runaways. Mitchum consequently found himself directing the children by default in several scenes. Shelley Winters had to reclaim her native Missouri accent for her role ("In this life we never forget our bad habits, Shelley," Laughton told her). Mitchum said Winters got what she deserved in her chilling underwater sequence, filmed in a studio tank. Other special effects included the hayloft scene, in which the children watch the preacher riding by on a plow horse; for reasons of perspective, Laughton used a midget actor on a pony for the scene. Much of Walter Schumann's musical score adapted folk tunes and themes from the Ohio Valley and West Virginia.

NIGHT OF THE LIVING DEAD. 1968. Filmed June–November 1967; Washington, D.C. Pennsylvania: Evans City; Pittsburgh: Hardman Associates; Latent Image Studio.

Cast: Duane Jones, Judith O'Dea, Russell Streiner, Karl Hardman, Marilyn Eastman.

Director: George A. Romero.

Mainline critics deemed this movie a new low in cynical exploitation filmmaking, and they deplored its effect on children. Made on a shoestring budget, George Romero's macabre horror film not only achieved an enormous popular success but introduced the concept of pure, unsubtle grossness as entertainment. It heralded an entire genre of explicitly gruesome films that went straight for throat and gut. The film's busy, flesh-eating zombies were all played by unknowns, mostly Romero's friends and advertising clients who had invested in the project. During months of on-again, off-again filming, its working title was simply *The Monster Flick*. Subsequent titles included *The Flesheaters* and *Night of Anubis*. Coproducer Karl Hardman said he played Harry Cooper in sharp contrast to what he considered the too-restrained style of lead actor Duane Jones. Hardman and Marilyn Eastman (playing Helen Cooper) were a real-life married couple, business partners in a Pittsburgh sound studio; and Karen Cooper, the daughter who devours them, was Hardman's own daughter Kyra. The residence used for the main set was an old farmhouse, formerly a church summer camp, about to be torn down near Evans City. Hardman recalled his death scene in the house, as Jones shoots him and he falls down the basement steps, as his most difficult. He said he kept tangling himself in the coat tree next to the basement door as he bounced off the piano, and for ten takes the coat tree followed him down the steps. He managed to avoid it on the eleventh take, by which time he was so exhausted from laughing he hardly had strength left to "die." The human flesh consumed by the zombies was actually lamb entrails from a local slaughterhouse, augmented with mannequin parts. Romero followed up with two sequels elaborating his hugely profitable premise that corpses aren't friendly: *Dawn of the Dead* (1979) and *Day of the Dead* (1985). John Russo's *The Complete Night of the Living Dead Filmbook* (1985) serves up all the gory details that one could hunger for.

NINOTCHKA. 1939. Filmed May–July 1939; MGM Studios, Culver City.
Cast: Greta Garbo, Melvyn Douglas, Ina Claire, Sig Ruman, Felix Bressart, Bela Lugosi.
Director: Ernst Lubitsch.

Garbo's twenty-sixth film (and first comedy) reminds us of the wit and sophistication with which Hollywood once handled confrontations between capitalism and communism. "Garbo Laughs!" headlined the movie ads; and well she might have, for the film proved a lifesaver after her career took a dive after *Conquest* (1937)—but she only acted in one more film before permanently retiring in 1941. Drink and drunks were anathema to the fastidious Swedish actress, and she refused at first to do her drunk scene; Ernst Lubitsch had a knack for directing difficult actresses, however, and he patiently cajoled her into it. Garbo became good friends with Ina Claire (playing the Grand Duchess), who had married Garbo's frequent costar and ex-lover John Gilbert in 1929 and was now his widow. (Gilbert died of drink and a broken career in

1936.) Look for Bela Lugosi (as Comrade Razinin) in one of his rare appearances outside a horror film. Spin-offs from this film included *Comrade X* (1940) and *The Iron Petticoat* (1956); *Silk Stockings* (1957) was a musical remake.

NORTH BY NORTHWEST. 1959. Filmed August–December 1958; New York: New York City; Phipps Estate, Old Westbury, Long Island. Chicago. Rapid City, South Dakota. California: Bakersfield; MGM Studios, Culver City.

Cast: Cary Grant, Eva Marie Saint, James Mason, Jessie Royce Landis, Leo G. Carroll, Philip Ober.

Director: Alfred Hitchcock.

Cary Grant's fourth and last film for Alfred Hitchcock was rated among the best of his career, but its plot was so complex that he often felt frustrated over the rationale for certain sequences. For example, the entire scene (filmed in Bakersfield) in which he is harassed by a crop-dusting plane left him bewildered, saying that such a role really belonged to David Niven. Hitchcock purposely withheld details of the plot from Grant and the entire cast in hopes their confusion would come across in performance. He admitted, with tongue planted firmly in ample cheek, that he intended this thriller as "one big joke"; even its title, based on a line from *Hamlet*, remained obscure. Hitchcock had first envisioned the film as a vehicle for James Stewart; but when the screenplay began to shape up as a spoof on spy thrillers, he realized that Stewart would be too earnest and dramatic for the lead role. During the filming, Grant separated from his wife, actress Betsy Drake, and they ultimately divorced. The studio had wanted Cyd Charisse for Grant's costar, but Hitchcock insisted on Eva Marie Saint, personally selecting her wardrobe and supervising every detail of her grooming. Jessie Royce Landis, playing Grant's mother, was almost a year younger than her 54-year-old "son." Hitchcock couldn't use the actual Mount Rushmore locale of Gutzen Borglum's sculptured presidential faces (except for background shots); the U.S. Dept. of Interior said such use would be "patent desecration." He was only allowed to recreate studio mock-ups of the faces below chin level for close-ups. (Hitchcock hated to part with his original idea of giving Grant a sneezing fit in Lincoln's nostril.) The

Long Island estate where an early sequence was filmed reappeared in *Love Story*. Look for the director's cameo appearance as a man crossing the street and missing a bus.

NOSFERATU THE VAMPYRE. 1978. Filmed 1977; the Netherlands: Delft; Schiedam.
Cast: Klaus Kinski, Isabelle Adjani, Bruno Ganz, Ronald Topor.
Director: Werner Herzog.

German director Werner Herzog's recreation of F. W. Murnau's silent classic *Nosferatu* (a film that subtly predicted, Herzog believed, the rise of Nazism in Germany) is a haunting mood piece, a succession of chilling tableaux as different from *Dracula* (1931) as a nightmare from a ghost story. Klaus Kinski, Herzog's perennial leading man, played the title role in heavy makeup that exactly duplicated Max Schreck's in the 1922 version. Some 11,000 specially bred white laboratory rats from Hungary, painted gray and used for the plague sequences, overran the set at Schiedam. The burgomeister at Delft had refused to permit the rodent invasion, insisting that the city had enough rats of its own to worry about. Citizens of Delft, which posed for the German city of Wismar in most scenes, had long memories of Nazi occupation and didn't exactly welcome German filmmakers, even without the rats. The final scene, filmed on a Dutch plain, used a trick shot of inverted clouds. Both German and English versions were shot, each with slightly different pictorial emphases as well as sound tracks; but the English one was pulled because the cast's unfamiliarity with the language resulted in unwanted laughs from filmgoers.

NOTHING SACRED. 1937. Filmed summer 1937; Selznick International Studios, Culver City.
Cast: Carole Lombard, Fredric March, Walter Connolly, Charles Winninger, Sig Ruman.
Director: William Wellman.

Ben Hecht wrote the screenplay (originally titled *Let Me Live*), one of Hollywood's most bitter and hilarious satires, aboard trains between New York and Los Angeles, creating the lead role of Hazel Flagg expressly for Carole Lombard. This was Lombard's only color film, and it remains one of her best. Her offscreen pranks, the practical jokes that passed incessantly between her and William Wellman, and her notoriously raw language kept the set in utter pandemonium. She didn't care much for Fredric March, who had once made a play for her, and she considered her love scenes with him her hardest chore in the picture. After one fight scene with him, she had to take the following day off to recuperate from bruises and scratches. To discourage his attentions, she invited him to her dressing room one night; after preliminary fumbling, March discovered to his disgust that she was wearing a rubber dildo. He never bothered her again. Walter Connolly was cast for the publisher's role at Lombard's suggestion. A 1953 stage musical version was entitled *Hazel Flagg*. This, in turn, was adapted for the screen as a Dean Martin-Jerry Lewis vehicle *Living It Up* (1954), with Lewis in the Lombard role.

NOTORIOUS. 1946. Filmed October 1945–February 1946; RKO Studios, Culver City.
Cast: Cary Grant, Ingrid Bergman, Claude Rains, Louis Calhern, Leopoldine Konstantin.
Director: Alfred Hitchcock.

Notorious was Cary Grant's second of four films for Hitchcock and his first of two teamings with Ingrid Bergman. Grant and Bergman made refreshing if not altogether likable lovers, while Claude Rains evoked sympathy as a villain. Among other memorable Hitchcockian moments was the prolonged kissing embrace of the costars. Hitchcock devised this three-minute sequence in defiance of the Hollywood censorship code, which prohibited any kiss lasting over three seconds. He got around the restriction by having Grant and Bergman kiss, then nibble, then talk and kiss again, holding each actual kiss no longer than three seconds. The scene proved ten times more erotic on screen than one long-held kiss would have been. Grant began this film still bearing a grudge against Hitchcock for fancied slights five years before, during the filming of *Suspicion*. He became one of Bergman's few costars who never fell in love with her, though they began a lifelong friendship on the set. Even Hitchcock was almost pathetically infatuated with her, but harmonica player Larry Adler occupied many of her offscreen hours at this time. Hitchcock had originally wanted Clifton Webb for Rains's role; and Ethel Barrymore had turned down the part of the victim's mother that went to Austrian actress Leopoldine Konstantin in her only American film. Hitchcock later claimed that he had been placed under FBI surveillance; during preparation for *Notorious* in 1944 and 1945, he created the plot device of having uranium ore stored in wine bottles—this, coincidentally, just before the A-bomb was exploded on Hiroshima and before the crucial role of uranium became public knowledge, thus alarming the government. His version of his own prophetic timing has, however, been disputed; the uranium factor was probably added to the screenplay after Hiroshima. Look for the director's cameo appearance as a party guest gulping a glass of champagne.

NOW, VOYAGER. 1942. Filmed spring 1942; California: Lake Arrowhead; Warner Bros. Studios, Burbank.
Cast: Bette Davis, Claude Rains, Paul Henreid, Gladys Cooper, Ilka Chase, Janis Wilson.
Director: Irving Rapper.

This Bette Davis film remains a classic of what Hollywood once labeled "women's pictures." She scrapped with her studio to land the lead role, which had originally been slated for Irene Dunne. One of the film's best remembered scenes involved the two-cigarette maneuver between Davis and Paul Henreid, in which he lighted both cigarettes in his mouth, then passed one to her. Henreid claimed to have originated this bit on the set, but it had apparently been used between George Brent and Davis herself in *The Rich Are Always With Us* (1932). Following *Now, Voyager*, at any rate, the fad caught on with the public, and Henreid couldn't go anywhere without being accosted by women begging him to "light me." Davis wore body padding and fake eyebrows for her early scenes. She formed lasting friendships with Henreid, Claude Rains, and Gladys Cooper, but she gave director Irving Rapper a hard time. Davis also reworked Casey Robinson's screenplay, determined to use as much of novelist Olive Higgins Prouty's dialogue as possible. (Title of both novel and film came from a poem by Walt Whitman.) Her friendship with Janis Wilson (playing Tina) resulted in Wilson later being cast in *Watch on the Rhine*. The sequences at Cascade, the sanitarium run by psychiatrist Rains, were filmed at scenic Lake Arrowhead.

The picture became a tremendous box office hit, and Davis said she received hundreds of letters from persons who strongly identified with her character's problems. Max Steiner received an Academy Award for his musical score.

O

ODD MAN OUT. 1947. Filmed summer 1946; Belfast, Ireland. Denham Studios, Denham, England.
Cast: James Mason, Kathleen Ryan, Robert Newton, F. J. McCormick, W. G. Fay, William Hartnell, Dennis O'Dea.
Director: Carol Reed.

Dublin's Abbey Theatre players made up most of the cast for this film that established Carol Reed's international reputation and gave James Mason—at the time, one of England's foremost matinee idols—the role that solidified his career. Mason, who always claimed this picture as his favorite, practiced for hours walking in time to William Alwyn's music, as he had to do in the film—and Reed also played recordings of Alwyn's score on the set to evoke the appropriate feeling. Reed always filmed in story sequence. This was Kathleen Ryan's screen debut (playing Kathleen) and Cyril Cusack's first appearance in a British film (he played Pat). American critic James Agee called the night scenes of Belfast some of the best city atmospherics ever filmed. After four decades, *Odd Man Out* remains topical in its story of Irish troubles, as those folk from the most Christianized island on Earth zealously continue to slaughter each other.

OF HUMAN BONDAGE. 1934. Filmed winter–spring 1934; RKO Studios, Los Angeles.
Cast: Leslie Howard, Bette Davis, Frances Dee, Reginald Owen.
Director: John Cromwell.

Katharine Hepburn, Ann Harding, and Irene Dunne had all turned it down. Bette Davis, however, succeeded in landing the role of slatternly waitress Mildred Rogers only after months of begging her studio chief, Jack L. Warner, to loan her to RKO for this adaptation of Somerset Maugham's novel. Warner couldn't understand why any young actress would crave such a part, but he finally acquiesced. And after twenty-one films she achieved the first major breakthrough of her career (to Warner's acute embarrassment). Leslie Howard and other British cast members strongly resented an American girl being cast as a Cockney and were barely civil to Davis at first; but when Howard saw her walking away with the picture, he quickly lost his icy indifference. Davis had prepared for weeks beforehand, hiring an Englishwoman to live in her home as dialect coach. The Britishers applauded her mastery of Cockney, and Maugham himself praised her performance. Rave reviews followed, but the movie faltered at the box office, and Davis was heartbroken not to be nominated for an Academy Award. But the resulting uproar among her colleagues gave her more publicity than if she had won the Oscar. As for Howard, he too regarded the film as one of his best. *Of Human Bondage* was twice remade (in 1946 and 1964), badly miscast both times. This one almost didn't make it to your VCR—for the original 1934 negative was unconscionably destroyed. In 1971, one 16-mm print was discovered, and the film received its first public showing in thirty-seven years.

OKLAHOMA! 1955. Filmed summer 1954–summer 1955; Arizona: Greene Cattle Company Ranch, San Rafael Valley. MGM Studios, Culver City.

Cast: Gordon MacRae, Shirley Jones, Charlotte Greenwood, Gloria Grahame, Gene Nelson, Rod Steiger, James Whitmore, Eddie Albert.

Director: Fred Zinnemann.

Rodgers and Hammerstein's long-running stage show came to the screen a decade after it opened on Broadway, becoming the durable prototype for flashy film versions of numerous stage musicals. "The mud is as high as a Cadillac's eye," sang crew members as daily rains fell on the Arizona locations crowded with the limos of worried studio executives. Arizona was chosen because the state of the title had too many oil derricks and noisy airplanes. Some interesting casting ideas—namely, Paul Newman and Joanne Woodward for the leads—

never worked out, and less interesting performers who could sing were chosen (though Rod Steiger, who had trained as an operatic singer before becoming an actor, excelled as Jud Fry, as did Gloria Grahame playing Ado Annie). Bambi Linn, playing Dream Laurey, was the only holdover from the stage cast. To create convincing cornfields, studio designers fashioned portable acres of ear corn, planting thirteen-foot stalks in boxes they hauled around on trailers for suitable placement. The longhorn cattle were brought in from California; an entire peach orchard was transplanted; and the wax peaches themselves were not without top-quality fuzz. This film marked several firsts: Rodgers and Hammerstein's first stage and screen collaboration, director Fred Zinnemann's first and only musical, and nineteen-year-old Shirley Jones's screen debut. (She and Gordon MacRae were reunited for *Carousel*.) The musical score won an Academy Award.

OLIVER! 1968. Filmed summer 1968; Shepperton Studios, Shepperton, England.
Cast: Mark Lester, Ron Moody, Oliver Reed, Harry Secombe, Shani Wallis, Jack Wild, Hugh Griffith.
Director: Carol Reed.

It was no accident that this became one of the few English musicals to make a hit with American audiences; it was American produced and aimed specifically toward our shores. Sweetly upbeat, unlike Dickens's *Oliver Twist*, on which the original stage musical was based, its incarnation as family entertainment was unlike anything else in Carol Reed's repertoire. He had wanted to cast Shirley Bassey as Nancy (played by Shani Wallis in her film debut), but Columbia Pictures vetoed her because a black actress, it was thought, would alienate audiences in the South. Ron Moody repeated his stage role as Fagin. Oliver Reed, the director's nephew, played Bill Sikes, while Welsh comedian Harry Secombe played Bumble; and nine-year-old Mark Lester took the title role, his fourth screen appearance. When Fagin opened his treasure box, Carol Reed had difficulty getting a suitable reaction shot from Lester; deciding that the lad had to be truly startled, Reed suddenly pulled a white rabbit from his jacket while filming the scene and got the reaction he wanted. The eighty-four rambunctious boys on the set, carefully selected by Reed for their street-waif looks and not for good behavior, occupied the full-time attentions of several harried handlers—getting them lined up on time, hushing them, herding them through scenes, drying tears, squashing sudden fisticuffs. This enormously successful film won six Academy Awards, among them, for best picture, best director, and best song score.

OLIVER TWIST. Filmed summer–autumn 1947; Pinewood Studios, Iver Heath, England.
Cast: Alec Guinness, Robert Newton, John Howard Davies, Kay Walsh, Francis L. Sullivan, Anthony Newley, Henry Stephenson, Diana Dors.
Director: David Lean.

Probably the best of several film versions of Dickens's classic tale, this production grew from David Lean's success with *Great Expectations* (1946). Though he condensed and omitted vast portions of the novel, he retained much of Dickens's dialogue and tried to treat the story as realistically as possible. Lean tested over one hundred youngsters for the title role, finding that most of them looked much too well fed; at last he hired nine-year-old John Howard Davies. (Davies grew up to produce such BBC-TV series as *Fawlty Towers* and *Monty Python's Flying Circus*.) Britain's child labor law would have prevented his being cast if the labor ministry hadn't winked at the violation. Alec Guinness's interpretation of Fagin proved extremely controversial, especially in the U.S., where an uncensored cut of this film couldn't be seen until 1970. Mainly at issue were charges of anti-Semitic stereotyping. (The film also provoked a West Berlin race riot on this account in 1949.) The role launched Guinness on his career of enacting odd people in various disguises. In his screen debut, Anthony Newley played the Artful Dodger.

ON GOLDEN POND. 1981. Filmed July–September 1980; Lake Squam, Laconia, New Hampshire.
Cast: Henry Fonda, Katharine Hepburn, Jane Fonda, Dabney Coleman, Doug McKeon.
Director: Mark Rydell.

The Fondas, father and daughter, performed together for the first and only time in this film, the rights to which Jane Fonda had purchased expressly "as a present to my father." It was also the first pairing for veteran costars Henry Fonda and Katharine Hepburn, as well as seventy-five-year-old Henry

Fonda's last big screen appearance. (In fast-deteriorating health from a heart condition, he appeared in one more made-for-TV movie before his death in 1982.) Highly publicized conflicts in the Fonda family gave a particular emotional edge to the father-daughter scenes, some of which the cast members and observers on the set found hugely affecting. Henry Fonda later remarked that he wasn't a religious man, but that "I thank God every morning that I lived long enough to play that role." No hatchling herself, Hepburn came to the role of Ethel Thayer in considerable pain; but her recent operation for a shoulder injury, suffered during a strenuous game of tennis, didn't slow her down much. In response to Hepburn's taunting, Jane Fonda learned to backflip dive; so for that scene a stuntwoman was not used. Hepburn gave Henry Fonda an old hat of Spencer Tracy's, the first of three that Fonda wore in the film; the hat had been given to Tracy by John Ford. Both costars received Academy Awards—Fonda's first, Hepburn's fourth—and Ernest Thompson's screenplay also won an Oscar.

ON THE BEACH. 1959. Filmed winter–spring 1959; Melbourne, Australia. California (exteriors): San Francisco; San Diego.

Cast: Gregory Peck, Ava Gardner, Fred Astaire, Anthony Perkins, Donna Anderson.

Director: Stanley Kramer.

Remember 1964? That was the year posed by this film for nuclear catastrophe. One of the first and grimmest dramas about the aftermath of atomic war, *On the Beach* was yet another of Stanley Kramer's message films. The Pentagon refused to lend the use of an atomic submarine, crucial to the story, on the curious grounds that real nuclear war would not wipe out most of the world's population, but only five hundred million or so, and that therefore the screenplay was inaccurate. Gregory Peck, playing the submarine commander, strongly objected to the consummation of his affair with Ava Gardner in the film, feeling it out of character; but Kramer insisted on this twist. Another person unhappy with Kramer's filmic interpretation was Nevil Shute, author of the novel, who boycotted the entire venture. Gardner found her off-camera time in Melbourne unbearably dull, telling a reporter that, for making a picture about the end of the world, "this is the place to do it." Fred Astaire, who celebrated his sixtieth birthday in Melbourne, performed his first straight dramatic role in this film. For his drunk scene, he imbibed a few slugs of real bourbon. Though not generally released in the Soviet Union, the film was well received by selected audiences there.

ON THE TOWN. 1949. Filmed March–July 1949; New York City (exteriors). MGM Studios, Culver City.
Cast: Gene Kelley, Frank Sinatra, Jules Munshin, Ann Miller, Betty Garrett, Vera-Ellen.
Directors: Gene Kelly, Stanley Donen.

This first of three Gene Kelly-Stanley Donen collaborations brilliantly set the stereotype for a whole bagful of Hollywood musicals about happy guys on an amorous spree before the ship/plane/train leaves or the cops/nerds/wives catch up. Filming on actual location was unique at the time; movie musicals heretofore had been stage-bound productions, and MGM was dubious about the idea of using real streets as backdrops for a song or dance. Thus the studio only allowed Kelly one week in Manhattan to film all the familiar sights, usually with a camera hidden in a station wagon. Certainly one innovative thing was fitting thirty-four-year-old Frank Sinatra with "symmetricals," a pair of padded buttocks to fill out his sailor pants—a need that, along with his hairpieces, he found humiliating and about which he became exceedingly defensive. After appearing with Kelly in *Anchors Aweigh* (1945), Sinatra had sworn that "they're not going to get me into another sailor's suit!" —but Kelly prevailed. The scene on the tiny rooftop of the Loew's Building was agony for Jules Munshin. Terrified of heights, he resisted until codirector Stanley Donen tied a rope around him beneath his sailor's suit, the other end held by an off-camera crewman. The musical score, though it won an Academy Award, used only four songs from the Broadway stage hit. Alice Pearce (playing Lucy Shmeeler) was the only holdover from the original cast.

ON THE WATERFRONT. 1954. Filmed September–December 1953; Hoboken, New Jersey.
Cast: Marlon Brando, Eva Marie Saint, Rod Steiger, Karl

Malden, Lee J. Cobb, Martin Balsam, Fred Gwynne. Director: Elia Kazan.

Because Marlon Brando played a good-guy informer, some critics unkindly suggested that this film was Elia Kazan's defensive response to turning informer himself when he went before the House Un-American Activities Committee, which ruined so many Hollywood careers. Kazan himself admitted as much, and despite his roster of future successes, he never lived down (or apologized for) this action that cost him much honor and many friendships. Playwright Arthur Miller refused Kazan's request to write the screenplay, so Kazan went to a fellow Congressional songbird, writer Budd Schulberg. Brando's reaction, like that of many others in the film industry, was mixed—anger at Kazan for informing, but solid admiration for him as a director. He felt that the classic scene in the taxicab between himself and Rod Steiger came across as phony; each improvised his part through seven takes of the scene, with Brando at first muffing his lines, then Steiger succumbing to tears. A disgusted Brando finally walked off the set instead of helping Steiger through his close-ups, a breach of filming etiquette for which Steiger never forgave him. Grace Kelly had been offered the female lead but decided to do *Rear Window.* Most of the key roles were based on actual persons—Brando's on whistle-blowing longshoreman Anthony De Vincenzo; Karl Malden's on waterfront priest John M. Corridan; and Lee J. Cobb's on mobster Albert Anastasia. Heavyweight boxers Tami Mauriello and Tony Galento were cast as union toughs, and many actual longshoremen blended with the cast as extras. This film was TV actress Eva Marie Saint's screen debut (also Martin Balsam's), and the music was Leonard Bernstein's first film score. Frank Sinatra thought he had been promised the lead role, and he sued producer Sam Spiegel for breach of contract when Brando was cast. (Sinatra's bitterness over being passed up strongly affected his relationship with Brando when the two later costarred in *Guys and Dolls*.) The mob still ruled the Hoboken docks during filming, and so fervid was the threat of actual violence that police protection was required for cast and crew. The film won eight Academy Awards: for best picture, Brando as best actor, Saint as best supporting actress, Kazan's direction, and Schulberg's screenplay, among others. Many union leaders, however, denounced the film.

ONE FLEW OVER THE CUCKOO'S NEST. 1975. Filmed autumn–winter 1974–75; Oregon State Hospital, Salem, Oregon.

Cast: Jack Nicholson, Louise Fletcher, Will Sampson, William Redfield, Brad Dourif, Michael Berryman, Scatman Crothers, Sydney Lassick.

Director: Miloš Forman.

Kirk Douglas bought the rights to Ken Kesey's novel in the early 1960s, intending to play the lead role of McMurphy himself (as he did on Broadway). He failed to interest a studio in the project, however, so he finally turned the package over to his son Michael, who succeeded in selling it and also co-produced the film. One wing of the Oregon State Hospital was loaned out to the company, and Jack Nicholson, cast as McMurphy (after Marlon Brando, Gene Hackman, and Burt Reynolds, among others, had refused the role), spent two weeks there familiarizing himself with hospital routines. Nor was Louise Fletcher's key role of Nurse Ratched easily cast; Anne Bancroft, Ellen Burstyn, Colleen Dewhurst, Angela Lansbury, and Geraldine Page all turned it down, apparently because they felt the part antithetical to the women's movement. Fletcher said she envied the rest of the cast their freedom, while her part required her to be constantly repressed and controlled. Will Sampson, a six-foot-five Creek Indian also noted as a Western artist, was doing manual labor in a national park when he was offered the role of Chief Bromden. Several actual patients of the hospital played extras; hospital superintendent Dr. Dean R. Brooks believed that the therapeutic benefits for these participating patients outweighed the risk factors inherent in the movie's theme. Brooks himself was enlisted to play his film counterpart, Dr. Spivey; and former Oregon governor Tom McCall played a news commentator. This film won five Academy Awards in all major categories—for best picture, Nicholson as best actor, Fletcher as best actress, Forman as director, and Lawrence Hauben and Bo Goldman for screenplay—only the second film to do so. (The first: *It Happened One Night*.) Barely mentioned during the award ceremonies was Ken Kesey, who made known his unhappiness with the film.

ORDINARY PEOPLE. 1980. Filmed autumn 1979; Illinois: Lake Forest; Fort Sheridan; Chicago.
Cast: Donald Sutherland, Mary Tyler Moore, Timothy Hutton, Judd Hirsch, Elizabeth McGovern.
Director: Robert Redford.

They weren't really, one hopes, *very* ordinary (except maybe to Robert Redford and his milieu), but this somber drama about the family problems of affluent folks nevertheless struck a large response. Redford, in his directorial debut, said he sought "the dark side of Mary Tyler Moore" and wouldn't let her affect the mannerisms she cultivated for years on TV. Moore effectively subverted her lovable image in her role as the neurotic mother, Beth Jarrett. Not without family problems herself at this time, she permanently separated from noted producer Grant Tinker, her husband of seventeen years, during the filming. Lee Remick had been considered for the role. The studio had wanted to cast Redford himself as Calvin, eventually played by Donald Sutherland, who was originally slated for Judd Hirsch's psychiatrist role. Timothy Hutton, son of actor Jim Hutton, made his screen debut at age nineteen as the son Conrad. Well-heeled residents of Lake Forest, where most scenes were filmed, played bit roles in the party sequence. Academy Awards went for best picture, to best supporting actor Hutton, to director Redford, and to Alvin Sargent's screenplay.

OUT OF AFRICA. 1985. Filmed January–June 1985; Kenya: Nairobi area; Masai Mara Game Reserve.
Cast: Robert Redford, Meryl Streep, Klaus Maria Brandauer, Michael Kitchen, Michael Gough, Rachel Kempson.
Director: Sydney Pollack.

While Sydney Pollack couldn't film this picture on Danish writer Isak Dinesen's own former coffee plantation in Kenya, he did use nearby locales that closely resembled those of her African reminiscences. Kenya newspapers branded the novelist a "downright racist" and strongly criticized the presence of the film company even though it pumped thousands of dollars into the local economy. Kurt Luedtke created the screenplay from Dinesen's memoirs with Meryl Streep in mind for the lead role; he thought that Robert Redford's role, however, wasn't big enough for such a superstar and tried to dissuade him from it. Kenya-born actor Mike Bugara, playing a servant, was so nervous working with Redford that in the scene where he spills a bottle of wine, he spilled it wrong six times. The hundreds of African extras were members of Masai and Kikuyu tribes, and most spoke no English. Because Kenya law forbade the use of wild animals, Pollack imported six trained lions and an eagle from California. In the panoramic scene of the coffee plantation, the blossoms on the plants are really dabs of shaving cream; the company couldn't wait for flowering season and collected all available aerosol cans of shaving cream for the shot. The film won seven Academy Awards—among them, best picture, direction, screenplay, and cinematography.

OUT OF THE PAST. 1947. Filmed autumn 1946; Mexico: Mexico City; Acapulco. Nevada. New York City. California: Los Angeles; San Francisco; Bridgeport; Lake Tahoe; RKO Studios, Culver City.

Cast: Robert Mitchum, Jane Greer, Kirk Douglas, Rhonda Fleming, Richard Webb.

Director: Jacques Tourneur.

Its title until just before release was *Build My Gallows High*, and the studio sought Humphrey Bogart for the lead role of detective Jeff Bailey. John Garfield and Dick Powell also turned it down. Robert Mitchum proved right for the part, establishing his macho persona and himself as a major star (though novelist-screenwriter Geoffrey Homes thought Mitchum looked "a little fat" for the role). Kirk Douglas, in his second film appearance, engaged in upstaging contests with Mitchum throughout, but old sleepy eyes always came out ahead. Jane Greer, in her first major starring role, recalled a love scene with Mitchum in which she noticed a thin brown line around his mouth; she didn't record her reaction when he told her "that's my chawin' tobaccy." The movie achieved a reputation as one of Hollywood's most notable film noir efforts. In 1984, Greer acted in its remake, *Against All Odds*, playing the mother of her original character.

THE OX-BOW INCIDENT. 1943. Filmed 1942; 20th Century-Fox Studios, Los Angeles.

Cast: Henry Fonda, Henry Morgan, Jane Darwell, Anthony Quinn, Dana Andrews, Frank Conroy.

Director: William Wellman.

This classic almost never got made. Studio chief Darryl F. Zanuck fought against it from the start, certain it wouldn't make money. (He was correct.) But Henry Fonda and William Wellman believed so strongly in the project that, in exchange, each agreed to film a picture that neither cared for; Fonda did *The Magnificent Dope* and Wellman directed *Thunder Birds*. Both pictures were released before *The Ox-Bow Incident*. Fonda wardrobed himself for his role weeks before filming began, then practically lived in the period clothing. Many Hollywood stars at this time were enlisting or being drafted for military service; though Fonda could have taken a deferment on account of his family, he chafed at his civilian status and immediately after filming was completed, he joined the navy. He didn't serve, however, until after a string-pulling Zanuck fetched him back to make *The Immortal Sergeant* (1943), ostensibly for the war effort—"a silly picture," said the furious actor. Fonda always considered *The Ox-Bow Incident* one of his best films.

P

THE PAPER CHASE. 1973. Filmed autumn–winter 1972–73; Toronto. California: Malibu; 20th Century-Fox Studios, Los Angeles.

Cast: Timothy Bottoms, Lindsay Wagner, John Houseman, Graham Beckel, Edward Herrmann, Craig Richard Nelson, James Naughton.

Director: James Bridges.

Stung by adverse reactions to the soporific *Love Story*, which was filmed at Harvard, officials at the university refused to take another chance, so director Bridges made this film mostly in Canada. Bridges, a former protégé of John Houseman, tried and failed to get James Mason, Edward G.

Robinson, Melvyn Douglas, Sir John Gielgud, or Paul Scofield for the role of redoubtable Professor Kingsfield, finally begging his seventy-one-year-old mentor to take the part. Stage and film producer Houseman had never considered himself an actor but entered the production enthusiastically. He said he remained painfully conscious of the disparity between his authoritarian role and his real feelings of inferiority in the troupe of highly professional, much younger performers. Also, he had little time to research his role, in contrast to the actors playing his students, some of whom had spent preparatory weeks at Harvard Law School. He credited John Jay Osborn, author of the novel, with helping him realistically portray Kingsfield. Despite all his qualms, Houseman not only received an Academy Award as best supporting actor but reprised his waspish role in the resultant TV series. Lindsay Wagner, playing Kingsfield's daughter, made her screen debut here.

PAPER MOON. 1973. Filmed summer 1972; Hays, Kansas. St. Joseph, Missouri. Paramount Studios, Los Angeles.
Cast: Ryan O'Neal, Tatum O'Neal, Madeline Kahn, John Hillerman, P. J. Johnson, Randy Quaid.
Director: Peter Bogdanovich.

Tatum O'Neal, nine-year-old daughter of Ryan, teamed with her dad in her acting debut as smart-mouth con artist Addie Pray. Peter Bogdanovich's effort to recreate the look and feel of grainy 1930s films struck some critics as pretentious. The elder O'Neal confirmed that Tatum's cigarette smoking scenes turned her green and nauseous. For himself, O'Neal said he hoped this movie would "exonerate" him from having made *Love Story*, a film he found hard to live down. Fifteen-year-old P. J. Johnson, playing the maid Imogene, was as irrepressible offscreen as on. ("They say I'm the greatest black actress since Ruby Dee. Who is she?") John Huston was originally scheduled to direct Paul Newman and Newman's daughter Nell Potts in this film; but when Huston backed out, the entire deal was revamped. Tatum O'Neal's Academy Award for best supporting actress made her the youngest Oscar winner ever in a regular category.

PAPILLON. 1973. Filmed February–October 1973; Fuenterrabia, Spain. Montego Bay, Jamaica. Joseph and Royale islands, French Guiana. Maui, Hawaii.

Cast: Steve McQueen, Dustin Hoffman, Victor Jory, Don Gordon, Anthony Zerbe, George Coulouris.
Director: Franklin J. Schaffner.

Henri Charrière, whose memoirs about the French penal colony of Devil's Island inspired this film, visited the prison set built in Jamaica and found it "all too realistic." Franklin Schaffner filmed the story in sequence, beginning with an unfinished script while screenwriter Dalton Trumbo tried to keep ten pages ahead of the camera. (Trumbo also appeared briefly as the prison commandant in his last film work.) Steve McQueen vacillated before reluctantly accepting the title role, giving perhaps the best performance of his film career. Accompanying him to the locations was actress Ali MacGraw, whom he married midway during the filming. Papillon's climactic leap from a cliff into the ocean was not a thing that high-priced stars do; stuntman Dar Robinson doubled the jump for McQueen after Schaffner went to Hawaii to find a suitable cliff. Dustin Hoffman, playing convict Louis Dega, found the physical and emotional demands of his role so rigorous that he lost twenty pounds during production. His wife, Anne Byrne, made her screen debut here as Dega's wife. By far the better actor of the costars, Hoffman managed not to arouse the wary McQueen's well-known insecurities, and the two related well. Victor Jory, playing his umpteenth Indian chief, appeared here in his final screen role. Cast and crew found location work not much less strenuous than serving a term on the actual Devil's Island. Some six hundred German-descended Jamaican farmers served as the French prisoners. For the butterfly-chasing sequence, 2,500 blue morphos butterflies were imported from South America; not one survived. Allied Artists financed this production mainly from the profits of *Cabaret*.

A PASSAGE TO INDIA. 1984. Filmed November 1983–spring 1984; India: Bangalore; Marabar Cave.
Cast: Judy Davis, Victor Banerjee, Peggy Ashcroft, James Fox, Alec Guinness, Nigel Havers, Richard Wilson.
Director: David Lean.

Sir David Lean's treatment of E. M. Forster's enigmatic novel formed an elegant capstone to his brilliant career. Lean was never one of those countless directors who never know the kind of scene they want until they see it performed. *Pas-*

sage, consequently, was filmed with great economy and with well-rehearsed framing of scenes (unfortunately often aborted by TV screen size), enabling Lean to capture what he wanted in usually one or two takes. But shaping high-powered actors to his intense vision involved many conflicts. Sir Alec Guinness, much of whose part as the Brahman mystic was cut from the finished version, remained simultaneously angry, fond, and respectful toward the director after battling with him in six films. Bengali actor Victor Banerjee, in his first Western screen appearance, fought the director (and won) on the issue of an appropriate English accent to adopt for his character of Dr. Aziz. Banerjee found inconsistencies in his role as written, but his performance made him the first Indian actor since Sabu to win international fame. Asian viruses plagued cast and crew except for the oldsters Lean, Guinness, and Dame Peggy Ashcroft, all over seventy. Lady Sandra Hotz Lean, the director's wife, performed extensive liaison work and also briefly appeared as James Fox's wife, Mrs. Fielding. Among many prizes won by the film, Ashcroft (playing Mrs. Moore) took an Academy Award as best supporting actress, and Maurice Jarre's musical score also won an Oscar.

PATHS OF GLORY. 1957. Filmed summer 1957; West Germany: Pucheim (interiors); Geiselgasteig Studios, Munich.
Cast: Kirk Douglas, Adolphe Menjou, Ralph Meeker, George Macready, Wayne Morris.
Director: Stanley Kubrick.

One of the most powerful and controversial antiwar films ever made, *Paths of Glory* was Stanley Kubrick's first major production, the one that brought him international fame. The screenplay frightened every studio he took it to, so he offered it to Kirk Douglas, who finally had the clout to raise financing from United Artists. But Douglas (who played Colonel Dax) almost backed out of the picture when Kubrick rewrote the script; in the end, however, Douglas stayed and the original version stuck. After weeks of preparation, Kubrick staged the crucial Battle of Ant Hill in a country pasture near Pucheim. Workmen dug acres of shell craters, littered the field with battle debris, and wired it with explosive charges. Soldiers' trenches were dug six feet wide (instead of the regulation four feet) to allow for tracking camera movements. Kubrick divided the battlefield into five zones, instructing each group of the eight hundred German policemen who played French troops as to their specific "dying zones" during the battle, which he filmed with six cameras. His meticulous attention to detail became notorious; he demanded an unheard-of fifty-six takes for the execution scene before he pronounced it okay. After all this effort, the film flopped on its initial release. Authorities in France, incensed at the portrayal of French officers, banned the film for years, and it was even excluded briefly from American military bases. Such reactions are often accurate indicators of a film's high quality as well as reliable forecasters of eventual classic status—and so it was with *Paths of Glory.* German actress Suzanne Christian, who played a frightened German girl in the final sequence, subsequently married the director.

PATTON. 1970. Filmed February–May 1969; Spain: Almería; Pamplona; Riofrío; Segovia; Seville Studios, Madrid. Greece. Sicily. Marrakech, Morocco. Knutsford, England. 20th Century-Fox Studios, Los Angeles.
Cast: George C. Scott, Karl Malden, Stephen Young, Michael Strong, Michael Bates, Tim Considine.
Director: Franklin J. Schaffner.

If knowing that this was Richard Nixon's favorite movie won't prejudice you against it, you'll see a finely drawn performance by George C. Scott of controversial World War II general George S. Patton, Jr. Actually this film pleased and enraged hawks and doves alike, each finding in it a confirmation of strongly held opinions about Vietnam. Franklin Schaffner insisted *Patton* was basically an antiwar film—while others, like Nixon and Ronald Reagan, viewed it as a grandly patriotic, pro-military hymn. General Patton's surviving family fiercely opposed the project at first—then, instead of suing the studio as promised, abruptly about-faced and lavishly praised the film. A long roster of famous actors turned down the title role before it came to Scott—among them Burt Lancaster, Robert Mitchum, Lee Marvin, and Rod Steiger. John Wayne eagerly sought the role, but its complexity was deemed beyond him. Scott took pains to create an authentic physical resemblance to Patton, shaving his head and changing his facial contours by adding a false nose and upper plate and caps of teeth. For Patton's gestures, speech, and mannerisms, he studied old newsreels. No easier on the people around him than was Patton himself, Scott frequently displayed his well-known tempestuous side during production, often turning his tension and frustrations to the benefit of his portrayal. He entirely ad-libbed the scene in which he directs the tank traffic. Believing that Karl Malden's portrayal of General Omar Bradley was much too pleasant, Scott took to calling Malden "Old Smiley" on the set. The real Bradley, still alive in 1969, served as a script source and consultant on the film. (Mrs. Bradley had wanted Charlton Heston to play her husband.) Location shooting occurred on seventy-one sites in six countries and three continents. Because of its ample supply of vintage American equipment from World War II, Spain provided most of the film locales. Battle of the Bulge sequences used Segovia for snow scenes, while amphibious landings were staged on coasts of Greece and Sicily. The film won seven Academy Awards, among them for best picture, director, and screenplay. Scott refused his best actor Oscar, a highly publicized move that no doubt won him vastly more attention than his gracious acceptance would have. General Patton would have slapped his face.

THE PAWNBROKER. 1965. Filmed autumn–winter 1964; New York City: Spanish Harlem; Lincoln Center; Movietone Studios (interiors). Jericho, Long Island, New York.
Cast: Rod Steiger, Geraldine Fitzgerald, Brock Peters, Jaime Sanchez, Thelma Oliver, Juano Hernandez.
Director: Sidney Lumet.

Rod Steiger's first big league starring role brought him an Academy Award nomination for what he considered one of his best screen portrayals, the repressed holocaust survivor Sol Nazerman. He took a risk, he said, when "I did that silent scream" at the end of the film, realizing how foolish he would have looked if it hadn't worked. Steiger recalled the frightened objections of various studios to doing the film: one wanted to eliminate the concentration camp scenes; another questioned whether Steiger's character had to be Jewish. Pushed by the expanding market for much less prudish European films, movie industry censors finally permitted (for probably the first time in a mainstream American feature) the exposure of nude female breasts, a key element in the story.

But the film, despite its present near-classic status, didn't escape censure. The Catholic Legion of Deceny objected to the brief nudity; Jewish groups labeled the film anti-Semitic; and blacks condemned Brock Peters's convincing gangster performance. A film that offended so many guardians of morality, one must conclude, has to be worth watching.

THE PETRIFIED FOREST. 1936. Filmed autumn 1935; Warner Bros. Studios, Burbank.
Cast: Leslie Howard, Bette Davis, Humphrey Bogart, Dick Foran, Porter Hall, Charley Grapewin.
Director: Archie Mayo.

Both Leslie Howard and Humphrey Bogart had played their respective roles in Robert E. Sherwood's play on Broadway in 1935. For the film version, however, the studio wanted Edward G. Robinson in Bogart's role of the vicious killer Duke Mantee. Only Howard's ultimatum—that either Bogart play the role or Howard would take a walk—saved not only Bogie's role but, in all probability, his future as a film actor. His snarling performance drew voluminous attention. Many critics still believe it his best work. While that performance typecast him for many years as one of Hollywood's most reliably nasty sorts, it also gave him his first big role, a foretaste of stardom. Not for nothing, said Bogie years later, did he name his daughter Leslie. Without studio permission, Bette Davis darkened her hair to its natural ash-blonde for her role of waitress Gabby Maple. In contrast to Howard's snobbish behavior when they made *Of Human Bondage*, the British actor became practically chummy toward Davis. There was much ado about how the film should end. Howard finally pulled rank to establish the ending we see—but not before some wild ideas were bandied about. At one point, Archie Mayo suggested (jokingly, one assumes) that a female evangelist like the real-life Aimee Semple McPherson suddenly emerge from the desert to convert everybody. *Escape in the Desert* was a 1945 remake, and *Key Largo* (1948), starring Bogart, used the same basic plot situation.

THE PHILADELPHIA STORY. 1940. Filmed July–August 1940; MGM Studios, Culver City.
Cast: Katharine Hepburn, Cary Grant, James Stewart, Ruth Hussey, Roland Young.

Director: George Cukor.

Katharine Hepburn worked closely with Philip Barry when he wrote the original play, which she performed on stage both before and after the film was made. Despite studio reluctance to cast her because of her waning box office appeal at the time, Hepburn's part-ownership of the play settled the matter. Modifications for the screen included a dry-eyed Hepburn at the end; George Cukor refused to allow her the tears scripted in the play. Hepburn had wanted either Clark Gable or Spencer Tracy for the role that finally went to Cary Grant. She especially liked the hostile scenes; in one bit, after she enthusiastically shoved Grant out the door, he ended up with genuine bruises. Grant insisted on top billing and salary, then donated his $125,000 from the film to the British War Relief Fund. Van Heflin had performed James Stewart's role in the stage play, and a bitter Heflin considered the switch a betrayal. Stewart's performance won him an Academy Award for best actor; many (including Stewart himself) felt it came as a deferred prize for *Mr. Smith Goes to Washington* (1939). Hepburn's performance marked a quick upswing in her career. *High Society* (1956) was a musical remake.

PICNIC. 1955. Filmed summer 1955; Kansas: Halstead; Hutchinson; Salina. Columbia Ranch, Burbank.
Cast: William Holden, Kim Novak, Rosalind Russell, Arthur O'Connell, Susan Strasberg, Cliff Robertson.
Director: Joshua Logan.

Joshua Logan had directed William Inge's play on Broadway and wanted Janice Rule to recreate her role of Madge for the movie. He was apparently overruled, however, by studio chief Harry Cohn, who saw his protégée, Kim Novak, as star material; but others thought Cohn was tossing an inexperienced Novak to the wolves. Novak was, at any rate, terrified to the point of paralysis at being cast in her first starring role. Her lack of self-confidence and withdrawn behavior created tension on the set. William Holden gave up trying to help her after she rebuffed him (or so he thought), and their offscreen relationship became a silent, armed truce. A crisis for Novak was the romantic waterfall scene filmed at Salina. In a state of utter panic she halted the action and told Logan she couldn't cry, as required for the scene. She then insisted that he pinch her hard on the arms to bring tears. The baffled, reluctant director finally did so, then filmed the scene in seven takes; between takes, makeup people swabbed Novak's arms to hide her black-and-blue marks. Logan said he threw up after it was over. Novak's later story was that Logan physically abused her in order to film the scene, a charge the director vehemently denied. Whatever the specifics of this episode, Rosalind Russell said that, in the collective effort to help make Novak look good, the entire cast suffered. Part of this effort included Russell's own ghastly makeup, camouflaging her natural beauty in her role as the haggard, desperate Rosemary. She played her marvelous drunk scene in one take. Holden strongly balked at doing the long, languid dance sequence with Novak, saying he absolutely couldn't dance. Despite long rehearsals with stand-ins, this proved to be correct; the only way that cinematographer James Wong Howe could finally film the scene was to shoot the hopelessly awkward couple from the waist up, making his camera dance instead of the actors' feet. Holden—who at the age of thirty-seven thought himself too old for this role—was required to shave his chest for his topless scenes because the production code censors had labeled hairy chests "dirty." Cliff Robertson made his screen debut as Alan, while Susan Strasberg turned seventeen on the set of her second film. Two thousand fascinated townspeople of Hutchinson served as extras in the actual picnic sequence. Howe's spectacular sunset shot, an unexpected bonus on the location, presaged a rip-roaring Kansas tornado that interrupted filming while cast and crew took to the ditches. The film made the song "Moonglow" a popular hit. Playwright Inge didn't care for the upbeat ending and later wrote an unsuccessful second version of his play titled *Summer Brave*.

PICNIC AT HANGING ROCK. 1975. Filmed spring 1975; Australia: Hanging Rock; Victoria; Strathalbyn and Clyde; Marbury School, South Australia; South Australian Film Corp. Studios, Norwood.

Cast: Rachel Roberts, Dominic Guard, Helen Morse, Jackie Weaver, Vivean Gray, Kirsty Child.

Director: Peter Weir.

Welsh actress Rachel Roberts, in one of her final screen performances, was a last-minute choice for the role of Mrs. Appleyard. She supplanted Vivien Merchant, who had been originally cast for the part but had to bow out owing to emotional distress over the breakup of her marriage to playwright Harold Pinter. The story was supposedly based on a true incident that occurred at the film's locale of Hanging Rock in 1900, but facts in the matter remained elusive despite the picture's semidocumentary pretensions. This enigmatic film brought director Peter Weir—and Australian filmmaking generally—to the forefront of international attention.

THE PICTURE OF DORIAN GRAY. 1945. Filmed autumn 1944; MGM Studios, Culver City.
Cast: Hurd Hatfield, George Sanders, Donna Reed, Angela Lansbury, Peter Lawford.
Director: Albert Lewin.

In some prints of this black-and-white film based on Oscar Wilde's novel, the final view of Dorian Gray's portrait explodes onto the screen in a dazzling burst of Technicolor. The twin American artists Ivan and Malvin Albright painted four canvases to represent the progressively changing portrait, using fresh chicken blood for the last. They also visited asylums and alcoholic wards to sketch properly dissolute faces. Sir Cedric Hardwicke's voice is heard speaking the narration. Angela Lansbury was cast as Sybil Vane because her face was said to resemble the Victorian ideal of feminine beauty, especially (according to critic James Agee) as seen in pornographic prints of the era. Lansbury's mother, stage actress Moyna MacGill, briefly appeared as the duchess. Years later, Lansbury said that her song in the film, "Goodbye Little Yellow Bird," had become a constant refrain in her career as people kept reminding her of it. This film gave Hurd Hatfield his only major starring role. Cinematographer Harry Stradling won an Academy Award.

PILLOW TALK. 1959. Filmed February–March 1959; Universal-International Studios, Universal City.
Cast: Doris Day, Rock Hudson, Tony Randall, Thelma Ritter, Nick Adams, Julia Meade.
Director: Michael Gordon.

Provisionally titled *Any Way the Wind Blows*, this first of three Doris Day-Rock Hudson teamings started the singer-actress on her successful string of squeaky-clean sex comedies, graduating to James Garner and Cary Grant as costars after

Hudson. Each of these romantic formula films seemed to contain at least one Doris Day "mad scene." This movie was the first in which she was able to wear clothing styles that enhanced rather than hurt her image and role. Ironically, at a time when few people knew that Hudson was homosexual, his playboy character pretends to be gay for part of the film. In his first comedy role, Hudson entered the project with serious misgivings about his ability to do the part. The costars, along with Tony Randall, became good friends on the set, however, and enjoyed themselves immensely. For the many takes of the final sequence in which Hudson carries Day to the street, she actually rode on a small shelf hooked over Hudson's shoulders so that he held only her legs and upper body. Dwayne Hickman had been slated for the part of Tony Walters but came down with flu on the day filming began, so Nick Adams stepped into the role. Day's final contented line—"All apartments look alike in the dark"—never got beyond the initial screenplay draft. In all, at least four writers worked on the screenplay, which won an Academy Award.

THE PINK PANTHER. 1964. Filmed autumn 1963; Paris. Italy: Rome; Cortina d'Ampezzo.
Cast: David Niven, Peter Sellers, Robert Wagner, Capucine, Claudia Cardinale, Brenda De Banzie, John Le Mesurier, Fran Jeffries.
Director: Blake Edwards.

This first of Blake Edwards's seven Pink Panther farces was the only one in which Peter Sellers, as the bumbling Inspector Clouseau, played a subordinate role. (While the Pink Panther title eventually came to represent Clouseau himself, it originally identified the precious stolen diamond hunted by the detective.) The role of Clouseau was slated for Peter Ustinov, who bowed out before filming began. For Sellers, playing Clouseau and enjoying the film's success relieved a period of deep melancholy following the failure of his first marriage. At first, Ava Gardner was considered for the role of Clouseau's wife Simone, played by French actress Capucine. David Niven entered the project assuming that the film would be primarily his vehicle, and he grew incresasingly dismayed as he watched Sellers steal the picture. More hilarious than anything on screen was Niven's account of a concurrent offscreen episode while filming on location in the Italian Alps. In preparing for one brief skiing scene, he hurtled down a mountain slope on an abnormally cold day. En route, he suddenly realized that, in his thin movie outfit, his penis had become frostbitten. When he reached the bottom, the excruciating pain of trying to thaw out the affected member led him to dunk it in a full brandy snifter that he took inside a hotel lavatory. His pain was not abated by the curiosity of bystanders. To the question "What *are* you doing?" Niven replied: "Pissing in a brandy glass. I always do." *The Pink Panther Strikes Again* (1976) was probably the best of the sequels; an animated cartoon series further obscured the title's genesis.

PINOCCHIO. 1940. Filmed summer–autumn 1939; Walt Disney Studios, Los Angeles.
Cast: Voices of Dickie Jones, Cliff Edwards, Christian Rub, Evelyn Venable, Walter Catlett.
Directors: Ben Sharpsteen, Hamilton Luske.

Disney's second animated feature (after *Snow White and the Seven Dwarfs*, 1937) is also one of the few major Disney cartoon productions that exists on video. Some critics consider *Pinocchio* his supreme achievement. Its visual detail and technical virtuosity surpassed all of Disney's previous (and much of his later) work. Twelve-year-old Dickie Jones voiced the title character, while old vaudeville entertainer Cliff Edwards (also known as Ukulele Ike) sang and spoke the film's Greek chorus part, Jiminy Cricket. Animator Ward Kimball, who created Jiminy, had been on the verge of quitting Disney Studios in disgust because much of his work had been cut from *Snow White*; but with the cricket, he came into his own. As a frequent character device used in subsequent Disney features, Jiminy foreshadowed such descendants as Thumper the Rabbit in *Bambi* (1942) and Tinker Bell in *Peter Pan* (1953). Veteran Austrian actor Christian Rub not only voiced the part of Gepetto the woodcarver, Disney artists also modeled the character on Rub's own actual appearance. Evelyn Venable, as the Blue Fairy, separately recorded all her lines, which were then intercut with the other voices. Her character was modeled after actress-dancer Marjorie Belcher (later known as Marge Champion), who had posed for the Disney rendition of Snow White. Dissatisfied with the way this film was shaping up, Disney scrapped the production when it was about half finished and ordered a fresh start. A technical innovation was his first extensive use of the multiplane camera, in which animation was accomplished by photographing cutouts placed at varying distances from the camera, using up to twelve planes of perspective in order to give added dimension to the frame. In the credit titles, note T. Hee, listed as one of the sequence directors. That's not a leg-pull; Thornton Hee managed the Stromboli scenes. Jiminy's song "When You Wish Upon a Star" won an Academy Award for Leigh Harline, its composer.

THE PIRATE. 1948. Filmed May–August 1947; MGM Studios, Culver City.
Cast: Judy Garland, Gene Kelly, Gladys Cooper, Walter Slezak, The Nicholas Brothers.
Director: Vincente Minnelli.

One of MGM's best musicals, adapted from a Lunt-Fontanne stage hit of 1942, was also one of Judy Garland's best. She performed mainly on raw nerve, for her personal life at the time was a shambles. Existing day-to-day on the verge of total physical and emotional breakdown, she consumed staggering quantities of sleeping pills and uppers, smoked four packs of cigarettes a day, and suffered perpetual malnutrition and fatigue. Her late arrivals and absences on the set, her testiness with cast and crew, and her periodic episodes of hysteria and paranoia—accusing Gene Kelly and Vincente Minnelli of conspiring to ruin her career—all reflected the depths of her anguish. It didn't help that her role was probably the most strenuous one of her career; and that her marriage with a seemingly unsympathetic Minnelli was also on sharp rocks. Before the climactic "Be a Clown" number, Minnelli told jokes to get Garland laughing hysterically. Immediately after completing her work in the film, the actress entered a sanitarium for a respite from work and life. Liza Minnelli, born in 1946, made her brief screen debut on her mother's lap in this film, which was the second of four Garland-Kelly teamings. Kelly, whose pirate ballet spoofing Douglas Fairbanks, Sr., was filmed last, did all his own dangerous stunt work in that sequence. Songwriter Cole Porter expressed final disappointment with his own music for the film—and Garland's antipathy also included him, finally. Several Southern cities cut the "Be a Clown" number from the film because of Kelly's teaming with the black Nicholas Brothers.

A PLACE IN THE SUN. 1951. Filmed October 1949–March 1950; California: Lake Tahoe; RKO Ranch, Encino; Paramount Studios, Los Angeles.

Cast: Montgomery Clift, Elizabeth Taylor, Shelley Winters, Keefe Brasselle, Raymond Burr, Anne Revere.

Director: George Stevens.

This second filming of Theodore Dreiser's novel *An American Tragedy* (the first came in 1931) defanged Dreiser's powerful social indictment, turning it into a commercial if compelling love story. This was the first of three teamings for Montgomery Clift and Elizabeth Taylor; it was their best and certainly most erotic movie. Stunningly beautiful Taylor at age seventeen had just emerged from the child-actress category, was still chaperoned by her mother, and remained blissfully ignorant of Dreiser's novel and the fact that George Stevens meant to make her *act*. Clift's intensity and obsessive concentration on his role fascinated her, and she promptly developed a huge schoolgirl crush on him. The twenty-nine-year-old Clift, though fond of Bessie Mae, as he called her, didn't reciprocate, but the two began a close, lifelong platonic friendship. One especially strenuous sequence for Taylor was her swimming scene with Clift (the first sequence of the movie to be filmed) at Lake Tahoe; the water was freezing cold, and Taylor was suffering from menstrual cramps. For this "summertime" scene, which required hours to film, Stevens had patches of surrounding snow shoveled away. He played mood music to prepare his costars for their intimate close-ups. Clift readied himself for his climactic sequence by spending a night locked in the San Quentin Penitentiary death house. Taylor's farewell scene in the prison with Clift, filmed last, became a true emotional trauma for her, signifying in some sense a real-life, as well as movie, parting. Shelley Winters had all but hog-tied Stevens to land one of her major screen roles as the frumpish Alice; but she soon developed mixed feelings toward the director for making her look so unglamorous alongside Taylor. Her role, moreover, typecast her in mousy or brassy parts. Winters said she drove white Cadillac convertibles (similar to Taylor's in the film) for years afterward to compensate for her intense feelings of inferiority while making the film. Raymond Burr, as the savage prosecutor Marlowe, eventually found himself inhabiting courtrooms regularly as TV's popular Perry Mason. Anne Revere played Clift's mother; a descendant of patriot Paul Revere, she became another victim of the Hollywood blacklist, not appearing again on screen until 1970. Academy Awards went to director Stevens and for the film's screenplay, cinematography, music, editing, and costumes.

PLACES IN THE HEART. 1984. Filmed September–December 1983; Waxahachie, Texas.
Cast: Sally Field, Danny Glover, John Malkovich, Lindsay Crouse, Ed Harris.
Director: Robert Benton.

This Depression drama, a Reagan-era sermon about how hard work finally surmounts all sorts of human disaster, was loosely based on Robert Benton's own family album. He filmed it in Waxahachie, his Texas hometown, he said, in order to have a reason to go back there. (*Tender Mercies* had been filmed in the same town two years previously.) Sally Field, in the lead role modeled on Benton's great-grandmother, had difficulty in playing a character so vastly different from herself, citing the woman's veiled sexuality and basic emotional frailty as examples of those differences. John Malkovich made his screen debut here as the blind boarder, Mr. Will. Field's Academy Award for best actress inspired her now-famous line at the award ceremonies: "You really *like* me!" Benton's screenplay also took an Oscar.

PLANET OF THE APES. 1968. Filmed May–August 1967; Page, Arizona. Lake Powell, Utah. California: Century Ranch, Malibu; Point Dume; 20th Century-Fox Studios, Los Angeles.
Cast: Charlton Heston, Roddy McDowall, Kim Hunter, Maurice Evans, James Whitmore, Linda Harrison.
Director: Franklin J. Schaffner.

Getting into the skin of his character, said Maurice Evans, proved a tall order when that skin was an orangutan's. He accepted the part of autocratic Dr. Zaius when Edward G. Robinson had to turn down the role because of ill health; Robinson also was unable to deal with the special latex makeup forming the mobile ape masks worn by almost all the cast. About twenty percent of the budget went into that makeup, which took three hours each day to apply and was extremely uncomfortable. Prop designers created a special rifle (the Rea Voom 88) to accommodate an ape's paw. Desert scenes were filmed in remote areas of Arizona and Utah; the greenbelt sequences, filmed at the studio ranch, used the same waterfall seen in *Doctor Dolittle* (1967); and Point Dume served as the final beach locale. Charlton Heston underwent more rough handling than usual in this picture, finding that his role tested his considerable stamina. One of his worst days occurred when filming the sequence in which he was caged and subdued by a fire hose; he had caught a cold, and his rasping voice as he screamed his last speech of the sequence was hardly faked. Equally taxing was the hunt sequence, wherein he ran naked through poison-oak undergrowth at Century Ranch. Three alternative versions were suggested for the startling climax, but Heston's own version won out. Several sequels catapulted the series into self-parody. John Chambers won an Academy Award for makeup design.

PLATOON. 1986. Filmed March–May 1986; Philippines.
Cast: Charlie Sheen, Tom Berenger, Willem Dafoe, Keith David, Kevin Dillon, John C. McGinley.
Director: Oliver Stone.

It took ten years for writer-director Stone to get *Platoon* made. Based on his own combat experiences in Vietnam, Stone presented, by critical consensus, the most brutally honest and compelling picture of that soul-sucking war, an effort ranking with the classic war films of Jean Renoir and Stanley Kubrick. Hollywood studios refused to touch it, and major financing—as with most of the serious films about Southeast Asia—came from foreign producers. Just before production started, ex-Marine Captain Dale Dye (playing a captain in the film who calls an air strike on his own defeated position) led the cast through a grueling, two-week boot camp in Philippine jungles. He demanded authentic sweat, discomfort, and military procedures; and Stone began filming the stinking, sore-footed performers without giving them rest or break from their suffering. Recalling the scene in which he savagely beat a crippled peasant, Kevin Dillon (playing Bunny) said he wasn't positive the Filipino extra in the part knew that "we were just filming a movie." Military hardware came from the Philippine government. Charlie Sheen, playing Chris, is the son of actor Martin Sheen (who appeared in his own Vietnam War role in

Apocalypse Now), and Anthony Quinn's son, Francisco, played Rhah. Stone himself briefly appeared as an officer in a bunker. Numerous veterans lauded *Platoon* as the first film about Vietnam that matched the truth of their own experiences. Others, including Veterans Administration officials, feared that the picture would reawaken nightmares and stress symptoms of combat vets. And many conservatives blasted the film as anti-American. It won four Academy Awards, including Oscars for best picture and best director.

POPEYE. 1980. Filmed January–June 1980; Malta: Anchor Bay; Kalkara; Filfla; Comino.
Cast: Robin Williams, Shelley Duvall, Ray Walston, Paul Smith, Paul Dooley.
Director: Robert Altman.

Dustin Hoffman had agreed to play the title role in this offbeat musical based on E. C. Segars's classic comic strip, but he backed out because of creative differences with screenwriter Jules Feiffer. The casting of TV comic Robin Williams as Popeye was a sudden inspiration of producer Robert Evans. Williams had to work himself up to the sailorman's supreme self-confidence ("I yam what I yam"). Hesitant and frightened at first, he walked out of Evans's office repeating to himself, "Yes, I can. *Sure I can*. I felt like the little actor that could." He watched old Popeye cartoons and worked on lowering his voice, comparing the effort to gargling with pebbles. He also undertook a strenuous program of workouts, tap dance, and acrobatics, dropping weight and getting limber for the role. The swollen forearms worn by Williams and Ray Walston (playing Poopdeck Pappy) were foam-rubber and latex sheaths, extremely uncomfortable and in constant need of "rehairing" and touching up; for Williams it was like "wearing two hot loaves of French bread." A small piece of latex glued over his eyelid helped him keep his right eye "squinky." Shelley Duvall was cast as Olive Oyl after Gilda Radner proved unavailable: her stiff, black ponytail required two hours of daily construction. During the filming, Duvall formed a romantic attachment with Stan Wilson, who played the barber. Cast as Wimpy, Paul Dooley made a valiant effort to add pounds by gorging on pasta but ended up wearing a padded fat-suit to fill in his frame. As the "infink" Swee'pea, director Altman cast his own year-old grandson,

Wesley Ivan Hurt; the baby's one-sided grin was the result of a partial facial paralysis, not a permanent condition. The entire movie village of Sweethaven was built to resemble a tacky Cape Cod shanty town on a deserted inlet located on the jagged northwest coast of Malta. Because the island is quite treeless, almost every stick and board had to be imported. Most of the props were plaster models, built by craftsmen on the set; tons of breakaway furniture and glass, as well as numerous special effects and creative stunt work, went into the roughhouse sequences. The Pirate's Cove sequence used the large special-effects tank at Kalkara that was previously used in *The Bedford Incident* (1965) and *Orca* (1977). Sea chase and boat ramming sequences occurred at open sea near Filfla and Comino islands. Bridget Terry's book *The Popeye Story* (1980) gives fascinating production background.

THE POSEIDON ADVENTURE. 1972. Filmed summer 1972; California: HMS *Queen Mary*, Long Beach; 20th Century-Fox Studios, Los Angeles,

Cast: Gene Hackman, Ernest Borgnine, Red Buttons, Carol Lynley, Roddy McDowall, Stella Stevens, Jack Albertson, Shelley Winters.

Director: Ronald Neame.

First (and probably best) of the spectacular disaster films that Seventies audiences found so appealing, *Poseidon* combined actual shipboard scenes with creative special effects to deliver the last full measure of vicarious danger. The real ship was the old luxury liner *Queen Mary*, permanently docked at Long Beach since 1967 as a floating museum; she never moved, but the rocking camera and decks awash from sideline hoses will make you believe she did. Upside-down sets for representing interiors of the capsized ship were built to exact scale from *Queen Mary* photos and blueprints. For the rising-water sequences, sets were placed on a giant sled and eased into a studio reservoir at a thirty-five degree angle. The radio room set could swing 180 degrees from the horizontal on an axle, permitting a most believable illusion of capsize. After the disaster episode, Ronald Neame directed the picture in story sequence, and the cast spent the rest of their weeks damp or drenched, shrouded in steam and smoke. The film won an Academy Award for best song ("The Morning After"). Sequel: *Beyond the Poseidon Adventure* (1979).

THE POSTMAN ALWAYS RINGS TWICE. 1946. Filmed autumn 1945; California: Laguna Beach; MGM Studios, Culver City.

Cast: Lana Turner, John Garfield, Cecil Kellaway, Leon Ames, Hume Cronyn.

Director: Tay Garnett.

This film noir derived from James M. Cain's novel gave Lana Turner one of her best parts. Director Tay Garnett dressed her entirely in white for her steamy role of Cora, hoping thereby to give her a patina of purity and fend off the production code censors. His ploy worked well. Suggestive sexuality also decorated off-camera scenes; Garnett (who fell off a three-year wagon during the filming, interrupting production while he dried out) recalled "some fairly raw kidding" on the set and received a fur-lined jockstrap from Turner after the filming. Turner's romance with the married Tyrone Power flamed hot about this time (years later, she claimed that Power had insisted on her having an abortion in South America shortly after this film was completed). Cameron Mitchell almost got John Garfield's role; only the latter's timely release from military service owing to his bad heart permitted him to join the cast. Previous versions of Cain's novel included the French *Le Dernier Tournant* (1939) and the Italian *Ossessione* (1942). In 1981 it was remade with Jack Nicholson and Jessica Lange under its 1946 title.

THE PRIVATE LIFE OF HENRY VIII. 1933. Filmed spring 1933; Elstree Studios, Borehamwood, England.

Cast: Charles Laughton, Merle Oberon, Robert Donat, Binnie Barnes, Elsa Lanchester, Wendy Barrie.

Director: Alexander Korda.

It's thick-sliced ham all the way, a bit overcured for today's tastes, but interesting for what was considered an Oscar-winning performance in 1933. Charles Laughton, at age thirty-three, spent weeks at Hampton Court Palace researching every known aspect of the much-married British monarch—studying portraits, taking lessons from a professional wrestler for his wrestling scene, and outfitting himself with authentic clothing from surviving sketches and from Henry's suits of armor in the famed Tower of London collections. The production was low budget. All of the cast received deferred salaries, and Laughton feared that the flimsy canvas and cardboard sets would collapse. Alexander Korda began making the film with no certainty that he could finish it. Costs forced him to refuse Laughton's demand for ample rehearsal time, and he ended the film vowing that he would rather die than direct Laughton again. Merle Oberon, playing Anne Boleyn, fell deathly ill before her turn came on camera; she lapsed into a coma and later claimed to have undergone an out-of-body experience during the crisis. Incensed at the brevity of her part, which Korda had offered her on impulse, she swore to make the audience "remember those two minutes" of the film, which helped establish her as a star. The song voiced by Binnie Barnes, playing Katherine Howard, was reputedly written by Henry VIII himself. As Anne of Cleves, Elsa Lanchester, wife of Laughton, said she made herself as ugly as possible in a blonde wig. This film won Britain its first international acclaim in cinema, thanks to Laughton's Academy Award as best actor, and inspired a succession of historical costume dramas. Laughton played Henry VIII again in *Young Bess* (1953). And Korda, who later wed Oberon, built a colossal production empire on the foundations of this picture's popularity.

THE PRIVATE LIVES OF ELIZABETH AND ESSEX. 1939. Filmed spring–summer 1939; Warner Bros. Studios, Burbank.

Cast: Bette Davis, Errol Flynn, Olivia de Havilland, Vincent Price, Donald Crisp, Henry Daniell, Leo G. Carroll.

Director: Michael Curtiz.

Most actresses of the time panted to costar with Errol Flynn. But after playing opposite him in *The Sisters*, Bette Davis wasn't eager to replay the experience in this film based on Maxwell Anderson's play *Elizabeth the Queen*. Davis thought Flynn miscast for the role of Essex, and her no-nonsense professionalism seems to have quite intimidated him. Their animosity grew as filming progressed. According to Davis, in all their scenes together, she pretended that he was Laurence Olivier. Flynn maintained that she slapped him unnecessarily hard with her bejeweled hand during a rehearsal for their public confrontation scene, causing him to throw up twice. Only his sincere threat to slug her back finally persuaded her to fake the crucial blow. Flynn also demanded rewrites of his own lines, saying he couldn't memorize Anderson's blank-verse dialogue. Davis threatened to quit the picture unless its original punnish title was changed from *The Lady and the Knight* (Flynn had proposed *The Knight and the Lady*); despite studio misgivings that the new (i.e., present) title sounded too British, the change was made to placate her. And neither costar liked being directed by blustering Michael Curtiz. Olivia de Havilland, playing Lady Penelope Grey, said she was miserable throughout the filming; all her concentration was on how to convince studio chief Jack Warner to loan her out for David O. Selznick's upcoming *Gone With the Wind*. The film won high praise, especially for Davis's acting and care for authenticity in her role. Horrified studio opposition could not prevent her from having her hairline shaved back two inches in order to preserve the illusion of baldness beneath the various red wigs she wore. This was Davis's first color film. She reappeared as Elizabeth I—giving a much better performance, she believed—in *The Virgin Queen* (1955). Look for Nanette Fabares (later Fabray) in her first adult screen role as Lady Margaret Radcliffe. Many sets of this film were recycled the following year for another Flynn vehicle, *The Sea Hawk*.

PRIZZI'S HONOR. 1985. Filmed autumn 1984; New York City. Los Angeles.
Cast: Jack Nicholson, Kathleen Turner, Anjelica Huston, William Hickey, John Randolph.
Director: John Huston.

Jack Nicholson gained thirty pounds and adopted a Brooklyn accent for his role of mobster Charley Partanna. He joked that John Huston completed the film with "more one-takes than since I worked with Roger Corman" (in *The Raven*, 1963). Nicholson's housemate Anjelica Huston, the director's daughter, played Maerose Prizzi. John Huston had wanted to cast an old friend, ninety-year-old character actor Sam Jaffe, as the family don; but Jaffe's untimely death resulted in the part being assigned to William Hickey. Anjelica Huston won an Academy Award as best supporting actress.

THE PRODUCERS. 1968. Filmed May–July 1967; New York City.
Cast: Zero Mostel, Gene Wilder, Dick Shawn, Kenneth Mars, Estelle Winwood, Lee Meredith.

Director: Mel Brooks.

Writer-director Mel Brooks originally titled his "high-class low comedy" *Springtime for Hitler*, the name of the musical produced by Zero Mostel and Gene Wilder within the film (derived from the old summer-stock favorite, *Springtime for Henry*); but distributor Joseph E. Levine insisted on the title change. Brooks wrote the part of lunatic Nazi playwright Franz Liebkind with the idea of playing it himself. Dustin Hoffman also wanted the role but chose instead to do *The Graduate*, and Kenneth Mars was finally selected. (Brooks did appear, however, as one of the Nazi chorus boys.) This was Brooks's first film, and explosions of temper and frustration resounded as the frenetic, neophyte director clashed head-on with veteran stage comedian Mostel, who cherished his own agenda for burlesquing legitimate Broadway. Both exterior and interior theatre sequences were filmed at Manhattan's Playhouse Theatre. Brooks won an Academy Award for his screenplay.

THE PROFESSIONALS. 1966. Filmed autumn 1965; Valley of Fire State Park, Overton, Nevada. California: Death Valley; Indio; MGM Studios, Culver City.

Cast: Burt Lancaster, Lee Marvin, Jack Palance, Robert Ryan, Woody Strodc, Claudia Cardinale, Ralph Bellamy.

Director: Richard Brooks.

Dust storms and Lee Marvin's boozing binges got production of this Western off to a slow start, but it was also Marvin who taught Italian actress Claudia Cardinale the rudiments of riding. All the lead players in this expensive effort had served as enlisted men in the marines or army, causing Marvin to muse on the fact of "all those millions riding on the backs of Pfc's." At age fifty-three, circus acrobat Burt Lancaster performed all his own stunts, including his cliff-scaling sequence.

PSYCHO. 1960. Filmed December 1959–January 1960; California: Revue Studios (interiors) and Universal Studios, Universal City; Los Angeles.

Cast: Anthony Perkins, Janet Leigh, Vera Miles, John Gavin, Martin Balsam, Patricia Hitchcock, John McIntire.

Director: Alfred Hitchcock.

Psycho brought a sharper, more urgent focus on terror—something spinning out of control, gone wildly berserk—than had any previous Hitchcock chiller. It also marked a new peak of his obsession with violence toward women, today an endless topic of Hitchcock seminars. He closed the studio lot during filming, demanding utter secrecy from cast and crew—a publicity ploy that naturally provoked extraordinary interest in the picture long before its release. Thereupon he maintained this intrigue by insisting that no moviegoer be seated once the show began. The director said his aim was to draw the audience into an accessory role in the action. In Janet Leigh's famous shower scene, Hitchcock created the suggestion of violence rather than an outright display of it. That crucial scene was a dynamic montage of skilled camera work—seventy-eight separate shots in forty-five seconds that took a week to film. The blood washing down the drain was really chocolate sauce. (Studio executives, reported Hitchcock, seemed much more disturbed about the unprecedented sound and view of the flushing toilet in the bathroom scene than about the implicit savagery.) Anthony Perkins was absent during filming of the shower sequence; a stand-in replaced his shadowy figure. Making his character a compulsive candy eater was, he said, his own idea. The voice of Mother Bates was dubbed by actress Virginia Gregg. The staircase scene in which the killer attacks Martin Balsam was also artful camera trickery. As he seemed to lose his balance atop the stairs, Balsam was actually safe in a chair, merely throwing up his arms, with the careening staircase projected on a transparency screen behind him. John Gavin (who became U.S. Ambassador to Mexico in 1980) expressed embarrassment about having to play his hotel room scene without a shirt; screenwriter Joseph Stefano finally convinced him to use those feelings of shame in his role of Leigh's lover. This film marked the final screen appearance of the director's daughter Pat, who played Leigh's office coworker. Hitchcock's own cameo appearance came as a man in a cowboy hat waiting for a bus. *Psycho* was Hitchcock's biggest box office success. The menacing Bates mansion, built only two-thirds natural size to heighten dramatic effect, reappeared (as did Perkins) in the sequels *Psycho II* (1983) and *Psycho III* (1986).

THE PUBLIC ENEMY, 1931. Filmed February–March 1931; Warner Bros. Studios, Burbank.

Cast: James Cagney, Jean Harlow, Eddie Woods, Joan Blondell, Mae Clarke, Donald Cook.

Director: William Wellman.

This is the film in which an enraged James Cagney smashes a half grapefruit in Mae Clarke's face, a one-take scene that neither performer was ever allowed to forget. Several versions exist as to how it originated, but the Cagney-Clarke account sounds most plausible. The scene, they said, was actually staged as a practical joke on the film crew, just to get their stunned reactions, with no thought of using it for the completed print. But it was, and for years afterward Cagney couldn't go into a restaurant without receiving a complimentary half-grapefruit (which he usually ate). Women's groups protested the scene. Though Clarke performed in some ninety subsequent films, she always remained known as the Grapefruit Girl, maintaining that the citrus industry missed a cue by not enlisting her to do commercials. (Rumors circulated that Clarke's ex-husband, Monte Brice, a brother of Fanny Brice, would laugh so hysterically during the grapefruit scene that he had to be ushered out of movie houses.) Louise Brooks had been originally cast for Clarke's role. Cagney, basing his portrayal on Chicago gangster Dion O'Bannion and two New York toughs he had known as a boy, earned himself stardom, but also typecast himself as a cocky hood in this film. He worried about the effect of his performance on his aged mother, writing to remind her that the whole thing was, after all, only make-believe. Cagney and Eddie Woods (playing Matt Doyle) began the film with reversed roles, then were recast. Donald Cook (playing Mike Powers), instead of faking his punch, actually hit Cagney on the jaw, breaking a tooth, an action that Cagney believed was instigated by director William Wellman. Real bullets crumbled the wall beneath Cagney's feet in one scene. (The practice of using live ammunition in films was never questioned until a few years later.) Filmmaking was never more ungentle an art than in some of these early Hollywood sound productions that seemed almost as rowdy on the make-believe set as the times and characters they portrayed.

PYGMALION. 1938. Filmed spring 1937; Pinewood Studios, Iver Heath, England.
Cast: Leslie Howard, Wendy Hiller, Wilfrid Lawson, Scott Sunderland, Jean Cadell.
Directors: Anthony Asquith, Leslie Howard.

George Bernard Shaw, author of the original play, raged and fumed at most screen versions of his works that were made during his lifetime. For this classic, however, he not only gave enthusiastic support but also wrote additional dialogue. He did think Leslie Howard miscast as Professor Higgins and would have preferred Charles Laughton; but he insisted that Wendy Hiller was the only one to play Eliza Doolittle. That role, Hiller's second on screen, made her a prominent star. Confronted with such monumental theatre figures as Shaw, Howard, and Anthony ("Puffin") Asquith, she was initially anxiety-ridden. In the ballroom sequence (written by Shaw expressly for the film), she performed while suffering from a bad toothache. Though not a frequent screen actress thereafter, she appeared in another filmed Shaw play, *Major Barbara*, in 1941. Anthony Quayle, as a French hairdresser, also made one of his first screen appearances here. *Pygmalion* won Academy Awards for Shaw's screenplay and its adaptation. The musical remake, *My Fair Lady*, proved even more popular than the original.

Q

THE QUIET MAN. 1952. Filmed June–August 1951; Cong, County Mayo, Ireland. Republic Studios, Los Angeles.
Cast: John Wayne, Maureen O'Hara, Barry Fitzgerald, Ward Bond, Victor McLaglen, Mildred Natwick, Arthur Shields.
Director: John Ford.

One of John Ford's best movies became a sentimental labor of love when the director (whose real surname was O'Feeney) returned to the "ould sod" of his parents to make this Irish-green film, his self-styled "first love story." Many of the characters possessed Ford family names, and the clannishness extended to the casting itself. Ford's brother, early silent-screen star Francis Ford, played the white-bearded man (though the brothers had fallen out years before and hardly spoke to each other on the set); Ken Curtis, playing Dermot Fahy, was Ford's son-in-law; Maureen O'Hara's younger brother, Charles FitzSimmons, played Forbes; Barry Fitzgerald and Arthur Shields (who played Reverend Playfair) were look-alike brothers; and John Wayne's two sons and two daughters played youngsters. Wayne, Ward Bond, and Victor McLaglen were old Ford regulars, having performed together in many of the director's Westerns. To get McLaglen sufficiently enraged for his big fight scene with Wayne, Ford pulled a trick on him that must have made the burly McLaglen recall similar treatment when they made *The Informer* together; on the eve of filming the scene, Ford lambasted the actor unmercifully for giving a poor performance up to that point. McLaglen stewed all night and came out fuming and violent in the morning, as Ford knew he would. Probably the longest fight sequence in cinema history, it took four days to film. Wayne later proudly cited the fact that neither he nor McLaglen had actually touched each other, so well did they fake their punches. Ford won his fourth Academy Award for direction, and cinematographer Winton C. Hoch took his third.

QUO VADIS? 1951. Filmed spring–summer 1950; Cinecittà Studios, Rome.
Cast: Robert Taylor, Deborah Kerr, Peter Ustinov, Leo Genn, Patricia Laffan.
Director: Mervyn LeRoy.

Whereas it took Nero only six days to burn Rome in A.D. 64, director Mervyn LeRoy and his technicians needed twenty-four nights to capture the holocaust they created for the camera. This fourth version of an old warhorse—the popular Christians-vs.-lions novel by Henryk Sienkiewicz (the title, uttered by the apostle Peter, means "Whither goest thou?")—was originally scheduled to be produced in 1939, but World War II intervened. Robert Taylor and Deborah Kerr replaced Gregory Peck and Elizabeth Taylor in the postwar casting lineup. John Huston, who had cowritten a far different screenplay than MGM studio chief Louis B. Mayer wanted, took his script and also bowed out of the director's slot, calling the final result "another dreadful spectacle." It was the first of four major epics that Hollywoodized the Roman empire with huge box office success (*Ben-Hur*, *Spartacus*, and *Cleopatra* followed). Rounding up the usual experts to provide authentic statuary and clothing, LeRoy admitted he went a bit overboard on Kerr's rich costuming. (She played lion bait Lygia.) As for the lions, such a tired bunch of cats—some fifty of them assembled from shows and circuses throughout Europe—had rarely been seen. Even when hungry they yawned at the Christians, so LeRoy took to stuffing meat into Christians' clothing to tempt them; the lions finally ate, but the scenes looked like—well, lions eating robed meat. Thus the only fierce cats on view are studio-built fake ones, rigged up to move somewhat lionlike. Fiercer by far was the Roman summer heat, causing cast and crew to swelter. Peter Ustinov, playing Nero, felt that the film's "inevitable vulgarities" actually contributed a large dose of authenticity and that "no nation can make Roman pictures as well as the Americans." LeRoy told Ustinov to think of Nero as "a guy who plays with himself nights." Robert Taylor's eleven-year marriage to Barbara Stanwyck was busting up at the time; on the set and for months afterward, he kept company with Italian actress Lia DiLeo, who played the pedicurist in the film. Former heavyweight boxer Buddy Baer played the athlete Ursus. He trained for months with Portuguese matadors, learning the *furcado*—the art of grappling a bull by its horns—for his arena sequence with Kerr. The fighting bull selected was, however, replaced by a chloroformed cow. Both Elizabeth Taylor and Sophia Loren performed as extras in crowd scenes; Taylor, honeymooning at the time with her first husband Nicky Hilton, was made up as a slave girl in the Colosseum sequence and did it for a lark; and Loren played a slave girl praying in the catacombs in her brief screen debut. Walter Pidgeon is the offscreen narrator.

R

RAGING BULL. 1980. Filmed April–October 1979; New York City. Los Angeles Auditorium, Los Angeles (fight scenes).

Cast: Robert De Niro, Cathy Moriarty, Joe Pesci, Frank Vincent, Nicholas Colasanto.

Director: Martin Scorsese.

Jake LaMotta's life story was a grim tale, and Robert De Niro's authentic portrayal of the middleweight boxing champion resulted in probably the best boxing film ever made. Even the long-retired LaMotta agreed. At first angry and upset at seeing himself so negatively mirrored, he soon expressed admiration for the authentic depiction of himself and the fight game. De Niro, in his typical, almost masochistic quest for realism, trained with LaMotta each day for a full year before production began. At the end of that year, the old fighter carried a few more scars—De Niro had blackened his eyes, broken his upper teeth caps, and damaged his chin during sparring bouts—and he considered the actor ready to qualify as a ranking middleweight fighter. Martin Scorsese halted production for four months so that De Niro could gain weight for his portrayal of the retired LaMotta. The actor went on a massive eating binge, quickly rising to 215 pounds from 160 (and lost the entire gain in the four months following wrap-up). Cathy Moriarty, a stunning nineteen-year-old model discovered by Joe Pesci, had never acted before. With platinum-bleached hair, she closely resembled the boxer's ex-wife, Vikki; the two women later promoted the film together on a European tour. Pesci, a sometime actor, was running a Bronx restaurant when Scorsese cast him as Joey LaMotta. He also, in sparring with De Niro, came away aching from the latter's obsession for realism, having suffered two cracked ribs. De Niro won an Academy Award as best actor.

RAGTIME. 1981. Filmed August–December 1980; New York: Mount Kisco; New York City. Spring Lake, New

Jersey. Shepperton Studios, Shepperton, England.
Cast: Howard E. Rollins, Jr., James Cagney, James Olson, Brad Dourif, Elizabeth McGovern, Mary Steenburgen, Pat O'Brien.
Director: Milos Forman.

James Cagney, lured out of a twenty-year retirement at age 81, played his final big-screen role as police commissioner Rhinelander Waldo. This film also marked veteran actor Pat O'Brien's last screen appearance (playing lawyer Delmas) and Howard E. Rollins's first. O. J. Simpson had wanted the part of Coalhouse Walker that went to Rollins, and George C. Scott had sought the father role played by James Olson—but director Forman termed both actors "not vulnerable enough." Robert Altman, originally scheduled to direct, was fired by producer Dino De Laurentis during pre-production; Altman had intended to make a film trilogy of E. L. Doctorow's novel, a scheme approved by Doctorow, who was extremely unhappy with the switch in directors. Novelist Norman Mailer, eager to act, was cast as playboy architect Stanford White for a brief scene; and Mailer's wife, Norris Church, is seen as his table companion. Just before playing his assassination scene, Mailer received word of the shooting of ex-Beatle John Lennon. He said that the real event made him lose his enthusiasm for performing a fake one. Trustees of New York's Morgan Library, the setting of much of the action, refused to permit filming there (they didn't like the idea of the place being held for ransom in the movie), so the Library and Madison Avenue sets were built at Shepperton Studios. A rented clapboard mansion at Mount Kisco was furnished with Victorian decor for the family home; and Atlantic City scenes used Spring Lake locales and residents. While the film won several Oscar nominations, it proved a financial disaster.

RAIDERS OF THE LOST ARK. 1981. Filmed June–September 1980; Tunisia: Tozeur; Kairouan. Kauai, Hawaii. La Rochelle, France. Elstree Studios, Borehamwood, England.
Cast: Harrison Ford, Karen Allen, Denholm Elliott, Wolf Kahler, Paul Freeman, Ronald Lacey, John Rhys-Davies.
Director: Steven Spielberg.

Modeling this cliffhanging adventure epic after the old serials once popular at Saturday matinees, Steven Spielberg said he tried to make it a film equivalent of a ride at Disneyland, good for more than one go-round. The numerous special-effects "toys," typical of Spielberg pictures, included the huge boulder—a 300-pound chunk of fiberglass, wood, and plaster—that chases Harrison Ford. Among plenty of live threats, too, were some 7,500 pythons, cobras, and boa constrictors, as well as fifty tarantulas. Karen Allen was so terrified in her snake-pit scene that she couldn't scream properly, so Spielberg dropped a snake on her from overhead scaffolding; thereafter she reportedly screamed on cue. Ford's role of Indiana Jones (producer George Lucas had named the character after his malamute dog) was originally slated for Tom Selleck, who proved unavailable. All South American scenes were filmed in Hawaii; the archaeological sequences occurred in 130-degree Tunisian desert heat at the same locale where Lucas had filmed canyon scenes for *Star Wars*; while the submarine pens, which had actually been used by Nazi U-boats during World War II, were found in coastal France. To Ford, the film was "really about movies, a real tribute to the craft." Spielberg and Ford followed up this huge box office success with its prequel, *Indiana Jones and the Temple of Doom* (1984), a much grimmer display of tricks.

RAIN MAN 1988. Filmed May–July 1988; Cincinnati, Ohio, and cross-country locations. MGM/United Artists Studios, Culver City.

Cast: Dustin Hoffman, Tom Cruise, Valeria Golino.
Director: Barry Levinson.

In his nineteenth film at age fifty-one, Dustin Hoffman won his second Oscar for his portrayal of autistic savant Raymond Babbitt. First offered the part of the brother Charlie, ultimately played by Tom Cruise, Hoffman preferred the more challenging role of the robotlike Raymond. Characteristically immersing himself into every aspect of the production and intensively researching his role for a full year, he changed Raymond's disability from mental retardation to autism, patterning his look and walk after an autistic man named Kim. The production was slow in starting, running through several writers and three less-than-enthused directors—including Steven Spielberg and Sydney Pollack—before Barry Levinson eagerly signed on. (Levinson also played a minor unbilled role, that of a pompous psychologist.) All participants agreed that only Hoffman's stubborn tenacity got the film made. Hoffman, who passed up the chance to star in *Midnight Run* in order to stick with *Rain Man*, knew he had finally mastered his role when he could improvise as Raymond; during rehearsals, he and Cruise would often exchange parts in order to sort out various aspects of their characters. In the end, Hoffman felt that Ratso Rizzo in *Midnight Cowboy* (1969) and Raymond in this film would be the two roles for which he would be remembered. Academy Awards also went for best picture, to director Levinson, and for the screenplay by Ronald Bass and Barry Morrow.

RASHOMON. 1951. Filmed summer 1950; Japan: Nara vicinity; Komyoji Temple forest and Daiei Studios, Kyoto.
Cast: Toshiro Mifune, Masayuki Mori, Machiko Kyo, Fumiko Homma.
Director: Akira Kurosawa.

Its title signifies the ancient gateway of the city of Kyoto, but Akira Kurosawa's medieval setting framed the most modern of questions: what is truth? Each eyewitness sees the same event as something different. The eye of the beholder has never received such rigorous inspection. This film, even though it failed in Japan, brought Kurosawa an international reputation. Like so many classics, *Rashomon* resulted both because and in spite of a baffled, reluctant studio. Throughout production, Daiei executives stalled and harassed the director, whose innovative use of forest light and shadow upset all sorts of conventional cinema wisdom. He broke the taboo, for example, against filming the sun directly, dispelling the myth that direct rays through the lens would burn the film. Machiko Kyo, a former dancer, was the first Japanese film actress to project sex appeal (at least deliberately), thus breaking another tradition—women in the Japanese cinema had heretofore been largely restricted to wifely domestic roles. Cast and crew found the virgin mountain forest near Nara infested with leeches that dropped from trees and crawled up legs; each day began with a salt rubdown to repel the creatures. Kurosawa required only two studio sets, the city gate itself and a courtyard wall. But the gigantic gate set that arose on the Daiei lot confounded the economy-minded studio officials, who accused the director of misleading them by building one mammoth set that cost more than a hundred ordinary ones. Kurosawa disingenuously replied that his image of the gate had started out much smaller but had grown larger the longer the studio had delayed him in starting the picture. *Rashomon* won an Academy Award as best foreign film. *The Outrage* (1964) was an American remake.

THE RAVEN. 1963. Filmed January 1963; California: Monterey; Producers Studio, Los Angeles.
Cast: Vincent Price, Peter Lorre, Boris Karloff, Hazel Court, Olive Sturgess, Jack Nicholson.
Director: Roger Corman.

Fifth of Roger Corman's eight low-budget thrillers based on the works of Edgar Allan Poe (all of them starring Vincent Price), this one spoofed the entire Poe genre. Here four old masters of horror—Price, Boris Karloff, and especially Peter Lorre—played for laughs. Price and Lorre "drove Boris a little crazy," recalled Corman, startling the aged, line-perfect actor with sudden improvised dialogue and bits of business. Off-camera, the screams were of laughter as Corman and his cast devised outrageous one-liners to insert. Corman, always broke and racing the calendar, filmed the picture in fifteen days, using revamped portions of his previous Poe sets. After filming was completed, he still had Boris Karloff under contract for three days, so he used him (along with the same rented sets) for a few scenes in his next quickie, *The Terror* (1963). Karloff had starred in a rather more serious version of *The Raven* in 1935. This was Jack Nicholson's third film, Lorre's third from last (he died in 1964); Karloff still had fifteen more to go.

THE RAZOR'S EDGE. 1946. Filmed May–August 1946; 20th Century-Fox Studios, Los Angeles.
Cast: Tyrone Power, Gene Tierney, Clifton Webb, Anne Baxter, Herbert Marshall, John Payne.
Director: Edmund Goulding.

This is the film that studio chief Darryl F. Zanuck wanted to be remembered for. Instead of accepting the lead role in *Gentleman's Agreement*, which went to Gregory Peck, Tyrone

Power chose this film to resume his career after his discharge from the Marine Corps. The character of questing mystic Larry Darrell not only excited and intrigued him but led him, for a time, to identify closely with the role. Offscreen he took to wearing white clothes and, according to one friend, walked around the lot "looking dreamy" (until his attachment to Lana Turner marked the end of that "phase"). Studio publicists tried to promote romance between Power and Gene Tierney, both of whom were parting from spouses; but while the two became good friends, the romance stayed in the screenplay. (Tierney was seeing much of the young John F. Kennedy during this period; in the meantime, her estranged husband, Oleg Cassini, designed the costumes for the film.) Real champagne, an arrangement that Power made with the prop man, added a special authenticity to the Paris nightclub sequence. Anne Baxter, playing Sophie, won her role by default after Alice Faye, Bonita Granville, Susan Hayward, and Maureen O'Hara proved uninterested or unavailable. Major surgery kept Baxter from the set for several weeks; when she returned, she found herself somewhat apart from the cast togetherness—but she incorporated her outsider status into the role. The lavish sets and props included so much expensive silver for a wedding scene that Pinkerton guards were hired to watch it. Critics found much irony in the contrast between the sumptuous decor (coupled with the studio's loud bragging about it) and the nonmaterialistic concerns of the story, based on Somerset Maugham's novel. (Herbert Marshall played the role of Maugham in the film.) Despite having been last choice for her role, Baxter won an Academy Award as best supporting actress. The film's 1984 remake starred Bill Murray.

REAR WINDOW. 1954. Filmed November 1953–January 1954; Paramount Studios, Los Angeles.

Cast: James Stewart, Grace Kelly, Thelma Ritter, Raymond Burr, Wendell Corey.

Director: Alfred Hitchcock.

Hitchcock said he was feeling "very creative" when he made this film, one of his personal favorites. With most scenes restricted to a single set of thirty-one apartment windows seen from James Stewart's own window, the localized focus of the picture was reminiscent of Hitchcock's earlier *Lifeboat*, which confined itself to an even closer space. The director, who often seemed to consider actors a necessary nuisance, profoundly admired Stewart, an esteem that Stewart thoroughly reciprocated. Toward Grace Kelly, as with several of his leading actresses through the years, Hitchcock developed an eccentric infatuation, emotionally distant yet domineering and apparently rich in fantasy rewards. He closely supervised each costume choice, at one point demanding that Kelly be fitted with falsies to fill out her figure. The actress refused. Conspiring with costume designer Edith Head, she merely tucked and rearranged; and Hitchcock, seeing his orders apparently obeyed, never knew the difference. Kelly, who said her role reminded her of Nancy Drew in the stories of her childhood, had either turned down or was refused the part that went to Eva Marie Saint in *On the Waterfront*, hence her availability for *Rear Window.* Hitchcock is seen briefly as a butler winding a clock.

REBECCA. 1940. Filmed September 1939–January 1940; Selznick International Studios, Culver City.
Cast: Joan Fontaine, Laurence Olivier, Judith Anderson, George Sanders, Nigel Bruce, Gladys Cooper, Florence Bates, Reginald Denny, C. Aubrey Smith.
Director: Alfred Hitchcock.

This was Alfred Hitchcock's first American-made film, though his leading cast members (except for Joan Fontaine and Florence Bates) came mainly from the large British colony of performers residing in Hollywood. Just as the picture began filming, England declared war on Germany, an act that posed quandaries for many of these people. Could they best serve their country at home or by aiding in fundraising and propaganda from Hollywood? (Most of them stayed.) Fontaine complained that her British colleagues were a clique who generally excluded her from their off-camera sociability. At age twenty-two she felt herself on trial and said that the tears she shed onscreen were genuine. Part of her problem was apparently fostered by Hitchcock, who believed in divide and conquer and had made derogatory remarks to Laurence Olivier about her. The two costars, consequently, hardly became friends. Fontaine, who had narrowly won her role over Anne Baxter and whose marriage to British actor Brian Aherne was only days old, said that Hitchcock's moral tyranny kept her off balance but that this finally helped her performance. *Rebecca* established her as a major star. Ronald Colman had refused the male lead accepted by Olivier. In addition to Hitchcock's fears about the safety of his family back in England, he was harassed by running feuds with his producer and studio chief, David O. Selznick, who insisted that Hitchcock remain absolutely faithful to Daphne du Maurier's novel. Their conflicts slowed production and gave Hitchcock a lasting distaste for being bossed. Yet this was the only Hitchcock film ever to win an Academy Award for best picture; George Barnes's cinematography also won an Oscar. Look for the director's cameo as he passes by a telephone booth occupied by George Sanders.

REBEL WITHOUT A CAUSE. 1955. Filmed March–May 1955; Los Angeles: Griffith Park Planetarium; John Marshall High School; Getty Mansion. Warner Bros. Studios, Burbank.

Cast: James Dean, Natalie Wood, Sal Mineo, Jim Backus, Dennis Hopper, Nick Adams, Ann Doran.

Director: Nicholas Ray.

This was the second of James Dean's three starring roles (after *East of Eden* and before *Giant*). In retrospect, the picture seemed jinxed. Four of the principal cast members died violent or accidental deaths—Dean by a car crash later in 1955, Nick Adams by a drug overdose in 1968, Sal Mineo by murder in 1976, and Natalie Wood by drowning in 1981. In 1982, Jim Backus (who played Dean's father) said he experienced a "terrible feeling of doom" during the production. The tragic fates of these actors added a chilling mystique to its cult status as the first of a popular genre, the troubled-youth syndrome. Nicholas Ray intended this picture (originally titled *Blind Run*) as an adolescent's view of adolescence, a revolutionary slant at the time. And Dean's own distinctive style of mannered self-consciousness seemed just right for conveying a pained identity struggle. (The studio had wanted to cast Tab Hunter and Jayne Mansfield in the lead roles.) In their knife fight scene, Dean and Corey Allen (playing Buzz) used real switchblades and wore protective vests beneath their shirts. For the police station scene, the cast cooled their heels while Dean psyched himself up in his dressing room by drinking wine and playing his bongo drums. The swimming pool in the scene with Dean, Wood, and Mineo was the same one used for *Sunset Boulevard*—on the old Getty estate, where the deserted-mansion sequences were also filmed. Wood, who graduated from high school just after filming was completed, strongly identified with the family problems of her character. Her parents had disapproved of her participation in the picture, which they viewed as a slam against parents generally. She recalled that both she and Dean, who became good friends (though Adams became her first steady boyfriend), were shy and embarrassed about filming her first screen kiss. Dean's vocal imitation of the cartoon character Mr. Magoo was a spontaneous tribute to Backus, who voiced Magoo for years in the UPA series. Ray himself (also a reputed flame of Wood's) appears in the film's final shot as the lone figure walking up to the planetarium. *Rebel* was banned in Britain and Spain, where it was feared that the film might incite young people to violence.

THE RED BADGE OF COURAGE. 1951. Filmed August–September 1950; California: John Huston Ranch, Tarzana; Sacramento River, Chico; MGM Studios, Culver City.

Cast: Audie Murphy, Bill Mauldin, Douglas Dick, Royal Dano, John Dierkes, Andy Devine.

Director: John Huston.

"There's no *story*!" maintained studio chief Louis B. Mayer, who steadfastly fought the acquisition of Stephen Crane's novel over the successful opposition of producer Gottfried Reinhardt and director John Huston. Though its stature has grown through the years, the film you see is far from the version that Huston intended. In order to increase the movie's commercial appeal after a disastrous preview showing, the studio gutted several key scenes, added a narration by James Whitmore, and rearranged material to "fix" the story. Some of that lost original footage might have been saved, enabling an intact video reissue, had not Huston abandoned the field in order to shoot *The African Queen* in the Congo. In a production loaded with high hopes, studio politics, and final disappointment (all richly detailed in Lillian Ross's book *Picture*, 1952), the final irony was that the vaunted badge of courage remained wanting in the filmmakers themselves on their own important battlegrounds. The youthful soldier role was probably World War II hero Audie Murphy's best. A strange, taciturn little man who had been a virtual killing machine in combat, Murphy had made a postwar career of playing good guys in B-Westerns. Even though Huston's intended message in the film was that heroism, like cowardice, is entirely situational, Murphy's casting as a coward must have given the actor pause. Prominent editorial cartoonist Bill Mauldin played the loud soldier. Most of the battle scenes were filmed on Huston's own seven-acre ranch. Despite Mayer's correct dire prophecy of box office failure, the battle lines he had drawn around the production finally forced his own retirement from the industry he had helped found.

RED RIVER. 1948. Filmed September 1946–January 1947; Arizona: Elgin; Whetstone Mountains; San Pedro River. Selznick International Studios, Culver City.
Cast: John Wayne, Montgomery Clift, Joanne Dru, Walter Brennan, Coleen Gray, John Ireland.
Director: Howard Hawks.

This classic—Howard Hawks's first Western and Montgomery Clift's screen debut—marked what John Wayne at the time considered his own swan song, falsely believing himself destined for minor character parts because of his age (forty-one). As it turned out, he said, his favorite director, John Ford, "never respected me as an actor until I made *Red River*." Hawks had wanted Gary Cooper, who declined, for the lead; and Cary Grant turned down the role that went to John Ireland, an actor who antagonized Hawks. Accounts differ as to whether the source of trouble between them was booze or a woman. Hawks ordered the actor's part cut to the bone after accusing him of drinking and smoking pot on the set—while Ireland charged the married director of jealousy over Ireland's personal interest in Joanne Dru (who had replaced pregnant Margaret Sheridan as Tess Millay). Ireland and Dru, at any rate, got married after completing the film. Wayne started out highly skeptical of the somewhat fragile Clift but gained huge respect for his acting talents as shooting progressed. Clift trained himself to become a proficient horseman before filming began, but he never learned to throw a punch properly. Knowing that Clift could never compete on a physical level with Wayne, Hawks taught him to underplay their scenes together. With the director's help, Clift established his familiar screen persona, cool and detached, an image that soon placed the actor on an unwanted pedestal, the subject of screaming adulation by bobby-soxers. Though critics applauded Clift's performance, the actor himself always disliked the film and himself in it. At age forty-two, Walter Brennan balked at removing his dentures; later, in countless Westerns and TV shows, his toothless geezer would become a familiar staple character. Hawks claimed that he based this film on accounts of the enormous King Ranch in Texas. Rain and dust storms abounded on the Arizona locations. Those were the days when movie directors could alter entire landscapes by command, and Hawks had five dams built in order to bring the San Pedro River to a convincing flood stage. Producer Howard Hughes sued Hawks over the climactic fight scene between Wayne and Clift, claiming that Hawks had lifted the episode from Hughes's film *The Outlaw* (1943); but he dropped the suit after a personal plea from Wayne. Veteran Western actor and Wayne sidekick Harry Carey, Sr., made his final screen appearance here as an Abilene cattle buyer. Look for a then unknown Shelley Winters in a bit part as a dance hall girl; several years later, she would costar with Clift in *A Place in the Sun*.

THE RED SHOES. 1948. Filmed summer–autumn 1947; France: Cap Martin; Cap Ferrat; Paris. Monte Carlo, Monaco. Pinewood Studios, Iver Heath, England.
Cast: Anton Walbrook, Moira Shearer, Marius Goring, Robert Helpmann.
Directors: Michael Powell, Emeric Pressburger.

The ultimate ballet picture, its virtues have attracted a much larger audience than just lovers of classical dance. In her first screen role, twenty-one-year-old Scottish ballerina Moira Shearer felt she was prostituting her art. Moviemaking didn't seem to interest her, said codirector Powell, "except for the money." The Sadler's Wells ballet company heavily pressured her not to compromise herself by performing in the film medium; but when Powell told her that he was also looking at American dancers for the role, she speedily made up her mind. Later her condescending attitude changed, and she danced in several more films through the 1950s. Anton Walbrook's role of Lermontov was, of course, based on the Russian impresario Diaghilev. Robert Helpmann, who played Ivan Boleslawsky, was also responsible for the choreography. In addition to winning Academy Awards for set design and Brian Easdale's musical score (most of which he composed in one week), this film proved highly inspirational to Gene Kelly in planning *An American in Paris*.

REDS. 1981. Filmed August 1979–December 1980; Spain: Guadix; Sevilla. England: Twickenham; Camber Sands. Helsinki, Finland. U.S.: Washington, D.C.; New York City.

Cast: Warren Beatty, Diane Keaton, Jack Nicholson, Edward Herrmann, Maureen Stapleton, Jerzy Kosinski, Paul Sorvino, Gene Hackman.

Director: Warren Beatty.

Real-life acquaintances of journalist John Reed, the subject of this lengthy period piece set during the 1917 Russian Revolution, framed the story and added authenticity. Called "witnesses," these thirty-one interviewees remained unidentified by name in the film; some of the best-known figures included historian Will Durant, showman George Jessel, novelist Henry Miller, socialist Scott Nearing, writer Adela Rogers St. John, and novelist Dame Rebecca West. Warren Beatty, who directed and also played Reed, had film-interviewed some of these people several years before he began making the movie, which underwent title changes from *The John Reed Story* to *Comrades* to *Reds*. Beatty's obsession for historical realism led him to learn the Russian language in preparation for his role. He wanted to film in the Soviet Union but was refused permission. His perfectionism on the sets, where he often required thirty or more takes of a single scene, often infuriated cast and crew (at one point, the normally sedate Maureen Stapleton, playing Emma Goldman, shouted "Are you out of your fucking mind?"). He gave complete scripts only to Diane Keaton and Jack Nicholson, doling out the dialogue to all other cast members only hours before shooting a particular scene. After Beatty lectured a group of extras about Reed's labor theories in preparation for filming the Bakun conference, the extras decided they liked what they heard and promptly went on strike for higher wages (and got them). By the end, Beatty was sick with exhaustion. Another casualty was his offscreen romance with costar Keaton; they fought on the set over her characterization of feminist Louise Bryant and parted company before the film was released. The novelist

Jerzy Kosinski played Zinoviev, and Soviet bureaucrats in the film were actually Russian emigrés in Spain. In the festive peoples' congress sequence, filmed at Sevilla's famed Alcazar, a group of Soviet tourists wandered into the street crowd as filming began; they departed highly bewildered at the strange, yet oddly familiar goings-on. The film was not a box office success. A few conservative groups picketed it as Communist propaganda, but it won three Academy Awards: for Stapleton as best supporting actress, Beatty's direction, and Vittorio Storaro's cinematography.

REPULSION. 1965. Filmed summer 1964; England: London (exteriors); Twickenham Studios, Twickenham.
Cast: Catherine Deneuve, Ian Hendry, John Fraser, Patrick Wymark, Yvonne Furneaux.
Director: Roman Polanski.

The Polish director's first film made in the West is, in the judgment of some critics, his best to date. A psychological chiller, it cast French actress Catherine Deneuve in the lead role as a woman descending into madness. Roman Polanski's oft-remarked sadistic tendencies toward his female stars were again evident as he prepared Deneuve for her role. He wanted her "love-starved"; so, weeks before filming, he sequestered her in London, making sure that she had no access to men. For her violent attack scene with the candlestick, he provoked her to such genuine explosive fury that she swung at him, whereupon he proceeded to film the sequence. Polanski felt that Yvonne Furneaux's interpretation of Helen was "too bloody nice"; he badgered her to tears in order to make her convincingly bitchy. Polanski's special effects (which he later judged "sloppy") included movable walls and passages in the apartment set to reflect Deneuve's distorted vision. For blood, the director used his "secret formula," a mixture of cochineal and Nescafé shot from a bicycle pump. The road accident scene was staged in London without police permission, and the producer drew a hefty fine. Polanski didn't share in the high critical opinion of his film, regretting his necessary artistic compromises with the budget.

RICHARD III. 1955. Filmed summer–autumn 1954; Spain. Shepperton Studios, Shepperton, England.
Cast: Laurence Olivier, John Gielgud, Ralph Richardson,

Claire Bloom, Cedric Hardwicke, Stanley Baker, Alex Clunes, Pamela Brown, Michael Gough.
Director: Laurence Olivier.

While Shakespeare's portrayal may have done large historical injustice to the enigmatic Yorkist monarch, the play as adapted by Sir Laurence Olivier made splendid film drama. As usual when making his Shakespearean films (this was his third after *Henry V* and *Hamlet*), Olivier managed to self-inflict some real wounds—this time in the Bosworth battle sequence (the first sequence of the picture filmed, on a bull farm near Madrid, where Spanish extras made up the opposing armies). The stunt archer aiming for the actor's side-padded horse instead put an arrow straight into Olivier's left calf, thus making the king's limp throughout the rest of the picture authentic indeed. Olivier spent three hours daily applying his intricate makeup, including false nose, hunched back, false hand, and pageboy wig. His wife, Vivien Leigh, was incensed that he had not cast her as Lady Anne (played by Claire Bloom) and suffered a mental relapse during principal photography. In her precarious emotional state, she convinced herself that her age (forty-two) was the reason she hadn't been chosen and that Olivier and Bloom were having an affair; and she strongly tried to persuade Olivier to drop the picture. Knighthood truly flowered for this film. With Olivier, Gielgud, Richardson, and Hardwicke, it joined more British theatrical knights together than any previous production. (There would have been a fifth if Olivier had had his way, for he had wanted Sir Carol Reed to direct.) Olivier afterward deplored his choice of Richardson for the Duke of Buckingham role; the actor "wasn't oily enough" for the part, he said, regretting that he hadn't cast Orson Welles instead.

RIFIFI. 1955. Filmed winter 1953–54; Paris.
Cast: Jean Servais, Carl Möhner, Magali Noel, Jules Dassin, Robert Manuel.
Director: Jules Dassin.

Much of this film proceeds without the use of dialogue. The title is French slang for *brawl* or *trouble*. Made in the tradition of *The Asphalt Jungle* on a basement budget, this ultimate jewel-heist film was probably the best of the genre. Blacklisted in Hollywood, director Jules Dassin—also playing César the safecracker under his pseudonym Perlo Vita—

moved to Europe, which became the locale of his best work. *Rififi* reestablished him as a director of international repute after years of forced inactivity, also triggering countless imitations from less talented directors. Several later films that used this title as part of *their* titles were not true sequels. Dassin himself lightheartedly repeated the theme in *Topkapi*, while the Italian *Big Deal on Madonna Street* parodied the original.

THE RIGHT STUFF. 1983. Filmed March 1982–January 1983; California: Edwards AFB; Hamilton AFB; China Basin; Burlingame; San Francisco area.

Cast: Sam Shepard, Scott Glenn, Ed Harris, Dennis Quaid, Charles Frank, Fred Ward, Lance Henriksen, Scott Paulin.

Director: Philip Kaufman.

How the seven Mercury astronauts became transformed from competent technicians into straight-arrow American media icons was the subject of this film based on Tom Wolfe's book of the same title. Expert technology, aided by NASA and other government agencies, also marked the production. The use of models and miniatures, along with stock footage of rocket flights and realistic locales, gave an air of historic authenticity. Stunt parachutist Joseph Svec was killed during the filming of a scene where he ejected from an experimental plane and failed to pull his rip cords. To recreate the astronauts' space suits, silver fabric left over from costume material for flamboyant singer-actress Cher was used. Sam Shepard played pioneer test pilot Colonel Chuck Yeager. (The real Yeager, having advanced to general, served as technical advisor and also played the bit part of Fred.) At the time the film was released, the real John Glenn (played by look-alike actor Ed Harris) had become a U.S. senator and was campaigning in presidential primaries; his political opponents felt that the movie gave him an unfair publicity advantage, but election results proved their fears groundless. Journalists on the set were amused to note that the press corps in the film was played by a commedia dell'arte troup of jugglers, mimes, and dancers known as I Fratelli Bologna. Cape Canaveral sequences were filmed at Hamilton AFB. The film crashed at the box office. (Americans had become rather blasé about instantly concocted national heroes during the Reagan years.) It nevertheless won four Academy Awards.

RIO BRAVO. 1959. Filmed May–July 1958; Old Tucson, Arizona. Warner Bros. Studios, Burbank.
Cast: John Wayne, Dean Martin, Angie Dickinson, Walter Brennan, Ricky Nelson, Ward Bond, Claude Akins.
Director: Howard Hawks.

Both John Wayne and Howard Hawks had strongly criticized *High Noon* (1952) and *3:10 to Yuma* (1957) for their depiction of Western lawmen as false to the macho stereotype of good American gunfighters; and Hawks intended this film as a response to such heresy. He filmed much of the picture in studio interiors, where he gave it the look and feel of a gangster movie, including the moll (named Feathers) played by Angie Dickinson. Wayne, seemingly aware of his function as a symbolic holdout for the type of frontier hero he so frequently played, even wore the same belt buckle that held up his pants in *Red River*. Dean Martin, according to the director, was hung over during much of the filming, a condition appropriate to his role. Martin's love for telling jokes on the set, according to cinematographer Russell Harlan, slowed the production considerably. Harlan tried to give the film the effect of frontier paintings by Charles M. Russell. The Arizona location, where *Gunfight at the OK Corral* (1957) was also shot, not only blistered in 120-degree heat, but was plagued by a huge invasion of grasshoppers; they caked on walls, littered the boardwalks, and fried on the hot lights. To film outdoor scenes before the powerful lighting attracted swarms of them, Hawks tried to make each scene a one-take, and he largely succeeded. Hawks liked this film so much that he remade it, more or less, twice: as *El Dorado* (1967) and *Rio Lobo* (1970). *Assault on Precinct 13* (1976) was a modernized remake by director John Carpenter.

ROAD TO BALI. 1952. Filmed spring–summer 1952; Paramount Studios, Los Angeles.
Cast: Bob Hope, Bing Crosby, Dorothy Lamour, Murvyn Vye, Peter Coe.
Director: Hal Walker.

This sixth of the seven Bob Hope-Bing Crosby *Road* pictures (originally titled *Road to Hollywood*) was also the first of the series in color and is the only one available to date on video. Spontaneous gags, Hollywood in-jokes, and fast improvisation marked the interplay between the costars in all these films. In this one, Crosby put up a brave front, for his first wife, actress Dixie Lee, was terminally ill with cancer (she died about three months after filming ended). Several cameo appearances included those of Humphrey Bogart, mocking his character in *The African Queen*, Dean Martin and Jerry Lewis, and Jane Russell. This was the only Crosby film in which his brother, bandleader Bob Crosby, also appeared. The script kept changing as filming proceeded; the leads worked on the picture for months before they knew the plot. Dorothy Lamour refused to make a record album of songs from the movie because financial arrangements would have shorted her in comparison with Hope and Crosby's take. When those two underhandedly went ahead and made the album anyway (using Peggy Lee for Lamour's song parts), Lamour was understandably miffed.

THE ROARING TWENTIES. 1939. Filmed summer 1939; Warner Bros. Studios, Burbank.
Cast: James Cagney, Priscilla Lane, Humphrey Bogart, Jeffrey Lynn, Gladys George.
Director: Raoul Walsh.

Originally titled *The World Moves On*, this gangster classic was probably the first film attempt to see the lawless Prohibition era, only five years in the past, for the national trauma that it was. It also marked (a) the end of James Cagney's first decade in films; (b) his final hoodlum role for another decade; and (c) the last of three movies in which he and Humphrey Bogart appeared together. Cagney's role was based on New York gangster Frank Fay, who had also inspired F. Scott Fitzgerald's *The Great Gatsby.* One of the actor's improvised bits was his two-for-one gimmick: after popping one thug on the chin, his head jerks back and conks the thug behind him on the forehead. Gladys George, playing Panama Smith, based her part on famed speakeasy hostess Texas Guinan; she was final choice for the role after Ann Sheridan, Lee Patrick, and Glenda Farrell had turned it down. The church steps in the final scene were the same ones used in the granddaddy gangster movie *Little Caesar*. For showing in Russia, the Soviets titled the film *The Fate of a Soldier in America*.

ROCKY. 1976. Filmed February–March 1976; Philadelphia. Los Angeles.

Cast: Sylvester Stallone, Talia Shire, Burt Young, Carl Weathers, Burgess Meredith.
Director: John G. Avildsen.

Scripted by Sylvester Stallone, this Cinderella story about an underdog boxer who triumphs reflected Stallone's own trials in getting the film made. An unknown actor at the time, he wrote the screenplay in four days but withheld it, despite tempting offers, until he was guaranteed the title role himself. He had never had formal boxing instruction but trained for five months before filming began. All the fight scenes, staged in the Los Angeles Sports Arena, were precisely choreographed and shot with three cameras including the hand-held Steadicam, the first use of this new camera in a feature. Made on a shoestring budget, the picture was inspired by the 1975 heavyweight title fight between Muhammad Ali and Chuck Wepner; former pro football player Carl Weathers modeled his role of Apollo Creed after Ali. Stallone brought his family into the picture, too. His father Frank played a timekeeper, and his brother Frank, Jr., performed as a street singer. Even his bull mastiff, Butkus, got into the act as Rocky's dog. The film was a huge success, bringing Stallone overnight stardom. It also cheered Burgess Meredith, who celebrated his first smash hit (playing Mickey the trainer) in a career of over one hundred films. *Rocky* won the best picture Oscar plus Academy Awards for direction and editing. Stallone made three sequels (*Rocky II*, *III*, and *IV*), the last in 1985. *Rocky IV* surpassed them all at the box office.

ROMAN HOLIDAY. 1953. Filmed summer 1952; Rome (exteriors and Cinecittà Studios).
Cast: Gregory Peck, Audrey Hepburn, Eddie Albert.
Director: William Wyler.

Hollywood studios still took a dim view of making movies on actual location in 1952, and William Wyler was offered his choice: make this film in color on home studio sets, or in black-and-white if you go overseas. Wyler chose Rome above color for this fairy-tale romance, which was Audrey Hepburn's American screen debut; it brought her instant stardom at age twenty-three. Gregory Peck, cast mainly for his name value, had originally turned down the picture because it was clearly intended as Hepburn's vehicle, but he finally agreed to costar and ended up insisting that Hepburn receive equal top billing. The film proved one of his favorites. Stalling the production at the outset, the Italian ministry in charge of issuing permits for location filming balked at the prospect of Italians being ridiculed in the film; Wyler convinced the officials, however, that all spoofing would be multinational, an assurance that satisfied them. Cast and crew had to contend with noisy crowds watching location photography, as well as bursts of gunfire from gangs of battling Fascists and Communists in the surrounding city area. The worst problem, however, was Rome's brutal heat that summer, melting makeup and short-fusing tempers on the sets. Peck separated from his first wife Greta during the filming, but also met French reporter Véronique Passani, who became his second. Hepburn won an Academy Award as best actress.

ROMEO AND JULIET. 1968. Filmed 1967; Italy: Pienza; Gubbio; Artena; Tuscania.
Cast: Leonard Whiting, Olivia Hussey, Milo O'Shea, Michael York, John McEnery.
Director: Franco Zeffirelli.

Franco Zeffirelli cast his own version of this much-filmed play with two London teenagers, performers who came closer in age to Shakespeare's characters than any previous Romeo and Juliet on screen. In portraying the milieu of Montagues and Capulets, the director said he tried to convey what he viewed as two Italian types—the gentle, aristocratic features of the nobles, and the dark, gothic faces of the peasantry. Authentic period costuming was carefully researched and recreated. Leonard Whiting, age seventeen, took fencing, riding, and walking lessons, while sixteen-year-old Olivia Hussey had to go on a potato diet to fill out her figure. Sir Laurence Olivier, unbilled at his own request, spoke the prologue and epilogue. The film aroused controversy because of Zeffirelli's arbitrary cuts in major passages of dialogue; notwithstanding, many critics declared this effort as some of the best Shakespeare on film. Interviewed in 1988, both costars looked back on the film as the high point of their since-declined careers. Pasquale de Santis won an Academy Award for his cinematography.

ROOM AT THE TOP. 1959. Filmed spring–summer 1958; England: Bradford; Shepperton Studios, Shepperton.
Cast: Laurence Harvey, Simone Signoret, Heather Sears,

Donald Wolfit, Hermione Baddeley, Donald Houston.
Director: Jack Clayton.

First of the British kitchen sink dramas, this film strongly indicted the rigid class system, a powerful dose of social realism for 1959. John Braine, author of the novel of the same name, thought Laurence Harvey an excellent choice for the role of Joe Lampton because the ruthlessness of the character's ambitions matched Harvey's own. Offscreen, the tremendously insecure actor was noted for his ludicrously affected mannerisms; but his performing talents were prodigious and *Room* brought him international stardom. He shocked the Yorkshire locals, many of whom were employed as extras, with his bawdy language and acid wit. Heather Sears, playing the young woman he woos, feared his caustic tongue and stayed away from him whenever possible. Though married to Margaret Leighton at the time, Harvey began a brief affair with the much-older Hermione Baddeley, whom he had cajoled into accepting the part of Elspeth. Harvey used no stunt double for the fight scene in which he gets tossed into a canal by three toughs. Filmed at 3 A.M., the action alarmed Bradford residents, who called the police. The "muggers" (imported from London), mild men in real life, included a bird breeder and an animal welfare volunteer. Simone Signoret, playing Alice, had been badly smeared in America by McCarthyists for her espousal of left-wing causes. She declined to join the cast until she was assured that no American was involved in the production, and the film relaunched her sagging career. Knowing its priorities, the busy wool town of Bradford permitted street filming only on Sundays so as not to interfere with local commerce. *Room*'s earthy language and frank treatment of extramarital sex, though modest by later standards, caused the film to be banned in various places. Signoret won an Academy Award as best actress; Neil Paterson won for his screenplay. Two sequels—*Life at the Top* (1965) and *Man at the Top* (1973)—followed.

ROPE. 1948. Filmed January–February 1948; Warner Bros. Studios, Burbank.
Cast: James Stewart, Farley Granger, John Dall, Cedric Hardwicke, Joan Chandler, Constance Collier.
Director: Alfred Hitchcock.

James Stewart's first of four films with Alfred Hitchcock

was also the director's first color production. Hitchcock had hoped to sign Cary Grant for the lead, and he wanted Montgomery Clift for the part of Brandon, which went to John Dall. (Grant was unavailable, and Clift turned him down.) Loosely based on the infamous Leopold-Loeb case of 1924, the film provided Hitchcock with an opportunity for trying out some new techniques (which he later disavowed); and this aspect was almost his sole interest in the project. His primary gimmick lay in filming the action as one continuous shot for the picture's entire eighty-minute length (corresponding to the actual passage of time in the story), accomplished by splicing together eight ten-minute takes. Such lengthy, unbroken scenes involved unusual problems. Each ten-minute segment had to be meticulously rehearsed; walls and furniture had to slide on cue for the tracking camera; and many retakes were needed in order to get satisfactory performances of such length. Stewart complained that the demanding rehearsals were intended more for camera than cast. All dialogue was postdubbed. Hitchcock especially liked the Manhattan skyline cyclorama, an accurate miniature construction using tiny incandescent bulbs and two hundred neon signs; look for one of these signs announcing a product called Reduco, showing before-and-after silhouettes of the portly director. His real cameo, however, comes just after the main title at the beginning, when we see him crossing a street. Public response to the film was lukewarm at best. Several social and educational organizations condemned it as dangerous, and it was initially banned in Chicago and Memphis.

ROSEMARY'S BABY. 1968. Filmed summer–autumn 1967; Dakota Apartments, New York City. California: Marina, Playa del Rey; Paramount Studios, Los Angeles.
Cast: Mia Farrow, John Cassavetes, Ruth Gordon, Maurice Evans, Sidney Blackmer, Ralph Bellamy, Patsy Kelly, Angela Dorian.
Director: Roman Polanski.

This horror film viewing childhood as a deceptive source of satanic evil inspired an entire genre that further elaborated the notion. Not accidentally, claimed some critics, it appeared at a time when young people were making daily headlines by protesting government gospel, opening a generation gap between themselves and their elders. Roman Polanski had originally hoped to cast his wife, Sharon Tate, in the part of Rosemary; he also strongly considered Jane Fonda and Tuesday Weld for the role. For Guy, Rosemary's husband, he wanted Robert Redford or Warren Beatty. Both Laurence Harvey and Jack Nicholson desired the part, but Polanski settled on John Cassavetes, a decision he regretted. Mutual dislike erupted in shouting matches; Cassavetes, a brilliant director himself, objected to doing a nude scene with Mia Farrow and wanted more creative space than the autocratic Polanski would allow. Farrow had her own problems with her then husband Frank Sinatra, who impatiently awaited her release from the picture so he could cast her opposite him in *The Detective*; the part finally went to Lee Remick. After giving her an ultimatum, Sinatra had his lawyer deliver divorce papers to her on the set during filming of the party scene. Devastated, Farrow nevertheless continued her work in the best show-must-go-on tradition. British actor Maurice Evans, playing Hutch, recalled with distaste the flamboyant Polanski's habit of wearing a cowboy outfit and twirling a six-shooter on the set. Angela Dorian, playing Terry, had been previously known as Victoria Vetri in a 1967 *Playboy* centerfold exposure—Farrow mentions Terry's resemblance to Vetri in the film. Veteran screenwriter Ruth Gordon rejuvenated her acting career as Minnie and received an Academy Award as best supporting actress. This film was roundly condemned by Catholic groups, and parts of it were censored in London.

RULES OF THE GAME (LA RÈGLE DU JEU). 1939.
Filmed February–June 1939; France: La Ferté-St. Aubin, Sologne (exteriors); Saint-Maurice Studios, Joinville.
Cast: Nora Gregor, Marcel Dalio, Jean Renoir, Mila Parély, Pauline Dubost.
Director: Jean Renoir.

First exhibited in a France soon to fall to the Nazis, this bleak satirical comedy caused a riot at its Paris premiere, and the government quickly banned the film as "demoralizing." It was seen as an attack on France's ruling circles, laying bare their cynicism and corruption. Director Renoir said he intended "an exact description of the bourgeois of our time," but many French viewed the film as simply unpatriotic in a bad year. Renoir, who played Octave in the film, originally wanted Simone Simon for the lead role taken by Nora Gregor, an Austrian princess in real life. His improvisational methods and constant script revisions at times bewildered the cast and slowed production. The rabbit-shooting sequence, for example, took two months to film and sacrificed many rabbits. France's Nazi occupiers continued the ban on the film, and an Allied air raid destroyed the original negative in 1942. In 1946, a virgin print was discovered, but a complete version of the film as Renoir intended it did not appear in Paris until 1965. With such a traumatic history, the film had to have been a masterpiece—and it was and is.

S

SABOTEUR. 1942. Filmed winter–spring 1942; New York City. Boulder Dam, Arizona. Universal Studios, Universal City.

Cast: Robert Cummings, Priscilla Lane, Otto Kruger, Norman Lloyd.

Director: Alfred Hitchcock.

Not to be confused with Alfred Hitchcock's earlier *Sabotage* (1936), *Saboteur* became his main contribution to World War II propaganda. Hitchcock had little choice over the casting; he wanted Gary Cooper and Barbara Stanwyck for the leads (both turned him down) and Harry Carey, Sr., for the master spy role that went to Otto Kruger. Carey's wife, it seems, had violently objected to this part for her husband, saying that it would undermine Carey's vital image as a role model for children, a mantle she claimed he had inherited since the death of Will Rogers. Robert Cummings was miscast, thought Hitchcock, mainly because of a face that hardly conveyed anguish. The director's own anguish resulted from constant conflict with his boss, David O. Selznick, who had loaned him out to Universal—at a huge profit for Selznick but little for Hitchcock—to make this picture and from the death in a plane crash of his good friend and Hollywood neighbor, Carole Lombard. Hitchcock said he had the fascist America First group in mind when he wrote the scenario. Subtitled in its advertising as *The Man Behind Your Back* (playing on wartime paranoia), the film was in many ways a thematic forerunner of *North by Northwest*. The context of the brief newsreel shot of the capsized *SS Normandie* at its Manhattan pier evoked huge displeasure from the U.S. Navy; the scenario seemed to imply that the ship had been sabotaged and the navy was thus derelict in its duty to protect it. (Both assumptions were probably correct.) Radio City Music Hall, scene of the shootout, was a wry inclusion: almost every Hitchcock movie of the Forties and Fifties premiered there. The director appeared in his cameo bit at a newsstand.

SAN FRANCISCO. 1936. Filmed winter 1935–36; California: San Francisco (backgrounds); MGM Studios, Culver City.
Cast: Clark Gable, Jeanette MacDonald, Spencer Tracy, Jack Holt, Jessie Ralph.
Director: W. S. Van Dyke.

Both Clark Gable and Spencer Tracy, in their first of three film pairings, had qualms about doing this picture—Gable because he hated being sung at by the likes of Jeanette MacDonald, and Tracy because his role of the priest, Father Mullin, troubled his Irish Catholic soul. (Tracy had disappointed his father by not entering the priesthood.) But the attractive parts and a director they admired finally enticed them into doing this film that would prove a highlight of both their careers and make a star of Tracy. Friendly rivals, the two were also a mutual-envy society; Gable wished he had Tracy's acting talent (the latter accomplished most of his scenes in one take), and Tracy longed for some of the public adulation heaped on Gable. Screenwriter Anita Loos based Gable's character, Blackie Norton, on the witty bon vivant and screenwriter Wilson Mizner, who died in 1933. It was MacDonald, however, who brought it all together; cast before the others, she wanted Gable for her leading man and she held out patiently, waiting for him to make up his mind. When he did, he ignored her when they weren't filming a scene together, his indifference made plain. While her reputation as a prima donna had preceded her, she apparently did nothing to provoke this mysterious behavior from a man who adored most of the women he worked with, and it greatly upset her. The look of surprise on her face during their first kissing scene in the film was genuine; Gable was reeking of garlic, an offense he had earlier accused her of. Director W. S. Van Dyke hired many unemployed actors and show people of silent-film days for bit parts; among them, Jean Acker, first wife of Rudolph Valentino and (as the Professor) old-time vaudeville star Al Shean. He also assigned film pioneer D. W. Griffith to direct one scene, probably a crowd sequence. Special visuals for the twenty-minute earthquake and fire sequences included the opening-pavement effect, accomplished by cables pulling apart two hydraulic platforms, with water hoses beneath to simulate ruptured pipelines. The epilogue scene, showing 1936 San Francisco with the Golden Gate bridge under construction, was added after the premiere, in order to improve audience reaction to the finale.

THE SANDS OF IWO JIMA. 1949. Filmed July–August 1949; California: Camp Pendleton; Camp Del Mar; Republic Studios, Los Angeles.

Cast: John Wayne, John Agar, Adele Mara, Forrest Tucker, Arthur Franz, Julie Bishop.

Director: Allen Dwan.

Thousands of California-based Marines took part in the authentic combat sequences staged by Allen Dwan in recreating the 1945 battle of Iwo Jima. The film's Mount Suribachi, where the American flag was raised, was actually an artillery observation post at Camp Pendleton; beach landing scenes were filmed at Camp Del Mar. Actual combat footage added to the Tarawa battle sequences. John Wayne seldom played anyone other than a Western or war hero, and his lead role here made him the nation's foremost box office star. Three survivors of the actual flag-raising on Suribachi (an action captured in the famous Pulitzer Prize photo by Jack Rosenthal) were enlisted to play themselves in the film and to recreate that historic event: John H. Bradley, René A. Gagnon, and Ira H. Hayes (the American Indian who would be portrayed, in 1961, by Tony Curtis in *The Outsider*). Also playing themselves were Captain Harold Schrier, who had led a platoon up the slopes, and Colonel David M. Shoup, who became Marine Commandant in the Fifties.

SATURDAY NIGHT FEVER. 1977. Filmed winter–spring 1977; New York City: Manhattan; Bay Ridge, Brooklyn.

Cast: John Travolta, Karen Lynn Gorney, Donna Pescow, Barry Miller, Julie Bovasso.
Director: John Badham.

The film that inspired the disco dance craze brought twenty-three-year-old TV actor John Travolta stardom as a strutting young stud who lets loose on Saturday night—a 1970s version of *Marty*, no less, with strong inspiration from the British-made *Saturday Night and Sunday Morning* (1960). Travolta, who learned disco dancing from scratch for this film, trained rigorously for his physically demanding role, dancing and running for hours each day over a five-month period. Karen Lynn Gorney, who made her screen debut at age twelve in *David and Lisa* (1963) and acted in TV soap operas, also put herself through a strenuous fitness program; so these were hardly your average, just-for-fun weekend disco jocks. Affecting Travolta emotionally during the filming was the sudden death (from cancer) of his lover, actress Diana Hyland. Helen Travolta, the actor's mother, played a bit part as a woman in a paint store. The film's sequel, *Staying Alive* (1983), attempted to resurrect Travolta's film character and his own teen-idol status, to sad effect.

SAYONARA. 1957. Filmed January–April 1957; Japan: Imperial Summer Palace grounds, Kyoto; Tokyo; Kobe; Osaka; Isle of Takamatsu. California: Malibu; Warner Bros. Studios, Burbank.
Cast: Marlon Brando, Red Buttons, Miyoshi Umeki, Miiko Taka, Ricardo Montalban, James Garner, Martha Scott.
Director: Joshua Logan.

This update of the Madame Butterfly theme, based on James A. Michener's novel about racial prejudice in postwar Japan (the title means *good-bye* in Japanese), brought several newcomers and relative unknowns together with Marlon Brando, then at the peak of his career. Miyoshi Umeki and Miiko Taka—the latter a Nisei from Los Angeles—made their screen debuts. Playing Hana-ogi, Taka was cast after a long search by Joshua Logan; he had first offered the role to Audrey Hepburn, who refused it. Taka, who had never previously acted, began work in an absolutely terrified state. Her fears threatened to disrupt the filming schedule until Brando and Logan worked closely with her to calm her down. Ricardo Montalban, playing a Japanese Kabuki actor, mastered the intricate movements of this style by intensive training with a Kabuki teacher. When the Japanese audience applauded his performance after filming, he cited it as "one of the great moments" of his professional life. James Garner had sought the starring role but happily settled for the part of Captain Bailey, just for the chance to work with Brando. Brando took pains to put his fellow performers at ease but gave Logan plenty of headaches. After refusing the role at first, he stalled his final acceptance to the point of Logan's utter frustration. Their stormy power struggles on the set coincided with the beginning of Brando's public involvement in various underdog causes. He insisted on script changes to avoid the appearance of racial put-downs and to give the film an upbeat ending, also ad-libbing and improvising in many scenes. Brando detested all of Logan's previous work, lost faith in him as a director during production, and largely threw up his hands long before completion. (Years later, however, he amended his opinion of Logan's direction, admitting that the director had often been right.) A compulsive eater at times, Brando fought a constant weight problem. Japanese cultural agencies took a dim view of filming Michener's novel and blocked Logan's efforts to use well-known dance troupes, so the director sought obscure, freelance companies—one of them a Communist puppet troupe. The film proved highly popular, winning five Academy Awards—among them, best supporting Oscars for Umeki and Red Buttons.

SCARFACE. 1932. Filmed spring–November 1931; Los Angeles.

Cast: Paul Muni, Ann Dvorak, George Raft, Boris Karloff, Karen Morley, Osgood Perkins.

Director: Howard Hawks.

Several different elements went into Paul Muni's portrayal of savage gangster Tony Camonte. Director Howard Hawks and screenwriter Ben Hecht based the character on Chicago mobster Al Capone, then at the height of his notoriety; but Hawks also intended the lead roles to represent updated Borgias; and Hecht viewed the drama as a modernized *Macbeth*. This film noir classic made major stars of Muni and George Raft, both relative unknowns at the time. Most characters and events in the film had their real counterparts in the lawless Prohibition decade that spawned *The Shame of a Nation* (the film's subtitle, insisted upon by censors who worried about the glamorous gangster images portrayed). And, as during the making of *The Godfather* decades later, that real-life world impinged upon the movie itself. Raft, for example, heretofore a bit actor and dancer in Manhattan speakeasies, owed his role of Guido Rinaldo (based on Capone's bodyguard Frankie Rio) to bootlegger Owney Madden, who talked Hawks into giving his boy a break. A phenomenal womanizer, Raft almost lost the part when he went after actress Billie Dove, unaware that she was producer Howard Hughes's girlfriend. Capone's own men kept a close eye on the filmmaking, some of them applying for jobs as extras and "advisers." Capone himself hugely enjoyed *Scarface*, owned a print of it, and threw a party for Hawks afterward in Chicago. Ann Dvorak's smoky dance in the party scene recreated a spontaneous bit between her and Raft that had occurred at an actual party, where Hawks had seen it. Raft practiced for days to perfect Guido's coin-flipping habit. He picked up the mannerism from one of Dutch Schultz's mobsters; for years afterward, he watched it become a favorite bit of George Raft impressionists. In the scene where Raft is shot, he actually hit his head on the door when he fell, the pain making his eyes roll, and Hawks didn't repeat the take. A worse casualty on the set was Gaylord Lloyd, a unit director and brother of film comic Harold Lloyd; during the garage massacre scene, copper splinters from exploding dynamite caps (simulating machine-gun fire) put out his eye. Real machine-gun bullets riddled the coffee shop set, tearing it to pieces, a scene technically superimposed with the actors. Boris Karloff, playing Gaffney, would become known for his monster role in *Frankenstein*, made just after *Scarface* but released long before. Censorship problems delayed release of *Scarface* for almost a year but notably aided box office returns. Muni could hardly tolerate character actor Vince Barnett, who, in his screen debut, played Muni's gunsel Angelo. Muni claimed that Barnett constantly tried to upstage him by stupid tricks and demanded at one point that Barnett be fired. Hawks apparently kept him on just to keep Muni sharp by antagonizing him; and Barnett became the bane of Muni's life in Hollywood, turning up in several later films with him. Osgood Perkins, playing Johnny Lovo, was the father of actor Tony Perkins. Note the recurrent X-motif that occurs throughout, a distinctive

Hawks touch. Hawks himself played a bit part as a man in a hospital bed. Producer Hughes, unhappy with Hawks, locked up the distribution rights for forty-seven years and wanted to confiscate all copies of the film. Only in 1979, after Hughes's death, could it be seen again. *Scarface* was remade, to much less effect, in 1983.

THE SCARLET PIMPERNEL. 1934. Filmed summer–autumn 1934; England: rural areas; Elstree Studios, Borehamwood.

Cast: Leslie Howard, Merle Oberon, Raymond Massey, Nigel Bruce, Anthony Bushell.

Director: Harold Young.

One of the few examples of a film being better than the original novel (by Baroness Orczy in this case), this movie was also unusual in England for its time in its use of outdoor location scenes. Producer Alexander Korda made Harold Young the director in name only, actually helming most of the film himself. Leslie Howard, something of a Don Juan off-screen, indulged in a brief romantic affair with Merle Oberon when Korda wasn't looking. (As a long-time Trilby to Korda's Svengali, she finally married Korda five years later.) Raymond Massey, playing the evil Chauvelin, said he "never had such fun working in a movie." The picture was seen, and probably intended, as a veiled comment on a rising Nazi Germany, with the French Revolutionists posed as the bad guys. *The Return of the Scarlet Pimpernel* (1937), a sequel, kept only Bushell from the original cast. Remakes included *Pimpernel Smith* (1941) and *The Elusive Pimpernel* (1950), as well as a 1982 TV movie using the original title.

THE SEA HAWK. 1940. Filmed January–April 1940; California: Point Magu; Warner Bros. Ranch, Calabasas; Warner Bros. Studios, Burbank.

Cast: Errol Flynn, Flora Robson, Claude Rains, Brenda Marshall, Donald Crisp, Henry Daniell, Alan Hale, Una O'Connor.

Director: Michael Curtiz.

At the apex of his career, Errol Flynn reprised his *Captain Blood* role in this swashbuckler loosely based on Rafael Sabatini's novel. The studio intended it as a patriotic flag-waver for Britain, which was threatened at the time by German invasion.

Despite Flynn's apparently superb physique and the fact that he did his own rope swinging and some of his own sword work, he was not a well man, and the role pushed him to his physical limits. High fevers and weakness, probably a recurrence of malaria, sidelined him for several days; these absences plus his chronic lateness on the set and his refusal to memorize dialogue slowed the production. His costar, Flora Robson, whom he liked very much, finally took him to task, saying the delays might prevent her doing a play in New York, at which news he shaped up. As on most of their pictures together, Flynn and director Michael Curtiz scrapped constantly; the actor played practical jokes on the director, who, in turn, regarded the actor as little more than a bum. Producer Hal Wallis admonished Curtiz at one point for filming so many scenes of brutal whippings of "slaves" in the Spanish galleys; this all-too-painful realism also upset Flynn. Henry Daniell, cast as Wolfingham, was found hopeless at handling a sword, according to studio memos, and his duelling scenes had to be doubled and, for close-ups, filmed from the elbows up. Brenda Marshall, soon to marry actor William Holden, played Maria in her second screen appearance, her singing voice dubbed by one Sally Sweetland. The film used several sets from a previous Flynn-Curtiz film, *The Private Lives of Elizabeth and Essex*, augmented with intercut miniatures and action footage from *Captain Blood*. Panamanian footage was filmed at the Warner ranch, using a set previously constructed for *Juarez* (1939). Two full-scale sailing vessels floated in the studio's new indoor ocean, a 100-×-170-foot tank first used in this picture. The vessels, however, were intact only on one side; hydraulic rocker machinery, designed to simulate wave motion and sinking, anchored the ships to the tank floor from the vessels' opposite sides. The resulting seasickness suffered by many actors in these bobbing models was much more authentic than the ships. This was one of British prime minister Winston Churchill's favorite films.

THE SEARCHERS. 1956. Filmed February–August 1955; Utah: Monument Valley; Mexican Hat. Aspen, Colorado. RKO-Pathé Studios, Burbank.

Cast: John Wayne, Jeffrey Hunter, Vera Miles, Ward Bond, Natalie Wood, Lana Wood.

Director: John Ford.

John Wayne thought this film embodied his best screen work, and many critics agreed. Wayne liked fanatical hero Ethan Edwards so much that he named his third son John Ethan. His second son, Patrick, played Lieutenant Greenhill, and eighteen-year-old Natalie Wood developed a schoolgirl crush on him. (Lana Wood played her big sister's role of Debbie Edwards as a child.) Other familiar faces included Ward Bond as Reverend Clayton and Ken Curtis of *Gunsmoke* fame; as Charlie McCorry, he used the drawling hillbilly accent he would later employ as Festus in the TV series. Olive Carey, cast as Mrs. Jorgensen, was the widow of veteran character actor Harry Carey, Sr., who had appeared in many Wayne movies. As a private salute to his old sidekick, Wayne postured himself in a typical Carey stance of crossed arms as he stood in a doorway in the climactic scene. Harry Carey, Jr., appeared as Brad Jorgensen. Look for Mae Marsh, a leading lady of the silent screen, as a woman at the fort. Spectacular Monument Valley was Ford's favorite location for filming westerns—he made nine there—but it wasn't paradisiacal; heat, wind, and sandstorms often made camera work difficult or impossible. Ford was noted, however, for using whatever conditions existed without waiting for weather to clear, shooting only occasional retakes.

THE SEVEN SAMURAI. 1954. Filmed 1952–53; Japan: various locations; Toho Studios, Tokyo.

Cast: Toshiro Mifune, Takashi Shimura, Yoshio Inaba, Isko Kimura.

Director: Akira Kurosawa.

Akira Kurosawa's masterpiece, this epic of feudal Japan was also the director's favorite in his imposing body of work. His aim, he said, was to make a film "entertaining enough to eat," and it provides one of those cinematic experiences that may be savored repeatedly. Lack of funds and sufficient numbers of horses slowed production so that actual filming took more than a year. Kurosawa expressed deep disappointment in the film's Americanized remake, *The Magnificent Seven*. *Battle Beyond the Stars* (1980) transferred the story to outer space.

THE SEVEN YEAR ITCH. 1955. Filmed August–November 1954; New York City. 20th Century-Fox Studios, Los Angeles.

Cast: Marilyn Monroe, Tom Ewell, Evelyn Keyes, Sonny Tufts, Robert Strauss.
Director: Billy Wilder.

The only way that the studio would let Marilyn Monroe achieve her dream of being directed by Billy Wilder, one of Hollywood's legendary best, was by requiring her presence first in *There's No Business Like Show Business*. Wilder much preferred to make his movies in black and white, only agreeing to do this one in color because Monroe's contract demanded it. On the set, her late arrivals and inability to get a scene right without a dozen or more takes bemused the director, who serenely adapted to her ways and guided her step-by-step. The famous scene of Monroe's skirt blowing up as she stood on a subway grating was filmed at 2 A.M. outside the Trans-Lux Theatre in Manhattan. Some 4,000 spectators—among them, her grim-faced husband Joe DiMaggio, sickened at the sight of the loud, leering crowd—watched take after take from the sidelines as an electric fan below the grate billowed her clothing. Their marriage was on its last shaky legs by this time, and they officially separated less than a month later; she divorced DiMaggio before the picture was completed. A week after the separation announcement, she returned to work, astonishing everyone by her sudden punctuality, line retention, and amiable cooperation that enabled Wilder to film the rest of her scenes in one or two takes apiece.

THE SEVENTH SEAL. 1956. Filmed July–August 1956; Sweden: Hovs Hallar; Svensk Filmindustri Studios, Råsunda.
Cast: Max von Sydow, Gunnar Bjornstrand, Nils Poppe, Bibi Andersson, Bengt Ekerot.
Director: Ingmar Bergman.

One of Ingmar Bergman's most allegorical and stylized early films was *The Seventh Seal*. It was also an important milestone of Bergman's own spiritual journey; making this film and *Winter Light* (1962), he said, "freed me from my own fear of death." Except for the commercial success of his comedy *Smiles of a Summer Night* (1955), *The Seventh Seal* would not have been filmed, for the studio had previously turned down his screenplay. Popular stage comedian Nils Poppe, playing Jof, made his screen debut here at age fifty. Bengt Ekerot, who often acted for Bergman, played Death;

Ekerot himself died shortly thereafter. For extras in the village tavern scene, the director hired residents of a Stockholm geriatric home. The climactic Dance of Death on the hilltop was totally improvised in ten minutes after the regular working day, when most of the actors had gone home. A beautiful cloud appeared in the sky; Bergman hastily dressed his working crew in the actors' costumes and filmed the sequence quickly. (Union regulations would now prevent such spontaneity.)

SHANE. 1953. Filmed summer–October 1951; Jackson Hole, Wyoming. Paramount Studios, Los Angeles.
Cast: Alan Ladd, Jean Arthur, Van Heflin, Brandon de Wilde, Jack Palance, Ben Johnson, Edgar Buchanan.
Director: George Stevens.

This enormously popular Western ranks as one of George Stevens's best films, giving Alan Ladd the best role of his career. A dour actor who specialized in silent suffering types, he played the title role of a lone stranger with a past too heavy for words—a hero who rides in from nowhere to save the beleaguered homesteaders. Ladd was a morose, insecure man with a huge inferiority complex about his acting ability; but he loved working with Stevens and regarded *Shane* as a strange, wondrous fluke in his career. Despite opportunities, he never again collaborated with a director of Stevens's caliber. He established a close friendship with Van Heflin on the set, one that lasted until Ladd's apparent suicide in 1964. This film marked Jean Arthur's final movie appearance after a thirty-year career. Brandon de Wilde at age nine was a terror on the set; his idea of fun, recalled Ladd's daughter Carol, was jumping up and down in puddles, splashing mud all over everyone, and she marveled at Stevens's patience with him. Ladd's younger daughter, eight-year-old Alana, joined the cast for a bit part as a child lugging a sack of potatoes. In one of his most villainous roles, Jack Palance, playing the gunfighter Wilson, instantly typecast himself as Hollywood's meanest and nastiest. Stevens, always a stickler for authentic detail, made sure that clothing and even haircuts were true to the period. To Ladd's disappointment but scant surprise, he failed to win an Academy Award, or even a nomination, for his performance; though Loyal Griggs took an Oscar for his cinematography.

SHE WORE A YELLOW RIBBON. 1949. Filmed November–December 1948; Monument Valley, Utah. RKO Studios, Culver City.

Cast: John Wayne, Victor McLaglen, Joanne Dru, John Agar, Ben Johnson, Harry Carey, Jr., Mildred Natwick.

Director: John Ford.

Never a director to film two takes if the first seemed all right, John Ford created this frontier classic at breakneck speed in spectacular Monument Valley, a frequent locale for his Westerns. One reason he often filmed there was to aid the local Navajo economy with employment and services that a Hollywood production could bring. In late 1948, this effort proved a particular godsend to the native people, actually saving lives, as a freak blizzard had plunged the isolated settlements into crisis. John Wayne, in essaying a role nineteen years older than his own age (forty-one), reversed his usual policy of playing younger and turned in one of his better performances. (He himself believed it his "best achievement in pictures" and expressed keen disappointment at not being nominated for an Academy Award.) Shooting one scene in an Indian camp, Wayne experienced his closest call in a lifetime of pretend heroics, taking a bad fall when his saddle worked loose and his horse threw him. Knocked out, he narrowly escaped being trampled by about fifty horses. Ford wanted the picture to bear the look of Frederic Remington paintings. At one point, wishing to take advantage of a scenic purple sky and horizon lightning, he instructed cinematographer Winton C. Hoch to film the vista. Hoch, a by-the-book cameraman who was packing up his gear for the day, did so under furious protest and filed a complaint against Ford to his union. That scene, as it turned out, helped Hoch win an Academy Award, the film's only Oscar. Actor-director Irving Pichel narrated the film.

SHIP OF FOOLS. 1965. Filmed June–September 1964; Pacific Ocean (exteriors); Paramount and Columbia studios, Los Angeles.

Cast: Vivien Leigh, Oskar Werner, Simone Signoret, José Ferrer, Heinz Ruhmann, Lee Marvin, José Greco, George Segal, Elizabeth Ashley, Michael Dunn.

Director: Stanley Kramer.

If not for Spencer Tracy's bad health, Katharine Hepburn

might have accepted the role ultimately given to Vivien Leigh; but Hepburn decided against returning to films while Tracy was dying. Leigh came to her final movie role in precarious mental health, again playing a Southern Gothic character, this one derived from Katherine Anne Porter's novel. Increasingly subject to episodes of manic-depressive psychosis and bouts of alcoholism, Leigh received periodic shock treatments. Though she could be irrationally abrasive toward fellow cast members during these spells, she remembered nothing after their occurrence; her colleagues on the set treated her supportively and affectionately, as befitted her talent and normally open, friendly nature. After some initial verbal fireworks with Lee Marvin over his stale whiskey breath on the set, she warmed especially to him—probably the most unlikely friendship she could have developed, given their differing ages, backgrounds, and lifestyles. Playing the vicious ex-baseball player Bill Tenny, Marvin was also dealing with the breakup of his first marriage and sowing seeds for a future crisis—the palimony suit brought against him fifteen years later by Michelle Triola; they first met during production of *Ship of Fools*. Because Oskar Werner, as the ship's doctor, refused to play stage left in a bar scene, Stanley Kramer had to rebuild the set to suit this difficult actor. Spanish flamenco dancer José Greco, in his film debut as Pepe, said he felt awkward and self-conscious playing to a camera and didn't enjoy the experience. Nor was Elizabeth Ashley, playing Jenny opposite George Segal, happy with her own second film performance. Kramer, whose uplifting message pictures never left doubt as to the sermon intended, said that he met "a very stony reception" in West Germany, where he went to cast the Jew Lowenthal—for the Germans recalled Kramer's *Judgment at Nuremberg* not at all kindly. Kramer finally chose Heinz Ruhmann, who had been a popular star in pre-Hitler Germany, not Jewish himself but anti-Nazi and eager to play the part. Ernest Laszlo won an Academy Award for cinematography.

THE SHOOTIST. 1976. Filmed January–April 1976; Carson City, Nevada. Burbank Studios, Burbank.

Cast: John Wayne, Lauren Bacall, Ron Howard, James Stewart, Bill McKinney, Richard Boone, John Carradine, Scatman Crothers, Hugh O'Brian, Harry Morgan.

Director: Don Siegel.

Playing a dying gunfighter in his last film, John Wayne himself had declined in health to the point where he could no longer mount a horse without help. Tiring quickly, he spent most of his off-camera location time resting in his hotel room. He formed a special empathy with Ron Howard, playing young Gillom. Part of the poignancy of this film lay in its implicit reprise of Wayne's career, with excerpts from his pictures *Red River*, *Hondo*, *Rio Bravo*, and *El Dorado* and the reminder of his own battle with cancer in 1964. (He made eighteen movies after that operation, but cancer finally did claim his life in 1979.) Indications are that, despite Wayne's loudly stated plans for future projects, he knew this would be his final appearance and consciously intended it as his summary performance. Having missed ten days of work on the set because of ailments, he finished his last scenes in severe pain from an ear infection.

SINGIN' IN THE RAIN. 1952. Filmed June–November 1951; MGM Studios, Culver City.
Cast: Gene Kelly, Donald O'Connor, Debbie Reynolds, Jean Hagen, Cyd Charisse, Millard Mitchell, Rita Moreno, Douglas Fowley.
Directors: Gene Kelly, Stanley Donen.

Gene Kelly's masterpiece, perhaps the greatest movie musical of all, received its title from producer Arthur Freed before any rain scenes were planned. Kelly and codirector Stanley Donen thought the idea ridiculous; Freed could only say that he'd always wanted to make a film of that title. So Kelly agreeably built his foremost dance number in the picture around the title song (previously used in *The Hollywood Revue of 1929* and the 1940 *Little Nellie Kelly*). Despite the classic image of utter joy he projected in this number, Kelly was suffering with a bad cold during the two days required to film it, and he feared that, as the chilly "rain" poured on him from overhead spray pipes, he would catch pneumonia. Also, he had trouble coordinating movements of his umbrella with the music. This was probably also Donald O'Connor's best dance work in films. Freed had wanted to cast Oscar Levant in the role of Kelly's sidekick, as in *An American in Paris*. Kelly wasn't pleased at the casting of nineteen-year-old Debbie Reynolds as Kathy, mainly because the relatively unknown actress had never sung or danced before and Kelly had to train her from scratch. Kelly taught her how to be a perfectionist, Reynolds attested later. In their number "You Were Meant For Me," she was profoundly embarrassed when Kelly leaned his head back on a wad of gum she had quickly stuck on a ladder rung just before the take; that occasion marked the end of her chewing-gum days. The jalopy driven by Reynolds early in the film was the same one that Mickey Rooney drove in the Andy Hardy series. Kelly's mansion contained furnishings left over from Greta Garbo's silent classic, *Flesh and the Devil* (1926). As a musical satire of Hollywood's early sound era, the film used several characters based on actual persons: Hagen as Lina Lamont, modeled on actress Judy Holliday; Millard Mitchell as the studio boss, on Freed; Douglas Fowley as the director, on Busby Berkeley; and Madge Blake, playing Dora Bailey, on gossip columnist Louella Parsons. The Broadway ballet sequence, intended to feature O'Connor with Kelly, had to be revised when O'Connor left to keep a TV commitment. Cyd Charisse, made up to look like 1920s actress Louise Brooks, replaced him. A recent mother, she dieted off extra pounds and worked intensively to adapt to Kelly's dancing style, far different from her own. There was one more embarrassment: the song "Make 'Em Laugh," composed by Freed, bore startling resemblances to Cole Porter's "Be a Clown" in Freed's 1948 film *The Pirate*. The plagiarism was apparently quite unintentional; nobody, including Porter, ever wanted to discuss it.

SMILES OF A SUMMER NIGHT (SOMMARNATTENS LEENDE). 1955. Filmed summer 1955; Sweden: Jordeberge Castle, Malmö; Svensk Filmindustri Studios, Råsunda.

Cast: Gunnar Bjornstrand, Eva Dahlbeck, Harriet Andersson, Ulla Jacobsson.

Director: Ingmar Bergman.

One of Ingmar Bergman's few comedies, this was the director's frank attempt to counter the impression of being "gloomy." He added that he made the film "during one of my blackest periods" as more or less constant financial problems weighed on him. Ulla Jacobsson, playing Anne Egerman, was pregnant when filming began, and she wore specially designed costumes to mask her condition. If she grew too large for her role, as he expected she would, Bergman had promised then unknown Bibi Andersson the refilmed part. But Jacobsson stayed the course, and a somewhat embarrassed Bergman ended up casting Bibi Andersson (her screen debut) in a bit part as a nameless stage actress. This movie inspired Woody Allen's *A Midsummer Night's Sex Comedy* (1982) as well as Stephen Sondheim's Broadway musical version, *A Little Night Music*. Its commercial success enabled Bergman to film one of his great masterpieces, *The Seventh Seal* (1956).

SOME LIKE IT HOT. 1959. Filmed August–November 1958; California: Hotel del Coronado, San Diego; Los Angeles (exteriors); Samuel Goldwyn Studios, Los Angeles.

Cast: Marilyn Monroe, Tony Curtis, Jack Lemmon, George Raft, Pat O'Brien, Joe E. Brown.

Director: Billy Wilder.

Tony Curtis always believed he got short-shafted in this wonderful comedy. His first few takes of a given scene were generally his freshest and best. Marilyn Monroe, here playing showgirl Sugar Kane, didn't operate that way. She commonly needed forty or more takes just to begin functioning, by which time Curtis was frazzled and sick of it. Billy Wilder, grateful for one decent Monroe take out of scores, realized but wearily ignored this unfairness. Curtis, understandably, grew to despise the actress, who seemed so bound up with her own performance that she couldn't or wouldn't act *with* her costars. (Still, Curtis's oft-quoted remark that kissing Monroe was "like kissing Hitler" struck many as a bit extreme.) Monroe's daily tardiness and frequent absences, along with her inability to get through the simplest scenes without repeated errors, further antagonized her coworkers. The scene in which she walks into Curtis's room and says "Where's the bourbon?" required forty-seven takes because she either moved off cue, froze on her line, or spoke it wrong—even after Wilder pasted slips of paper with the dialogue in all the bureau drawers she opened. During the final month of filming, she read many of her lines from an off-camera blackboard; her eyes can be seen moving in the scene where she talks to Curtis on the phone. Monroe's severe depression following a miscarriage had prompted her husband, Arthur Miller, to encourage her to do the picture. Wilder's decision to film in black and white instead of color, because of the gaudy makeup applied to the boys in drag, irritated her from the outset. She again became pregnant during the filming, and again miscarried a few weeks after its completion. Psychosomatic stress took its toll on Wilder's health; he was hobbling around on a cane before production stopped. Later he had many harsh words about the actress. Wilder had originally wanted to cast Frank Sinatra in Jack Lemmon's role. Both Lemmon and Curtis had problems with their female attire, especially wearing high heels; at the end of a take, they often plunged their feet in ice water. George Raft, playing gangster Spats Columbo, parodied his own coin-flipping trick from *Scarface*. In this film, he gets killed by the son of his Hollywood rival in many gangster roles, Edward G. Robinson, Jr., playing Johnny Paradise. Raft balked at the scene in which he kicks a toothpick from the mouth of George E. Stone (playing Toothpick Charlie), fearing he would kick Stone in the head. After many takes, a furious Wilder demonstrated how he wanted it, aimed his kick, and put Stone in the hospital. The problem was solved by painting a nail to resemble a toothpick, and Raft kicked it from a bruised, nervous Stone in one take. Offscreen, old hoofer Raft gave tango lessons to Lemmon and Joe E. Brown for their dance scene. The movie's stunning last line was written only the night before shooting it, as screenwriters Wilder and I. A. L. Diamond sought a suitable tag for the picture because of Monroe's absence due to illness. An Academy Award went to the costume designer, Orry-Kelly, and the film inspired a later broadway musical, *Sugar*.

SONS OF THE DESERT. 1933. Filmed October 1933; Hal Roach Studios, Culver City.
Cast: Stan Laurel, Oliver Hardy, Charley Chase, Mae Busch, Dorothy Christy.
Director: William A. Seiter.

One of Laurel and Hardy's best feature-length comedies, satirizing lodge conventions, this film was based on their silent two-reeler *He Faw Down* (1928); its working title was *Fraternally Yours*. Director William A. Seiter filmed scenes mostly in the sequence in which they appear. For the convention scenes, some twenty members of the Hollywood American Legion post joined forty other extras playing Sons—among them, future MGM studio chief Jimmy (James T.) Aubrey. Comedienne Patsy Kelly had been cast in the role of

Laurel's wife, but a loan-out arrangement canceled her participation, and Dorothy Christy was a last-minute replacement. The large international organization of Laurel and Hardy devotees took the name for their group from this film's title.

SOPHIE'S CHOICE. 1982. Filmed March–June 1982; Jadran Studios, Zagreb, Yugoslavia. New York City: Bronx; Brooklyn; Camera Mart Studios, Manhattan.
Cast: Meryl Streep, Kevin Kline, Peter MacNicol, Rita Karin, Stephen D. Newman, Josh Mostel.
Director: Alan J. Pakula.

Alan J. Pakula had originally wanted Liv Ullmann for the role of Sophie, while novelist William Styron said he had always pictured Ursula Andress in the part. Marthe Keller and Barbra Streisand also sought the role, but after long indecision, Pakula half-reluctantly chose Meryl Streep, who had all but bribed him. Pakula was first to realize the wisdom of that choice; on European location, he gave up trying to direct her, saying that her self-direction had more authenticity and originality than he could offer. In preparing for her role, Streep made a bible of Styron's novel and learned to speak both German and Polish. She gained ten pounds for her Brooklyn scenes and shed twenty-five—plus shaved her head—for the Auschwitz sequences, which were filmed in Yugoslavia when Poland refused entry to cast and crew. It was she who suggested Kevin Kline for the role of her lover Nathan. Streep immersed herself so thoroughly into her role that she said the toughest part "was saying goodbye to it . . . I could have played it forever." Styron enthused over her performance, as did the Motion Picture Academy, which awarded her an Oscar as best actress. Note the muted colors of the flashback sequences; cinematographer Nestor Almendros said he sought to reproduce the German Agfacolor process of World War II films in these episodes.

SORRY, WRONG NUMBER. 1948. Filmed winter 1948; Paramount Studios, Los Angeles.
Cast: Barbara Stanwyck, Burt Lancaster, Ann Richards, Wendell Corey, Ed Begley.
Director: Anatole Litvak.

Agnes Moorehead had made this suspense thriller famous in a 1943 radio play, but she was not regarded as potent movie star material, so Barbara Stanwyck was assigned the part for the film. The screen role was by far the tougher job; in order to maintain a peak of hysteria, she asked director Anatole Litvak to film all of her most emotional scenes in sequence and at once. He did, and at the end of twelve consecutive days of acting nothing but terrified, she was wrung with exhaustion. Moreover, her natural hair color, from being prematurely gray-streaked, had turned completely white by the time filming ended. To indicate the character's wealth, a fortune in real gems was loaned to the production by a Beverly Hills jeweler —so everywhere Stanwyck went on the set, an armed guard followed. Burt Lancaster, as Stanwyck's husband Henry, talked himself into being (mis)cast for the role and said he "sweated bullets" in the part. Afterward, he admitted that he saw no recognizable part of himself on screen.

THE SOUND OF MUSIC. 1965. Filmed spring–summer 1964; Austria: Rossfeld; Salzburg area. 20th Century-Fox Studios, Los Angeles.

Cast: Julie Andrews, Christopher Plummer, Eleanor Parker, Richard Haydn, Peggy Wood.

Director: Robert Wise.

Few were more astonished at the phenomenal success of this massive musical confection from Rodgers and Hammerstein than the people who adapted and performed the screen version. (Mary Martin had starred in the 1959 Broadway hit.) Robert Wise came aboard reluctantly after William Wyler began, then withdrew from, the film. Julie Andrews thought at the outset that the movie version might be "awfully saccharine." According to Wise and others, however, the finished picture was considerably less dangerous to diabetics than it started out to be. Experiences of the real von Trapp family, who were operating a ski lodge in Vermont at the time the film was made, weren't quite so caloric, of course. Baroness Maria von Trapp, played by Andrews, herself appeared as an extra in one scene and liked the film. Andrews learned to strum the guitar for her role, bleached her hair blond, and found herself a top star when the film became a money mill. Canadian actor Christopher Plummer, as Captain von Trapp, almost backed out when he learned that his singing voice would be dubbed (by Bill Lee). Plummer's cynical working title for the picture was *The Sound of Mucus*. Look for Marni Nixon in her screen debut, playing Sister Sophia; for years Nixon had dubbed the singing voices for some of Hollywood's best-known female stars. (Here she also dubbed the singing of Peggy Wood, who played the mother abbess, though Wood herself was a former opera singer.) Rainy weather plagued much of the scenic Alpine shooting, including the opening sequence on Rossfeld mountain; thus most of the exterior shots were done under awnings in artificial light. Citizens of Salzburg, where much of the location work occurred, were about the only viewers of this film—apart from a grumpy, sugar-allergic pack of critics—who perversely didn't adore it. *The Sound of Music* won five Academy Awards, among them for best picture, Wise's direction, and Irwin Kostal's score adaptation.

SOUTH PACIFIC. 1958. Filmed 1957; Kauai, Hawaii. 20th Century-Fox Studios, Los Angeles.
Cast: Mitzi Gaynor, Rossano Brazzi, John Kerr, Ray Walston, Juanita Hall, France Nuyen.
Director: Joshua Logan.

The only thing this dated musical has going for it today, most critics agree, is the music itself. Despite the fact that Rodgers and Hammerstein's adaptation of James A. Michener's *Tales of the South Pacific* made more money than all the rest of Joshua Logan's films and stage productions combined, Logan himself deplored several key aspects of the production. He had desperately wanted Elizabeth Taylor for the lead role of Nellie Forbush; Taylor also wanted the part, but she froze up in her singing tryout before an intimidating Richard Rodgers. And Doris Day killed her chance at the role when she primly refused to sing on request at a party where Logan intended to audition her. To Logan's chagrin, Rodgers cast Rossano Brazzi as the French planter; chagrin turned to incredulous disgust when Logan found that the Italian actor couldn't carry a tune. Brazzi became highly incensed when he had to mouth words to opera singer Giorgio Tozzi's dubbing. He repeatedly flubbed the playback scenes of "Some Enchanted Evening," raging that he couldn't synchronize to such a "goddamn cheap shit voice"—at which point Logan lectured him sternly about certain moviemaking facts of life. Worst of Logan's disappointments, though, was the look of the film itself; the color processing, either by laboratory omission or commission, gave many scenes garish, glitzy hues that (in

Logan's view) "upset the whole chemistry." Mitzi Gaynor did her own singing, but John Kerr (as Lieutenant Cable) and Juanita Hall (as Bloody Mary, the only cast member to reprise her stage role) were both dubbed. The U.S. government loaned about 20,000 marines and navy men for the Thanksgiving show scene. Logan marveled at how well they provided audience reactions on cue to a performance that wasn't really there; the stage show footage was intercut later. The war sequences, produced on a remote Kauai beach, recorded actual war games being conducted by Hawaii-based marines. Look for Joan Fontaine in a brief, nonspeaking cameo and teenager Beverly Aadland, Errol Flynn's companion of his final years, playing a dancer

SPARTACUS. 1960. Filmed winter–spring 1959; Madrid area, Spain. California: Death Valley; Thousand Oaks; Chatsworth area; San Simeon; Universal-International Studios, Universal City.
Cast: Kirk Douglas, Jean Simmons, Laurence Olivier, Tony Curtis, Charles Laughton, Peter Ustinov, John Gavin, Woody Strode, Nina Foch.
Director: Stanley Kubrick.

Stanley Kubrick's *Spartacus* is generally regarded as one of Hollywood's better epics. Ironically, Kubrick, replacing Anthony Mann as director, operated here as an employee of Kirk Douglas, whose production company owned screen rights to Howard Fast's novel. Relations between director and producer-star became strained after Kubrick decided he wanted to rework Dalton Trumbo's screenplay and Douglas refused to permit it. Conflicts among the high-powered cast also resulted from Douglas's strange method of acquiring his major stars; to each he had sent a script version that subtly favored the recipient's part over the others. When the cast assembled and began comparing notes, verbal mayhem ensued, with the performers finally settling the dialogue details among themselves. Especially wary of each other were those two high-priced egos Sir Laurence Olivier (playing Crassus) and Charles Laughton (playing Gracchus), sharers of an old animosity. On the set, they circled and eyed each other with frosty politeness, each convinced of the other's veiled hostility. Peter Ustinov, who played Batiatus, recalled that Laughton seemed to sit around "waiting to have his feelings hurt," sulking over the nefarious influence that Olivier was supposedly exerting on Douglas. When Laughton refused to act the scenes given him, Ustinov was engaged to mediate, and he rewrote their shared scenes to Laughton's satisfaction. Douglas had wanted Elsa Martinelli for the slave girl role that finally went to Jean Simmons; Ingrid Bergman had turned it down as "too bloody," and Jeanne Moreau also refused it. Douglas in the title role did most of his own stunt work, including the dangerous sword and trident fight with Woody Strode. Some 8,000 Spanish infantrymen, trained in Roman legion maneuvers, acted in the battle scenes, though parts of the Silarus River battle sequence occurred in the studio, where 3,000 yards of earth were dumped on a sound stage to simulate ground contours. A main building of publisher William Randolph Hearst's lavish estate at San Simeon served as Olivier's Roman villa. The crowd noises you hear on the soundtrack were recorded at an October 1959 football game between Notre Dame and Michigan State (the Spartans). After years of Hollywood blacklisting and working under pseudonyms, screenwriter Trumbo finally received credit in his own name for his script. Among the film's four Academy Award winners, Ustinov took an Oscar as best supporting actor, and Russell Metty received one for cinematography.

SPELLBOUND. 1945. Filmed July–October 1944; Selznick International Studios, Culver City.

Cast: Ingrid Bergman, Gregory Peck, Leo G. Carroll, Michael Chekhov, Rhonda Fleming, Norman Lloyd.

Director: Alfred Hitchcock.

With this film emerged Alfred Hitchcock's favorite theme of guilt overshadowing and preventing love. Psychoanalysis was faddish in Hollywood at the time; Hitchcock and producer David O. Selznick were probably the first filmmakers to consider it a fit topic for a picture. Selznick, in analysis himself, waxed keenly enthusiastic (one of his secretaries suggested the film's title), visualizing a cast that included Joseph Cotten, Dorothy McGuire, and Paul Lukas. Ingrid Bergman initially refused her role because she didn't find the love story convincing. Playing opposite a younger man for the first time in her career (she was only a year older than Gregory Peck) disturbed Bergman, as did Hitchcock's iciness toward actors. Hitchcock didn't feel that Peck was right for the part of the amnesiac, but he finally had little to say about this casting choice. While rejoicing over the access to Bergman's audience he would gain in this film, Peck judged his own performance as "lousy." Michael Chekhov, nephew of the great Russian dramatist Anton Chekhov, played Dr. Alex Brulov. Rhonda Fleming, in her second film appearance, played Mary Carmichael. Most of artist Salvador Dali's dream-sequence footage was cut from the final version as too distracting. A startling flash of red Technicolor (one-twelfth of a second on film) still adorns the climactic scene in some video prints, a pure Hitchcockian touch. The director performed his cameo as a man emerging from a crowded elevator carrying a violin case.

STAGE DOOR. 1937. Filmed spring 1937; California: Biltmore Theatre, Los Angeles; RKO Studios, Culver City.
Cast: Katharine Hepburn, Ginger Rogers, Adolphe Menjou, Lucille Ball, Ann Miller.
Director: Gregory La Cava.

Screen Door would have been a more fitting title, insisted George S. Kaufman, coauthor of the original Broadway play. He was referring to the number of script revisions, many of them occurring on the movie set itself. Director Gregory La Cava had his own unique procedures, employing a pianist to play on the set between takes to create mood. Striving for realism through improvisation, he demanded that the cast wear their own clothing; one of his pet peeves about movies was that actresses were always dressed far beyond the means of the roles they played. He also had a stenographer record the performers' actual conversation between rehearsals, then incorporated this spontaneous chitchat into the script. For bit parts, La Cava hired many young actresses whose real-life stories matched episodes of futility and heartbreak referred to in the film. Phyllis Kennedy, playing Hattie, was one; a former dancer, she was told she'd never walk again after fracturing a vertebra; she recovered, though not to dance. Tensions flared among the high-powered female costars, and La Cava used their offscreen rivalry to advantage. To get Ginger Rogers to cry convincingly in the scene following Katharine Hepburn's calla lilies speech (a text Hepburn lifted from a 1933 play, *The Lake*, which she had performed some eighty times), La Cava filmed Rogers separately after dramatically telling her that her house had burned to the ground. Though

Lucille Ball's role of Judy Canfield proved a major breakthrough in her budding career, she didn't much care for her own performance. The film provided seventeen-year-old Ann Miller, playing Annie, with her first real acting challenge—illegally, for she was just under the child labor law age limit, only winning the part by faking her birth certificate. When word got out, producer Pandro S. Berman fumed, for the violation threatened to jeopardize the whole production. Rogers worried that Miller looked too tall in their scenes together and adjusted matters by wearing heels and top hats. For Berman and several of the cast, the filmmaking became a tortuous ordeal, owing not only to star temperaments but to La Cava's weakness for alcohol. He drank throughout the production, at one point falling off the Biltmore Theatre stage; and Berman feared the director, one of Hollywood's best comedic minds, would crack up before finishing the picture. Whitey, Eve Arden's pet in the film, was a white alley cat and a veteran performer, having been trained for two years to meow and purr on cue. The animal's salary was $25 per day.

STAGECOACH. 1939. Filmed November–December 1938; Monument Valley, Utah. Arizona: Kayenta; Mesa. California: Kernville; Muroc Dry Lake, Victorville; Fremont Pass; Newhall; Calabasas; Chatsworth; Republic Studios and Samuel Goldwyn Studios, Los Angeles.
Cast: John Wayne, Claire Trevor, Thomas Mitchell, Andy Devine, George Bancroft, Berton Churchill, John Carradine, Donald Meek, Tim Holt.
Director: John Ford.

Probably the first A-picture Western, this is one of those classic milestones whose impact has been eroded by frequent imitation and stereotyping of its characters. For thirty-one-year-old John Wayne, a relatively unknown cowboy actor at the time, the role of the Ringo Kid catapulted him to major stardom—but not without major harassment from the acidic John Ford, a director Wayne worshiped. The director bullied Wayne unmercifully, repeatedly ridiculing his walk and talk. By this roundabout psychology, he united cast and crew in support of Wayne, a tactic he often employed to forestall envy over casting a newcomer in a good role. The film marked Ford's first use of spectacular Monument Valley for location work, a place he used in many subsequent Westerns. Wayne always insisted that, contrary to Ford's account, he himself had accidentally "discovered" the area, leading Ford to what was then one of the least accessible locales in the Southwest. Ford used many old stagecoach trails in the area and employed some three hundred Navajo residents outfitted as Apaches (though Many Mules, who played Geronimo, was a genuine Apache who lived in a remote side canyon, and Chief John Big Tree, playing an Indian scout, was one of the models for the Indian head nickel). Ford filmed some of his long shots from high bluffs up to forty miles away from the traveling stagecoach. This vehicle was a sturdy, original Concord stage, which provided public transportation in the West during the years 1876–89; a studio mock-up on rockers, however, was used for scenes inside the coach. The horse falls were accomplished by "running W's," jerked cables attached to front-leg shackles, a practice that resulted in fatalities to many movie animals. (It has been discontinued on film sets.) Last filmed was the chase sequence over Muroc Dry Lake bed in Victorville. Thomas Mitchell, playing Doc Boone in the first rendition of the drunken-doctor character who appeared in many Ford films, won an Academy Award as best supporting actor. Original negative prints of this film were lost until 1970, when Wayne provided his own copy, thus permitting its rerelease and video production. The film suffered an inferior remake in 1966.

STALAG 17. 1953. Filmed February–March 1952; California: Calabasas (exteriors); Paramount Studios, Los Angeles.
Cast: William Holden, Don Taylor, Otto Preminger, Robert Strauss, Harvey Lembeck, Peter Graves.
Director: Billy Wilder.

The real World War II German POW camp called Stalag 17 stood near Krems, Austria. Charlton Heston was originally slated to play the role of Sergeant Sefton but became unavailable. William Holden declined the part at first, accepting when it was beefed up from the Broadway play version to his satisfaction. Typecasting himself in real life with the image of a Prussian disciplinarian, famed Austrian-born movie director Otto Preminger played the camp commandant in much the same way as he ran his own casts and crews, at least according to plentiful tales from those who worked with him. Robert Strauss (as Stosh) and Harvey Lembeck (as Harry) were the only cast members who recreated their stage roles. Their off-camera high-jinks annoyed Holden, who found their incessant comedy distracting. Holden won his only Academy Award as best actor in this film, which remained one of director Billy Wilder's favorites.

A STAR IS BORN. 1937. Filmed October–December 1936; California: Santa Anita Racetrack, Arcadia; Los Angeles (exteriors); Selznick International Studios, Culver City.
Cast: Janet Gaynor, Fredric March, Adolphe Menjou, Andy Devine, Lionel Stander.
Director: William Wellman.

Hollywood loves to mythologize about itself, and this durable story turns up once every generation or so to reaffirm the film colony's rather odd self-image. A revamp of *What Price Hollywood?* (1932), this version was the second of four. The costars had much in common with their roles—except in reverse. Janet Gaynor, playing the rising young actress, found herself at age thirty-one in a fast-fading career that all but ended a few years later, while Fredric March, playing Norman Maine, was still rising toward his peak years of stardom. A number of Hollywood has-beens and new up-and-comers performed bit parts. Owen Moore, playing director Casey Burke, had been a silent screen star and the first husband of Mary Pickford. Helene Chadwick, ex-wife of director Wellman, also played a small part. Among the new faces were Carole Landis and Lana Turner, both making their screen debuts as extras in the racetrack sequence. (The film eerily foreshadowed, in some elements, Landis's suicide in 1948.) March, playing one of his favorite roles, based his interpretation loosely on the downward-spiraling careers of John Gilbert and John Barrymore. His character's final end brought criticism from movie censors and church leaders. Gaynor's climactic line was based on an actual radio-show appearance by Mrs. Wallace Reid, widow of the actor who died of drug addiction in 1923. The film's early experimental Technicolor resembles the video colorization process lately reviled by filmmakers and serious cinephiles. An Academy Award went to screenwriters Dorothy Parker, Alan Campbell (Parker's husband), and Robert Carson.

A STAR IS BORN. 1954. Filmed October 1953–March 1954; California: Los Angeles (exteriors); Warner Bros. Studios, Burbank.

Cast: Judy Garland, James Mason, Charles Bickford, Jack Carson, Tommy Noonan, Amanda Blake.

Director: George Cukor.

Third time around, as if trying to get it right, this musical version of a Hollywood war-horse was generally regarded as the best. Always casting herself as a victim in real life, Judy Garland strongly identified with both lead roles, perhaps even more strongly with James Mason's than her own. Her career by this time had patterned itself into a series of long dips between comebacks. For her, Vicky Lester represented a desperate attempt to convey how cold and lonely it was at the top; she submerged herself with painful intensity into the part. She crash-dieted before filming began, and by the time it ended, she was again hooked on diet and sleeping pills, perpetually exhausted, showing up late on the set, and with her marriage to the film's producer, Sid Luft, on the rocks. Garland and Luft had wanted Cary Grant to play opposite her, and Grant was originally cast but finally, after much agonizing, withdrew, and Mason stepped in. Mason began work dizzy from an ear infection. He modeled his role on some of his own alcoholic friends and not, as he believed director George Cukor wanted, on a John Barrymoresque figure. Cukor had also filmed the story's first version, *What Price Hollywood?*—but this was his first of several musicals. After the studio fragmented the film by cutting some forty-seven minutes from the release version, Cukor furiously refused to see the picture. He was about to relent on the eve of the film's 1983 restoration of original footage (after painstaking work by film archivists), but he died before seeing that version—now available on videocassette. Ronald Haver's book *A Star is Born: The Making of the 1954 Movie and Its 1983 Restoration* (1988) also provides an enlightening view of how Hollywood handles its valuable properties. The latest remake was released in 1976.

STAR WARS. 1977. Filmed March–autumn 1976; Tikal National Park, Guatemala. Tunisia: Tozeur; Nefta; Matmata. England: Elstree Studios, Borehamwood; Shepperton Studios, Shepperton. California: Death Val-

ley; Industrial Light & Magic Corp., Van Nuys.
Cast: Mark Hamill, Harrison Ford, Carrie Fisher, Peter Cushing, Alec Guinness, David Prowse.
Director: George Lucas.

The runaway success of George Lucas's *American Graffiti* gave him the clout to acquire studio financing for this comic book space epic, a film that introduced entirely new concepts of miniature and optical effects. It also gave its title (despite Lucas's appalled fury) to Ronald Reagan's vaunted defense system. Lucas intended the film, basically a retread of Akira Kurosawa's eastern Western *The Hidden Fortress* (1958), as only one in a series of nine. (Subsequent entries included *The Empire Strikes Back*, in 1980, and *The Return of the Jedi*, in 1983). Many aspects of the project seemed almost overwhelmingly difficult for both director and cast. Lucas's relations with the British filmmaking crew were far from cordial, and he also treated his live performers aloofly, preferring to concentrate on the elaborate technology. The stilted dialogue of Lucas's screenplay frustrated the cast; often they actively ridiculed their lines. This was Hamill's screen debut. His character was called Luke Starkiller until the first day of filming, when the name was changed to Skywalker; Lucas apparently modeled the character on himself. Harrison Ford was working as a studio carpenter when Lucas tested him and, to Ford's astonishment, cast him as Han Solo—after rejecting Nick Nolte and Christopher Walken for the part. Carrie Fisher, nineteen-year-old daughter of Debbie Reynolds and Eddie Fisher, at first strongly believed herself miscast. Lucas had her breasts taped down for her role of Princess Leia; there was to be "no jiggling in the Empire," she discovered. Sir Alec Guinness accepted his role of the sage Obi-Wan Kenobi on the basis of a much larger part in the original screenplay. When Lucas revised the script to kill him off halfway through, Guinness angrily threatened to quit. Ironically, after decades of fine film acting, Guinness found himself better known for this role than any other in his career. David Prowse, as the evil Darth Vader, wore layers of canvas and leather, struggling for breath through his cowcatcher mask that allowed him to see only ten feet ahead; James Earl Jones, refusing screen credit, dubbed Vader's stertorous voice. Probably the most popular characters were the two android robots. British actor Anthony Daniels, sweltering inside his fifty-pound aluminum-steel-fiberglass costume as C-3PO, found the experience highly unpleasant. His vision inside this suit of armor was so restricted that he kept bumping into people and props. The entire weight of his arms rested on his thumbs, which stayed numb for weeks afterward. The other robot, R2-D2, was inhabited by midget actor Kenny Baker only when the robot stood still; the moving electronic models numbered seven in all. Lucas found seven-foot-two Peter Mayhew (who played the apelike Chewbacca) working in a London hospital; Mayhew, in his screen debut, performed in elevated boots. Elaborately masked and costumed actors in the cantina scene's motley gathering of planetary life forms found that their masks had no air vents, so each mask was quickly slit under the chin. Lucas packed *Star Wars* with an average of three special effects per minute. The film's merchandising spinoffs proved another gold mine. And seven Academy Awards included Oscars for music score, sound, and visual effects.

THE STING. 1973. Filmed 1972; Chicago. California: Pasadena; Santa Monica; Universal Studios, Universal City.
Cast: Paul Newman, Robert Redford, Robert Shaw, Charles Durning, Ray Walston, Eileen Brennan.
Director: George Roy Hill.

Initially neither Paul Newman nor Robert Redford fought to sign on for *The Sting*, but George Roy Hill convinced them that they might repeat the success they enjoyed in *Butch Cassidy and the Sundance Kid*, also directed by Hill. An accurate forecast. Hill had wanted Richard Boone for the part of mobster Doyle Lonnegan; but Boone turned it down, and Robert Shaw, though limping from a knee injury suffered in a handball game, was cast. Location scenes included Chicago's Union Station and a Pasadena neighborhood that was converted to the Joliet, Illinois of 1936. Those close-up, card-shuffling hands in the poker scene were not Newman's but ace gambling expert John Scarne's. Though Scott Joplin's ragtime piano music did not fit the period of the film (Joplin died in 1913), its use in the soundtrack sparked a renewed interest in this influential American composer. Among the film's seven Academy Awards were Oscars for best picture, Hill's direction, David S. Ward's screenplay, and Marvin Hamlisch's score adaptation. *The Sting II*, with writer Ward as the only holdover, was a 1983 sequel.

STRANGERS ON A TRAIN. 1951. Filmed October–December 1950; New York City (exteriors): Pennsylvania Station, Manhattan; West Side Tennis Club, Forest Hills. Danbury, Connecticut. Washington, D.C. California: Canoga Park; Chatsworth; Warner Bros. Studios, Burbank.

Cast: Robert Walker, Farley Granger, Ruth Roman, Leo G. Carroll, Patricia Hitchcock, Marion Lorne, Howard St. John.

Director: Alfred Hitchcock.

One of Alfred Hitchcock's scariest films is noted for its dual motif, pairing and juxtaposing things and people in twos. Raymond Chandler's original screenplay (from Patricia Highsmith's novel) was almost wholly rewritten by others after Hitchcock found that he couldn't work with the thorny writer. This was Robert Walker's last fully completed film, one that made him a major star just before his tragic death. (He died from a medically induced drug trauma during an alcoholic seizure in 1951; final scenes for his appearance in *My Son John*, released in 1952, were lifted from the final scenes of this picture.) Hitchcock had wanted William Holden for the role of Guy Haines but had to settle for Farley Granger. Tennis pro Jack Cushingham coached Granger (and acted as his tennis opponent in the film) in 97-degree heat at Forest Hills. The studio's insistence on casting Ruth Roman (playing Anne Morton) probably accounted for Hitchcock's constant harshness toward her on the set. But even toward his own daughter Patricia, playing Barbara Morton, his behavior could be inexplicably odd. On the amusement park set, he had her marooned at the topmost point of the Ferris wheel for an hour in total darkness, reducing her to trembling hysteria. That set, including the carousel of the climactic sequence, was built to the director's precise specifications on the Rowland V. Lee Ranch at Chatsworth. Special effects included the carousel explosion, filmed in miniature then enlarged on a huge rear-projection screen behind the actors, and the large, distorted lens constructed to represent a close-up of Laura Elliot's eyeglasses. Hitchcock's cameo appearance is that of a train passenger carrying a double bass fiddle. The film was remade as *Once You Kiss a Stranger* in 1969.

A STREETCAR NAMED DESIRE. 1951. Filmed August–October 1950; New Orleans, Louisiana (exteriors). Warner Bros. Studios, Burbank.

Cast: Vivien Leigh, Marlon Brando, Kim Hunter, Karl Malden.

Director: Elia Kazan.

Almost any Tennessee Williams play that has emerged on screen is a gutted, sanitized version, a situation that Williams himself bore with bemused tolerance. In the case of *Streetcar*, some sixty-eight script changes from the Broadway staging were required by production code censors; and negotiations with the Catholic Legion of Decency resulted in further cuts, most having to do with homosexuality and rape, the key elements crucial to the behavior of Vivien Leigh's character Blanche. Elia Kazan and his cast were all veterans of the 1947–49 Broadway run of the play (except for Leigh, who had performed her role on the London stage and was brought in as a recognized name, grievously disappointing Jessica Tandy of the original cast). Leigh, tired of the role, apparently accepted it again only to be near her husband, Laurence Olivier, who was in Hollywood to film *Carrie*—and also for the major factor of money. Olivier had directed her in the London staging of the play, and Kazan found it necessary to reshape her depiction of Blanche—though Leigh herself continued to give major credit to Olivier for her interpretation. As the only outsider to the established family of Broadway *Streetcar* players, Leigh was tense at first. She thought Marlon Brando affected, and he thought her impossibly stuffy and prim—but they soon became friends, and the cast worked together smoothly. Brando's role as the crude Stanley Kowalski was only his second film appearance. Though he purportedly detested the character, the film brought him instant stardom. Kazan had him arrange the apartment set to his own liking. Minor injuries plagued Brando: a dislocated right shoulder when Karl Malden (playing Mitch) shoved him under the shower in one scene; recurrence of an old knee problem when he spent hours in rehearsals and takes kneeling to beg Stella (played by Kim Hunter) not to leave him. Kazan filmed mainly in the chronological sequence we see on screen. The city of New Orleans resurrected one of its retired trams for one night of exterior filming, but most of the picture was made in the Burbank studio. Leigh won her second Academy Award as best actress (both times for playing American Southern belles), and Malden and Hunter took Oscars as best supporting players. Even Tennessee Williams liked this expurgated version of his play.

SUNDAY, BLOODY SUNDAY. 1971. Filmed winter–spring 1970; London: exteriors and Bray Studios.

Cast: Glenda Jackson, Peter Finch, Murray Head, Peggy Ashcroft, Maurice Denham.

Director: John Schlesinger.

Ménage à trois was the name of the game between two men and a woman in this film made possible by the commercial success of John Schlesinger's *Midnight Cowboy.* Not the woman (Glenda Jackson as Alex Greville) but the young designer (Murray Head as Bob Elkin) was the lover shared by Jackson and Peter Finch (as Dr. Daniel Hirsh). Ian Bannen had been originally cast as Hirsh but fell ill with viral pneumonia, resulting in Finch's casting. Finch so hated flying that he almost turned down the role because the schedule required him to fly quickly to London from his home in Rome; most of the clothing he wore in the film was his own, since there was no time for wardrobe fittings. Jackson's role was originally slated for Vanessa Redgrave, who instead accepted the leading role that Jackson had turned down in *The Devils*. Head described himself at age twenty as a flower child and gave Schlesinger plenty of difficulty on the set. On one occasion, he turned up with a severe burn mark on his nose; his girlfriend, he said, had stubbed out a joint on his face. He related well to the unconventional Finch, saying he considered the older actor a flower *man*, "and that's a lot harder to be!" The anxiously awaited kissing scene between Finch and Head greatly disturbed almost everybody on the set—especially technicians and crew—except for the two performers, who were so preoccupied with their roles they had no time to be abashed. "I did it for England," joked Finch. Head was also recording the part of Judas for the album *Jesus Christ Superstar* at the time. The film showcased what was probably the best work of Finch's career; some observers felt that his posthumous Academy Award for *Network* was really a belated tribute for his performance here. Critical opinion waxed much kindlier than box office receipts, however. Finch couldn't find work for eight months—and Head remained unemployed for eighteen—following this film. Look for silent movie star Bessie Love in a cameo role as an answering service clerk.

SUNSET BOULEVARD. 1950. Filmed April–June 1949; Los Angeles: Getty Mansion; Paramount Studios.
Cast: Gloria Swanson, William Holden, Erich von Stroheim, Nancy Olson, Fred Clark, Jack Webb, Cecil B. De Mille, Buster Keaton.
Director: Billy Wilder.

Silent film siren Gloria Swanson, at age fifty-two, marked a triumphant comeback in her role as faded star Norma Desmond. The part reflected Swanson's own life only insofar as she was one of many Hollywood performers whose careers had declined with the transition to sound films. She was actually fourth choice for the role. Mae West had indignantly rejected the notion of herself as passé, and Pola Negri also declined; Mary Pickford liked the concept but wanted the screenplay rewritten to suit herself. Totally enamored with her role, Swanson hated to have the picture end. During filming, she resumed many old friendships among the cast of veterans. Her climactic staircase scene brought tears and applause on the set. The silent-film extracts of Swanson were from *Queen Kelly*, directed by Erich von Stroheim in 1928, but unfinished by him and never released in the U.S. because of its risqué brothel scenes. Here playing Swanson's ex-husband, ex-director, and current butler, von Stroheim—one of cinema's most brilliantly creative directors—was idolized by Billy Wilder. A scene von Stroheim found especially exhausting was as Swanson's chauffeur, driving her to the studio. Since von Stroheim couldn't drive, the car was actually towed by ropes as he sat nervously behind the wheel. This film provided a breakthrough for thirty-two-year-old William Holden. Curiously, he was also fourth choice for his role of gigolo Joe Gillis. Montgomery Clift backed out of the part two weeks before filming began, enraging Wilder; then Fred MacMurray, finding the role demeaning, refused it; and Gene Kelly was unavailable. The swimming pool of the film's opening scenes was one that Wilder had constructed at the Jean Paul Getty mansion on Wilshire Boulevard in Los Angeles. (This same pool—and mansion—later appeared in *Rebel Without a Cause*; the house was demolished in 1957). Cecil B. De Mille, another famous director, played himself; his scenes were filmed on the set of *Samson and Delilah*, the biblical epic he was directing at the time. Academy Awards went for the screenplay and Franz Waxman's music.

SUPERMAN. 1978. Filmed March 1977–August 1978; Alberta, Canada: Drumheller; Stoney Indian Reservation; Kananaskis area; Barons; Blackie. New York City (exteriors). Gallup, New Mexico (exteriors). England: Shepperton Studios, Shepperton; Pinewood Studios, Iver Heath.

Cast: Christopher Reeve, Marlon Brando, Gene Hackman, Margot Kidder, Ned Beatty, Jackie Cooper, Glenn Ford, Phyllis Thaxter, Trevor Howard, Susannah York.

Director: Richard Donner.

Casting America's 20th-century hero archetype, a creature of comic books, was somewhat akin to casting Jesus Christ—who could do the part justice? Some two hundred actors and athletes considered for the title role included Robert Redford, Paul Newman, Steve McQueen, Clint Eastwood, Charles Bronson, Sylvester Stallone, and Bruce Jenner. Christopher Reeve, a TV soap opera actor, was finally selected when the producers decided to go for an unknown. Rather scrawny at the outset, the twenty-four-year-old Reeve began a strenuous pre-production physical regimen, adding thirty pounds of highly visible brawn. With no known neurotic traits, past sins, or personality quirks, the offscreen actor proved as dull as Clark Kent to studio publicists, but he fit the costume well and became at least as convincing a Superman as any previous actor in the role. (The first was Kirk Alyn in a 1948 Columbia serial; he and Noel Neill, the first film Lois Lane, emerged from retirement to play Lois Lane's parents in this movie.) Reeve's hardest task was to "fly" properly in the elaborate harness and belts that wafted him by crane above the sound stage; keeping his limbs ramrod straight demanded all those muscles he had developed, resulting in huge bruises and calluses. For some long shots of Superman flying, a midget with a latex Reeve mask and a tiny costume was used as a double. Canadian actress Margot Kidder, who narrowly won her role of Lois Lane over Lesley Ann Warren, had never read a Superman comic until the day before her screen test. She said she finally rid herself of lifelong claustrophobia during the sequence in which she is trapped inside her car, which is lodged in an "earthquake fissure" (actually a wedge-shaped hydraulic compressor that crushed the car in three stages); hours later, she still spat out dirt that had been poured on her for the scene. Marlon Brando's minor role as Jor-El evoked much publicity because of his unprecedented salary—almost $4 million for 13 days' work. Jack Klugman, Eddie Albert, and Keenan Wynn had each been cast in turn as editor Perry White; the first two changed their minds, Wynn fell ill, and Jackie Cooper was hired as a last-minute replacement. Joan Crawford was wanted for the part of Ma Kent but died before she could be signed, and Phyllis Thaxter took the role. Exhibiting all of the supernatural powers that being Superman involves was, of course, the realm of special effects, using miniatures, matte paintings, and optically processed shots. Kansas farm and missile base sequences were filmed in Alberta; while *Daily Planet* exteriors used the New York *Daily News* building. The film was dedicated to cinematographer Geoffrey Unsworth, who died shortly after production wrapped. About half the scenes for *Superman II* (1980) were shot during this production; *Superman III* appeared in 1983 and *Superman IV* in 1987. David Michael Petrou's book *The Making of Superman the Movie* (1978) details almost everything one could want to know about this hugely profitable blockbuster.

SUSPICION. 1941. Filmed winter–May 1941; RKO Studios, Culver City.

Cast: Joan Fontaine, Cary Grant, Nigel Bruce, Cedric Hardwicke, May Whitty, Isabel Jeans, Heather Angel, Leo G. Carroll.

Director: Alfred Hitchcock.

The studio-contrived ending was far different from the much more interesting one concocted by Alfred Hitchcock (who also wanted to title the film *Fright*); but nervous executives refused to tamper with moneymaker Cary Grant's pleasant image by launching him as a thoroughgoing villain. Grant wasn't happy making this picture, partly because he despised costar Joan Fontaine. (Her "bitchy behavior," he muttered, made her a perfectly believable target for murder by her husband. Also, he believed that Hitchcock favored the actress and let her dominate the film.) Grant avoided Fontaine for the rest of his life and Hitchcock for five years, by which time he had cooled sufficiently to make *Notorious* and, ultimately, two more movies for the portly director. To focus attention on the questionable glass of milk that Grant carries upstairs to an ailing Fontaine, Hitchcock installed a small light in the tumbler; milk alone wouldn't have glowed so incandescently. Nigel Bruce, not yet settled for life into his role of Dr. Watson to Basil Rathbone's Sherlock Holmes, played Grant's cloddish chum Beaky. Fontaine, younger sister of Olivia de Havilland, won a best actress Oscar for her performance. The film was remade in 1988.

SWING TIME. 1936. Filmed winter–spring 1936; RKO Studios, Culver City.

Cast: Fred Astaire, Ginger Rogers, Victor Moore, Helen Broderick, Eric Blore, Betty Furness.

Director: George Stevens.

Long regarded as a minor opus in the Fred Astaire-Ginger Rogers canon (their sixth of ten pairings, one which Astaire himself regarded as far from their best), this film has gradually assumed classic status. For dance numbers alone, it is often cited as among their greatest. Astaire didn't like the script, much of which he dismissed as "stupid" and which remained unfinished when filming began. Working titles included *I Won't Dance* and *Never Gonna Dance*; lyricist Jerome Kern suggested the title finally chosen. Astaire appeared here for the only time in blackface doing his trick-screen "Bojangles of Harlem" number, a takeoff-tribute to the still-living Bill "Bojangles" Robinson (though Astaire was not overly impressed by Robinson's dancing skills). Rogers, now at a point where she yearned for greater control of her own career apart from her constant association with Astaire, delayed rehearsals by renegotiating her contract, setting the stage for her eventual release from the partnership. Studio gossip linked her at the time with George Stevens, here directing his first musical. The film's climactic stairway number, "Never Gonna Dance," filmed in one continuous camera shot, was one of the most strenuous sequences that either costar ever performed. They performed forty-seven takes through a ten-hour day, changing shirt and skirt repeatedly, before Astaire was finally satisfied. (Their dance on the stairway landing was filmed separately.) Two big nightclub sets were based on actual clubs in Manhattan. Betty Furness, who sold refrigerators on TV two decades later, played Margaret Watson; the director's father, Landers Stevens, played Judge Watson. Kern's song "The Way You Look Tonight" won an Academy Award. Astaire, however, detected the beginning of the end for the team, not only in Rogers's increasing independence but in declining box office returns compared to their previous films.

T

A TALE OF TWO CITIES. 1935. Filmed summer 1934; California: Bakersfield; MGM Studios, Culver City.
Cast: Ronald Colman, Elizabeth Allan, Edna May Oliver, Reginald Owen, Basil Rathbone, Blanche Yurka, Donald Woods.
Director: Jack Conway.

The first sound-film version of Charles Dickens's novel cast Ronald Colman in what he claimed as his all-time favorite role, that of heroic dissolute Sydney Carton. Though his appearance in the film occupies relatively little screen time, the role was one he had wanted to play ever since he began acting. For only the second (and last) time in his film career, he shaved off his trademark mustache. Unlike most actors, who shoot their own scenes and go home, Colman was so intrigued with the project that he lingered on the set for almost the duration. Elizabeth Allan, playing Lucie Manette, said that Colman's charm was such that she couldn't look him in the eye during his impassioned romantic speeches to her; the only way she could act indifferent to him (an aspect of Lucie's character she never understood) was to look aside. Czech-American actress Blanche Yurka, as the sinister Mme. De Farge, was the sixty-seventh actress to test for the role, her screen debut. She had to learn how to knit, having never even held a pair of knitting needles before. Her fight sequence with Edna May Oliver required two days to film and was so strenuous that both actresses took to their beds for several days. Yurka gave herself a sixtieth birthday party on the set. Isabel Jeans was cast as the seamstress by producer David O. Selznick over the strenuous objections of director Jack Conway, who believed that her image as a comedienne disqualified her for the part. Selznick, a great admirer of Dickens, took pains to insure period authenticity in every detail of clothing, furnishings, even tableware. Enormous sets of the Bastille and other Paris landmarks arose on the studio lot. For the Bastille storming sequence, some 17,000 extras were hired to play the enraged mob. Success of this film gave Selznick the freedom to depart MGM and establish his own studio, Selznick International, in 1936. *Tale* was remade to much less effect in 1958, starring Dirk Bogarde and Dorothy Tutin.

TARZAN, THE APE MAN. 1932. Filmed October–December 1931; California: Toluca Lake area, North Hollywood; MGM Studios, Culver City.

Cast: Johnny Weissmuller, Maureen O'Sullivan, C. Aubrey Smith, Neil Hamilton.

Director: W. S. Van Dyke.

Johnny Weissmuller, Olympic swimming champion of 1924 and 1928, made his major screen debut as the brawny jungle hero at age twenty-eight. Silent films based on the pulp novel series by Edgar Rice Burroughs had been turned out since 1918, but this was the first sound version, produced as a studio follow-up to the immensely successful *Trader Horn* (1931). Though many Tarzans came before and after Weissmuller, no other actor became so identified with the role. Alfredo Codona of The Flying Codonas, an aerialist act, doubled the actor for his tree-swinging scenes, which were used repeatedly in subsequent Tarzan adventures. This film was the first of six pairings for Weissmuller and Irish actress Maureen O'Sullivan; Weissmuller made five more Tarzan movies without O'Sullivan. Playing Jane, the future mother of Mia Farrow was just beginning, at age twenty, her own long film career. After testing hundreds of actors and athletes for the title role, director Van Dyke chose football star Herman Brix, who fractured his shoulder just before he was to sign for the part. Weissmuller (who had previously appeared in bit roles) replaced him—but only after an initial hassle. For when Weissmuller sought release from his advertising contract with BVD underwear manufacturers to act in the film, the BVD company refused to let him go. MGM finally solved the impasse by agreeing to let all its players be photographed in BVD's, a less-than-thrilling prospect for the thespians. Brix (later known as Bruce Bennett) subsequently appeared in two films as Tarzan. Studio jungle sets included Indian elephants rented from circus herds; the beasts were rendered African by the attachment of large plastic extensions to their ears and tusks. Novelist Burroughs later expressed dismay that Weissmuller's portrayal became the prototype for all Tarzan performances. As for Weissmuller, when asked the secret of his success in the role, the Northwestern University graduate replied, "My grunt."

TAXI DRIVER. 1976. Filmed 1975; New York City.
Cast: Robert De Niro, Cybill Shepherd, Jodie Foster, Peter Boyle, Albert Brooks, Harvey Keitel.
Director: Martin Scorsese.

A film reflective of the post-Vietnam urban violence uniquely characteristic of American streets, *Taxi Driver* encapsulated this mad, mean streak in the person of Robert De Niro's Travis Bickle, a psychotic loner aching to explode. Another loner, John W. Hinckley, watched this film some fifteen times, forming a weird, fantasy rescue agenda for an appalled Jodie Foster. Hinckley so identified with Bickle and his loony attempt to "rescue" the teenage prostitute Iris (played by twelve-year-old Foster) that he shot Ronald Reagan. The young actress, a veteran of three Walt Disney movies, came reluctantly to her role, fearing not its possible emotional trauma, but the reaction of her peers. Before filming began, she underwent a long psychiatric interview to gauge her stability for the role, and a welfare worker accompanied her each day on the set. Her protectors need not have feared; she so distanced herself emotionally from the part—so foreign to any life experience of her own—that the risk to her well-being was minimal. Her sexually explicit scenes were doubled by her twenty-year-old sister Connie. Method actor De Niro, on the other hand, always adopted his characters to an intense degree. In preparation for his role, he dropped thirty-five pounds, drove a cab, and read books on the Green Berets, achieving a repressed, ticking-time-bomb manner that seemed menacing enough to his colleagues even offscreen. Screenwriter Paul Schrader brought elements of his own experience to the character of Bickle. A former Calvinistic ministerial student, Schrader had undergone major depression, withdrawal, and hospitalization. Martin Scorsese himself appeared in the film as an angry, gun-toting passenger in the cab; De Niro's wife, Diahnne Abbott, played a bit part behind the concession stand in the porno theatre sequence. The music was veteran film composer Bernard Herrmann's last of sixty-one film scores; he completed it the day he died.

TENDER MERCIES. 1983. Filmed November–December 1981; Texas: Waxahachie; Palmer.
Cast: Robert Duvall, Tess Harper, Betty Buckley, Wilford Brimley, Ellen Barkin, Allan Hubbard.
Director: Bruce Beresford.

This was Australian director Bruce Beresford's first American film, one he almost quit during filming as a result of conflicts with Robert Duvall, who deplored Beresford's "dictatorial way" and had little kind to say about him then or later. Duvall roamed Texas rural areas in preparation for his country singer role, even took a brief job singing in a good-ole-boy bar. He wrote eight of the songs he performed in the film. Tess Harper made her film debut here as Rosa Lee. The town of Waxahachie, a major locale for the picture, later hosted the filming of *Places in the Heart*. Duvall received an Academy Award as best actor, and Horton Foote won for his screenplay.

TERMS OF ENDEARMENT. 1983. Filmed 1983; Lincoln, Nebraska. River Oaks, Texas.
Cast: Shirley MacLaine, Debra Winger, Jack Nicholson, Jeff Daniels, John Lithgow.
Director: James L. Brooks.

The offscreen verbal missiles that constantly flew between the competitive, high-powered costars achieved the stuff of Hollywood legend. A real generation gap apparently existed between Shirley MacLaine and Debra Winger, as well as huge differences in acting involvement and technique. To Jack Nicholson fell the offscreen role of diplomacy. Winger (who won her role over contender Sissy Spacek) credited him as "the glue of the production," further stating that such conflicts as existed between herself and MacLaine, though overemphasized, had been useful for their roles. Playing Emma Horton, Winger insisted that MacLaine call her by her character name off-camera. She wore, even slept in, pregnancy pads for three months, all for the sake of two small scenes of Emma's pregnancy. MacLaine modeled Emma's mother, Aurora, on a turbulent personality she admired, the late Martha Mitchell. Five Academy Awards included those for best picture, MacLaine as best actress ("I really deserve this"), best supporting actor Nicholson, and best director and screenwriter James Brooks.

THEM! 1954. Filmed 1954; California: Mojave Desert (Palmdale); Warner Bros. Studios, Burbank.
Cast: James Whitmore, Edmund Gwenn, Joan Weldon, James Arness.
Director: Gordon Douglas.

The world must have seemed a pretty scary place during the McCarthy era. Giant mutated ants were *Them!*, first and probably best of the killer insect movies, a box office smash and forerunner of numerous films about fellow earth dwellers out to getcha (*Tarantula*, in 1955 and *The Deadly Mantis*, in 1957, to name two). Originally scheming it for color photography using purple ants, the studio lost interest and went for low-budget black and white, little anticipating public response to the film. A crew of off-camera propmen yanked on pulleys and levers to control various portions of giant ant anatomies, including two twelve-foot-high models—one entire, one a front section only. No stop-motion or animation techniques were used. Promotion blitzes for local theatres capitalized rather blatantly on the prevailing mood of Commie paranoia, suggesting gun displays and civil defense tie-ins. The unknown James Arness, playing Graham, was about to launch himself to fame as Marshal Matt Dillon in TV's *Gunsmoke*. Other future TV heroes included Fess Parker as the pilot Crotty and a young Leonard Nimoy as a desk sergeant.

THERE'S NO BUSINESS LIKE SHOW BUSINESS. 1954. Filmed June–August 1954; 20th Century-Fox Studios, Los Angeles.
Cast: Ethel Merman, Marilyn Monroe, Donald O'Connor, Dan Dailey, Mitzi Gaynor, Johnnie Ray.
Director: Walter Lang.

Show biz folk never tire of telling us how unique they are; actually there's no business like roofing and pest extermination either, but these practitioners largely mute their self-congratulations. In this case, however, the film title seemed quite apropos. Ethel Merman's shouting exuberance, always belting to the last row from her Broadway leather lungs, made all of her scenes seem like theme and variations of "Hail, Hail, the Gang's All Here." Her opinions were as strong as her voice. She felt that Marilyn Monroe was miscast as Donald O'Connor's love interest; a better match, she believed, would have been Mitzi Gaynor and O'Connor. And Johnnie Ray playing the son entering the priesthood just somehow "didn't ring true," she thought. Monroe also complained about her pairing with O'Connor, that he looked younger than she (he was actually a year older) and stood three inches shorter. Monroe felt inadequate and intimidated—especially by Merman—in this company of professional song-and-dancers. She constantly blew her lines, fought with choreographer Robert Alton, and collapsed three times on the set and had to be sent home. She didn't trust Walter Lang as a director and showed her displeasure by frequent tardiness. For Monroe, this film represented little more than an agonizing commitment she had to fulfill before the studio would let her star in *The Seven Year Itch*, which she began filming immediately upon completion of this picture. Her marriage to Joe DiMaggio was tottering; and her voice coach, Hal Schaefer, later confirmed that he and Monroe were having an affair at this time. There's no business like it.

THEY SHOOT HORSES, DON'T THEY? 1969. Filmed January–May 1969; California: Lick Pier, Ocean Park, Santa Monica; Warner Bros. Studios, Burbank.

Cast: Jane Fonda, Michael Sarrazin, Susannah York, Gig Young, Red Buttons, Bruce Dern.

Director: Sydney Pollack.

Far from the glamorous sex kitten Jane Fonda had usually played in films heretofore, she became a seedy, desperate creature searching for a reason to go on living; she lived the part of despondent marathon dancer Gloria so intensely that she was moody and depressed throughout much of the filming. About to end her marriage to French director Roger Vadim, she withdrew from normal social life, isolating herself in a small trailer adjacent to the Ocean Park set. To catch the despairing Depression mood, Sydney Pollack showed his cast movies from the 1930s. Before starting each day's work, he made cast members run around the set several times to get them properly fatigued. The endurance sequences took great physical and emotional toll on Fonda and her costars. ABC

Pictures executive Marty Baum insisted on casting Gig Young and Red Buttons over the producers' objections; Young's part, as Rocky the announcer, had been written for Lionel Stander. Young, whose real name was Byron Barr, had appeared in dozens of forgettable light-comic roles from 1940, taking his stage name from the character he played in *The Gay Sisters* (1942). His role here, for which he won an Academy Award as best supporting actor, marked the peak of a career that ended in tragedy when he murdered his fifth wife and shot himself in 1978. At least twenty producers had refused the project because it seemed such a downer; but Pollack insisted on maintaining the integrity of time and place. Even so, Fonda criticized the editing of certain sequences, saying it compromised the film's honesty. Pollack filmed the sixty-four day dance marathon largely in script sequence at Lick Pier, where the marathon set was an exact replica of the old Aragon Ballroom (later Lawrence Welk's Make-Believe Ballroom) at Ocean Park. Film director Mervyn LeRoy, who showed up on the set one day, made a brief, uncredited appearance as an audience member introduced by Young.

THEY WERE EXPENDABLE. 1945. Filmed February–April 1945; U. S. Coast Guard Station, Key Biscayne, Florida. MGM Studios, Culver City.
Cast: Robert Montgomery, John Wayne, Donna Reed, Jack Holt, Ward Bond, Marshall Thompson.
Director: John Ford.

John Ford had long wanted to make this adventure about navy patrol boat crews in World War II, but he didn't want to take leave from the wartime navy himself to do it. Finally at the urging of government officials during the last stages of the war in Europe, he and Robert Montgomery (who had actually commanded PT boats in the Pacific and a destroyer on D-day) took leaves of absence from the navy to make the film, which was based on real individuals and events. John Wayne, one of Ford's favorites, was keenly sensitive, even heartbroken, over his own failure to qualify for military service on family, age, and physical grounds. (He had a bad shoulder from an old football injury.) He joined this project well aware that play-acting could hardly compare with the real-life heroism of his two colleagues. Wayne blew up at one point when a boat windshield of real glass, mistakenly placed instead of safety glass by a technician, shattered in his face as it was being "strafed" by ball bearings; unhurt but enraged, Wayne went for the off-camera technician, and only Ford's quick intervention narrowly averted a fistfight. Ward Bond, another Ford staple, played "Boots" Mulcahey on crutches because of a recent auto accident. Ford himself fell off a scaffold and broke a leg before he finished the picture, and Montgomery replaced him as director during the last two weeks. Despite Ford's gung ho intentions, however, the real-life heroes the film was based on didn't consider themselves *that* expendable. Lieutenant Robert B. Kelly, on whom Wayne's part was modeled, sued MGM for what he claimed was an unfair depiction and was granted $3,000. Lieutenant Beulah Greenwalt, Donna Reed's character, did better, winning $290,000 from the studio.

THE THIN MAN. 1934. Filmed 1934; MGM Studios, Culver City.
Cast: William Powell, Myrna Loy, Maureen O'Sullivan, Nat Pendleton.
Director: W. S. Van Dyke.

William Powell and Myrna Loy in their second of thirteen films together—but their first of six as the debonair detective couple Nick and Nora Charles—transformed these Dashiell Hammett characters into probably the best-known husband and wife team in movies. The inspiration for the film came largely from director W. S. Van Dyke, who fought with studio mogul Louis B. Mayer to bring his portrayal of a happy (if somewhat boozy) marriage to the screen, in contrast to the unpleasant marriages depicted in most Hollywood films of the period. Mayer thought Loy all wrong, wanted Laura La Plante for the part, but Van Dyke's concept and casting finally won out. Filmed in only sixteen days by order of a disgruntled Mayer as a low-budget B picture—with hardly time to film more than one take per scene—the film proved a runaway box office success, astonishing everyone concerned with it. Van Dyke urged his players to improvise lines and add details to their roles in ways that felt right to them. Both costars freely did so, Powell later admitting that Nick Charles came closer to his own personality than any role he ever played. Though no romantic interest ever existed between the costars offscreen, they formed a close lifelong friendship and always enjoyed working together. Loy was nervous about her opening scene, in which she trips and falls with a load of packages; the scene was completely unrehearsed, and she attributed her success in making it a one-take to her dance training. She had problems, however, with the movie dog Asta, whose real name was Skippy and whose appearance set off a national craze for wirehaired terriers. He wasn't a loving dog—movie animal trainers didn't allow actors to make friends with their charges—and even bit Loy once. This was the same dog that appeared in *The Awful Truth* (1937) and *Bringing Up Baby* (1938), as well as in the succeeding *Thin Man* films.

THE THING (FROM ANOTHER WORLD). 1951. Filmed winter 1950–51; Glacier National Park area, Montana. California: Los Angeles; RKO Studios, Culver City.
Cast: Margaret Sheridan, Kenneth Tobey, Robert Cornthwaite, Douglas Spencer, James Arness.
Director: Christian Nyby.

This science-fiction classic, heralding an entire genre of space-alien films, cast a still unknown James Arness in the title role—all three minutes of it—some five years before he began his long-running performance on TV's *Gunsmoke*; he was the only cast member who went on to bigger if not always better *things*. Four-inch boot heels added to his six-foot-five normal height. Famed director Howard Hawks produced the film and—despite Christian Nyby's credit line—probably directed much of it as well. He brought several of the cast, including Robert Cornthwaite (playing Professor Carrington), from radio. Another soon-to-be familiar face was that of George Fenneman, playing the scientist Redding; he became Groucho Marx's longtime announcer-sidekick on *You Bet Your Life*. The U. S. Air Force refused Hawks's request for cooperation, saying that such a film would run counter to its claim that flying saucers didn't exist. Some Arctic scenes used the same Los Angeles icehouse where parts of *Lost Horizon* and *The Magnificent Ambersons* were filmed. Frigid temperatures at Montana locations ranged to 30 below. John Carpenter's 1982 remake used footage from this original version.

THE THIRD MAN. 1949. Filmed September–October 1948; Vienna. Shepperton Studios, Shepperton, England.
Cast: Joseph Cotten, Alida Valli, Orson Welles, Trevor Howard, Bernard Lee.

Director: Carol Reed.

This classic suspense thriller, written by Graham Greene, reunited Joseph Cotten and Orson Welles in their fourth film together. Coproducer David O. Selznick had wanted Noel Coward for the small but crucial role of Harry Lime, but Carol Reed held out for Welles. Welles took the job because he needed money for financing his film version of *Othello*. Italian actress Alida Valli, playing Lime's mistress, proved helpful off screen as a translator between English and German speaking cast and crew members. Welles, while confessing that this was the only one of his films that he ever watched on TV, was chagrined that his public usually identified him more with Harry Lime than with any of the films he directed. Trevor Howard, who discovered street musician Anton Karas playing his zither in a *weinstube* at Hietzing, played Major Galloway in one of his first major roles. During a break from filming, while still uniformed, Howard was arrested in another *weinstube* for impersonating a British officer, requiring some hasty explanations from himself and Reed. The final scene was entirely improvised without script by Reed, holding the camera on Cotten long after the latter expected the scene to end; only after an exasperated Cotten tossed his cigarette to the ground did Reed finally cut the scene. Karas, whom Reed signed despite studio objections to compose and perform the music, proved an enormous sensation, as did the stringed zither instrument itself. The film was especially popular in Europe, where thirty years later Cotten attended a memorial reunion with the Vienna sewer police. Robert Krasker's cinematography won an Academy Award.

THE THIRTY-NINE STEPS. 1935. Filmed January–March 1935; London: (exteriors) and Lime Grove Studios.
Cast: Robert Donat, Madeleine Carroll, Peggy Ashcroft, Wylie Watson, Helen Haye.
Director: Alfred Hitchcock.

Spy novelist John Buchan was miffed that Alfred Hitchcock used only the title and about ten percent of his book—not including the *steps* themselves. Here emerged one of Hitchcock's recurring motifs, sexual bondage, symbolized by the handcuffs binding the costarring couple. To prepare Robert Donat and Madeleine Carroll for the sequence, the director handcuffed them together, then disappeared for the day. The two were virtual strangers and both reacted angrily to the embarrassment and humiliation of the sadistic episode, which Hitchcock laughed off; he had, as usual, his reasons—presumably aimed toward helping them give convincing performances. On another occasion, during actual filming, his method was more direct. Donat and Peggy Ashcroft (playing Margaret) ruined five takes of their crofter's cottage scene by erupting into giggles. Suddenly Hitchcock, without a word, walked over to a studio lamp and smashed it with his fist. The pair sobered instantly and completed the scene. The herd of sixty-two Hertfordshire sheep that Hitchcock brought inside the studio literally ate up props and sections of sets before harried stagehands could finally drive them out. Many of Hitchcock's original cinematic tricks here became clichés among later filmmakers. Until 1941, when Buchan's estate was liquidated and withdrew this film from general distribution, it was known among exhibitors at small American theatres as a "mortgage lifter," so reliable an audience puller that they would feature it for several days whenever the rent came due. Remakes of this film in 1960 and 1978 lacked the inimitable Hitchcock touch.

THIRTY SECONDS OVER TOKYO. 1944. Filmed February–June 1944; Hurlburt Field at Eglin Field, Naval Air Station, Pensacola, Florida. California: San Francisco-Oakland area; MGM Studios, Culver City.

Cast: Van Johnson, Robert Walker, Spencer Tracy, Phyllis Thaxter, Scott McKay, Robert Mitchum, Don Defore.

Director: Mervyn LeRoy.

This story of the first U.S. bombing raid on Tokyo in 1942 gave Van Johnson, playing Captain Ted Lawson, his first major screen role. It was also Phyllis Thaxter's film debut (as Ellen Lawson) and Steve Brodie's as well (he played an MP), while Robert Mitchum played his last minor role (as Bob Gray). Robert Walker, who would die of alcoholic trauma seven years later, played Thatcher; though he dated Thaxter at the time, he still carried a highly visible torch for his estranged wife, Jennifer Jones. Spencer Tracy, feeling that his recent parts were typecasting him as a war hero, was reluctant to add the role of Lieutenant Colonel James H. Doolittle to his résumé, finally accepting mainly to help boost his friend Johnson's career. Much of the location filming at Pensacola occurred on the same airfield where Doolittle had trained his crew. The presence of the actors (some of them rather rowdy and few of whom actually served in uniform) provoked some hostility at the base from air corps regulars, who saw them wearing insignia and living in barracks just as if they were real officers. Director Mervyn LeRoy recalled his own embarrassment there when he discovered that his radioed instructions from the ground to a B-25 squadron leader—"Bring them in while the sun's out"—had blared into every airport tower in Florida, mystifying dozens of air controllers. The army loaned about twelve B-25 bombers to the production along with personnel to fly them, but many of the aircraft carrier scenes were ingenious blends of newsreel footage, rear projection, studio mock-ups, miniatures, and special effects. Aerial shots of the Japanese homeland were actually filmed over the San Francisco-Oakland Bay area in California; smoke from a refinery fire in East Oakland provided some excellent Tokyo bombing footage. Some of the aerial footage reappeared in *Midway* (1976). Look for future comedy director Blake Edwards in the role of a second officer and for Kay Williams, who would become Clark Gable's wife, as a girl in the officers' club. The film won an Academy Award for special effects.

THIS GUN FOR HIRE. 1942. Filmed October 1941–January 1942; Paramount Studios, Los Angeles.
Cast: Veronica Lake, Alan Ladd, Robert Preston, Laird Cregar.
Director: Frank Tuttle.

This film, intended as a routine vehicle for Veronica Lake, made both the morose Alan Ladd and the fluffy Lake into popular stars; though wooden performers both, this particular screenplay uniquely suited their acting styles. Studio publicity mills tried to get something going between the two offscreen, but both were very aloof people and both, moreover, were married. This was the first of three teamings for the pair, a suitable match insofar as Lake was one of Ladd's few costars whom the pint-size actor didn't have to stand on a box to kiss; she stood three inches shorter than his five-foot-four. With no singing or dancing experience, Lake took lessons from a professional magician for her magic show act. Director Frank Tuttle required a punishing sixty-four takes of the magic act

—and infuriated Lake by finally using the fourth. The monkey Josephine didn't treat her any better, biting her twice on the arm during those takes. Robert Preston, whom Tuttle had originally intended to cast as the male lead but then rejected as too tall, gave Lake her first screen kiss; she was so nervous that, again, the scene required many takes, to Preston's gallant delight. Ladd, his blond hair dyed black for his role of Phillip Raven, also began wearing the worn trench coat that would stamp his later performances. As production wound down, he collapsed with a life-threatening case of pneumonia and remained out of action for several weeks. Yvonne de Carlo made her screen debut here in a bit part as a show girl. *Short Cut to Hell* (directed by James Cagney) was a 1957 remake.

THE THREE MUSKETEERS. 1948. Filmed winter 1948; MGM Studios, Culver City.
Cast: Lana Turner, Gene Kelly, June Allyson, Van Heflin, Angela Lansbury, Frank Morgan, Vincent Price, Keenan Wynn, Gig Young, Robert Coote.
Director: George Sidney.

Third of four sound-film versions of the Alexandre Dumas adventure epic, this lavish costume drama represented the conventional MGM all-star approach to filming classics. In vigor it surpassed many of the other treatments. Lana Turner initially refused the role of Lady DeWinter and was suspended from the studio; negotiations brought her back when her part was beefed up. She finally warmed to the role. Beneath all those cloaks and bodices, she wore slacks and street shoes—which may not have aided her physical comfort, since the cast sweltered in bulky clothes and hot studio sets during the filming. Angela Lansbury, playing Queen Anne, had earlier sought Turner's lead role. Gene Kelly, as D'Artagnan inspired by Douglas Fairbanks, Sr., spent two months learning to fence; despite blunted sword edges, he lost half of his fake mustache one day on the set when a blade nicked him. The entire film was physically taxing for him because he did all his own stunt work and swordplay—viewing them as extensions of his dancing—and he carried multiple bruises home to prove it. He claimed the role as his favorite in nonmusical films. June Allyson, as Lady Constance, was perhaps the only totally disgruntled performer; uncomfortable playing in costume drama, she simply wanted out of her contract-forced assignment. The most controversial role belonged to Vincent Price, as the villainous Cardinal Richelieu. The Catholic Legion of Decency had urged total elimination of the part, but MGM compromised with the church (and history) by demoting Richelieu to a layman cavalier—a move that angered Keenan Wynn (playing Planchet), the only true Dumas buff in the cast.

TO BE OR NOT TO BE. 1942. Filmed October–December 1941; United Artists Studios, Los Angeles.
Cast: Carole Lombard, Jack Benny, Robert Stack, Felix Bressart, Lionel Atwill, Sig Ruman.
Director: Ernst Lubitsch.

This satiric masterpiece gave both Carole Lombard and Jack Benny their best film roles—for Lombard, her last and in a film she never saw. Her death in a Nevada plane crash less than a month after production was completed shattered Clark Gable, her husband, as well as the entire Hollywood community. Making the film was, she reported, the happiest experience of her career. She had replaced Miriam Hopkins at Benny's suggestion when Hopkins withdrew. (Director Ernst Lubitsch had envisioned the film as a comeback performance for Hopkins, but Benny had not relished the prospect of working with the temperamental actress.) This was Lubitsch's first venture into controversy, strongly satirizing the Nazis at a time when America was officially neutral (though the bombing of Pearl Harbor ended that policy about two weeks before filming finished). Lubitsch had problems finding financial backers for the picture, in fact. The title referred to Poland's newly questionable existence as well as to Shakespeare. Lubitsch had Benny in mind from the outset for the role of actor Joseph Tura. Known primarily as a radio comedian, Benny paced the set and chewed his nails from nervousness, asking even a young Robert Stack for acting suggestions. Stack, playing Lieutenant Sobinski, was an old friend of Lombard's and received his role on her recommendation. Lombard's death cast a pall over studio promotion of the picture. (A line from Lombard to Benny, cut from the finished film: "What can happen in a plane?") And the film's volatile satire angered some critics. Probably the main source of controversy lay in a line referring to Benny spoken by Sig Ruman as a Nazi colonel: "What he did to Shakespeare, we are now doing to Poland."

Many critics felt this to be insensitive scavenging at the expense of a blitzed nation: but Lubitsch defended the line as a necessary showpiece of crude Nazi humor. A 1983 remake starred husband-wife team Mel Brooks and Anne Bancroft.

TO HAVE AND HAVE NOT. 1944. Filmed March–May 1944; Warner Bros. Studios, Burbank.
Cast: Humphrey Bogart, Lauren Bacall, Walter Brennan, Hoagy Carmichael, Dolores Moran, Marcel Dalio.
Director: Howard Hawks.

This first pairing of Humphrey Bogart and Lauren Bacall predated their 1945 marriage. It was Bacall's screen debut; at age nineteen and totally innocent of sound stages, she was so nervous she trembled. That famed smoldering look, in fact, originated from her nervousness in the scene where she first meets Bogart; the only way she could stop her tremors was by holding her head low and looking up. The Bacall image, however, was largely the creation of director Howard Hawks. He became her Svengali before production started, changed her first name from Betty to Lauren, and made her practice reading aloud to lower the timbre of her voice. All through the filming, she did screaming and shouting exercises, the result being the famed Bacall huskiness. "If you want anything, just whistle . . ."—the most famous line of her film career—was not in the original screenplay but *had* been part of her initial screen test weeks before and was later inserted in the script. Even the costars' nicknames in the film—Steve and Slim—were pet names that Hawks and his wife used for each other. Bacall hid from her director the fact that she was Jewish, Hawks (and even Bogart to some extent) being noted for dropping casual anti-Semitic remarks. As filming progressed and the costars' offscreen romance grew increasingly visible, Hawks resentfully lectured his protégée on the dangers to her budding career of becoming involved with Bogart, who was still married to actress Mayo Methot. Hawks filmed in chronological sequence, working only a few days ahead of William Faulkner's revised pages of script. The film itself, based on Ernest Hemingway's novel, resulted from a wager Hawks had made with the novelist, that he could make a decent movie from Hemingway's worst book. (Neither seems to have disagreed on which book that was.) The U. S. government, however, threatened to withhold the picture's export license to overseas markets because its Cuban setting might embarrass the Batista regime; that's why the story location became French Martinique instead. Composer Hoagy Carmichael also made his screen debut here, as the pianist Cricket. Marcel Dalio, playing Frenchy/Gerard, had fled France as war broke out; unknown to him, his Rumanian Jewish parents were, at about this time, being exterminated in a Nazi concentration camp. With this film, the studio was frankly aiming to reprise the atmospherics of its highly successful *Casablanca* (1942), and certain similarities are obvious. Remakes include *The Breaking Point* (1950) and *The Gun Runners* (1958).

TO KILL A MOCKINGBIRD. 1962. Filmed spring 1962; Universal Studios, Universal City.

Cast: Gregory Peck, Mary Badham, Philip Alford, John Megna, Brock Peters, Robert Duvall, William Windom.

Director: Robert Mulligan.

Gregory Peck was awarded a best-actor Oscar for his portrayal of small-town lawyer Atticus Finch. Rock Hudson had discovered Harper Lee's novel based on her childhood reminiscences, but the studio turned down Hudson at the time and only later bought the screen rights for Peck. For novelist Lee, the casting was precisely right. "That film was a work of art," she glowed. Before beginning the picture, Peck went to Alabama and met the real Atticus Finch, Lee's aged father Amasa Lee, who died during the filming. Lee herself coached Peck in handling the pocket watch he wore. In gratitude for his performance, she presented him with her father's own watch, a gift that greatly moved the actor. Playing Finch's children, Jem and Scout, were thirteen-year-old Philip Alford and nine-year-old Mary Badham, both screen newcomers from Birmingham, Alabama. Dill Harris, played by nine-year-old John Megna, was a character based on Lee's childhood friend Truman Capote. Robert Duvall made his screen debut here in a brief but pivotal role; in fond memory of the part, he named a succession of his dogs Boo Radley. Frame houses came from a rundown area of Los Angeles and were reconstructed on the studio lot to represent the backwater town of Maycomb. Actress Kim Stanley narrated the film (as the grown-up Scout). In addition to Peck, screenwriter Horton Foote and the set designers also won Academy Awards.

TOM JONES. 1963. Filmed summer 1962; Cerne Abbas, England.
Cast: Albert Finney, Hugh Griffith, Susannah York, David Warner, Edith Evans, Joan Greenwood.
Director: Tony Richardson.

Henry Fielding's 1749 novel became a best seller again following the release of this film. Albert Finney made no effort to mask his Lancashire accent in the title role. Several improvised bits included the scene of Finney picking flowers in the rain, a case of director Tony Richardson using a torrential downpour that occurred during filming. For the public hanging sequence, Richardson had many of the crowd extras remove their dentures to lend an extra touch of 18th-century authenticity. Most of those extras were farmers and residents of Cerne Abbas, a tiny Dorchester village. Dame Edith Evans, playing Miss Western, expressed much discomfort over the working habits of Hugh Griffith, who played Squire Western; Griffith, she claimed, was drunk from lunchtime onward, and she thoroughly disapproved. David Warner, playing Blifil, made his screen debut here, as did Lynn Redgrave in the bit part of Susan. (Richardson, married to Vanessa Redgrave, was Lynn's brother-in-law.) This film contains probably the most erotic eating scene in movie history, between Finney and Joyce Redman. Irish actor Micheal MacLiammoir narrated the film, which won four Academy Awards: for best picture, Richardson's direction, John Osborne's screenplay, and John Addison's musical score.

TOOTSIE. 1982. Filmed April–August 1982; New York City.
Cast: Dustin Hoffman, Jessica Lange, Teri Garr, Dabney Coleman, Charles Durning, Bill Murray, Sydney Pollack.
Director: Sydney Pollack.

Dustin Hoffman, in drag as aspiring actress Dorothy Michaels, continued his career pattern of reaching for roles that most established actors would shrink from. In this comic masterpiece, his complex female makeup—as well as the lighting problems it entailed—gave him considerable trouble. The cosmetics he had to wear irritated his skin to the point of acne, and everybody on the set joined in an informal beard watch for signs of erupting whiskers during long days of filming. A variety of materials for his false breasts was tried; at one point, bits of packing foam floated everywhere on the set, sticking to objects and people—until a suitable substance was finally concocted. Between takes, Hoffman enjoyed flirting with the crew, blowing kisses, and mincing outrageously. As in all his films, his very precise ideas as to how he should play his character often conflicted with the director's views; but Hoffman and Sydney Pollack had huge respect for each other and, through sometimes tense confrontations, worked out their differences. Stage and TV actress Polly Holliday coached Hoffman in his Southern accent. The actor played part of his role with an injured hand (he had somehow caught it under a door) and carried his arm in a sling between takes. Comedian Buddy Hackett had discovered the original screenplay, hoping to play the hypertensive agent George Fields himself. Pollack had wanted Dabney Coleman (who was finally cast as Ron, the sexist TV director) for this part, but Hoffman insisted on Pollack himself for the role, and the latter finally agreed. The film's original title—*Would I Lie to You?*—was renamed by Hoffman himself (his mother had called him Tootsie as a child). Jessica Lange almost turned down her role: her title performance in *Frances*, she said, had depressed her to the point of inertia. On the advice of actress Kim Stanley, however, she took the role of Julie for self-therapy. For her work here she won an Academy Award as best supporting actress. Susan Dworkin's book *Making Tootsie* (1983) charts the film's evolution from script to screen.

TOP HAT. 1935. Filmed May–June 1935; RKO Studios, Los Angeles.

Cast: Fred Astaire, Ginger Rogers, Edward Everett Horton, Helen Broderick, Eric Blore.

Director: Mark Sandrich.

This fourth of the ten Fred Astaire-Ginger Rogers films ranks among their best. A tireless perfectionist, Astaire demanded and got meticulous dancing performances from himself and his partners. A legendary blowup occurred on the set of this film between the normally even-tempered costars. Rogers had insisted on wearing a long-feathered "dream dress" for the couple's "Cheek to Cheek" number. During rehearsals, Astaire grew increasingly irritated with the swirls of ostrich feathers that blinded him and made him sneeze. He finally declared an ultimatum: no dream dress. The episode brought Rogers's combative mother, Lela Rogers, storming onto the set, ready for battle. After a day of stalemate, Astaire compromised by allowing Rogers to wear the costume if the designer would sew each feather separately into place—and that's the gown we see Rogers wearing (not without an occasional floating feather). Astaire soon made peace with his co-star and playfully nicknamed her Feathers; but from that point on, he made sure that his contracts gave him final approval rights over his partners' costumes. Offscreen, the Astaire-Rogers relationship was usually pleasant but never more than casual. This is the film that gave Astaire his screen image as debonair, dressed-up man about town. He never again seemed quite himself without sporting white tie and tails. For his "Top Hat" number, he used the last of thirteen canes that had been supplied for rehearsals and filming; he broke twelve of them, and propmen sighed with relief when the final cane survived the second and last take of his number. Helen Broderick, who played Madge Hardwick, was the mother of actor Broderick Crawford. Look for Lucille Ball as a flower clerk in her fourth screen-credited role (though *Top Hat* was actually her eighteenth film appearance). *The Fred Astaire & Ginger Rogers Book* (1972), by Arlene Croce, gives interesting production details on all the Astaire-Rogers films.

TOPKAPI. 1964. Filmed summer 1963; Istanbul. Paris (interiors). Kaválla, Greece.
Cast: Melina Mercouri, Maximilian Schell, Peter Ustinov, Robert Morley, Akim Tamiroff.
Director: Jules Dassin.

Recovering from a long illness and not enamored with her role, Greek actress Melina Mercouri said this was the first film she truly didn't enjoy making. Director Jules Dassin, her husband, spoofed his own caper film *Rififi* with this one, originally titled *Man in the Middle*. (The release title refers to the palace museum in Istanbul, where much of the filming occurred.) Dassin's adult son and daughter both appeared in bit parts, as did the director himself. Peter Ustinov, playing Arthur Simpson, won his second Academy Award as best supporting actor. He opined that Dassin could have had a more remarkable career had he not devoted himself so exclusively to Mercouri's.

TOPPER. 1937. Filmed spring 1937; California: "Topper" House, Pasadena; Hal Roach Studios, Culver City.
Cast: Cary Grant, Constance Bennett, Roland Young, Billie Burke, Alan Mowbray.
Director: Norman Z. McLeod.

Producer Hal Roach wanted W. C. Fields and Jean Harlow to costar as George and Marian Kirby, the rollicking ghost couple whose style of boozy frolics owed much to William Powell and Myrna Loy in *The Thin Man*; but neither Fields nor Harlow was available at the time. This was Cary Grant's first real box office hit, though he never appeared in the sequels. According to Roach, Grant "wasn't too keen" on Constance Bennett as his costar—an attitude Roach attributed to the fact that Grant was in love with Ginger Rogers at the time and didn't want to play love scenes with anyone else. Roland Young, in the title role, was also a last-minute choice. The film gave studio technicians ample opportunity to exhibit lots of special effects and trick photography as the ghosts appeared and disappeared throughout the movie. The costars spoke much of their dialogue entirely offscreen. In Pasadena, the house used in many scenes later hosted locales for the *Batman* TV series and the film *True Confessions* (1981). Only Billie Burke, playing Mrs. Topper, remained for both sequels, *Topper Takes a Trip* (1939) and *Topper Returns* (1941).

TOUCH OF EVIL. 1958. Filmed February–April 1957; California: Venice; Universal-International Studios, Universal City.
Cast: Charlton Heston, Orson Welles, Janet Leigh, Marlene Dietrich, Akim Tamiroff, Dennis Weaver, Joseph Calleia, Mercedes McCambridge.
Director: Orson Welles.

Both Charlton Heston and Janet Leigh grabbed at the chance to work with Orson Welles, and the latter also had no trouble persuading such well-known friends as Marlene Dietrich, Joseph Cotten, and Keenan Wynn to appear in brief scenes. At age forty-one, Welles played the corrupt police chief Hank Quinlan in heavy makeup, including plastic bags under his eyes, an ugly nose, and lumpy padding beneath his clothes to increase his already impressive bulk of about three hundred pounds. Location filming in a run-down section of Venice occurred mostly at night. Welles accidentally fell into a canal at one point, giving him sprains and bruises, and he wore a sling and arm splint for much of the time when not on camera. Leigh was a prior casualty, having broken her left arm on the set of a TV movie she had just completed. The cast she wore was concealed in various ways and, for certain scenes, was temporarily removed. Dietrich, an inspired last-minute casting choice as the prostitute Tanya, rejoiced working with Welles, saying "I was never better in my life." Her gypsy makeup included a costume of exotic fragments collected from her roles in previous films, and her black wig was one formerly worn by Elizabeth Taylor. Studio executives, always anxious about Welles projects because he never let them feel like supervisors, were flabbergasted to see Dietrich in the picture; she was increasingly choosy about her screen appearances. Mercedes McCambridge, as the gang leader, was filmed on the same day that Welles called her up to ask her to join the cast. He rubbed black shoe polish into her hair to make it kinky. Dennis Weaver, who accepted the role of the wimpy motel clerk at Heston's urging, largely improvised his character. Welles's cinema techniques, as usual, proved ahead of their time—most notably in the film's opening shot under the screen credits, which incorporated multiple scenes and actions in one continuous tracking shot that spanned three city blocks. And Welles's jump-cut editing anticipated by decades a common story technique. Unfortunately, as happened so often with Welles's work, he lost control of post-production decisions. The studio gave the film a smoother, more conventionally linear editing and insisted on having director Harry Keller film some linking retakes with Heston and Leigh. Despite this tampering, Welles felt that the final product ended up *almost* as he wanted it; the present video version has restored much of Welles's original footage.

THE TOWERING INFERNO. 1974. Filmed May–August 1974; California: San Francisco; Century Ranch, Malibu.

Cast: Steve McQueen, Paul Newman, William Holden, Faye Dunaway, Fred Astaire, Susan Blakely, Jennifer Jones, Richard Chamberlain, O. J. Simpson, Robert Vaughn, Robert Wagner.

Directors: John Guillermin, Irwin Allen.

Movie audiences of the 1970s craved catastrophe, the bigger the better; and this film, one of Hollywood's best-known disaster epics, merged spectacular fire and flood sequences to give the customers what they wanted. Special-effects teams had a field day, creating elaborate combinations of miniatures, painted backgrounds, process photography, mock-ups, propane jets, water ramps, and smoke bellows, all serviced for multiple camera crews. Of the fifty-seven sets built, only eight remained standing at the end of production. Los Angeles fire fighters stood by to make sure that flames—actually confined at any one time to rather small studio areas—never got out of control, and not one cast member suffered injury despite numerous hazards. The most dangerous sequence was the climactic deluge of a million gallons of water, forcefully spilling from tanks above the twenty-five-foot-high set onto some of Hollywood's highest priced flesh. Recorded by twelve cameras stationed at various points, the flood demolished the set with no chance for second shots. The Hyatt-Regency Hotel in downtown San Francisco doubled for exterior and lobby scenes of the 138-story skyscraper; a full-size mock-up of four building floors was constructed at the Fox ranch. Owners of modern office buildings weren't happy to see this film and tried to have a disclaimer inserted, saying that such a disaster couldn't actually happen. (But only months after its release, fire gutted six floors of Manhattan's World Trade Center.) This film was the first merged effort of two major studios, Warner Bros. and 20th Century-Fox. Each had begun similar productions based on two similar novels, but the anticipated expenses were so steep that the studios decided to join rather than compete. Steve McQueen, playing the fire chief, had originally been offered Paul Newman's role of architect but preferred the more macho part—insisting, however, that he have exactly the same number of lines to speak as Newman. McQueen did his own stunt work. William Holden felt humiliated at having to take third billing; his irritation focused mainly on Faye Dunaway, whose chronic tardiness upset him. Fred Astaire, in one of his final dramatic roles, said he enjoyed playing a con man. Scott Newman, twenty-four-year-old son of Paul, played a nervous fireman. This was Jennifer Jones's last film appearance. The song "We May Never Love Like This Again" and the cinematography won Academy Awards.

THE TREASURE OF THE SIERRA MADRE. 1948. Filmed March–July 1947; Mexico: Tampico; San José de Purua area; Durango. California: Bakersfield; Warner Bros. Studios, Burbank.

Cast: Humphrey Bogart, Walter Huston, Tim Holt, Bruce Bennett, Barton MacLane, Alfonso Bedoya.

Director: John Huston.

John Huston's involvement with this classic began as early as 1941, but World War II intervened and the production was shelved until 1947. Casting his sixty-two-year-old father, Walter Huston, as the old prospector Howard, he convinced the reluctant elder to part with his dentures for the role. John himself appeared in the film as the white-suited American, his close-up scenes directed by Bogart—who, maliciously enjoying his brief power, made him do the scenes over and over. Bogart's scene in the barber chair was probably the last time his real hair was seen in a film. He was losing it in patches at this time and wore partial hairpieces; afterward, he wore a full frontal toupee. Producer Henry Blanke had wanted John Garfield for Tim Holt's role of Curtin, but Garfield was unavailable. The film's mixed reviews prompted Holt to forget about an A-picture career and go back to making cowboy films. Ronald Reagan had wanted the part that went to Bruce Bennett, but studio chief Jack Warner had other ideas. Mexican actor Alfonso Bedoya, cast more-or-less on impulse as the bandit chieftain Gold Hat, had little acting experience (and practically no familiarity with English); he approached his role in near panic, which the director eased by applying hypnosis. Bedoya's bandit *compadres* (one of them had actually been a bandit) took a violent dislike to him. Though half his size, they ganged up on him, gave him bloody noses and black eyes, and generally terrorized him at every opportunity. Bedoya later became a familiar stock character in Westerns. Huston filmed the bandits' raid sequence on a studio lot, heaping sixty tons of earth to create a mountainside and transplanting a forest on it. Most of the picture, however, was filmed in a remote area of Mexico, causing both the city-loving Bogart and the elder Huston to complain about the director's perverse love for tropical weather, insects, and steep mountain trails. During the filming, John Huston worked closely with the mysterious B. Traven, whose novel formed the basis for the movie. Look for a quick appearance by an actress who *may* be Ann Sheridan as Bogart leaves the barber shop; for little Bobby Blake, later Robert Blake of TV's *Bar-*

etta; and for Holt's father, veteran character actor Jack Holt, as a flophouse bum. Both Hustons won Academy Awards: Walter as best supporting actor and John for screenplay and direction.

TRIUMPH OF THE WILL (TRIUMPH DES WILLENS). 1935. Filmed September 1934; Nuremberg, Germany. Director: Leni Riefenstahl.

Adolf Hitler himself commissioned this film and suggested its title to chronicle the 1934 Nazi party congress in Nuremberg—at a time when he was still consolidating his power. After the Night of the Long Knives three months previously, in which he had bloodily purged and rendered impotent the SA organization, which he believed was about to launch a coup, he needed a strong propaganda vehicle to resolidify party unity and authority. Another means to this end was his elevation of the black-uniformed SS and its leader Heinrich Himmler, who was prominently displayed in the film. The quasi-religious ceremonies, the obvious symbology and overpowering spectacle of the event, and the skill of Leni Riefenstahl's film crews resulted in the most impressive propaganda film ever made, despite the barbaric monstrosity of the regime portrayed. As a relatively unknown director, also politically naive and never a Nazi Party member herself, Riefenstahl had never made a documentary film before and was reluctant to undertake this one. (Her main interest at the time was Spain, where she was preparing to film *Tiefland*.) Hitler's propaganda minister, Joseph Goebbels, had opposed choosing her for the job because of her lack of political commitment, her age (thirty-one), and the fact that she was a woman. But Hitler had liked her 1932 film *The Blue Light* and ordered her to make this one as a "personal favor" to him, aiming it mainly toward German domestic consumption. Thirty cameras plus a supplementary crew of twenty-nine newsreel cameramen were included in her team of 172 people recording the event. While the filmed party activities gave the impression of having been staged primarily for the cameras, they were not. The Nuremberg congress was an annual political event that occurred through 1939, and Hitler gave the director absolute freedom as to emphasis, style, and editing of the sixty-one hours of film recorded. In at least twelve sequences, her cameras may be seen, their operators dressed in SA uniforms. She estimated that about half the finished film was composed of footage from the camera of famed cinematographer Sepp Allgeier. Hitler himself viewed this film in March 1935 and praised it, as did Goebbels. The Nazis did not show it so widely, however, as its present reputation might suggest. Charles Chaplin mercilessly lampooned portions of the film in *The Great Dictator*, and parts of it were also used by the Allies in various anti-Nazi propaganda films. No public screenings of it have been allowed in Germany since 1945. Riefenstahl, arrested after the war for her associations with the Nazi regime, maintained her innocence of political involvement and underwent denazification hearings in 1948 and 1952, which acquitted her. But her career, despite several postwar projects, never recovered from the tarnish of her deification of a monster. Richard M. Barsam's book *Filmguide to Triumph of the Will* (1975) gives numerous production details.

TRUE GRIT. 1969. Filmed September–December 1968; Montrose, Colorado. California: Mammoth Lakes; Paramount Studios, Los Angeles.

Cast: John Wayne, Glen Campbell, Kim Darby, Jeremy Slate, Robert Duvall, Dennis Hopper.

Director: Henry Hathaway.

The "best scene I ever did," said John Wayne, was the one in which, as aging, one-eyed marshal Rooster Cogburn, he reminisces with Kim Darby about his life. He also believed Marguerite Roberts's screenplay the best he had ever worked from. His silver and leather hatband in this film had belonged to Gary Cooper, who had given it to Henry Hathaway. Wayne used a new eye patch for each day of filming. This was the first appearance of his horse Dollor, who also appeared in five subsequent Wayne Westerns, the last time in *The Shootist*. At age sixty-two, Wayne had hoped to direct as well as star. (Charles Portis's novel had been written with the Duke in mind.) Producer Hal Wallis had tried to cast Mia Farrow as Mattie Ross; Farrow accepted but changed her mind when Robert Mitchum frightened her with tales about Hathaway's abrasive style of direction; later she said her refusal was the biggest personal and professional mistake of her life. Tuesday Weld also turned down the role. TV actress Darby at age twenty-one had settled into family life and only reluctantly accepted the part after Wallis practically begged her. Hathaway did give her a hard time, but the main conflicts on the set occurred between Hathaway and Robert Duvall (playing the outlaw chief), who hated imperious directors. Several fiery exchanges between them helped clear the air, but Duvall carried away no fond memories. This was pop-singer Glen Campbell's screen debut. Wayne, who received his only Academy Award as best actor for this film, reprised the role in *Rooster Cogburn* (1975).

TWELVE ANGRY MEN. 1957. Filmed 1956; New York City.
Cast: Henry Fonda, Lee J. Cobb, Ed Begley, E. G. Marshall, Jack Klugman, Martin Balsam, Jack Warden.
Director: Sidney Lumet.

Henry Fonda also produced this film, adapted from a TV play, and he considered it one of his three best (*The Grapes of Wrath* and *The Ox-Bow Incident* being the two others). He chose Sidney Lumet to direct—it was the latter's first big-screen assignment—and hand-picked the cast of eleven other actors to play the deadlocked jury. Most of the action occurred on a single set, an actual jury room in a Manhattan courthouse, which involved huge problems of camera mobility and lighting. Such problems required that each close-up speech had to be filmed consecutively for each actor, one at a time, no matter its final order in the movie—a lengthy process designed to test any film performer's skill. After long rehearsals, the actual filming was completed in twenty days. The film was made on an absurdly low budget and promptly sank at the box office. Its European reception, however, was phenomenal, and it won several prizes there as well as in Australia and Japan. Eleanor Roosevelt praised the film lavishly, and it won three Oscar nominations; but Fonda vowed never to produce another film himself, and didn't.

20,000 LEAGUES UNDER THE SEA. 1954. Filmed winter 1954; New Providence, Bahamas. Long Bay, Jamaica. Walt Disney Studios, Burbank.
Cast: Kirk Douglas, James Mason, Paul Lukas, Peter Lorre.
Director: Richard Fleischer.

This film based on Jules Verne's futuristic novel was the first live-action drama produced by Disney Studios after years of creating animated cartoons and features. James Mason, playing Captain Nemo, delayed acceptance of his role because of a top-billing dispute with Kirk Douglas, finally agreeing to second billing. Despite his opinion that the part was far from his best, he admitted that "unlike most of my films, it made mountains of money." Elaborate special effects and interior sets marked Disney's effort to abide as closely as possible to Verne's own descriptions, especially of Nemo's super-submarine *Nautilus*. The giant squid, a creation of studio technicians, fought with the actors in a special studio tank. Academy Awards went for art direction and special effects.

2001: A SPACE ODYSSEY. 1968. Filmed December 1965–winter 1968; England: Shepperton Studios, Shepperton; Elstree Studios, Borehamwood.
Cast: Keir Dullea, William Sylvester, Gary Lockwood, Daniel Richter, Leonard Rossiter, Margaret Tyzack.
Director: Stanley Kubrick.

With *2001* and director Stanley Kubrick came a new dynasty of film creator-engineers who found more satisfaction in tinkering with electronic gadgetry and devising intricate process shots than in directing actors. First of the high-tech science fiction epics that would prove so popular over the next two decades—but far more intelligent than most that followed—*2001* evolved from an Arthur C. Clarke story. The screenplay by Kubrick and Clarke further inspired Clarke's novel of the same title, which appeared simultaneously with the film's release. Kubrick introduced marvels of the cinema age in his use of elaborate special effects and visual techniques. Two innovative procedures, significant for future filmmakers, included the front-projection system (a new way of using a still photograph as background for a scene) and a streak-photography process, designed for the psychedelic stargate sequence. The Ferris-wheel-shaped centrifuge, inside which the astronauts live on the space ship *Discovery*, was built especially for the film. Scenes of the performers walking up the walls and upside-down were achieved by rotating the entire set, to which the camera was attached; actors actually walked a treadmill at the bottom. (The same effect is seen in the shuttle *Aries* sequence with the stewardess, using a smaller rotating drum.) Except for two baby chimpanzees, the apes in the dawn of man sequence were all played by exceptionally thin actors, mimes, and dancers. Precise combinations of models and miniatures with full-size mock-ups, transparency screens, and matte paintings gave realistic impressions of space travel. Pervading life aboard the Jupiter-bound spacecraft was the aural presence of the computer HAL. Kubrick had originally named the computer Athena, which would speak with a woman's voice; then he decided to name it by combining the acronym of *heuristic* and *algorithmic*, the two principal learning systems; some critics suggested that HAL was actually IBM, by means of a backup by one position in the alphabet of each letter. Kubrick found actor Martin Balsam's voice "too emotional" for HAL's speech, and Canadian Shakespearean actor Douglas Rain voiced the part without seeing any of the film. The film's only Academy Award went for special effects. Of the original cast, only Keir Dullea performed in the 1984 sequel, *2010*. Books providing behind-the-scenes data include Jerome Agel's *The Making of Kubrick's 2001* (1970) and Carolyn Geduld's *Filmguide to 2001* (1973).

U

UMBERTO D. 1952. Filmed 1952; Rome: exteriors and Cinecittà Studios.

Cast: Carlo Battisti, Maria Pia Casilio, Lina Gennari.

Director: Vittorio De Sica.

Carlo Battisti, playing the title role, was a nonprofessional actor, a university professor in real life. Screenwriter-director Vittorio De Sica dedicated this film to the memory of his father, also named Umberto. De Sica said he modeled his visual style on that of American documentary pioneer Robert J. Flaherty—"true, poetic, and limpid"—who had died in 1951. This film is regarded by many critics as the most sensitive, yet unsentimental screen treatment of lonely old age.

V

VERTIGO. 1958. Filmed September–December 1957; California: San Francisco; Santa Cruz; San Juan Bautista; Paramount Studios, Los Angeles.
Cast: James Stewart, Kim Novak, Barbara Bel Geddes, Tom Helmore, Henry Jones.
Director: Alfred Hitchcock.

Many critics rank this as Alfred Hitchcock's masterpiece, though it was far from his biggest moneymaker. In its brooding obsession with female identity and transformation, the film disclosed more of the director's own lifelong hang-ups than he perhaps intended. He had hoped to cast Vera Miles, whom he had carefully groomed for stardom, believing that the film's success depended upon her. His disgust and resentment knew no bounds when she became pregnant and had to back out. (Actually she had given birth by the time filming began, but Hitchcock refused to reconsider.) When the studio insisted on replacing her with Kim Novak, Hitchcock said he lost interest in both the character and the film. An insecure performer at best, twenty-four-year-old Novak received no help from the director concerning her role or its interpretation, though she begged more than once. She rebelled (to no avail) against wearing a gray outfit and black shoes in the opening scenes, believing the colors didn't suit her; and she went braless (Hitchcock said she was proud of that) in many of her scenes. The director seemed to take perverse delight in ordering multiple retakes of Novak leaping into the bay—actually a studio tank. What she finally gave him, however, was apparently satisfactory. This was James Stewart's fourth and final movie for Hitchcock, playing the acrophobic Scottie Ferguson. His vertigo attack in the bell tower, one of Hitchcock's most famous visual sequences, was achieved by a new technique originated by the director, that of pulling the camera away while simultaneously zooming in with the lens. The stairway was a miniature turned on its side. California locations included two old Spanish missions: Mission Dolores and

Mission San Juan Bautista. For his own cameo, Hitchcock appeared as a pedestrian crossing a street.

W

WALL STREET. 1987. Filmed spring–summer 1987; New York: Bridgehampton; New York City.
Cast: Michael Douglas, Charlie Sheen, Daryl Hannah, Martin Sheen.
Director: Oliver Stone.

This portrayal of a subculture in which money is sacred, but ways of getting it are not, brought major stardom to Michael Douglas, son of actor Kirk Douglas and heretofore mainly known as a producer. The subject of Yuppie greed infecting the New York Stock Exchange was current, as major trading scandals rocked the money temple repeatedly during the Reagan years (the film's original title was simply *Greed*). As lizardlike stockbroker Gordon Gekko, Douglas based his nine-minute paean to avarice on a speech once actually given by the felonious Ivan F. Boesky, who went to jail for insider trading. The beachfront house used in the film was the mansion of another fraud artist, Owen Morrissey. Father and son Martin and Charlie Sheen also played father and son in the film. Oliver Stone, son of noted stockbroker Louis Stone, had rebelled early against a business career but finally decided to try fulfilling the elder's wish for him to make "an intelligent business movie." Many behind-the-scenes Wall Street advisers helped add authentic details to the production, while junior cast members educated themselves on the workings of a brokerage house at Salomon Brothers, one of the country's biggest. Douglas himself probably owed his role to his own experience in the business end of filmmaking. Reaction to the film from stock exchange members varied. Most gave it high marks for its portrayal of the Wall Street lifestyle but thought that it grossly overemphasized the sordid aspects of the business. A few, however, granted that the film version was altogether too true. Douglas won an Academy Award as best actor.

WAR AND PEACE. 1956. Filmed summer–autumn 1955; Cinecittà Studios, Rome.
Cast: Audrey Hepburn, Henry Fonda, Mel Ferrer, Vittorio Gassman, John Mills, Herbert Lom, Anita Ekberg.
Director: King Vidor.

Leo Tolstoy's epic novel received lavish screen treatment here despite some obvious miscasting. Henry Fonda never believed himself right for the pivotal role of Pierre. Fonda's interpretation differed markedly from King Vidor's romantic conception of Pierre, and the two clashed frequently. Not helping matters was Fonda's abysmal mood; his wife, Susan Blanchard (third of five), left him during the filming. Audrey Hepburn, playing Natasha, deeply immersed herself in both the novel and her part, supervising each detail of her makeup and clothing for authenticity. During filming of the violent battle sequences, she suffered nightmares, and the typically noisy Italian sets, the frequent distractive interruptions, and the necessity of performing scenes out of script sequence shattered her nerves. At one point, she almost walked off the set; and in the end, she thought her work unsatisfactory. Thousands of Italian soldiers were recruited as extras. Tons of cornflakes dipped in gypsum (the standard Hollywood recipe for snow) served to winterize the Moscow sets in hot summer Rome. Vidor was proud of the spectacular horse falls filmed during the Battle of Borodino sequence. These were achieved by using thinly covered, oblong, three-foot deep pits, into which the horses would run and stumble; not a horse, claimed the director, was ever injured. The 1968 Russian remake, much more faithful to the novel, was more than twice as long as this version.

WAR OF THE WORLDS. 1953. Filmed December 1951–February 1952; Florence, Arizona. California: Simi Valley; Paramount Studios, Los Angeles.
Cast: Gene Barry, Ann Robinson, Les Tremayne, Henry Brandon.
Director: Byron Haskin.

Based more on Orson Welles's epochal 1938 radio broadcast about space invaders than on the H. G. Wells novel, this science fiction thriller used state-of-the-art special effects (for which the film won an Oscar). Mass destruction sequences displayed intricate combinations of glass paintings, miniatures, and matte work. The Martian spacecraft, their shapes reputedly inspired by manta rays, were copper bowls traveling on wires over a scale model of Los Angeles. Look closely and you may see an occasional wire that didn't get hidden. Arizona National Guardsmen functioned as army troops. Stuntman "Mushy" Callahan, playing a soldier struck by a heat ray, was badly burned in one sequence. The Flying Wing bomber that drops an A-bomb on the Martians remains the only such aircraft in existence, housed today at the Smithsonian Institution. Charles Gemora not only played the Martian creature while standing on his knees; he also designed the papier-mâché and rubber-tubing outfit he wore. Carolyn Jones played a dumb-blonde bit part here at the dawn of her career, and the film's producer, George Pal, played a bum. As for his two lead players, Gene Barry and Ann Robinson, director Byron Haskin judged their performances "terrible!" Sir Cedric Hardwicke spoke the narration.

WATCH ON THE RHINE. 1943. Filmed summer 1942; Warner Bros. Studios, Burbank.

Cast: Paul Lukas, Bette Davis, Geraldine Fitzgerald, Lucile Watson, George Coulouris, Donald Woods.

Director: Herman Shumlin.

Paul Lukas, George Coulouris, Lucile Watson, and director Herman Shumlin all came to the film from the Broadway stage version of Lillian Hellman's anti-Nazi play. Bette Davis, insisting that Lukas receive top billing, eagerly sought the role of Sara Muller after Irene Dunne refused the part, for Davis felt the message of the picture vital for wartime America. Fatigued from having just completed *Now, Voyager*, she argued throughout with Shumlin, a stage director unfamiliar with cinema techniques. (Veteran cinematographer Hal Mohr became virtual codirector at the request of producer Hal Wallis.) But Hellman expressed delight with Davis's casting and with the film generally, for which she added a few scenes. Canadian actress Watson, known for her extremely vocal right-wing views, played the dominating matriarch in ironic contrast to her real feelings, which Davis found tiresome and annoying. Davis brought Janis Wilson, whom she had befriended on the set of *Now, Voyager*, to the cast in the role of her daughter, Babette. The studio had sought Charles Boyer for the male lead, but the French actor didn't trust his German accent and turned it down. Lukas was so offended at the studio insistence of tacking on a new ending required by the Hollywood production code that he never showed up to film it—hence the reference to his character's possible "disappearance" at the end. He won an Academy Award as best actor for his performance.

THE WAY WE WERE. 1973. Filmed autumn 1972; New York: Union College Campus, Schenectady; New York City. Exteriors and Columbia Studios, Los Angeles.
Cast: Barbra Streisand, Robert Redford, Bradford Dillman, Lois Chiles, Viveca Lindfors.
Director: Sydney Pollack.

Screenwriter Arthur Laurents adapted his own novel especially for Barbra Streisand, fashioning her role as an analogy to the actress's own creative development as he had observed it. Streisand had sought Robert Redford for her costar from the beginning; she turned down Ken Howard for the role, and Warren Beatty declined. Redford himself, however, was reluctant to type himself as a romantic idol and required eight months of persuasion by Sydney Pollack before he agreed to costar. Even then, he demanded numerous script changes, reflecting his mistaken belief that the picture was to be primarily his, rather than Streisand's, vehicle. The actress, who seldom related very well to her male leads, stood in total awe of Redford—a worship that blinded him to the fact that he was not, as he thought, stealing the film from her. With daily rewrites amending the script even as filming proceeded, tension mounted on the set until, near the end, one observer described the atmosphere as "doing overtime at Dachau." Note Streisand's preference for her left profile before the camera. Academy Awards went to Marvin Hamlisch for his musical score and title song.

WEST SIDE STORY. 1961. Filmed March–July 1960; New York City. Exteriors and Samuel Goldwyn Studios, Los Angeles.
Cast: Natalie Wood, Richard Beymer, Rita Moreno, George Chakiris, Russ Tamblyn.
Directors: Robert Wise, Jerome Robbins.

Shakespeare never dies. This adaptation of the Broadway musical landmark, updating *Romeo and Juliet*, proved one of the most popular musicals ever made. Neither a singer nor a dancer, Natalie Wood felt extremely insecure in her lead role of Maria. Thus she didn't do much of either one. Studio vocalist Marni Nixon dubbed her singing voice, and dance choreographer Robbins gave her easy steps disguised by artful camerawork. Richard Beymer's songs were also dubbed (by Jimmy Bryant). Many sequences were filmed in run-down tenement areas of west Manhattan, where old buildings scheduled for razing had been granted a reprieve for the picture. This was street gang turf, but the only problems encountered by the crew came not from teenage rumblers, who quietly observed the proceedings, but from younger kids, who threw stones and verbally harassed the intruders. A Los Angeles skid row area backgrounded the film's climactic gang-fight sequence. John Astin made his screen debut here as Glad Hand, the social worker. The film's ten Academy Awards included Oscars for best picture, best directors, Rita Moreno and George Chakiris as best supporting players, cinematography, and musical score. The film proved especially popular in France, running for five years straight in Paris.

THE WESTERNER. 1940. Filmed spring 1940; Tucson area, Arizona. Samuel Goldwyn Studios, Los Angeles.
Cast: Gary Cooper, Walter Brennan, Doris Davenport, Fred Stone, Forrest Tucker, Chill Wills, Dana Andrews.
Director: William Wyler.

Though top billed, Gary Cooper played an essentially supporting role here to Walter Brennan's Judge Roy Bean. Cooper professed puzzlement as to why he was needed at all. The reason, of course, was that he was an enormous box office draw. The film's anti-Western maturity, however, presaged Cooper's later classic attack on Western stereotypes, *High Noon*. Plagued by an aching back, the thirty-nine-year-old actor suffered each time he mounted a horse. X-rays disclosed that he had actually fractured a hip in an auto accident when he was seventeen, an event that also gave him his unique, stiff-legged gait. Doris Davenport, plucked from the Goldwyn chorus line by Samuel Goldwyn himself, was forced on William Wyler for the role of Cooper's love interest; Wyler had wanted to cast his wife, Margaret Tallichet. Davenport disappeared from movies without a trace after her screen appearance here. Two other first-timers who lasted were Dana

Andrews (playing Bart Cobble) and Forrest Tucker (as Wade Harper). Andrews, a longtime Cooper admirer, said that a Cooper silent movie, *Legion of the Condemned* (1928), had initially inspired his own acting ambitions. Brennan won an Academy Award for best supporting actor, his third in a space of five years.

WHAT EVER HAPPENED TO BABY JANE? 1962. Filmed August–September 1962; California: Santa Monica; exteriors and Producers Studio, Los Angeles.
Cast: Bette Davis, Joan Crawford, Victor Buono, Anna Lee, Maidie Norman.
Director: Robert Aldrich.

Aging Hollywood beauty queens seemed to outdo themselves during the Sixties, going to the other extreme to play haggard, often evil old women. This low-budget film started a trend of what might be termed Gothic horror geriatrics—though both Bette Davis and Joan Crawford were only in their fifties at the time. Considered as professional rivals throughout their careers, they had never performed together, and Crawford thought it time they did. For years, she had been strongly attracted to Davis, sending her gifts and trying to ingratiate herself. Davis did not reciprocate and seemed rather to dislike this actress who, almost more than any other, cultivated a movie star image of herself and tried at all times to live up to it. Davis recalled the beach scene, in which she had to fall on a reclining Crawford, as "like falling on two footballs"; Crawford, she claimed, owned three sizes of bosom and was wearing her largest size that day. But the two actresses really didn't have much in common, either personally or professionally, and their so-called rivalry was probably more press-agentry than anything else. Davis originated her own ghastly makeup for the title role of Baby Jane Hudson. To represent the early careers of both reclusive sisters, Robert Aldrich used clips from the early Davis films *Parachute Jumper* (1933) and *Ex-Lady* (1933), and from Crawford's *Sadie McKee* (1934). Davis's fourteen-year-old daughter, B. D. Merrill, played the neighbor girl Liza. (B. D. would grow up to write a scathing memoir of her mother.) Massive twenty-four-year-old Victor Buono made his screen debut here. This film's huge success rejuvenated the careers of both Crawford and Davis.

WHITE CHRISTMAS. 1954. Filmed summer–autumn 1953; Paramount Studios, Los Angeles.
Cast: Bing Crosby, Danny Kaye, Rosemary Clooney, Vera-Ellen, Dean Jagger.
Director: Michael Curtiz.

A sort of remake of *Holiday Inn*, in which Bing Crosby had introduced Irving Berlin's "White Christmas," this film was made chiefly as a reprise for Crosby and the song, though Berlin wrote nine new tunes for it, too. It also bore strong resemblances to a previous Michael Curtiz-directed film, *I'll See You in My Dreams* (1952). Screenwriters Norman Panama and Melvin Frank, called in to beef up Danny Kaye's part in Norman Krasna's screenplay, recalled the filming as "eight terrible weeks of shouting and screaming." As third choice for his role of Phil Davis, Kaye was feeling a bit prickly about the whole thing and not disposed to taking a back seat to Crosby. The studio had wanted Fred Astaire to repeat his sidekick role as in the 1942 film, but the old hoofer decided he was now *too* old for such a part and refused. Then Donald O'Connor hurt his back and couldn't dance, so Kaye was cast. Dean Jagger, playing the general, said he felt better bald and hated wearing a hairpiece in the movie. One of the few bright spots during filming involved Hungarian-born Curtiz's infamous accent and chopped diction. The screenwriters had to explain each joke in the script to Curtiz, a laborious effort that most often left him none the wiser. Despite its thin story line, however, *White Christmas* proved one of Crosby's biggest moneymakers. This film ranks historically as the first made in VistaVision, a new deep-focus process.

WHITE HEAT. 1949. Filmed summer 1949; California: Torrance; Warner Bros. Studios, Burbank.
Cast: James Cagney, Virginia Mayo, Edmond O'Brien, Margaret Wycherly.
Director: Raoul Walsh.

The last of James Cagney's classic gangster performances was one of his best. He based his psychotic character Cody Jarrett on Arthur "Doc" Barker, one of the infamous Ma Barker's boys. Cagney always sneered in contempt at Method acting techniques. "You just go out and do it," he said—not very helpful advice for aspiring actors, but it worked well for him. Climbing into the lap of Ma Jarrett (played by Margaret

Wycherly) was his own improvised idea, a scene that neither he nor director Raoul Walsh were sure would pass the censors but which they thought added depth to the character. Cagney also improvised other bits as well as much of his own dialogue. Climactic scenes were filmed atop a large butane tank in Torrance. Look for former Olympic champion Jim Thorpe, playing a bit part as a prisoner.

WHO'S AFRAID OF VIRGINIA WOOLF? 1966. Filmed July–December 1965; Smith College campus, Northampton, Massachusetts. Warner Bros. Studios, Burbank.

Cast: Elizabeth Taylor, Richard Burton, George Segal, Sandy Dennis.

Director: Mike Nichols.

Edward Albee's lacerating play about domestic violence, campus faculty style, gave Mike Nichols his first shot at film direction and brought Elizabeth Taylor her first screen role in which she not only downplayed but subverted her glamour image. She and her husband, Richard Burton, were at the peak of their glitzy popularity at the time, darlings of both jet set and scandal-mag journalism. Albee had wanted Bette Davis and James Mason for the lead roles. Several actors, including Jack Lemmon, Glenn Ford, and Robert Redford had refused the male lead. Only thirty-three, Taylor courageously aged herself to a frumpy mid-forties by means of makeup and weighing in at a hefty 155, while Burton, seedy and gray in his makeup, celebrated his fortieth birthday during production. The corrosive screenplay affected everyone. Taylor frequently exploded in huge if brief bursts of frustration as Nichols demanded more from her than any director ever had. And Burton gave himself low marks for what he labeled an "indifferent" performance. Both had a hard time shaking off their roles of George and Martha after filming ended—and they never really did, for their marriage went downhill from then on, culminating in their 1974 divorce. This was Sandy Dennis's second film; pregnant at the time, she lost the baby soon after filming ended. Five Academy Awards included Oscars to Taylor as best actress (her second), Dennis as best supporting actress, and Haskell Wexler's cinematography.

THE WILD BUNCH. 1969. Filmed March–July 1968; Mexico: Parras; Duranzo Arroyo; El Rincon del Montero; El Romeral; Torreón.
Cast: William Holden, Ernest Borgnine, Robert Ryan, Edmond O'Brien, Warren Oates, Ben Johnson, Strother Martin.
Director: Sam Peckinpah.

This controversial Western from one of Hollywood's most iconoclastic directors roused much criticism for its seemingly gratuitous violence (which appears pretty tame by today's standards). Warner Bros. and the producers hacked the finished film to pieces, to Sam Peckinpah's helpless fury, but most of the footage has been restored in the video version. Many critics believed that Peckinpah, a devotee of Robert Ardrey's *African Genesis* theories of human nature, was trying to say something significant about mankind; but few of them could finally agree on just what that message was. The director's first choice for the lead role of Pike Bishop was Lee Marvin, who chose instead to act in *Paint Your Wagon*. So William Holden was cast in the part. This actor, whose bouts with the bottle were legendary, managed to stay relatively sober throughout the filming by drinking only beer. Ernest Borgnine, in the role of Dutch, limped throughout the production from a walking cast on his left foot, which had been broken during filming of *The Split* (1968). Strother Martin, playing the psychotic Coffer, said he seemingly couldn't do anything right for the volatile director. The girl being trampled by Holden's horse was actually stuntman Whitey Hughes, who "got so sore I could hardly move" after repeated takes of the scene. Bo Hopkins made his screen debut here as Crazy Lee. Mexican soldiers were used as extras. It is said that more blank ammunition was fired during the filming of this picture than real bullets during the entire period of the story, the Mexican Revolution of 1914.

THE WILD ONE. 1954. Filmed summer 1953; Columbia Studios Ranch, Burbank.
Cast: Marlon Brando, Mary Murphy, Robert Keith, Lee Marvin, Jay C. Flippen.
Director: Laslo Benedek.

Not a very well-made film, it was nevetheless important for Marlon Brando's performance and its faddish influence on a whole generation of actors and public alike. All biker films trace to this one, as did the greaser hair styles and mumbling incoherence affected by the youth culture of the Fifties. Based on a 1947 incident that occurred in Hollister, California, the original screenplay by John Paxton enthralled Brando at the outset. Always interested in making social statements in his films, Brando soon soured on the project as Hollywood censors, believing that the script glorified violence, gutted most of the commentary that had attracted Brando in the first place. He honored his commitment, however, even agreeing to speak the film's prologue much against his will, contemptuously assuming a phony Southern accent for the speech. In preparation for his role, he hung out with cycle gangs and spent time in Hollister, and he drove his own cycle in the film. Many actual gang members blended in with the cast. The scene between Brando and Mary Murphy (playing Kathie) conversing in the café was entirely improvised in one take, with Murphy responding out of thin air to his ad-libs. She later confessed to having a huge crush on her costar. Brando and Lee Marvin, cast as Chino, didn't like each other much; by picture's end, they were trading barbed names for each other: Marlow Brandy and Lee Moron. Finally, Brando declared *The Wild One* an artistic failure that had "missed badly." He credited it, however, with helping him personally realize and vent his own violent feelings at the time. England banned the film (for its violence) until 1968.

WILD STRAWBERRIES (SMULTRONSTÄLLET). 1957.
Filmed July–August 1957; Sweden: Lake Vättern; Lund; Dalarö; Ångö; Svensk Filmindustri Studios, Råsunda.
Cast: Victor Sjostrom, Ingrid Thulin, Bibi Andersson, Gunnar Bjornstrand, Naima Wifstrand, Gunnar Sjöberg.
Director: Ingmar Bergman.

Veteran actor Victor Sjostrom (also known as Victor Seastrom) performed his final screen role at age seventy-eight. Though often forgetful of his lines and somewhat querulous on the set, Sjostrom (as Uncle Isak Borg) and twenty-one-year-old Bibi Andersson (playing Sara) formed a close bond of kinship and mutual teasing and flirtation. Considering himself retired, Sjostrom had been exceedingly reluctant to join the cast, and Ingmar Bergman had to use all his powers of persuasion to enlist the elderly actor. Once working, however, Sjostrom visibly enjoyed himself. The only time he became cranky was when Bergman held him on the set beyond the customary hour of his evening whiskey. One such time was the meadow scene in which Sjostrom stands with a benign expression of spiritual calm; in actuality, said Bergman, the old man was boiling mad because he was going to be late for his glass of whiskey. Lena Bergman, the director's daughter, played a twin—and her mother Else Fisher, Bergman's ex-wife, also appeared in a bit as a mother in a distance shot. Gunnar Sjöberg's role of engineer Ahlman was based on film critic Stig Ahlgren, who had often attacked Bergman's work. Bergman said the idea for this film originated from a 1956 trip he took to Uppsala, revisiting nostalgic scenes of his childhood. *Wild Strawberries* ranks among the best—some critics believe it *the* finest—of the Swedish master's career.

WITNESS. 1985. Filmed spring–summer 1984; Pennsylvania; Philadelphia; Lancaster County.

Cast: Harrison Ford, Kelly McGillis, Lukas Haas, Danny Glover, Alexander Godunov.

Director: Peter Weir.

Australian director Peter Weir's first American film gave Harrison Ford a chance to show what he could do beyond his superhero typecasting of previous films. The entire filming company encountered passive resistance from the local Amish residents of the Pennsylvania rural locale. Forbidden to see movies or be photographed themselves, they avoided all contact with the filmmakers and entirely disowned this project, with its story line that involved so much of the Amish way of life. Kelly McGillis, cast as Rachel Lapp after Weir had considered "planeloads of Italian actresses" for the role, worked to master the Amish dialect and actually lived, briefly, with an Amish family—until she was summarily evicted when they discovered she was preparing for a film role. After trying unsuccessfully to rent an Amish dairy farm to use as a main locale, Weir had to settle for a non-Amish farm. He received help, however, in creating authentic farm and household details from several ex-Amish members. The film received Academy Awards for screenplay and editing.

WITNESS FOR THE PROSECUTION. 1957. Filmed May–October 1957; Samuel Goldwyn Studios, Los Angeles.
Cast: Charles Laughton, Marlene Dietrich, Tyrone Power, Elsa Lanchester, John Williams.
Director: Billy Wilder.

Agatha Christie's stage hit also became a popular screen thriller in the skillful hands of Billy Wilder and three of Hollywood's best-known scenery chewers: Marlene Dietrich, Charles Laughton, and Tyrone Power. Eager to play the role of Christine Vole, Dietrich modeled her part at Laughton's home, also taking lessons in Cockney speech from the British actor. (A legend persists, however, that another actress made up to look like Dietrich finally stood in for her in her scene as the English tart.) Wilder insisted that he couldn't cast Dietrich unless she sang at least one song, which she did ("I'll Never Go Home Anymore")—only one instance of the director's additions to the original screenplay. This was forty-three-year-old Tyrone Power's last film; in November 1958, he died while filming *Solomon and Sheba* in Spain. Dietrich's infatuated attentions to Power embarrassed the actor. Power, Wilder, and Laughton got along so well that they took a holiday trip to Europe together after finishing the picture. Elsa Lanchester, Laughton's wife in real life, played the nagging Miss Plimsoll. London's Old Bailey courtroom, recreated from original plans and sketches on stage 4 of the Goldwyn lot, was accurate to the last detail (except for movable walls and flooring installed to facilitate camera movement). Note the jury reaction shots; they were all filmed in one day with Laughton, off camera, reading *all* the speeches, at his own request. Agatha Christie, highly pleased with the film, said it was the first good screen adaptation of any of her tales.

THE WIZARD OF OZ. 1939. Filmed October 1938–March 1939; MGM Studios, Culver City.
Cast: Judy Garland, Ray Bolger, Bert Lahr, Jack Haley, Margaret Hamilton, Billie Burke, Frank Morgan.
Director: Victor Fleming.

This musical classic adapted from L. Frank Baum's series about the magical land of Oz made a star of sixteen-year-old Judy Garland in her seventh film. The film was not well received; most serious critics thought it dreadful. MGM never expected to do more than break even on it, in fact, intending it more as a prestige film than a moneymaker. The film took twenty years to recoup its investment, not achieving its present status until carefully spaced TV showings, beginning in 1956, drew huge audiences. The studio had wanted Shirley Temple for the key role of Dorothy, but 20th Century-Fox refused to loan her. By studio order Garland fasted on alternate days to become a sufficiently gaunt eleven-year-old. She was also tightly bound and corseted to mask her budding womanhood. Tensions flared on the set. Some observers felt that the four male stars, vaudeville oldtimers all, were subtly hostile toward Garland, fearing she might upstage them. Ray Bolger, for one, expressed astonishment in later years when he heard Garland bitterly cite her memories of unhappiness and ill-treatment while making the film, and others also recalled her sunny disposition and apparent enjoyment. Buddy Ebsen was originally cast as the Scarecrow and Bolger as the Tin Woodman—then they switched roles, but the aluminum dust powdered on Ebsen's face put him in the hospital with a severe allergic reaction, and Jack Haley replaced him. Bolger, Haley, and Bert Lahr sweltered under their heavy makeup and the brutally hot studio lights—Bolger with a foam-rubber bag glued to his head and tied at his neck; Haley with chalk-salved face and a stiff buckram outfit in which he could not bend; Lahr in a heavily padded fur suit, wig, and facial prosthesis. Margaret Hamilton's skin acquired a greenish tinge from the copper-based makeup she wore as the Wicked Witch of the West. In the scene where she departs Munchkinland in a burst of fire and smoke, a near-fatal accident occurred. Timing of the explosion was off by a split-second; when she dropped below stage on the elevator built by special-effects technicians, she was in flames. Her face and right hand were burned so severely that she remained off work for six weeks. Upon her return, still in pain, she refused to do any more scenes involving fire, despite studio assurances and threats. Thus her stunt double, Betty Danko, did the broomstick ride. Sure enough, the broomstick pipe exploded, putting Danko in the hospital and scarring her legs. In those days, studios often treated their props better than their employees; Hamilton said she never sued the studio "for the simple reason that I wanted to work again." Veteran actor Frank Morgan, playing the Wizard and Professor Marvel, came to work each morning with a small suitcase containing his miniature bar, but his drinking remained circumspect. For Professor Marvel's seedy coat with velvet collar, studio costumers came up with a true find: L. Frank Baum's own coat, coincidentally discovered in a Chicago used-clothing store and with his name label attached. The midgets playing the munchkins—all hypopituitary "very raunchy people," according to screenwriter Noel Langley. Tales of sex orgies and drunken sprees at their Culver City hotel plagued studio personnel, who sighed with relief when they left. The Kansas tornado was actually a thirty-five-foot-high muslin wind sock hooked to an overhead gantry, with air and dust fed into the bottom. This film, employing ten writers and four directors hardly before a camera turned, also marked Garland's first performance of what became her theme song, "Over the Rainbow." Studio chiefs almost cut it from the film, saying it slowed the action too much, but it won the film's only Academy Award. Intriguing details fill Aljean Harmetz's book, *The Making of the Wizard of Oz* (1978).

THE WOLF MAN. 1941. Filmed summer 1941; Universal Studios, Universal City.
Cast: Lon Chaney, Jr., Maria Ouspenskaya, Evelyn Ankers, Claude Rains, Ralph Bellamy, Bela Lugosi.
Director: George Waggner.

Originally titled *Destiny*, this film set the lycanthropic style for the many werewolf films to follow from Hollywood's horror factories—but it was itself based on an earlier film, *Werewolf of London* (1935). The stolid Lon Chaney, Jr., whose acting rang somewhat more wooden than a railroad tie (which he otherwise resembled), lurched to horror film stardom as the baneful canine and played the role four more times, appearing in company with his pals Dracula and Frankenstein's monster. It was, he said, his favorite role—certainly it distinguished him finally from his father, Lon Chaney, Sr., maybe even one-upped that redoubtable silent-film master of disguises. The biggest horror for these early monster actors was the studio makeup room. Jack Pierce, the makeup artist responsible for turning Boris Karloff into a walking mass of rivets in *Frankenstein*, also undertook the hairier job with Chaney, requiring five hours daily to apply rubber snout, fangs, claws, and (you'd never guess) genuine yak hair. Time-lapse transformation scenes, in which man changes to wolf, occupied twenty hours of applying a tuft here, a tooth there, starting and stopping the camera many times. British actress Evelyn Ankers, playing Gwen, became known as "The Screamer" for her superb talents in this direction. A queen of horror pictures, she and Chaney got off on the wrong paw, as it were, when the studio assigned her his former dressing room, which he and his pal Broderick Crawford had smashed up during a transformation due to alcohol the night before. Ankers fainted once on the set—those misty moorland and graveyard fogs of B-movies were lethal concoctions of studio chemists, and she inhaled a bit much during the chase sequence. Universal released this film only two days after the Japanese bombed Pearl Harbor, resigning itself to a total wipeout at the box office. To its astonishment, a public in sore need of distraction flocked to the movie, making it one of the most popular horror films in years.

WOMAN OF THE YEAR. 1942. Filmed August–October 1941; MGM Studios, Culver City.

Cast: Katharine Hepburn, Spencer Tracy, Reginald Owen, Fay Bainter, William Bendix.

Director: George Stevens.

Most of the nine films that Katharine Hepburn and Spencer Tracy made together were at least mildly sexist in tone, but the couple's performances generally outweighed objectionable aspects of the screenplays. This film was their first teaming. Each came to it a perfect stranger to the other (though Hepburn had long idolized Tracy's work and refused to consider making this film unless he consented to play opposite her). By the time filming ended, they were lovers, beginning an affair that lasted until the still-married Tracy's death in 1967. Opposites in many ways, they remained an unlikely combination—Hepburn's upper-class New England background and fiercely independent lifestyle, as contrasted with the cantankerous Tracy's midwestern upbringing, his tortured Irish-Catholic conscience, and a severe drinking problem that sent him off on ugly periodic binges. They were cautious with each other at the beginning. When Hepburn initially expressed her fear that she was too tall for him, he replied, "Don't worry, Miss Hepburn, I'll cut you down to my size." Tracy took a dim view of women who wore trousers, and their acting styles were far different, with Hepburn preferring long rehearsals, while Tracy performed on instinct and seldom surpassed the quality of his first take of a scene. Hepburn did the most adjusting. She had dated director George Stevens for months, but as the costars warmed to each other, Stevens gracefully stepped aside. Hepburn's role was modeled on journalist Dorothy Thompson (designated Woman of the Year for 1935). Hepburn despised the sexist breakfast-scene ending that Stevens and producer Joseph L. Mankiewicz insisted upon, but she could finally do nothing about it. Look for an actor named Joe Yule playing a small role as the building superintendent; he was the father of Mickey Rooney. This was William Bendix's film debut. The screenplay won an Academy Award.

THE WOMEN. 1939. Filmed spring–summer 1939; MGM Studios, Culver City.
Cast: Norma Shearer, Joan Crawford, Rosalind Russell, Mary Boland, Paulette Goddard, Joan Fontaine.
Director: George Cukor.

Only two of the all-female cast (135 actresses) of Clare Boothe's Broadway play performed in the film version: Phyllis Povah as Edith Potter and Marjorie Main as Lucy. Most critics preferred the movie over the play. Norma Shearer, the widow of legendary producer Irving Thalberg, played the lead role of Mary Haines. A grande dame of Hollywood, she permitted Joan Crawford's name to be top billed with hers but balked at including Rosalind Russell in the starring credits. For the first and only time in her career, Russell called in sick and stayed sick until Shearer experienced a sudden conversion in the matter and welcomed Russell aboard. Cukor, who had achieved a reputation as a woman's director, had originally wanted Ilka Chase from the Broadway cast for the role of Sylvia, described as the "arch-bitch of all time"; but Russell fought hard to test for the role and was cast. She credited it as establishing her as a comedienne. She said her fight scene with Paulette Goddard (playing Miriam) left scars on her shins. As two massive egos, Shearer and Crawford were thoroughgoing rivals who ached for chances to upstage each other; and tensions, continually dampened by Cukor, often flared on the set. Boothe's comedy play wasn't a very flattering portrayal of women generally. Each main actress was identified with a supposedly corresponding animal—tigress, cat, lamb, for example—in the opening credits. A Technicolor fashion-show sequence in this black-and-white picture was strenuously opposed by Cukor as unnecessary and distractive, but MGM insisted that such a film couldn't possibly be shown without one. *The Opposite Sex* (1956) was a musical remake.

WOMEN IN LOVE. 1970. Filmed autumn 1969; Zermatt, Switzerland. England: Derby; Sheffield; Newcastle.
Cast: Alan Bates, Oliver Reed, Glenda Jackson, Jennie Linden, Eleanor Bron, Alan Webb.
Director: Ken Russell.

Not usually noted for his subtlety, Ken Russell used much of the dialogue from D. H. Lawrence's novel for the film, which proved to be one of his most polished and artistic efforts. (Larry Kramer was credited with the adaptation.) Russell had qualms about most of his female cast. He thought Jennie Linden, for example, "too pert" for the part of the dullish Ursula; and his opinions of Glenda Jackson, playing Gudrun, often shifted; at various times, he thought her ugly, plain, and beautiful. The Greek ballet sequence by Jackson, Linden, and Eleanor Bron (whose part of Hermione was based on the English socialite, Lady Ottoline Morrell) was a satirical thrust at the dancing style of Isadora Duncan, about whom Russell had filmed a documentary in 1966. Jackson and Oliver Reed (playing Gerald Crich) didn't relate well, especially in the sequence with the cattle, in which Jackson suffered from the cold and her own dislike of cows. The film's most startling sequence—the nude wrestling contest between Reed and Alan Bates—was staged over three days, with both actors initially reluctant to engage. It was Reed, however, who convinced Russell that the filmed sequence should stay faithful to the novel. Not the friendliest of chums off-camera, Reed and Bates got roaring drunk on vodka at a pub the night before and began filming the sequence next day amid much off-color humor designed to embarrass the script girl. Reed was already a judo expert, and Bates had taken lessons in it, but both ended up bruised head to toe, Bates with a dislocated thumb. Playing Rupert, Bates represented the figure of Lawrence himself. Jackson won an Academy Award as best actress.

WUTHERING HEIGHTS. 1939. Filmed autumn–winter 1938–39; California: Chatsworth; Samuel Goldwyn Studios, Los Angeles.

Cast: Laurence Olivier, Merle Oberon, David Niven, Geraldine Fitzgerald, Flora Robson, Donald Crisp.

Director: William Wyler.

This screen version of Emily Brontë's novel brought international stardom to Laurence Olivier. Virtually unknown in America, he only reluctantly accepted the role of Heathcliff, the more so after Vivien Leigh, his lover at the time, was refused the costarring role of Cathy. She in turn refused the part of Isabella that went to Geraldine Fitzgerald—and Merle Oberon, to Olivier's annoyance, became his leading lady. The friction between the two soon erupted into open hostility, with Olivier treating her coldly, even refusing to speak to her off-camera. For Oberon, who had wanted Douglas Fairbanks, Jr., as her costar, the entire production was an ordeal. Besides contending with Olivier's boorishness, she fell extremely ill during repeated takes of the violent storm scene; the studio-concocted rain and wind chilled her to the bone. Upon her recovery, the sequence was repeated using warmed air and water. She also twisted her ankle in a scene, and with Olivier's severe case of athlete's foot, both stars hobbled for a time. Moreover, she felt uneasy being cast with David Niven (playing Edgar); the two had ended a year-long affair in 1936. Niven, too, almost turned down his role of cuckolded husband. As one of Hollywood's best-known playboys, he didn't like the scripted image; but his worst fears stemmed from being involved again with William Wyler, who cowed actors by outbursts and demands for numerous takes and had so directed Niven in *Dodsworth* (1936). Wyler jovially assured the actor that it wouldn't happen this time—but once on the set, he spared nobody his harassment, and Niven gritted his teeth. The Yorkshire moorland was recreated on a 540-acre tract near Chatsworth. Some 14,000 tumbleweeds and a thousand actual heather plants were transplanted there, growing about three feet higher in the California climate than on the actual English moors. Throughout, studio chief Samuel Goldwyn continually sought to Hollywoodize the production by glamorizing the stars and hoking up the story. Wyler and his cast strongly resisted these efforts and mostly succeeded—until the film's final scene, showing the lovers together at last in heaven. Wyler absolutely refused to film this scene and always discounted it thereafter; the actors shown were doubles. Cinematographer Gregg Toland won an Academy Award. Luis Buñuel remade the film in 1954 as *Abismos de Pasion*, and a British-made version appeared in 1970.

Y

YANKEE DOODLE DANDY. 1942. Filmed winter 1941–42; Warner Bros. Studios, Burbank.
Cast: James Cagney, Joan Leslie, Walter Huston, Rosemary de Camp, S. Z. Sakall, Eddie Foy, Jr.
Director: Michael Curtiz.

Playing show biz legend George M. Cohan was not James Cagney's idea of a good role, and he, like Fred Astaire, refused it. But coproducer Hal Wallis, along with Cohan himself, finally persuaded Cagney to do the part for which he won his only Academy Award (as best actor) and which he always claimed thereafter as his favorite. Also, his brother and the film's coproducer, William Cagney, thought it high time that Jimmy do a patriotic picture to help deflect criticism of his outspokenness as a Roosevelt liberal. Though one of Hollywood's great versatiles, Cagney hadn't danced in years and felt rusty; he worked with a Cohan associate, Johnny Boyle, to perfect Cohan's stiff-legged technique—but aside from trying to imitate Cohan on stage, Cagney said he made no attempt to carry the imitation into offstage sequences of the film. Cagney, as usual, changed and improvised many of his scenes to his own satisfaction. The final scene of his wing dance at the White House was almost spontaneous, and almost all of his scenes were one-takes. An exception was his crying scene at the deathbed of his father (played by Walter Huston), so affecting Michael Curtiz that the latter's sobs ruined one take. (Cagney could always cry, genuinely, on cue.) Filming began the day after the Japanese bombed Pearl Harbor, and work on the picture became an emotionally charged effort for everybody involved. Rosemary de Camp (playing Cagney's mother, though she was actually fourteen years younger than the star) recalled the filming as a "patriotic frenzy," as if "sending a last message to the free world." Though the film romanticized Cohan's life considerably, the ailing old showman lived (barely) long enough to see himself portrayed by Cagney and to profess himself pleased. Cagney's own sister, Jeanne, played Cohan's sister Josie in the film. Eddie Foy, Jr., played his famous father. In 1955 Cagney again portrayed Cohan in *The Seven Little Foys*.

THE YEAR OF LIVING DANGEROUSLY. 1982. Filmed March–June 1982; Manila, the Philippines. Sydney, Australia.

Cast: Mel Gibson, Sigourney Weaver, Linda Hunt, Michael Murphy.

Director: Peter Weir.

The title, nowhere mentioned in the film itself, was Indonesian president Sukarno's prophetic phrase for the year 1965—but Peter Weir said it also aptly described his own year of preparing and directing this picture. A particular risk was the casting of Linda Hunt in a male role, that of the dwarf photographer Billy Kwan. After rejecting hundreds of male actors, he decided—only three weeks before filming began—that she was simply best for the part. And most audiences were astonished to discover in the end credits that he was, in fact, a she. This was only the second film appearance for the four-foot-nine actress. Filming began in Manila, but when cast and crew started receiving death threats from a radical Moslem group, Weir pulled out weeks sooner than expected and completed filming in Australia. He had hoped to make the entire picture in Indonesia, the film's locale; but technical reasons, not political ones, prevented it. Sigourney Weaver, playing Jill Bryant, stood a bit too tall for Mel Gibson, so he wore elevated shoes in their scenes. Weaver reported that they became good friends. C. J. Koch, author of the original novel and cowriter of the screenplay, grew increasingly unhappy with Weir's revisions as filming progressed; and at least one American journalist formerly based in Indonesia criticized the film severely for lapses of realism. Hunt won an Academy Award as best supporting actress.

THE YEARLING. 1946. Filmed summer 1945–February 1946; Florida: Marion County; Ocala National Forest.

California: Lake Arrowhead; MGM Studios, Culver City.
Cast: Gregory Peck, Jane Wyman, Claude Jarman, Jr., Chill Wills, Henry Travers, Forrest Tucker.
Director: Clarence Brown.

Filming originally began on this movie version of Marjorie Kinnan Rawlings's novel in 1941, with Spencer Tracy. Anne Revere, and Gene Eckman in the starring roles: but war intervened, and that effort was abandoned. Four years later, Gregory Peck, Jane Wyman, and Claude Jarman, Jr. stepped in. During the final days of filming, Peck was also filming *Duel in the Sun*; he'd go down the studio street, shed his "Southern cracker overalls" and his Southern accent, and put on cowboy clothes and adopt a Texas drawl. Ten-year-old Jarman, a non-actor from Tennessee, made his screen debut here, his first of about half a dozen films. Some thirty-two trained animals were used, including five fawns representing the one fawn, Flag. (Through almost ten months of principal photography, fawns had to be replaced as they aged.) Rawlings's own Cross Creek homestead, where she wrote the novel, was used for some location scenes; now a state historic site, it may be visited. The film won Academy Awards for cinematography and art direction.

YOUNG FRANKENSTEIN. 1974. Filmed spring 1974; 20th Century-Fox Studios, Los Angeles.
Cast: Gene Wilder, Peter Boyle, Marty Feldman, Madeline Kahn, Cloris Leachman, Gene Hackman.
Director: Mel Brooks.

Mel Brooks's intention in this broad, off-the-wall comedy was not so much to parody the original *Bride of Frankenstein* as to offer an affectionate valentine to the horror genre, especially the Universal classics of the Thirties. To that end, he transformed every last stereotype into something rich, strange, and hilarious—such as the monster's neck sporting a Courreges zipper instead of a bolt, and Igor's hump shifting sides. The idea for the film came from Gene Wilder, who played the title role. Kenneth Mars, playing the wooden-armed Inspector Kemp, parodied Lionel Atwill's role in *Son of Frankenstein*. Brooks himself briefly appeared as a leering gargoyle in the monster escape sequence. Also resurrected here, by happy coincidence, was the original *Frankenstein* laboratory set of

1931, which had been stored for many years in a garage. Brooks also used many archaic optical devices, including the old 1:85 aspect ratio for height and width of the frame. If Brooks's account is to be trusted, he said that Cloris Leachman (playing Frau Blucher) ended up eating her facial wart; it "fell in her tuna-salad and was swallowed in a glob of mayonnaise."

Z

Z. 1969. Filmed summer 1968; Algiers.
Cast: Yves Montand, Irene Papas, Jean-Louis Trintignant, Jacques Perrin, François Périer.
Director: Costa-Gavras.

No American studio would touch this political thriller (based on the 1963 assassination of pacifist leader Gregorios Lambrakis in Greece) when Costa-Gavras sought financing for it. Its coproducer, Jacques Perrin, who also played the journalist in the film, finally raised the money in France and Algeria. Its cast, too, except for Greek actress Irene Papas, was mainly French. The Greek-French director achieved international acclaim with this picture, his first in a string of powerful, highly controversial films that, like Jean Renoir's work of the previous generation, aimed for the gut of corrupt, repressive regimes. It was, of course, banned in Greece (also in Spain, India, and Brazil) and not shown there until the overthrow of the fascist military government in 1974. Since composer Mikis Theodorakis was being held under house arrest in Greece at the time, he could not contribute new music to the film score—so Costa-Gavras, determined to include his music, used adaptations of the composer's previous works plus a smuggled-out original song. The film won many awards, including Oscars for best foreign film and best editing.

ZIEGFELD FOLLIES. 1946. Filmed March 1944–February 1945; MGM Studios, Culver City.
Cast: Fred Astaire, Lucille Bremer, William Powell, Judy

Garland, Gene Kelly, Lucille Ball, Red Skelton, Fanny Brice, Lena Horne, Kathryn Grayson.
Director: Vincente Minnelli.

Showman Florenz Ziegfeld, mainly remembered for introducing the stage chorus line, was one of Hollywood's favorite people, as manifested by the fact that this was the third MGM film in a decade titled with his name (after *The Great Ziegfeld*, in 1936, also starring William Powell in the title role; and *Ziegfeld Girl*, in 1941, costarring Judy Garland). Fanny Brice, however, was the only member of this cast who had ever performed in an actual Ziegfeld stage show. This was Fred Astaire's first color film. He and Lucille Bremer filmed the beginning and end of the "Limehouse Blues" number on a revamped street set first used in *The Picture of Dorian Gray.* Astaire and Gene Kelly danced together here for the first of only two times in their careers; their styles were poles apart, but each had enormous respect for the other, and there was never any rivalry between them despite the best efforts of Hollywood publicity flacks. Kelly, perhaps the more deferential of the two, disliked the third section of their "Babbit and the Bromide" number. This was a number that Astaire and his sister Adele had performed together on Broadway back in 1927. Look for the white horse ridden by Lucille Ball in the carousel sequence—that's Silver (as in "Hi-Yo"), and his trainer almost sued MGM for "sissifying" the Lone Ranger's stallion by braiding his tail and adorning him with pink satin bows. If Silver was humiliated, Ball definitely felt likewise; at age thirty-five, she considered herself thoughtlessly miscast. Red Skelton's skit was one he had performed many times on radio. During its filming, the camera operator laughed so hard he fell off the crane, and a replacement quickly grabbed the camera to finish the shot. Lena Horne suffered doubly: she hated the racially stereotyped setting for her "Love" number and refused to record the song commercially—and movie exhibitors in Tennessee deleted the sequence anyway. Most of the big bubble show finale, which took weeks to film and almost asphyxiated everybody from the bubble gas, was edited out; only Cyd Charisse, in her second film appearance, remained in a fragment of the routine that was used. There was much patchwork involving retakes, cuts, and added scenes after the main filming was completed. All of Kathryn

Grayson's work, for example, was a last-minute insertion. Greer Garson had auditioned for the "Madame Crematon" number that parodied her own performances in *Mrs. Miniver* and *Madame Curie*; but the part finally went to Judy Garland, whose casting left the whole point of the routine somewhat mystifying. Vincente Minnelli had not yet married Garland, but they eventually named their daughter after the George Gershwin song "Liza" performed by Horne and Avon Long (a number that was cut from the release version). Born in 1946, Liza Minnelli, of course, became a prominent star in her own right.

ZULU. 1964. Filmed May–July 1963; Natal, South Africa.
Cast: Stanley Baker, Jack Hawkins, Ulla Jacobsson, James Booth, Michael Caine.
Director: Cy Endfield.

Based on the 1879 battle of Rorke's Drift in southern Africa, this film represented a final, flamboyant gasp of a once-thriving genre, the stiff-upper-lip, British-colonials-against-natives epic; but its colorful spectacle if not its underlying racism is much diminished on the small screen. Some four thousand Zulu tribespeople were used as extras, headed by Buthelesi, chief of all the Zulu nations, who played Chief Cetewayo in the film. Stanley Baker, who with director Cy Endfield coproduced the film, found the Zulus mystified at any notion of acting until he showed them an old Gene Autry Western; greatly amused by it, they instantly comprehended what they were supposed to do. Jack Hawkins, playing the fanatic missionary, thought he turned in a good performance but felt bitterly betrayed by Endfield in the way he finally appeared on screen. Hawkins claimed that he had no knowledge during filming that his character, the Reverend Otto Wit, would be used in context as a misguided buffoon. Calling this film a "fiasco" as far as he was concerned, Hawkins angrily stalked out of the premiere showing in London. This was Michael Caine's first major screen role. Playing Lieutenant Bromhead, his tense nervousness was such that he fell off his Basuto pony three successive times as it reared up in the river fording scene. He said he suffered from the broiling weather and from "the trots" during most of the location work, later attributing his illness mostly to nerves. He was also distressed to find himself aloofly treated; playing an officer, he discovered, means that "people don't speak to you." An entire Zulu village was built for the film in Natal province, which encompassed the former kingdom of Zululand. Richard Burton voiced the narration. *Zulu Dawn* came as a prequel in 1979.

ABOUT THE AUTHOR

JOHN EASTMAN is a renowned researcher-writer for magazines, newspapers, and almanacs and he is an expert historian of films and film literature. He is the author of WHO LIVED WHERE (1983) and WHO LIVED WHERE IN EUROPE (1985). Mr. Eastman lives in Kalamazoo, Michigan.